FIRST FLIGHT

FIRST FLIGHT

THE WRIGHT BROTHERS AND THE INVENTION OF THE AIRPLANE

T. A. Heppenheimer

WILEY

John Wiley & Sons, Inc.

Photo credits: San Diego Aerospace Museum: 9, 60, 73, 76, 296, 310, 315; American Heritage: 40, 51 top, 58, 193, 290; Art by Cayley, reproduced by Charles Gibbs-Smith: 51 bottom; National Archives: 74, 77, 78, 81, 202, 280, 298, 311, 334; Library of Congress: 123, 126, 162, 171, 207, 228; U.S. Air Force: 285, 286; NASA: 351, 362; Art by Don Dixon and Chris Butler: 358, 360, 365, 369

ISBN 0-471-40124-2

Printed in the United States of America

10 9 8 7 6 5 4 3 2 1

CONTENTS

ONE

ENTER THE WRIGHTS

THE NAME OF WRIGHT is inseparable from that of their home-town of Dayton, Ohio, which is known for such institutions as Wright State University and Wright-Patterson Air Force Base. Indeed, ancestors of the Wright brothers were present at the city's founding, in 1796.

The townsite passed into American control in 1795, following a decisive victory in which General Anthony Wayne defeated Indians at the Battle of Fallen Timbers. It took its name from General Jonathan Dayton, one of its founders, who had been among the signers of the U.S. Constitution. Its location was promising, for it lay at the confluence of three rivers: the Mad, Great Miami, and Stillwater. This made it a natural center for trade. The first settlers came from Cincinnati, fifty miles to the south.

One Wright ancestor, John Van Cleve, had gained the unfortunate distinction of being the only white man to be killed by Indians within Cincinnati's city limits. His widow, Catharine, remarried and soon

1

became one of the first residents of Dayton, arriving in 1796. Her son Benjamin later became the town's first postmaster, its first school-teacher, and its first public librarian. Within the surrounding Montgomery County, he also was the first county clerk. His marriage in 1800 was the first to be recorded in that county.

John's sister, Margaret Van Cleve, stayed in Cincinnati. She married an innkeeper named George Reeder and had a daughter, Catherine. In 1818, when she was seventeen years old, this girl married a farmer named Dan Wright. The children of this marriage included Milton Wright, born in 1828. He became the father of the Wright brothers, Orville and Wilbur.

Milton Wright developed a strong interest in genealogy. He traced his own family name to John and Olive Wrighte, who had purchased an estate in England's Essex County in 1538. Samuel Wright, the first in the family to emigrate to America, was a Puritan who came to Massachusetts in 1636. Two centuries later, Milton was literally born in a log cabin. Dan and Catherine were living in Indiana; this state had joined the Union only a dozen years earlier, while Rush County, the site of the cabin, had only recently been organized.

Religion played a central role in the family's life. The father, Dan Wright—he never accepted being called Daniel—became a serious believer in 1830. He embraced abstinence; in a community where most men drank corn liquor routinely, he did not allow alcohol to pass his lips. He grew corn but refused to sell it to the local distillers, even though they were often ready to buy at the highest prices. Young Milton became a sincere believer as well.

Milton's mother shared his father's strong convictions. When he was eight years old and under her influence, Milton began to pray regularly and to attend church, where he listened attentively to the preaching. Then in 1843, at age fourteen, he was working in the family cornfield when he found himself called by God. He later wrote of "an impression that spoke to the soul powerfully and abidingly," bringing "a sweet peace and joy never known before." He went on to pursue a career in the church, and he was not alone. All three of his brothers made similar commitments to the ministry.

Dan Wright had refused to join an established church. He vigorously opposed slavery, but could not find a local congregation that shared this belief with sufficient enthusiasm. His son Milton also took time in making his own commitment. Then in 1846, as Milton was turning eighteen, an itinerant preacher whom he much admired led him to the Church of the United Brethren in Christ.

Here was a church to suit the religious attitudes of a frontier community. There was little emphasis on ritual; congregations were free to adopt any form of baptism they wished. Basic decisions concerning the church did not come down from a pope, but were settled by vote at a conference. Bishops did not hold their posts for life, but were elected to four-year terms at these same conferences. Church doctrine was strongly against alcohol and slavery, while emphasizing the importance of a moral life.

Milton continued to work on the family farm, earning a little extra money by teaching in local schools. He also became increasingly active within his new church, preaching his first sermon in 1850, on his twenty-second birthday. Three years later he was invited to join the local church governing body. During that same year he entered Hartsville College, which was run by the United Brethren. Although he attended classes for only a year before illness forced him to drop out, this background qualified him for ordination as a minister, which took place in 1856.

He was very much at an age where he could begin to think about marriage, though for several years this was as far as he went. He began by falling in love with a neighbor's daughter. He did not propose, deciding that she was not right for him, but to the end of his life he remembered her with the fondest of thoughts. But in 1853, soon after entering Hartsville, he met his future bride, Susan Koerner. She was two years younger than him and very shy, which made for a prolonged courtship.

Her father had grown up in Saxony, a part of Germany. He had emigrated to the United States in 1818, and it says much about German militarism that he left to avoid being drafted, in a time when the wars of Napoleon were at an end. He joined the United Brethren soon after arriving in Indiana. Susan took his religious commitment as her own, experiencing her own call to faith and joining the Brethren in 1845, at age fourteen.

In 1857, recently ordained, Milton Wright accepted an invitation to join a mission in Oregon. Local churches there were organized into groups called circuits; he was to travel from one to the next, preaching at each in turn. He asked Susan to marry him and accompany him to that distant land. She gave him her commitment but not her hand, declaring that she was not about to leave Indiana and would wait for his return. For Susan this brought a fiancé and the prospect of an eventual marriage. Moreover, she had plenty of time to make up her mind, without being pressed by an ardent and eager lover.

For several decades, settlers in Conestoga wagons had been making their way westward along the Oregon Trail. However, in 1857 it was possible to reach that territory using steam power. Milton's odyssey began by railroad to New York, followed by steamship to Panama. A new railroad line, which had entered service only two years earlier, now crossed that isthmus. Reaching Panama City, he took another steamer to San Francisco, stopping along the way in Acapulco, which he described as one of the "sorry towns." At San Francisco, another ship carried his party onward to Portland.

He was in Panama only briefly, but it was long enough to catch malaria. He recovered slowly, but although he expected to ride the circuits of the Willamette Valley, for a time he was too weak to do so. He took a teaching position at a nascent United Brethren college, and as his health returned, he went on the circuits as a preacher. In 1859, the year that Oregon joined the Union, he completed his tour of duty and returned to Indiana, again by the Panama route. He arrived back home in November, and his Susan was waiting. They had stayed in touch by exchanging letters. Ten days after his arrival they were married, knowing that they could look forward to raising a family.

All children grow up with something from the mother, something from the father, and something that is all their own. Milton and Susan entered their marriage with significant strengths that in time were to influence Orville and Wilbur, as well as their other children. At the outset, their pervading religious faith carried overtones of personal strength and seriousness of purpose, of making commitments and holding to them. This gave the young Wrights a good underpinning when they set out to accomplish difficult tasks.

By the time Milton was married, he had already done an uncommon amount of traveling. He had lived in faraway Oregon; he had seen New York, San Francisco, Jamaica in the Caribbean, Mexico. This proved to be a prelude to a life of travel, as he pursued his career within the church. As he stayed in touch by letter and told of his adventures upon returning, he gave the family a strong sense of the wider world.

He also brought a background as a teacher. In 1852 he had been certified to teach penmanship, grammar, reading, writing, arithmetic, and geography in local elementary schools. He took his teaching seriously, like everything else in his life, later remembering particular students with fondness and pride. He went on to teach his own children to read, relying on the widely used McGuffey readers.

Susan brought her own strengths. In an era when few women obtained formal education, she went to Hartsville College, where she studied literature while taking courses in mathematics, Latin, and Greek. She also developed skill as a carpenter; her father had been a carriage maker, and she had spent much time in his shop. When her boys wanted advice on a mechanical project, they often found that she, rather than Milton, was the one who knew what to do.

During the early years of their marriage, Milton worked by turns as a teacher and as a minister, riding the local circuits. He also kept his hand in as a farmer. The newlyweds lived on farms, particularly one in Indiana's Grant County that Milton had purchased several years earlier. The Civil War broke out less than a year and a half into their marriage, but this conflict did not directly touch them. Though Milton was of military age, being still in his early and mid-thirties during that war, he was a pacifist and an ordained minister. The draft passed him by.

His income was limited but adequate. He earned $25 per month teaching school; his salary from the church was separate and came to an additional $200 per year. He also earned as much as $50 per year from sales of timber and crops grown on his Grant County farm. The Wrights had received a wedding gift of several hundred dollars from their families, and they held on to it. In 1864 Milton used this money to purchase a second farm, of five acres, with a three-room house. He and Susan did not live on this property but rented it out for $20 per month. This rental income helped to tide them over during the long months of summer, when school was out.

Milton's income thus stood near $700 per year. It was enough to enable him to work full time as a circuit-riding preacher, as he and Susan lived in a succession of rented houses while he moved from circuit to circuit. He knew that he could always earn more by returning to the classroom. In addition, his modest financial stability gave a useful foundation when the babies began to arrive.

The first of several, a boy, was born in March 1861. Milton viewed the name Wright as commonplace and expected to compensate by giving his children distinctive Christian names. The newborn son thus became the first in the family to bear this cross. Milton named him Reuchlin, after the German scholar Johannes Reuchlin, a contemporary of Martin Luther who had advocated toleration for the Jews. Perhaps it helped that people called him Roosh.

The next Wright child, born late in 1862, was also a son: Lorin, named for a town picked from a map. Wilbur, the older of the famous Wright brothers, came into the world on April 16, 1867. His name came from Wilbur Fiske, a clergyman whom Milton admired; the family called their new son Willy. Twins, Otis and Ida, were born in March 1870, but Ida died at birth and Otis followed her a month later. However, Orville, the second renowned Wright brother, came on August 19, 1871. His name was also derived from an admired minister, Orville Dewey of the Unitarians. The last Wright baby, Katharine, was born three years after Orville. Her name honored her mother, whose middle name was Catherine; it also varied that of recent ancestors such as Catharine Van Cleve and Catherine Wright. The new baby made five surviving children out of seven.

Their birth dates spanned a decade and a half, from 1861 to 1874. During those years, Milton consolidated his position within the United Brethren Church. In 1868 the family returned to Hartsville College, where he took a position as professor of theology. He was the first to hold such a professorship in the history of the Brethren. From this base he soon became actively involved over an issue of considerable controversy: the attitude of the Brethren toward secret societies such as the Masons.

During the eighteenth century, a number of leading Americans had been Freemasons. However, the new century brought a widespread change of opinion, with many people coming to view the Masons as a conspiring group of elitists. People expected their leaders to rise on their merits; they were appalled at secret societies that embraced mystic rituals while offering unfair privileges in business and politics to their members. A political party called the Anti-Masons flourished for a time, drawing strength from a widespread belief that the Masons had murdered a man for disclosing their secrets. Prominent Anti-Masons included John Quincy Adams, a recent president, and William Seward, who became President Lincoln's Secretary of State. The Anti-Masons became a significant element within the Whig Party, which sent several presidents to the White House in the decades prior to the Civil War.

For Milton, strong opposition to Freemasonry was a family affair. His father Dan had abhorred such secret societies, and it didn't matter that few of their members ever reached the wilds of rural Indiana. After all, Dan had a similarly strong hatred of slavery, in a land where there were no slaves. When Milton was coming of age and looked for a church he might join, he learned that the United Brethren were strongly anti-Mason. Indeed, the church constitution prohibited members from joining a secret society. This gave him one more reason to choose this church as his own.

But by the time of the Civil War, the Masons themselves were ready to respond to this opposition. Rather than remaining small in numbers and elitist in outlook, local Masonic lodges reached for a broader membership, prefiguring their evolution into community and service clubs like the Kiwanis and Lions of the next century. Businessmen and professionals flocked to join, not because the Masons offered the advantages of Yale University's Skull and Bones but because the lodges provided places to go and things to do, along with pleasant companionship. In little more than a decade, membership in the Masons leaped from 5,000 to as many as 200,000.

This presented a challenge to the anti-Masonic United Brethren. This sect was not like the Catholic Church, which took nearly four centuries to remove the writings of Copernicus from its Index of Prohibited Books. Still, the issue of Freemasonry raised the question of whether the Brethren could change with the times. A group of younger ministers, known as the Liberals, advocated a softening in the church's strong anti-Mason position. The old guard, who would have no such nonsense, came to be called Radicals, for they intended to defend existing doctrine to its roots. For some time, the Radicals remained in the majority.

Milton Wright cast his lot with the Radicals. He despised secrecy on principle; he was well aware that a Masonic lodge swore its members to oaths that could not be divulged. He also understood that no man could serve two masters, and viewed such practices as turning the Masons into a competing church—which did not pray to Jesus. Milton had been quite liberal for his time, not only opposing slavery but advocating equal rights for women. But in opposing Freemasonry, he took an unyielding stand. Everyone knew that he'd never, never budge.

During the late 1860s the Radical position was still ascendant, but church leaders saw a need to buttress this position. One way to do this was to put a strong Radical in charge of the church's publication program. This program was centered in a well-equipped printing house, the United Brethren Printing Establishment, located in Dayton, Ohio. Its products included a weekly newspaper, *The Religious Telescope*, which presented the official church position to members of the Brethren. With Milton as a leading spokesman for the Radicals, the church convention of 1869 chose him as editor of *The Telescope*.

This sudden and unexpected development brought the Wrights to Dayton, where they soon bought a house. It was part of a real-estate development stemming from the work of two local entrepreneurs,

William Huffman and H. S. Williams. They owned large tracts of land, much of it undeveloped, and they expected that it would rise in value if they could provide transportation. They built the Dayton Street Railway, which featured horse-drawn streetcars.

Like the freeways of the 1950s, these streetcars made it possible for people to live in pleasant parts of town and to commute to their jobs. Williams and Huffman did not anticipate the twentieth century by building homes and business districts, in the fashion of William Levitt and his Levittowns. However, these landowners indeed saw the value of their holdings increase, and they divided some of their tracts into lots for sale to individual buyers. Local contractors proceeded to build homes to order.

The new Wright home was at 7 Hawthorn Street, and remained the family's principal residence until well into the next century. Its neighborhood certainly was no exercise in suburban sprawl, for the lots were quite narrow. The Wrights' property was only thirty-seven feet

The Wright home at 7 Hawthorn Street.

wide. The house stood only two feet from that of the immediate neighbors. It had plenty of windows, but in general appearance it was a rather ordinary two-story frame structure with painted exterior walls. Milton paid $1,800 for it.

He took his family to Dayton in June of 1869, living in rented dwellings for the next two years. The Hawthorn Street house was still under construction when he bought it, just before Christmas of 1870. They moved in during the following April. Then in August, Susan gave birth to Orville, at home and in an upstairs bedroom. (One pictures her in labor, without painkillers, in the heat of an Ohio summer.)

The bedroom was one of four on the second floor. The house also had an attic, along with a partial cellar beneath the rear. A staircase with a balustrade led to the upstairs. The downstairs accomodations included a parlor and sitting room—along with a walk-in closet with a window, which the young Wrights later came to know all too well. A dining room and kitchen completed the arrangement. A cistern held water for the sink; a water pump stood just outside the kitchen door. Kerosene lamps provided light. Coal stoves gave heat; the cook stove in the kitchen burned wood. An outhouse stood in the backyard.

From this domestic base, Milton pursued his personal and professional activities. He was very firm in his personal beliefs, but he did not treat his *Religious Telescope* as a personal fiefdom. He gave fair coverage of different viewpoints, thus strengthening his position as editor. He nevertheless remained a thoroughgoing Radical, winning increasing recognition as a leader in an anti-Masonic movement that by then was well past its peak of national influence.

With children to raise, the question of their education was a matter of priority. Home schooling was high on the agenda; Milton had been a teacher, while Susan had ample education of her own. When the boys were naughty, they served time in the downstairs closet. Yet this was also part of their education, for it held magazines and shelves of books, while the window gave light to read by.

Income was no problem for the Wrights; Milton's salary as editor was as much as $1,500 per year. He also continued to hold his Indiana farms, which returned some $50 per month from rents plus sale of crops. His annual earnings thus exceeded the purchase price of his home, in an era when federal and state income taxes still lay far in the future. Secure both professionally and financially, he proceeded to parlay his editorship into selection as a bishop.

This was the highest post within the United Brethren, and Milton pursued it by developing talent as a politician. His publishing house attracted numerous visitors, and he took care to entertain them at his home. He wrote their family details in a notebook so that he could ask about their wives and children by name during future meetings. He continued to travel on church business, making sure that he ate and slept as a houseguest in as many different homes as possible. His campaign paid off. At the church conference of 1877, he was elected to a four-year term as bishop of the West Mississippi District, which extended from the Mississippi River to the Rockies.

His new responsibilities greatly increased his need to travel. The family remained in Dayton for another year, but experience showed that Milton needed a more central location as his home base. During subsequent decades he again lived at 7 Hawthorn, but June 1878 he put the house up for rent and moved with his family to Iowa, living first in Cedar Rapids and then in Adair. During the years in Iowa, the younger boys Wilbur and Orville began to come into their own.

New boys in town sometimes have difficulty making friends, but this did not prove to be a problem for the Wrights. Soon after arriving in Cedar Rapids, Orville took command of an "army" of over a dozen schoolmates. He was the general, with others being colonels and captains, while Wilbur, age eleven, plotted strategy. For weapons, they removed loose pickets from the school fence. This threatened trouble, but the young General Orville got them to agree to stand together, all for one and one for all. This proved unnecessary, as they got away with it.

Much of their education continued at home, where Milton took the view that toys, adroitly chosen, could teach a great deal. At age five, Orville had received a gyroscope as a birthday gift, which did not topple over even when resting on the edge of a knife. Soon after moving to Cedar Rapids, Milton presented his boys with a gift that had considerably greater significance in the long run. It was a type of toy helicopter, with twin propellers powered by a rubber band.

Though merely a plaything, it drew on work by a serious French inventor, Alphonse Penaud. He had introduced the rubber band as a source of power for model aircraft. Orville took to this toy avidly, constructing several copies that also flew successfully. Soon he was envisioning larger versions.

One day in school, his teacher found him at his desk with two pieces of wood. She asked what he was doing; he replied that he was building a flying machine. He hoped that his enlarged helicopter would fly particularly well, and was disappointed when it didn't. It needed more power, which was not to be had by using rubber bands.

That toy and its homebuilt successors did not lead Wilbur and Orville directly to aviation. Still, they gave the boys an initial step in that direction, and the memory stayed with them. Decades later, testifying in court, Orville stated that their earliest interest in flight "began when we were children. Father brought home to us a small toy actuated by a rubber spring which would lift itself into the air."

Inventors need ingenuity, and Orville displayed a good mind in Cedar Rapids, where he entered second grade. He quickly showed promise, winning a prize—a picture of his teacher—for having the best penmanship in class. His schoolmates were using McGuffey's Second Reader, but he grew bored with it, stating that he wanted to move on to the Third. He got his wish when the principal announced that any students who were sufficiently proficient might indeed advance to that level by passing a test. It called for Orville and other selected students to stand in front of the class and read a passage from the Second Reader aloud, with the teacher and principal close at hand. Orville was so flustered that he held the book upside down. However, he had memorized his portion, which enabled him to pass.

The Wrights stayed in Iowa until 1881, when Milton experienced a professional setback. He had given up his editorship when he became a bishop, but in his new position he failed to keep his political fences mended. He had won his 1877 election through his fair-minded editorship of *The Religious Telescope* and by making good first impressions when meeting people. But the United Brethren still cherished the democracy of the frontier, and in his day-to-day work as a bishop he had proved to be an Old Testament patriarch, convinced that his way was the only way. He had never held support among Liberals, but he lost ground among his own Radicals. At the 1881 church conference, he did not win a second term as bishop.

He still counted as an elder of the church, but he had lost both his bishopric and his newspaper. He moved his family from Iowa and retreated to Indiana, returning for a time to his old work as a circuit-riding preacher. They lived on a farm near Richmond, where Milton soon renewed his involvement with newspapers by founding a Radical monthly publication, *The Star*. It kept his name in the Brethren limelight, and encouraged him to hope for better days.

The move to the Richmond area brought Susan close to her family. Her father had prospered, with his farm growing to include over a dozen buildings, including a carriage shop. Wilbur and Orville were especially interested in this shop's foot-powered lathe. In what proved to be their first successful exercise in craftsmanship, they built a similar lathe in Milton's barn, with neighborhood friends counting it a privilege to work the foot treadle that provided power. Then Wilbur decided that he could improve its design by installing ball bearings. His balls were marbles made of clay rather than glass or steel; their races were metal rings taken from a horse's harness. This makeshift arrangement failed to work, but it showed anew that the boys had an inventive spirit.

Orville had somewhat more success when he began flying kites. He soon began building his own, which were so good that he made others to sell to his friends. This helped him earn spending money. It also helped him to appreciate the importance of light weight in aeronautics. He made his kites' frameworks as thin as possible, so thin that they bent in the wind.

The boys found other ways to spread their wings. Orville found a friend in a neighbor, Gansey Johnston, whose father was fond of taxidermy. His stuffed birds and animals gave Orville an idea, which Gansey enthusiastically embraced: that they should use these specimens to put on a circus, complete with a parade through town. Wilbur prepared publicity in the form of a news release, which ran in the Richmond newspaper under the heading, "What Are the Boys Up To?"

They were up to a lot. Wilbur's news item promised a "colossal" and "stupendous" show, featuring "thousands of rare birds," all of them stuffed. In addition, Davy Crockett was to appear with a grizzly bear. The bear was also part of the Johnston taxidermy collection, while Davy proved to be Gansey's four-year-old brother, who found himself swimming in his dad's hunting clothes. The centerpiece of the parade was an old buggy stripped of its body, with planks forming a platform. Several of Orville's friends pulled it, with the platform providing room for the "rare birds" as well as for Davy Crockett and his grizzly. The show drew a big turnout, not so much for its spectacles, but because Richmond was a close-knit town where people were glad to see what their children could do. Overwhelmed by so much attention, Orville and Gansey escaped by turning their parade into an alley. However, they satisfied the crowd by continuing the performance with an exhibit inside the Johnston barn.

Wilbur, for his part, was well along at Richmond High School during the early 1880s, entering his senior year in 1883. The nineteenth century paid little heed to professional credentials; it was a time when a man could rise to the top in almost any field based on skill and good horse sense. Moreover, Richmond was merely a small town on the Ohio border. Even so, Wilbur's senior-year courses would do credit to a modern four-year college, for he took Greek, Latin, geometry, natural philosophy, geology, and composition. His grades averaged to 95 out of 100 and indicated real achievement, for grade inflation still lay a century in the future.

Then in 1884, Milton decided to move the family back to Dayton. He was ready to renew his push for a larger role within the United Brethren, and Dayton was a major center for church activity, as well as the home of its all-important publishing house. His ploy worked, after a fashion, for again he was elected a bishop. However, the Liberals now were much stronger, and his bishopric covered California, Oregon, and Washington state. This was tantamount to exile; he might as well have been posted to Siberia. A Dayton newspaper reported the words of one Liberal: that this selection "would send him clear across the Rocky Mountains, where he could not disturb them." Milton continued to make Dayton his home, but he spent six months out of each year on the West Coast.

Within Dayton, Orville followed Wilbur by excelling in school. He graduated from eighth grade with a particularly high mark in arithmetic. In high school, he did not restrict himself to the assigned textbooks, but consulted other books as well. This enabled him to accomplish such feats as producing alternative solutions to problems in elementary geometry.

In Richmond, Wilbur had completed his senior year in high school, though he regarded his diploma as a mere formality and did not stay to receive it. He had done so well that Milton hoped to send him to divinity school at Yale, but Wilbur wanted more preparation. He enrolled at Dayton's Central High School, intending to study trigonometry and to improve his knowledge of Greek. He scored in the eighties when he took courses in rhetoric and in the writings of Cicero, presented in the original Latin. He also joined the football team and ran track.

Suddenly, while playing a game resembling hockey, someone struck him in the face with a bat and knocked out his upper front teeth. He was not severely injured otherwise, and dental repairs proved feasible. However, for a time his diet was restricted to liquids along with eggs and toast. This led to a digestive disorder, which spread to produce palpitations of the heart. This was serious. It was all too common for an illness or accidental injury to produce complications that could spiral out of control, leading to disability or to an early death.

Wilbur retreated from much of his ongoing life as he fell into a considerable depression. He gave up thoughts of Yale; indeed, he never went to college. He ceased to continue at Central High. He had been seeing a girl at that high school; he gave her up as well. He became increasingly homebound.

An excellent home library gave continuing activity for his mind. Many of his father's books were in a wooden bookcase that stood next to the downstairs closet. Popular writings included works of Nathaniel Hawthorne, Washington Irving, Sir Walter Scott, as well as the fairy tales of Grimm and Andersen. Serious histories included Gibbon's *The Decline and Fall of the Roman Empire,* Guizot on France, Green on England, Boswell's *The Life of Samuel Johnson,* and Plutarch's *Lives.* Family holdings included the *Encyclopaedia Britannica* and *Chamber's Cyclopedia.* Wilbur had hoped to study for the ministry; works on theology were in a separate library, in Milton's study on the upper floor.

Letters from his father, who continued to travel extensively, reminded him of the wider world while stimulating his imagination. In California, Milton wrote of "pumpkins as big as boulders" and "grapes as big as plums." He also wrote of travel by railroad:

> The tunnel over the mountains is not in repair and we went up
> the steepest grades I ever saw cars climb. We had two locomotives
> before, and one behind, and all their strength moved us very
> slowly. The ascent was in the midst of the wildest mountain
> scenery, and the track had a horse-shoe bend and some very short
> curves. The descent was more gentle, but the scenery wild all the
> way to Missoula, and indeed to Clark's Fork of the Columbia.[1]

Wilbur also made himself useful by helping his mother. Susan's health had never been robust, but in 1883 she contracted tuberculosis. The disease advanced only slowly, but it did advance, and she much appreciated his support. His brother Lorin suggested that Wilbur was merely a "cook and chambermaid," but by lifting some of Susan's burdens, he probably prolonged her life.

Milton was still caught up in controversies within the United Brethren, and as Wilbur gradually came out of his shell, he helped support his father's points of view with well-written essays. He proved to be a vigorous and effective writer, with one of his pamphlets being published and circulated in thousands of copies. Though barely into his twenties, he also showed that he would stand his ground when challenged by men who were far older and more experienced.

Milton's life took a major turn during 1889. Within the Brethren, the Liberals had continued to gain strength. Their agenda now ranged beyond the issue of toleration for secret societies, for they had pushed for reform in the church constitution, particularly in the manner of selecting representatives for its decision-making conventions. The Liberals also insisted on revising the church creed, or statement of belief. Milton, however, would have none of it. He insisted that the Brethren should hold to their old-time religion.

Matters came to a head at the convention of 1889. The Liberals won formal endorsement and enactment of all the points on their agenda, and by huge majorities. Milton joined with other leaders of the dwindling Radicals, as they staged a walkout and set up their own sect. It had only 15,000 members out of a total membership in the Brethren of some 200,000, but Milton was its undisputed leader. He was no more than a big fish in a small pond, but he now had a church that was all his own.

These events took place in May. Back home, Susan already was nearing death, at the age of fifty-eight. She died a few weeks later, and Milton described her passing in terse notes within his diary:

> July 3, 1889. Susan slept well tonight. Awoke at about 1:00 and got Susan a cool drink.
>
> July 4, 1889. About 4:00 I found Susan sinking and about five awakened the family. She revived about 7:00 somewhat, but afterward continued to sink until 12:20 afternoon, when she expired, and thus went out the light of my home.
>
> July 5, 1889. Bought a beautiful lot in Woodland, $135. Made arrangements as best I could for the funeral.
>
> July 6, 1889. Funeral at 2:00 in the afternoon. Bishop Halleck Floyd preached. Bury Susan in Woodland Cemetery about 4:00 p.m.[2]

Milton was sixty years old, still eligible, and there was no shortage of available widows. However, he had loved his Susan dearly for more than thirty years, and his heart had no room for someone new. Even so, he found that he needed a housekeeper and a companion. He found both in his daughter Katharine, who was not yet fifteen.

Milton was not a man to control his nearly grown children by sternly laying down the law. He didn't have to. He had raised them with a strong sense of duty, and with ample respect for the Fifth Commandment. Moreover, everyone in the family accepted not only that he had their truest interests at heart, but that he knew best. Even so, he gave them plenty of leeway as they grew. Thus, although he needed Katharine at home, he continued to live by his belief that she held an unquestioned right to pursue her education.

She attended Dayton's Central High, graduating in 1892. She went on to Oberlin Preparatory School, near Cleveland, entering that university and graduating with the Class of 1898. However, she took a year off during 1892 and 1893, and Milton had her work as his secretary, helping him with numerous details of church business. When she left Oberlin, she returned to Dayton, willingly taking up the role that Milton had laid out for her. She did not marry until well after Milton died, nearly thirty years later.

During the 1890s, Wilbur and Orville came of age to strike out on their own and to make their own marriages. However, that decade saw the Panic of 1893, with subsequent hard times that resembled the Great Depression of forty years later. With home and hearth providing an unrivaled combination of warmth, security, and freedom to try new things, the house at 7 Hawthorn continued to offer a highly attractive haven. Indeed, neither Wilbur nor Orville ever married.

In contemplating marriage, the younger Wrights had cause to reflect on the cautionary tales of their older brothers. Reuchlin had married in 1886, with his wife having a baby a year later. However, in 1888 Susan wrote that the in-laws were "sponging off" him, even though he had "no work, and no prospect of it." Reuchlin recouped by moving to Kansas City, where he indeed found work. Even so, Kansas City was a long way from Dayton.

Lorin also lit out for the territories, spending several months in Kansas during 1886 and then returning to that state early in 1887. Caught up in loneliness, he went back to Dayton after his mother died. He married an old sweetheart in 1892, and proceeded to have four children. He worked as a bookkeeper, but even with part-time second jobs, he found it hard to support his family.

Despite the Panic of 1893, Dayton continued to offer opportunities as it grew in population from 61,220 in 1890 to 85,333 in 1900. An important reason for this growth lay in a rapidly-prospering local company, National Cash Register. A Dayton inventor, James Ritty, had built the first mechanical cash register in 1879. A Dayton business-man, John Patterson, launched the company. People called it "the Cash"; it quickly grew into the city's economic mainspring.

In addition, Wilbur and Orville found more at home than the sim-ple warmth of family. As Wilbur later wrote, "From the time we were little children, my brother Orville and myself lived together, played together, worked together, and, in fact, thought together. We usually owned all of our toys in common, talked over our thoughts and aspi-rations so that nearly everything that was done in our lives has been the result of conversations, suggestions, and discussions between us."

In earnest of their intention to remain in Dayton, they carried out a program of home improvement. The house at 7 Hawthorn was func-tional but plain, with shutterless windows that stared outward like enor-mous eyes. They installed pale green shutters on those of the upper story. The house stood very close to the one next door, but in front and to the other side, there was room for a wraparound porch that resem-bled a southern veranda. Wilbur and Orville built it as well, with their craftsmanship being good enough to make it look as if it had been part of the house from the outset. Pillared and roofed, it stood two steps off the ground. A wooden railing lined the edge, with posts that the young Wrights turned on a lathe. Though straightforward in construction, it made the house look larger and considerably more attractive.

The experience of building that porch might have fitted them for work as construction contractors. Instead, they turned to a different activity: printing. They eased into it by degrees, amid considerable support within the family, taking initial steps and then proceeding to more demanding efforts. This prefigured their experiences a few years later, when they set out to invent the airplane.

Orville was the first to develop an interest in printing. He was twelve years old and the family was living near Richmond, Indiana. He saw line illustrations printed in magazines and wondered how they were made. He consulted articles in *Chamber's Cyclopedia,* which was part of the home library, and learned they were printed from carved wooden blocks. He proceeded to try his own woodcuts. Milton gave him both encouragement and help by presenting him with proper woodworking tools as a Christmas gift. Milton also allowed him to make prints by using a letterpress, a device that made copies of letters by pressing them strongly against damp paper, thus causing the ink to transfer.

When the Wrights returned to Dayton, Orville found that an old friend named Ed Sines was still in the neighborhood. During kindergarten Orville had played hooky at Ed's home, taking care to return to his own home right after school ended for the day. Soon afterward, the two young boys lit a fire in the Wright backyard that threatened to spread. Three-year-old Katharine saved the day by running to get her mother.

Ed already had a toy printing press. It could print only one line at a time, but it drew strong interest from Orville. He and Ed proceeded to set up a printshop in a corner of the Sines's kitchen. Soon Milton stepped in anew, offering a proposal for expansion. Two older brothers, Wilbur and Lorin, had built a rowboat and found an opportunity to trade it for a somewhat larger printing press. Milton arranged for the exchange to go through, then purchased twenty-five pounds of used type for Orville.

There was an obvious confluence between Orville's budding interest and Milton's professional activities. Indeed, their ventures proceeded side by side, for during 1885 Milton launched a new Radical publication, *The Christian Conservator.* Orville and Ed, for their part, found themselves in a position to print three-by-five-inch sheets using their new press. This spurred thoughts of publishing a four-page newsletter for their eighth-grade classmates. They quickly ran out of material to print, and when Milton saw that they had failed to put anything significant on page three, he refused to allow them to hand out the printed copies. He insisted that if they were to print material for distribution, even to their classmates, they had to do it right.

It was easy for Milton to keep an eye on them (when he was in town), for they had moved their shop to larger quarters at the Wrights'. Though their impromptu newsletter flopped, they soon purchased a quantity of display type and solicited orders from local shopkeepers. Handbills, business cards, and advertising circulars became their stock in trade. The boys were always glad to take payment in cold cash, but they weren't fussy. One customer paid a bill with two dollars worth of popping corn, still on the cob. Ed wanted to eat the profits, but Orville bought out his share, took the corn to a local grocer, and sold it for money.

Though Ed and Orville initially had come to printing merely as a hobby, their work acquired a tone of seriousness. Another neighborhood boy joined them as a general assistant, earning a wage of fifteen cents per week. The enterprise expanded anew, with Susan Wright clearing out an upstairs room for their use. The three-by-five-inch press quickly became inadequate, and Orville proceeded to acquire a larger one. Significantly, he did not save up money and buy it; he designed and built it himself. It was somewhat makeshift; for instance, a damaged gravestone from a marble dealer served as the press bed. Nevertheless, it could print single sheets as large as eleven by sixteen inches.

He moved toward a professional career as a printer during his high school years, spending two summers as an apprentice at a local printshop. He learned the art of stereotyping, pressing set type into sheets of wet cardboard to make a mold for hot lead, so as to create a plate suitable for use in printing. This enabled him to break up the columns of set type and redistribute them for further use, thus stretching his supply of type.

During 1888, at the age of sixteen, Orville set out to build a new press with a self-inking system for printing at high speed. He needed an array of folding bars that could hold the type in position while pressing it against the paper. The folding top of an old buggy gave him what he wanted. When his new press was up and running, it printed five hundred sheets per hour.

The boys had long been accustomed to working with Milton on his own publications: *The Star, The Conservator*. They had helped to prepare copies for distribution, with Wilbur having built a device powered by a foot treadle that folded the sheets neatly. When Wilbur wrote a broadside that supported his father's point of view in the ongoing controversies, Orville used his first large homebuilt press to print some of the copies. Now, with his new high-speed press, he could print complete issues of the *Conservator*, two pages to a sheet. He proceeded to bid for a number of lucrative church and business contracts, with Milton steering a good deal of new work to his son.

Early in 1889, Orville launched a new venture in the form of a four-page weekly community newsletter. The Wrights' neighborhood lay to the west of downtown Dayton, and he called it *The West Side News*. Much of its material came from publications such as *The Youth's Companion*, with little attention to copyright, but it also ran advertisements from local merchants, which helped to win their support. It quickly began to turn a profit. Orville responded by moving his operation out of household quarters and into rented space within a commercial building on Third Street, a few blocks away from home.

Wilbur also joined him, taking the post of editor while Orville listed himself as the publisher. Wilbur had already shown talent as a writer, for work he had written in support of his father had been published. The two brothers thus were on the masthead in July, when their mother died. They marked the occasion solemnly, running a front-page obituary that particularly noted the personal strength with which she had borne her illness.

After a year, the young publishers expanded their paper into a daily. As many as a dozen professionally published newspapers served the city of Dayton, but Orville and Wilbur hoped to gain a niche for themselves by emphasizing news that was genuinely local. They subscribed to a wire service. They ran editorials calling for street improvements while noting that the West Side had leaky sewers and inadequate streetcar service. Taking a leaf from William Randolph Hearst, they also used sensational headlines when they could. Thus, an account of a fire carried the head, "Roasted in Red, Roaring and Terrible Flames."

This enterprise did not succeed. It failed to compete with the city's mainstream newspapers. As losses mounted, the Wrights shut it down after less than four months. They returned to the business of operating a general printshop within their growing city, keeping their hand in this venture for several additional years. Along the way, they made a modest contribution to American literature.

Orville had a friend, Paul Dunbar, a black man who was working as an elevator operator for four dollars per week. However, the young fellow had talent. His parents had sent him to Central High, where he became class poet, editor of the school newspaper, and president of the debating club. He contributed poetry to *The West Side News,* and wrote doggerel that expressed his high regard for his publisher:

Orville Wright is out of sight
In the printing business.
No other mind is half as bright
As his'n is.[3]

The last line indicated Dunbar's preference for verses in dialect. He also wrote poems in a classic style, with "Ere Sleep Comes Down to Soothe the Weary Eyes" being cherished across a century and appearing in the modern *Norton Anthology of Poetry:*

Ere sleep comes down to soothe the weary eyes,
Which all the day with ceaseless care have sought
The magic gold which from the seeker flies;
Ere dreams put on the gown and cap of thought,
And make the waking world a world of lies—
Of lies most palpable, uncouth, forlorn,
That say life's full of aches and tears and sighs—
Oh, how with more than dreams the soul is torn,
Ere sleep comes down to soothe the weary eyes. . . .

When sleep comes down to seal the weary eyes,
The last dear sleep whose soft embrace is balm,
And whom sad sorrow teaches us to prize
For kissing all our passions into calm,
Ah, then, no more we heed the sad world's cries,
Or seek to probe th' eternal mystery,
Or fret our soul at long-withheld replies,
At glooms through which our visions cannot see,
When sleep comes down to seal the weary eyes.

In 1892 Dunbar took fifty-six of his poems to Orville and asked him to print them in book form. Orville lacked equipment for binding, but invited him to try the United Brethren publishing house in downtown Dayton. The book that resulted, *Oak and Ivy,* put the young poet on the map. He continued in this field, writing "Weary Eyes" in 1896. In time his home, the Paul Lawrence Dunbar House, became a museum.

Although Orville and Wilbur's newspaper did not last long, the overall success of their printshop showed them that they could measure up to the demands of challenging tasks by using their hands and their wits. They had reason to believe that their shop might develop into a publishing arm of Milton's religious sect. However, the young Wrights were not about to turn away from further opportunities. Very soon, a new one beckoned: bicycles.

They became important only late in the nineteenth century, even though pertinent technology had been at hand for thousands of years. The civilizations of antiquity had made good use of horse-drawn chariots, thereby demonstrating that they could build lightweight wheels as well as axles with low-friction bearings. When Ben-Hur ran his race in the Roman arena, it would have been quite possible for contemporaries to transform the chariot into a bicycle. Chain drive would have outstripped their capabilities, but pedals fixed to the front axle would have sufficed. A wooden frame, a seat, and a front wheel steered by handlebars would have completed the arrangement.

Still, even if ancient inventors had crafted such vehicles, they would have been defeated by rough roads. This proved to be the fate of two nineteenth-century developments that foreshadowed the modern bicycle. The first, known as the "swift-walker" or "hobby horse," looked somewhat like a bike without pedals. A rider sat on a small saddle and walked along, with the vehicle carrying much of the weight while the feet provided propulsion. A German inventor, Karl von Drais, introduced the first of them in 1817. They became briefly popular among fashionable young men. However, they lacked any semblance of a spring-mounted suspension. When a dandy rode his hobby horse over a bump in a bad road, it tended to give the seat a sudden upward thrust against his groin. This fad died out very quickly.

It experienced a brief revival after the Civil War, as new versions made their appearance, equipped with pedals. They were formally known as velocipedes, but many people preferred a more descriptive name: the "boneshaker." The use of pedals promised speed, but the ride again proved highly uncomfortable on anything but the smoothest pavement. The basic boneshaker design lived on in the child's tricycle, which added an extra rear wheel while retaining the pedals on the front axle. Within the world at large, however, the boneshaker soon went to the boneyard.

Even so, its use of pedals raised the question of whether a different type of pedaled bicycle might find a market. The answer came from England in the form of the high-wheeler, also called the "ordinary." Its enormous front wheel gave speed in the most direct fashion, for the big wheel rolled further with each turn of the pedals. The first such bicycle was the Ariel of 1871, patented by the English inventors James Starley and William Hillman. It had a 48-inch front wheel, with later versions expanding this diameter to as much as 63 inches.

Like its successors, the Ariel made use of wire-spoke wheels. These resembled the wheels of a modern bike. In place of the inflexible spokes of the boneshaker, the Ariel used steel wires that could all be put into tension. Such wires would bend when a rider went over a bump, which eased the jolt. With practice, a good cyclist could cruise at twenty miles per hour.

Even children rode them. When Orville Wright and his friend

Gansey Johnston were preparing their parade, they announced that they planned to lead it by riding on "iron horses," which turned out to be high-wheel bicycles. Still, while such vehicles were faster and rode more smoothly than a boneshaker, a bump in the road could easily pitch a rider over the top and make him fall headfirst to the ground. High-wheelers thus became largely a sport for young men of bravado, who laughed off such mishaps as "taking a header." Their vehicles thus were the motorcycles of their day, dangerous, exciting, and macho. They flourished for some twenty years, but never became practical as a serious form of personal transportation.

In this fashion, sixty years of inventiveness brought forth three types of bicycle-like vehicles, all of which failed to catch on because they were dangerous. The swift-walker and the boneshaker tended to kick a man in the testicles; the high-wheeler could actually break his neck. Still, the means were in hand for a reasonably comfortable ride. In addition to the bump-absorbing wire-spoke wheel, the high-wheeler also introduced saddles or seats mounted on coil or leaf springs. For inventors, the challenge now lay in reinventing the bicycle by shrinking the enormous front wheel to a more convenient size, while preserving the speed and the lack of pain.

The key proved to lie in chain drive, which now entered the bicycle realm for the first time. A large gear, fitted with pedals, could turn a much smaller gear mounted to the rear axle. This gave the high speed that previously had been achieved using the directly pedal-driven big front wheel. That wheel, in turn, could diminish considerably in size, restoring the bicycle's overall proportions to those of the boneshaker—and with considerably more comfort. Such vehicles were called safety bicycles, for they did not tip forward to cause a header. With modest refinements, they amounted to bicycles as we ride them to this day.

The first safety bicycles came from England's John Starley, nephew of James Starley of the Ariel, and his partner William Sutton. Their design converged rapidly to a definitive form; versions sold only a few years later differed only in fine detail from models that are advertised in today's catalogs. Still, there remained room for improvement. Early safety bicycles, like the high-wheelers, used solid rubber tires. They saved weight, but did little to cushion bumps. In 1888 an Irish inventor, John Dunlop, introduced the first inflatable tires. Another inventor, I. W. Boothroyd, developed a tire that was easy to repair following the inevitable punctures.

Despite the inconvenience of such punctures, inflatable tires gave a notably superior ride and quickly swept the field. In only four years, from 1890 to 1894, inflatables rose from barely one percent of the market to nearly 100 percent. Solid rubber tires, which had stood virtually without rival in 1890, virtually vanished.

A further refinement involved the pedals and chain drive. During the first decade of the safety bicycle, there was no freewheeling; the pedals, gears, chain, and rear wheel all turned as one system. This meant that on a downhill run, the motion of the bike forced the pedals to keep turning regardless of the rider's wishes. Bicycles of the era had footrests, allowing a rider to keep the feet out of the way of the whirling pedals, but this proved to be merely an interim solution. The true freewheeling gear was in hand by 1897, allowing for a considerably more convenient coasting ride.

The first safety bikes reached America in 1887, quickly sparking the rise of an important new industry. In 1890 some 40,000 were built in the United States; production peaked at 1.2 million only five years later. They gave people the mobility of a horse, at considerably less cost. Complementing the electric trolleys that by then were replacing the horse-drawn streetcar in a host of cities, bicycles neatly filled the gap between walking and traveling long distances by rail.

In important respects, bicycles foreshadowed the automobile. They demanded some mechanical skill, particularly when repairing a flat tire. This anticipated early motorcars, whose drivers were well advised to be able to carry out their own repairs and maintenance. Designers of bikes had gone far to accommodate the poor roads of the era, but the widespread use of bikes brought an increasing demand for paved roads of better quality. A tire industry developed; to this day, the name of Dunlop is associated with this product. This industry thus was ready when it faced a demand for automotive tires. Other bicycle technologies also found use with motorcars: electrical welding, ball bearings, chain drive. Moreover, as bicycle ownership spread, an increasing number of people came to experience the freedom of the open road. This presaged the even greater freedom of the automobile.

Orville and Wilbur came to bicycling much as they had come to printing, entering this new activity by degrees. Orville started in 1892 by paying $160 for a top-of-the-line model. His old friend, Ed Sines, became an active bicyclist as well; together they joined the YMCA Wheelmen, a national association, and began competing in races. Wilbur followed, picking up a used bike at an auction.

The young Wrights were well known locally for having built printing presses from scratch. They quickly found their mechanical talents in demand among their fellow cyclists, and Wilbur decided that they could find new opportunities by selling and repairing bikes. The demise of their newspaper in 1890 had left them with more time than the printshop could fill. Moreover, that shop was in good hands, for Ed Sines was still working there.

In December 1892 they rented a storefront. Bicycling was highly seasonal, with little activity during the winter but plenty during the warm months of each year. The Wrights thus had several months to order stock, including an extensive line of spare parts and accessories. Orville appreciated only too well that good bikes were costly; the $160 he had paid for his own cycle compared with the $1,800 that Milton had paid for the family house. The brothers therefore took care to sell brand names that were known for quality. They further encouraged sales by taking used bikes as trade-ins and by offering time-payment plans.

For a time they had the only bicycle shop on Dayton's West Side, and business boomed. Within a year, bicycles had outstripped printing as their primary activity. Indeed, as they turned increasingly to bicycles, they spent less time with Ed Sines at the printshop, so they hired their brother Lorin to help him. Calling their enterprise the Wright Cycle Company, they moved to a succession of larger buildings as their sales continued to expand.

They made good use of advertising. They had used their printing presses to help Milton in his religious work, and during the fall of

1894 they set out to help themselves, publishing a weekly newsletter directed at local cyclists. With the name *Snap-Shots of Current Events,* it promoted the Wright Cycle Company, while the brothers again sold advertising to other local merchants to cover their expenses.

High school students represented another potential market. At Central High, teachers gave written tests that followed a standardized format. A rumor got around that a student had stolen a copy of an upcoming test, and the Wrights responded adroitly. They printed up advertising sheets in the standard test format. However, the questions and answers sang the praises of Wright Cycle.

Still, there was only so much business to go around. The young Wrights had gotten an early start, but by 1895 there were fourteen bicycle shops in Dayton, three of which were within two blocks of the Wrights' location. Everyone was offering low, low prices, which meant that the Wrights could not compete by underselling the competition. Still, they could regain their edge in other ways. Their mechanical skills were as sharp as ever. They now held several years of close experience in selling and repairing the top brands, and were intimately familiar with their strong points. Drawing on this background, they set out to build custom models of superior design and craftsmanship.

This new venture promised to reawaken their creativity, within lives that were increasingly routine. Wilbur was in his late twenties in 1895, with Orville in his mid-twenties. Even so, despite their successes first in printing and then in bicycles, they both were living at home with their father. Both were bachelors and seemed well on their way to becoming confirmed bachelors, for neither of them had a sweetheart or a significant prospect for marriage. Nor did they attend college.

Wilbur, at least, might have gone on to college and pursued a professional career. His thoughts of Yale University's divinity school lay nearly a decade in the past, but in September 1894 he wrote a candid letter to his father, who was away on a trip at the time:

> I have been thinking for some time of the advisability of my
> taking a college course. I have thought about it more or less for a
> number of years but my health has been such that I was afraid that

it might be time and money wasted to do so, but I have felt so much better for a year or so that I have thought more seriously of it and have decided to see what you think of it and would advise.

I do not think I am specially fitted for success in any commercial pursuit even if I had the proper personal and business influences to assist me. I might make a living but I doubt whether I would ever do much more than this. Intellectual effort is a pleasure to me and I think I would be better fitted for reasonable success in some of the professions than in business. . . .

I have always thought I would like to be a teacher.[4]

His thoughts were in keeping with family expectations. Reuchlin and Lorin, the older brothers, had attended Hartsville College, the alma mater of both his parents, while his sister Katharine was a newly-enrolled freshman at Oberlin, in pursuit of a degree and of her own career as a teacher. Wilbur and Milton discussed the financial arrangements, with Milton offering to help. Then Wilbur got cold feet. Perhaps he had no wish to burden Orville with sole responsibility for both the printing and the bicycle business; perhaps he wanted not to leave home but to continue working with Orville as a twosome. He turned down his father's offer of financial help and stayed in Dayton.

But he joined in with enthusiasm when custom-made bikes emerged as the brothers' next venture. The Wrights prepared by setting up a machine shop. They installed a turret lathe, a drill press, and equipment for cutting steel tubing. They also put in apparatus for electric welding that they themselves had devised. To drive their machine tools, they placed a rotating shaft on the ceiling, with belts running down to their equipment. They needed a motor to power the shafting, and they designed and built that as well. It took form as an internal combustion engine with a single cylinder.

Engines of that general type dated to 1860. The first of them used a two-stroke cycle; that is, it took in fuel and air, burned them explosively to drive the piston's downstroke, then used its return stroke to exhaust the burned gases from the cylinder. A French inventor, Adolphe-Eugene

Beau de Rochas, described the more efficient four-stroke cycle in 1862. It promised to improve performance by taking in the fuel-air mix and then compressing it, with ignition occurring at the instant of greatest compression. In Germany, Nicolaus Otto built the first such motor in 1876. His colleague Gottlieb Daimler built a greatly improved Otto-cycle engine in 1886. Such engines soon became important within the nascent automobile industry.

Automotive engines burned gasoline and required a carburetor, to produce a good fuel-air mix for the cylinders. However, Otto's earliest four-stroke motor used illuminating gas made from coal, and the Wrights did the same. This bypassed the need for a carburetor, for the gas and air mixed readily. Within the Wrights' new shop, the coal gas came from a municipal line. The engine took shape as a joint effort. Orville worked on the valve lifters and the timing of the spark ignition, while Wilbur installed a governor and addressed the important problem of cooling.

Though their bikes were to be designed and sold as custom models, the Wrights took care to offer brand-name seats, tires, and handlebars. They made their own frames, building them from tubing and painting them meticulously with enamel. In April 1896, they used *Snap-Shots* to announce their new product with a blare of trumpets:

> The Wright Special will contain nothing but high grade materials throughout, although we shall put it on the market at the exceedingly low price of $60. It will have large tubing, high frame, tool steel bearings, needle wire spokes, narrow tread and every feature of an up-to-date bicycle. Its weight will be about 22 pounds. We are very certain that no wheel on the market will run easier or wear longer than this one, and we will guarantee it in the most unqualified manner.[5]

The Wrights constructed some three hundred bicycles during the next five years, and continued to introduce improvements. They were particularly proud of wheel hubs of their own design, describing them as "absolutely dust proof, and oil retaining to a degree that *one oiling in two years* is all they require." These hubs thereby accommodated the roads of rural Ohio, which were unpaved and dusty.

This new activity helped to fill their time during the slack winter months, when bicycling activity fell off sharply while sales and repairs diminished as well. A customer could have a bike made to order and it would be ready in time for the coming of spring. Business took a decided turn for the better, with the Wrights responding by selling their printshop in 1899. There was every reason to anticipate that they would make their living entirely through bicycles.

The bicycle was one of a number of inventions that marked the 1890s. In particular, some of the first automobiles took to the road. One of them was the work of Cordy Ruse, a friend of the Wrights. Orville helped him build it, but Wilbur was not impressed. He suggested that Cordy should fasten a bed sheet beneath his car to catch parts as they fell off while the vehicle was in operation.

Still, Wilbur and Orville had not exhausted their ingenuity with their one-cylinder engine and their custom bikes. By the end of the decade they were ready to pursue still another venture. They now wanted to build a flying machine, and to work within a realm of aeronautics that had seen people taking to the air for over a hundred years.

TWO

PROPHETS WITH SOME HONOR

ROUGH ROADS MAY EXPLAIN why bicycle-like vehicles were not invented until early in the nineteenth century, rather than in the time of the ancient Greeks. Yet this lack of creativity ran deeper, drawing on a widespread difficulty in making pertinent mental leaps even when opportunities were there to be seen. The advent of the hot-air balloon gives an illustration. Smoke rises; this has been known since the early use of fire, hundreds of thousands of years ago. Yet it was not until 1782 that anyone thought to trap warm smoke within a lightweight enclosure, thereby inventing the balloon.

Leonardo da Vinci might have done it. He held an ongoing fascination with aviation and with the flight of birds. He also sought to take advantage of the power of a rising column of smoke within a chimney, by having this smoke spin a windmill. This whirling propeller then was to provide power to turn a large joint of meat as it roasted over the fire. He invented this "smokejack" around the year 1500, but he never thought of a balloon.

But the eighteenth century marked the beginning of an age of inventiveness. Coal entered widespread use, replacing wood that had served in previous centuries. It demanded ingenuity, both to protect products from its fumes and to make use of its intense heat. Blast furnaces produced iron in substantial quantities. Scotland's James Watt built the first good steam engines after 1765, laying groundwork for an upsurge in the use of mechanical power. With the spirit of the times embracing new discoveries and innovations, the era was ripe for those who might find something new in rising smoke.

Two Frenchmen, Joseph and Etienne Montgolfier, were men who saw this. They were two of sixteen children born within the family of Pierre Montgolfier, a prosperous paper manufacturer near Lyon. Joseph, born in 1740, was a tall and strong fellow with a highly casual way about him. This applied to his clothes and to a tendency to forget basic things, as on an occasion when he left his wife at an inn without remembering to bring her with him. He was casual as well in his attitude to life, rarely becoming angry, and in his background, for he had spent some time as a vagabond. He showed similar lack of concern in his business dealings, borrowing and spending freely and then turning to his family to bail him out.

But he had a good memory for some things, readily learning long poems and songs. He also had shown a strong interest in chemistry and mathematics, eagerly reading textbooks on these topics and taking lengthy notes. A cousin had studied science in Paris and introduced him to the study of gases. These included carbon dioxide, "inflammable air" or hydrogen, as well as oxygen. They all differed sharply from common air, and each gas had its own properties and methods of preparation. Montgolfier found himself strongly drawn to these discoveries.

One evening in November 1782, sitting in his room, he found himself contemplating a picture of a recent siege of the British fortress of Gibraltar. Britain had won this stronghold some seventy years earlier, following the War of the Spanish Succession, but had been compelled to defend it against attack both by land and sea. Montgolfier now asked himself: might it be taken by air? He was sitting near a fire; he watched the hot smoke rise into the chimney. He already knew that hydrogen was buoyant, being much lighter than air, but he was also aware that this gas was difficult to prepare. He considered that fire-heated air might also be buoyant, and far easier to obtain.

His background would hardly have marked him for so original a thought, for he had been educated by Jesuits, who were quick to stamp out heresy and to discourage his forbidden studies of science. But his casualness extended to disdaining restraints on his freedom of thought. He built a lightweight framework of thin wood and covered it with taffeta fabric, leaving a large hole in the bottom. Crumpling up some paper, he placed it within the hole and ignited it. As he had hoped, the device, which looked like a box kite, rose from its support and reached the ceiling.

His next thought was for his brother Etienne, who was five years younger. His attitudes contrasted sharply with those of Joseph, for Etienne was a capable business manager who had been trained as an architect and had begun to build a practice in Paris. Although he was the youngest of the brothers, his father, Pierre, selected him as the next head of the paper factory. Now in charge of that plant, Etienne had introduced new manufacturing methods and was leading it to new prosperity.

Joseph wrote him a brief letter: "Get in a supply of taffeta and of rope or cords, quickly, and you will see one of the most astonishing sights in the world." He had been living in Avignon, but now he returned home to rejoin Etienne and to repeat the experiment with heated air, this time in the open air. He built a new fabric-covered box and sent it to a height of seventy feet, keeping it aloft for a full minute. Etienne indeed was astonished. Working with Joseph, he helped to craft a new and larger version that was nine feet across. It produced so much lift that it broke a restraining cord and flew into the air, flying for nearly a mile before it finally came down.

The free-spirited Joseph had lacked a commitment that could give focus to his life, and now he had one. Etienne had plenty of work at the factory, but he put some of it on hold as he joined his brother in a program of experiments. They learned to measure lifting force by having test versions break cords of known strength. They also abandoned the use of boxy wooden frames, turning to a simple cloth bag as the preferred design. The cloth needed a lining to hold the heat. Paper proved suitable, providing a new use for the family's stock in trade. The new invention merited a name. Choosing not to be fancy, the brothers called it simply a ball, or *ballon*.

In April 1783, they were ready with a big one, thirty-five feet across and holding more than a ton of air. It showed its power during an early experiment, as four strong laborers held it to keep it from rising. As a fire warmed its air, its lift increased so rapidly that two of the men let go of their ropes. The balloon then raised the other two off their feet. They avoided being lifted higher by releasing their own lines, whereupon the inflated bag again flew freely before coming down on a nearby farm.

A public demonstration was now in order, and the brothers arranged to conduct it in the marketplace of Annonay, their home town. A meeting of some importance was to take place in June, with members of the nobility in attendance, and a report of its proceedings was to be forwarded to Paris. The Montgolfiers hoped to put on a good demonstration for the attendees. The day proved to be rainy, but the brothers gamely piled dry straw and wool in a brazier, added alcohol, and set fire to this fuel. To achieve a dramatic flight, they attached this heater below the balloon's mouth so that it could continue to warm the enclosed air. The balloon rose to 3,000 feet and drifted with the wind for over a mile before landing in a vineyard.

Flight had now been achieved in the presence of witnesses, and the report from the meeting indeed included a discussion of this event. This document reached Paris later that month, where its readers included the powerful controller general of finance, Lefevre d'Ormisson. He read about the flight, decided that the matter was worth pursuing, and sent a letter to the Marquis de Condorcet, head of the Academy of Science. Condorcet set up an investigative panel that included Antoine Lavoisier, a founder of the science of chemistry.

Another member, Nicholas Desmarest, already was acquainted with Etienne through a mutual interest in papermaking. Indeed, Etienne had written letters to him describing their work with balloons.

The brothers were well aware that Paris was the place to seek serious attention, and they were gratified when the city's newspapers began to pick up the story. A particularly informative article appeared in the *Journal de Paris* late in July, with Condorcet's committee as a source. As the news began to spread, new people began to seek involvement. These included Jacques Charles, a well-born man with a strong interest in science. Widely known for his public lectures, he decided that he could build his own balloon and fly it as a public spectacle. Rather than use hot air, though, he decided to be bolder and to use hydrogen.

Often called "inflammable air" at the time, it had been discovered as recently as 1766. Lavoisier was familiar with it. This gas produced water when it burned, and he named it "hydrogene," the water former. Charles was also aware of it, for he had often prepared small quantities during his lectures, arranging for this gas to flow through a tube and to blow bubbles that rose to the ceiling. Hydrogen was difficult to prepare in quantity, and Charles at first had not stretched his imagination beyond bubbles. But when he learned of the balloon flight in Annonay, he made his own mental leap.

England's Henry Cavendish, the discoverer of hydrogen, had produced it by treating shavings of iron, zinc, or tin with sulfuric acid. His process remained the standard method, but it did not lend itself to ready use when this gas was needed in large quantities. It called for substantial amounts of iron, which was cheap but heavy, and of acid, which was highly corrosive. The reaction also produced heat, which could touch off the highly flammable hydrogen or cause some acid to evaporate, condensing inside the balloon and perhaps eating away its lining. Nor did anyone have experience in producing hydrogen in quantity; no one had ever done this. Charles nevertheless expected to keep the danger under control by diluting his acid. He anticipated that this would slow the reaction and reduce its production of heat.

People called his hydrogen balloon a *charlière*. It was thirteen feet across, considerably smaller than the *montgolfière* of Annonay. This reflected the fact that hydrogen had far more lifting power than the hot air of Joseph and Etienne. Even so, Charles needed a thousand pounds of iron and 500 pounds of acid to produce enough of this gas to fill the balloon to capacity. Charles nevertheless set August 27th as the date for the ascent, with his promoters proceeding to sell tickets for what they hoped would be a profitable public show.

Spectators began to enter the grounds in midafternoon, with the balloon still undergoing inflation. This took time; the crowd became impatient, and its mood did not improve as rain clouds gathered. Then at five P.M. a cannon fired and the fully inflated *charlière* leaped into the air. It remained in view for only two minutes before vanishing into the clouds, but then continued onward for fifteen miles. It finally came down in the village of Gonesse, where curious peasants watched it bounce upon landing as if it were a strange monster. Some of them smelled the foul odor of hydrogen sulfide, an impurity that produces the stench of rotten eggs. Clearly, here was the work of the devil, and the people set upon it with pitchforks.

By then Etienne was in Paris, having arrived during July. He met with members of Condorcet's commission, and secured funding from the Ministry of Finance. Within that ministry, Controller General d'Ormisson was an appointee of King Louis XVI, and was quite familiar with the king's court. He helped Etienne arrange for a new flight that was to take place at Versailles, in front of the royal family.

With this balloon launch taking place only two months after Etienne's arrival in Paris, it is tempting to view Louis XVI as prefiguring President John Kennedy, who personally met with astronauts following their missions. Louis indeed had intelligence, owning a library that filled several rooms and translating part of Gibbon's *Decline and Fall of the Roman Empire.* Yet he was not a serious man. He willingly indulged the extravagances of his queen, Marie Antoinette. At times he put aside statecraft for the pleasures of the hunt. His lack of seriousness extended to the national economy, which stood as *the* critical issue during his reign. The controller general of finance held the key post, dealing with taxes and spending as well as with forced donations of labor, which were stirring popular discontent. This office also held responsibility for the government's standing in financial markets, as well as for such basic issues as whether the people were to have bread to eat at affordable prices.

A century of wars and financial lavishness had brought France close to bankruptcy, and Louis had begun in promising fashion during 1774 by naming the reformer Robert Jacques Turgot as controller general. But when Turgot's new laws brought opposition among the wealthy and powerful, Louis fired him and returned to the status quo. During the 1780s, on the eve of the Revolution, four different men held this position. None of them lasted long enough to address the mounting financial crisis. D'Ormisson himself became caught amid this instability, being replaced later in 1783.

With the king unwilling even to face France's balance sheets seriously, he hardly was ready to display insight that could view the balloon as emblematic of the ingenuity that already had launched the Industrial Revolution. Instead he regarded it merely as entertainment, an afternoon's diversion for his courtiers. Jacques Charles had already provided such a spectacle for some 300,000 Parisians, who had seen his *charlière* ascend from the Champ de Mars, the city's military parade field. Etienne's *montgolfière* was considerably larger and promised to be correspondingly more impressive.

Jean-Baptiste Reveillon, an old friend of Etienne's, had been a client during his days as an architect. Reveillon owned a wallpaper factory that had plenty of room on the grounds for construction of the king's balloon, and contributed his artistic talents as well. For the king and queen, the design had to be elegant indeed, and Reveillon responded with panache. He colored the balloon azure blue, with King Louis's initial appearing as a letter L stylized in gold, along with painted bands and draperies.

The hydrogen-filled *charlière* had demonstrated free flight, but had carried no payload, which gave Etienne an opportunity to go further. He thought of having his balloon carry a sheep. His brother Joseph wrote him a letter and suggested instead that he "take a cow. That will create an extraordinary sensation." But cows were heavy, and Etienne stayed with his sheep, soon adding a duck and a rooster. All three of these animals rode within a cage, through which their heads or tails could protrude.

In a letter to his wife, Etienne himself describes the flight at Versailles:

> At one o'clock, we set off a round of ammunition and lighted the fire. . . . The machine filled in seven minutes. It was held in place only by ropes and the combined efforts of fifteen or sixteen men. A second round went off. We redoubled the gas, and at the third round, . . . everyone let go at once. The machine rose majestically,

Montgolfier's balloon lifts off from the Palace of Versailles in 1783.

drawing after it a cage containing a *sheep,* a *rooster,* and a *duck.* A few moments after takeoff a sudden gust of wind tilted it over on its side. Since there was insufficient ballast to keep it vertical, the top afforded the wind a much larger surface than the part where the animals were. At that instant I was afraid that it was done for. It got away with losing about a fifth of its gas, however, and continued on its way as majestically as ever for a distance of 1,800 fathoms where the wind tipped it over again so that it settled gently down to earth.[1]

Paris in 1783 resembled Brooklyn or the Bronx, with most of its people being workers who were preoccupied with the daily matters of making a living. But its wealthier residents had time for pleasure, and they went wild over the new invention. A baron wrote that "all one hears is talk of experiments, atmospheric air, inflammable gas, flying cars, journeys in the sky." The excitement even reached the realm of fashion. No elegant Parisian lady cared to look like a balloon, but one couturier designed a gown in *la mode au ballon.* Her fan showed drawings, while pumpkin-shaped furbelows decorated the hat, sleeves, and billowing skirt.

"The balloon excitement was now building toward a peak," writes the aviation historian Tom Crouch. "Hair and clothing styles, jewelry, snuffboxes, wallpaper, chandeliers, bird cages, fans, clocks, chairs, armoires, hats, and other items were designed with balloon motifs." Fashionable guests sipped *Crème Aerostatique* liqueur and danced the *Contradanse de Gonesse,* named for the village where the *charlière* had met its end.

Only one thing was missing: an actual flight of people. This was on the Montgolfiers's agenda, however, and they had volunteers who wanted to be aeronauts. One of them, Francois Pilatre de Rozier, had personal connections that included members of the royal family. Another, Francois d'Arlandes, was a minor nobleman who had known Joseph Montgolfier for over a decade. Following the flight at Versailles, Etienne took him on as a pilot and set him to work as a foreman, as he pursued his man-carrying project.

The place of construction again was the Reveillon wallpaper factory, and this balloon's decorations surpassed even those of Versailles. Reveillon started with his stylized gold bands and king's initial on a background of azure. He then added royal suns that recalled Louis XIV, the Sun King of a century earlier. Friezes at the top portrayed the twelve signs of the zodiac and also showed fleur-de-lis, a national symbol that also appeared on the flag of France. The bottom showed painted draperies and curtains, along with eagles whose outstretched wings were to carry the balloon into the air. These pretentious embellishments were far removed from present taste. Still they were appropriate for the time, for they represented a salute to the first manned aircraft ever to fly.

Etienne conducted several test flights during October, with the balloon tethered by a three-hundred-foot rope. Rozier then took over, making out his will and saying good-bye to friends. However, his own test flights also went well. For free flight, he attached a brazier to the bottom to permit continual heating of the enclosed air. He and d'Arlandes then became the first men to fly freely, on November 21st, with d'Arlandes setting down his discussion of the experience immediately afterward.

He had charge of the brazier, but as the balloon rose, he found himself distracted by the view. Early in the flight, Rozier chided him: "You're not doing a thing, and we're not climbing at all." D'Arlandes apologized, tossed some straw onto the burner, then went back to sightseeing. Soon they were over the Seine, and Rozier again called to him: "There's the river, and we're dropping. Come on, my good friend, the fire!" A new helping of straw surged into flame, and the men felt themselves "hauled up as if by the armpits."

Suddenly they heard popping sounds. D'Arlandes looked inside the balloon's envelope—and saw that sparks from the brazier had burned holes in the fabric. He dampened some smoldering edges by using a water-soaked sponge at the end of a pitchfork, then saw that threads were loosening within an important seam. "We've got to put down," he insisted. They couldn't; they still were over the city, and there was no open ground below.

Rozier assured him that there was no damage on his side. When d'Arlandes looked more closely, he saw that the seam was holding and the holes were not growing larger or more numerous. He agreed that they could continue to sail on. They entered the countryside and soon allowed the fire to diminish, for they expected to come down soon. Then, immediately ahead, they saw windmills. More straw on the fire gave it new strength and lifted them clear of the danger, allowing them to land just beyond a pond. They had spent close to half an hour in the air and had covered five miles.

Jacques Charles, with his hydrogen balloons, prepared his own manned flight. He too won royal favor, being granted permission to make his ascent from the palace of the Tuileries. To carry the weight of aeronauts in a gondola, he needed ten times more hydrogen than for the *charlière* of August, which raised anew the issue of obtaining an adequate supply. He addressed this by building a chemical generator that used several barrels, each filled with iron filings and dilute sulfuric acid. When any of them needed recharging, this could be done while the others continued to work.

In designing his balloon, he saw that he needed a means to relieve the internal pressure if an aeronaut rose too high. He installed a valve, operated by a cord, that could open to allow some of the hydrogen to escape. Then, because a pilot might release too much, he decided that balloons should carry ballast. If a flight started to descend prematurely, an airman could toss some of this weight overboard. In this fashion, Charles introduced methods of control that became standard.

He flew on December 1st, only ten days after the ascent of Rozier and d'Arlandes, with one of his associates as a companion. Once more he charged admission, drawing a record crowd. Just before liftoff he toasted the project by opening a bottle of champagne, with the two men filling glasses and lifting them high. The balloon soon lifted as well, approaching 2,000 feet in altitude as measured by an onboard barometer. Charles released gas through a long and narrow neck that he could open or close with his hand. He slowed his ascent and proceeded to drift with the wind. Nearly an hour after launch, he heard the report of a distant cannon. It was at the Tuileries, signaling that the balloon was lost to view.

It continued onward. Charles navigated by barometer, releasing gas and then dropping ballast to stay close to his desired altitude. It now was late afternoon; with the sun descending, it was time for the flight to descend as well. Flying over a clearing of fields, he allowed the balloon to sink slowly. The landing was smooth, with greeters that included several dozen curious peasants—and two dukes, who had kept the balloon in view while riding on horseback.

Paris lies at northerly latitudes, which means that the sun sets slowly late in the year. There still was light in the sky, and Charles saw that by ascending alone, without his companion, he could lighten his craft and soar aloft with ease. It took him only ten minutes to reach 9,000 feet. His barometer dropped by over nine inches, while the temperature, measured by an onboard thermometer, fell from fifty to twenty degrees Fahrenheit. He rose above the clouds, later writing of his "inexpressible delight, this ecstasy of contemplation":

> The cold was sharp and dry, but not at all unbearable. . . . I stood up in the middle of the gondola, and lost myself in the spectacle offered by the immensity of the horizon. When I took off from the fields, the sun had set for the inhabitants of the valleys. Soon it rose for me alone, and again appeared to gild the balloon and gondola with its rays. It was the only illuminated body within the whole horizon, and I saw all the rest of nature plunged in shadow.[2]

These two flights, on November 21st and December 1st, capped events in aviation that had taken place within no more than a few dramatic months. In addition, the *charlières* and *montgolfières* of 1783 brought more than mere public spectacle, for they gave vivid indication of what the free human mind might achieve. Charles Dickens later wrote that in this era, "it was clearer than crystal" in both England and France "that things in general were settled for ever." The work of Jacques Charles and the Montgolfiers now suggested strongly that this was no longer true. Benjamin Franklin, living in Paris as a diplomat from the nascent United States, wrote a letter that caught the new sense of possibility: "A few months since, the idea of witches riding through the air on a broomstick, and that of philosophers upon a bag of smoke, would have appeared equally impossible and ridiculous."

New pilots soon took to the skies, with Jean-Pierre Blanchard in the forefront. He had dreamed of wing-flapping flying machines and even tried to build one, and when he learned of the Montgolfiers, he found his calling. He became the world's first professional airman, earning his living through fees charged for his public ascents. He launched this career during 1784, making flights in May and July, and then set a goal that indeed was ambitious. He hoped to become the first man to fly across the English Channel.

He knew that a hydrogen-filled *charlière* could make this crossing; the first manned version, flown by Charles himself, had covered twenty-seven miles during its December 1st flight. This was more than the distance from Dover to Calais. Blanchard left for England in mid-August and proceeded to meet men of London who shared his interest in ballooning. These included John Jeffries, an expatriate American physician who had spent his early life in Boston but remained loyal to King and Crown during the War of Independence. When Jeffries saw Blanchard make an ascent, he came away enthralled. "I resolved to gratify this," he later wrote, "which had finally become my ruling passion."

Meeting with Blanchard, he agreed to cover the latter's expenses in return for the opportunity to accompany him on future flights. Jeffries first took to the air in November. An unexpected wind blew them against a building just after liftoff, sending a chimney-pot crashing to the street. Then they recovered and flew for two hours, traversing the whole of London. With this, the two adventurers agreed that they were ready for the Channel flight.

They left London on December 17th and reached Dover two days later. Then, amid bad weather and unfavorable winds, they waited through the Christmas and New Year holidays. Finally, early in the morning of January 7, 1785, Blanchard came into Jeffries's room and told him that the wind and weather were fair. Indeed, the day was beautifully clear; when they ascended, they were visible from the

French coast. Liftoff came shortly after one P.M. "We rose slowly and majestically from the cliff," Jeffries later wrote. They gained altitude; the balloon expanded, and they valved off hydrogen. Then, finding that they had released too much, they dropped ballast. Their gas bag appeared to have been leaky, for they kept dropping ballast until all of it was gone.

An hour into the flight, still not halfway across, they began to throw overboard some of the items they had brought with them. By 2:30 they had jettisoned their food supply. Blanchard had equipped his gondola with silk-covered aerial oars, a rudder, and a hand-cranked propeller. These all went over the side as well, followed by a bottle of brandy. Nearing the three-fourths mark, they threw grapnels and rope into the Channel, then dispensed with the heavy clothes that they had worn, to guard against the chill of January. Blanchard threw in his trousers, leaving them with little more than cork life jackets. Still they failed to climb, remaining below the level of cliffs near Calais. They had only four or five miles to go, and the wind was still fair. Even so, they felt that their only hope was to climb onto the balloon's ropes in an attempt to remain afloat once they hit the water.

Suddenly their luck turned, as a change in the wind carried them aloft once again. They crossed the French coast, still rising. They had done it; they had crossed the Channel! Then, while landing, the wind blew them into a tree. Jeffries grabbed a branch; Blanchard frantically valved gas, and the men worked their way from branch to branch until they could drop to the ground. They stood shivering in the cold, but a search party found them and gave them warm clothing. Extensive honors soon followed, including a visit to Versailles where they met the king and queen.

In this fashion, the first two years of ballooning established its broad forms according to patterns that persisted through subsequent centuries. There was plenty of risk; Rozier and a companion, Pierre Romain, became the first men to die in an air accident when their balloon caught fire and crashed. Yet, with care, a man might make dozens of flights and return to tell about them. Blanchard, for one, flew some sixty times, lived until 1809, and died in bed.

Safety in ballooning took a large step forward in 1797 with the invention of the parachute, which might have saved Rozier and Romain. Andre-Jacques Garnerin made the first such descent. His parachute was attached to his gondola; he remained within this aerial car as he released it from the balloon and descended from 2,300 feet into a Parisian park. For use with parachutes, hot-air balloons remained in vogue. They did not use costly hydrogen and did not fly far after a pilot bailed out, making them easy to recover.

The early flights of Charles, Blanchard, and the Montgolfiers cast a long shadow over the subsequent development both of ballooning and of aviation in general. In less than two years these men invented the hot-air and hydrogen balloons, along with a method for producing hydrogen in quantity. On the single day of December 1, 1783, Charles showed that a balloon could reach high altitudes and cover long distances. Such achievements, all accomplished by Frenchmen, gave their country a lasting claim to primacy in aviation. When heavier-than-air flight came to the forefront after 1900, there was a widespread view that France would bring forth a new Montgolfier to win this prize as well. When Louis Bleriot flew his monoplane from Calais to Dover in 1909, he did more than merely salute Blanchard. He ushered in a new era of unquestioned French supremacy in aviation.

Long after 1783, the role of the balloon continued to expand. Hot-air versions were fine for sport, but for serious ballooning, hydrogen remained in the forefront. An English inventor, Charles Green, cut its cost by introducing common coal gas, which was rich in hydrogen. In 1836 his balloon, *Royal Vauxhall,* took him and two companions from London to Germany's Duchy of Nassau, covering 380 miles and setting a distance record that stood for decades. For sheer size, no one could top *Le Geant,* built in 1863 by a famous Parisian photographer who called himself Nadar. It approached two hundred feet in height and lifted a two-story gondola that carried fourteen people.

Balloons also made voyages of exploration. The meteorologist James Glaisher rode with an experienced pilot in 1862 and claimed to have reached 37,000 feet on a flight from Wolverhampton. He didn't; they used no oxygen, and the historian Charles Gibbs-Smith writes that they may have reached "19,000 feet, or a bit higher." Thirteen years later, France's Gaston Tissandier tried to top this mark by using oxygen. The equipment did not work well, for he and two companions passed out at around 25,000 feet. He regained consciousness on the way down, but the others were dead. Even so, this flight showed that the heights indeed were within reach, if only it was possible to breathe.

The century ended with the dramatic flight of Sweden's Salomon Andree, who flew from Spitsbergen in July 1897 with two other men in an attempt to reach the North Pole. They went only one-third of the way before they had to set down on the ice, but salvaged their equipment and walked southward toward their base. They nearly made it, but all three of them died within sight of Spitsbergen, probably from eating the infected meat of a polar bear. The world learned of this in 1930, when hunters found their bodies, diaries, and camera film.

Significantly, the balloons of these flights did not differ fundamentally from those of Charles and Blanchard. In the wake of their achievements, the record flights of the subsequent century amounted largely to embellishments. Yet while the technology of balloons quickly matured, their flights also stimulated thoughts of true airplanes, powered perhaps by steam. Some of the most important thoughts were in print early in the nineteenth century, barely a quarter-century after the early ascents of balloons in France.

Charlières and *montgolfières* whetted appetites for flight, but fell well short of giving true satisfaction. Aeronauts could control their altitude and could rise or descend at will. However, in all other respects a balloon was a passive voyager that flew only where the winds might take it. If they were blowing from the wrong direction, a balloonist was out of luck. Inventors responded by trying to build dirigibles—and by nurturing visions of heavier-than-air machines that might fly against the wind.

The science writer Arthur C. Clarke notes a useful distinction. Some inventions, such as the spaceship, were predicted long in advance of their realization. Others—radio, X rays, atomic energy—lay beyond the imagination, and were not even properly envisioned until their technical basis was nearly in hand. Balloons fell into the second category, while airplanes definitely were in the first. Dreams of flight trace back to medieval times, as when the philosopher Roger Bacon wrote, "Flying machines can be made, and a man sitting in the middle of the machine may revolve some ingenious device by which artificial wings may beat the air in the manner of a flying bird." Bacon's anticipation of wing-flapping systems, called ornithopters, set the stage for several centuries of thought during which this remained the standard approach.

The ornithopter concept seemed obvious, but it could not be made to work. Though birds furnished a clear proof that wing-flapping flight was possible, ornithopters proved to stand on a par with trying to imitate horses by building carts or carriages that would walk on moving wooden legs. Leonardo da Vinci, for one, is renowned for having drawn designs of flying machines in the time of Columbus. Yet he was twice removed from valid aeronautical invention, for he not only restricted himself to ornithopters; he did not publish his writings, which were not found until 1893.

Nevertheless, between the early balloons and the Wright brothers, there was a long century during which serious people began to develop insights appropriate to true heavier-than-air flight. Even with gliders, however, this form of flight demanded far more than the cut-and-try techniques of the early balloonists. It needed a well-developed science of aeronautics, and the man who took the lead in its formulation was England's Sir George Cayley.

He traced his descent to Osborne de Cailly, a lord of Normandy who came to England in 1066 with William the Conqueror. A descendant, Edward Cayley, purchased the family estate, Brompton Hall, near Scarborough in Yorkshire, in 1622. Edward's son William received the title of baronet from King Charles I in 1643; Sir George, born in 1773, became the sixth in succession to hold that title. On his mother's side, he claimed descent from Robert the Bruce.

He was marked from birth for the life of a country squire. His mother often made the family's decisions; when he was fifteen, she sent him to board with a tutor in Nottingham. He was Reverend George Walker, a man of scholarly reputation who was a Fellow of the Royal Society. When George fell in love with Walker's daughter Sarah,

Mrs. Cayley became miffed and withdrew George from that household, sending him to a different tutor in London. Then in 1792 his father died, and George returned from London to inherit his title and landed estate. He also married his Sarah, with whom he had continued to exchange letters.

His interest in mechanics dated to his teenage years. He was a well-born gentleman, but he spent much time in a nearby village, where he formed a friendship with a watchmaker. His interest in aviation appears to date to 1796, when he constructed a model helicopter. It drew power from a stringed bow made of whalebone, with the string winding around a shaft of wood. Each end of the shaft held a cork, with feathers stuck in to act as propeller blades. The flexible bow pulled the string from both ends and rotated these propellers, with this small aircraft rising toward the ceiling. It thus resembled the toy helicopter that the Wrights flew, some eighty years later.

Next, in 1799, Cayley took a long step toward inventing the airplane. He did not offer a feasible and flightworthy concept, but he was the first man in history to break with the ornithopter tradition, and to introduce the most critical element of successful design. This was the separation of aircraft and powerplant, with the engine being distinct from the fuselage and wings. Ornithopter concepts had merged these elements, with their flapping wings being meant to provide both lift and power. Cayley's insight amounted to asserting that mechanical flight would have to follow its own principles, rather than seek to mimic the flight of birds.

He did not completely abandon the ornithopter, for he retained its moving wings in the form of oars, which a pilot was to pull back and forth to propel his craft through the air. Cayley might easily have envisioned the use of a propeller; windmills had been in use for centuries, and he had flown his helicopter with propellers only a few years earlier. Even so, the importance of his initial renderings is incalculable. If other inventors had been thinking of carriages with moving legs, he was the first to envision a wheel.

He set down his thoughts as a neat engineering drawing and as an engraving on a silver disk. Right at the start, however, he was well

Silver medallion of Sir George Cayley, 1799. The engraving shows a pilot rowing his airplane through the air.

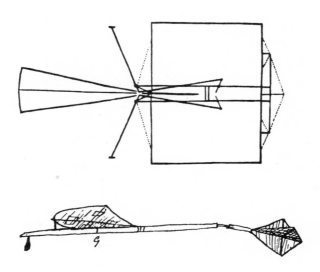

Aeronautical concepts of Sir George Cayley. Top, overhead view of an airplane powered by oars. Bottom, side view of a glider.

aware that these concepts did not represent the culmination of his work, but defined instead a point of departure for a program of research. Already the means existed to conduct studies in aerodynamics. Several decades earlier, the mathematician Benjamin Robins had invented what proved to be a key instrument for experiments: the whirling arm. Driven by power from a falling weight on a cord, this arm rotated rapidly through the air, with a model mounted to its end. The rotation rate was easy to measure by using a watch. Heavier weights made the arm turn more rapidly, while drag produced by the model provided a countering force that made it turn more slowly.

Robins presented two papers to the Royal Society in 1746, titled "Resistance of the Air" and "Experiments Relating to Air Resistance." This was only two decades after the death of Sir Isaac Newton, whose work in physics had laid the necessary groundwork. Robins's papers amounted to technical foundations in their own right, for they brought the formal study of aerodynamics as a new topic in science. A civil engineer, John Smeaton, built his own whirling arm and used it to study windmills. His model windmill sails lifted weights, which grew heavier as his designs improved. He also launched the study of wings with his own Royal Society paper in 1759. He considered a flat plate as a wing, a plane moving through the air at a gentle angle, and made the important finding that a curved or cambered wing—an airfoil, in modern parlance—gave more lift. He also made more measurements of the drag produced by square and rectangular sheets of metal.

Cayley adopted Smeaton's findings. Right at the outset, in his engraving of 1799, he showed a wing that was cambered. Then, during the first years of the new century, he carried out three types of experiments. He devised a whirling arm for his own use and revisited Smeaton's investigations, seeking to determine a critical quantity: the speed at which a surface of one square foot produces a drag of one pound. The drag of wings could be referenced to this measurement. In turn, determination of drag was critical to learning the amount of power needed for flight.

"I have tried many experiments upon a large scale to ascertain this point," he later wrote. He averaged the results of these tests and concluded that the pertinent speed was 23.6 feet per second. This was close to the modern value of 27.2 feet per second, showing that Cayley was a good experimentalist. Indeed, he was better than Smeaton, who had given the less accurate value of 21 feet per second.

Cayley also made measurements of lift. He treated his foot-square surface as a wing and placed it at an angle to the horizontal, then arranged for it to lift a weight. At 21.8 feet per second, and at an angle of three degrees, the weight supported was one ounce. At eighteen degrees, it topped five ounces. Like his studies of drag, this work also gave benchmark data. He knew that real wings would be cambered and would develop more lift, which he could measure by comparison with his flat-plate results. This opened the door for studies of cambered airfoils that might disclose a particularly effective shape.

Whirling-arm studies represented one phase of his work. In a second set of experiments he built and flew gliders. He started by using a kite as his wing, attaching it to a pole and throwing it down a hill like a spear. It quickly dived into the ground, and he responded with improvements. He gave the kite a small upward tilt by installing a stick as a support; he also added vertical and horizontal tail surfaces that amounted to fins. His device now flew much better.

His gliders grew in size and sophistication. The best of them used tail surfaces in a cruciform arrangement like the feathers of an arrow. The tail itself was angled slightly downward, which caused the glider to nose down. However, the wing was set at an upward angle and responded to the rapid downward glide by developing a good deal of lift. This was the first such craft in the history of aeronautics.

Cayley's third research topic dealt with shapes of minimum drag. Other inventors had watched the flights of birds, but he considered that dolphins had the appropriate form. To carry out experiments, he turned to an arsenal in nearby Scarborough and obtained a supply of gunpowder along with the use of a cannon. He considered that by introducing projectiles of reduced drag, he could increase their range. Cannonballs, spherical in shape, constituted the ordnance of his day, but his shapes had streamlined bodies and cruciform fins. His best tests showed increases in range of one-fourth of a mile, which was nothing to sneeze at. The three-mile limit, the traditional distance from shore over which nations claimed sovereignty, reflected the range of the heavy guns of that era.

In this fashion he dealt with the important issues of lift, drag, general layout of an airplane, and streamlining. Then in 1809 he was stirred by a report that Jakob Degen, a clockmaker in Vienna, had built an ornithopter and achieved man-powered flight. He hadn't; he indeed had flapped wings, but a hydrogen balloon had lifted his weight. Cayley didn't know this, and thought that Degen was stealing his thunder. He responded with a three-part paper, "On Aerial Navigation," within the *Journal of Natural Philosophy, Chemistry and the Arts.*

In words that might have been written by Newton, he summed up his goal: "The whole problem is confined within these limits, viz.—To make a surface support a given weight by the application of power to the resistance of air." Power indeed came forth as a central concern, as Cayley suggested, but did not design, a steam engine of one horse-power that was to weigh 163 pounds. Such a motor, having "the power of a horse and the weight less than that of a man," appeared suitable for his purposes. With this, he turned to aspects of aerodynamics and airplane design.

He presented results from his work with the whirling arm, supplementing his conclusions with data from France. He also touched on his gliders, the largest of which was five feet long and loaded with a weight:

> I have myself made a large machine on this principle, large enough for aerial navigation. . . . It was beautiful to see this noble white bird sail majestically from the top of a hill to any given point of the plane below it with perfect steadiness, and safety, according to the set of the rudder, merely by its own weight descending in an angle of about 8 degrees with the horizon. . . .
>
> I made a machine having a surface of 300 square feet, which was accidentally broken before there was an opportunity of trying the effect of the propelling apparatus, but its steerage and steadiness were perfectly proved, and it would sail downwards in any direction

according to the set of the rudder. Its weight was 56 lbs., and it was loaded with 94 lbs., thus making a total of 140 lbs., about 2 square feet to one pound.

Even in this state, when any person ran forward in it with his full speed, taking advantage of a gentle breeze in front, it would bear upward so strongly as scarcely to allow him to touch the ground, and would frequently lift him up and convey him several yards together.[3]

Cayley introduced the topic of aircraft stability, which he entered by reinventing the parachute. When Jacques Garnerin descended over Paris in 1797, his chute had lacked a hole in the center, a feature that would have allowed trapped air to escape. His chute could spill this air only by rocking strongly from side to side, "which is said to have endangered the bold aeronaut." Cayley declared that rather than designing a parachute as an inverted cup, it should have the form of a cone of broadly obtuse angle, pointing downward. He showed that such a shape would be stable, whereas Garnerin's was not, and invited his readers to demonstrate this result with a cone of paper: "Place a small weight in the apex, and letting it fall from any height, it will steadily preserve the position to the ground."

Turning to airplanes, he declared that they should have the shape of a broad letter V when seen from the front, as if cut from his conical parachute by making two slices across its diameter. He asserted that this shape, "with apex downward, is the chief basis of stability in aerial navigation." Wings therefore were to have "dihedral," being mounted at upward angles to form the V, which "most effectively prevents any rolling of the machine from side to side."

He certainly was on to something. Control of roll proved essential for practical flight, particularly when making turns. In turn, dihedral emerged as an important element of design, for it indeed promoted stability. Several inventors took Cayley at his word and built craft that sought to rely on dihedral alone, but experience showed that it was far from sufficient. Even so, Cayley showed considerable insight when he recognized the need for stability in roll.

In writing of wings, he discussed the center of lift, with half the lift being generated forward from this center and half behind it. Drawing anew on his experiments, he wrote that this point did not coincide with a wing's center of gravity, "but is considerably in front of it." Shifts in the location of the center of lift raised important issues in designing flyable aircraft, for such shifts could cause a flying machine either to stall with its nose pointing upward, or to dive into the ground.

He also noted that aircraft with engines would need maximum power at takeoff, drawing this conclusion from the observation of birds: "Many birds, and particularly water, run and flap their wings for several yards before they gain support from the air. The swift . . . is not able to elevate itself from level ground." We see this in today's airliners, which use peak power during takeoff before throttling back substantially for cruising flight.

Finally, he offered proposals for the construction of lightweight wings. He showed fabric stretched across a framework, with the frame also supporting a kingpost or vertical strut. Wires, running from the ends of structural members to the post, gave these members strong support. "Diagonal bracing is the great principle for producing strength without accumulating weight," he wrote. He might have been describing the wire-braced biplanes that flourished during World War I. He gave a diagram of a wing that "contained 54 square feet and weighed only 11 lbs.," with two such wings lifting a weight of 125 pounds. He added that wire bracing "produces but a trifling resistance in the air and keeps tight in all weather." Subsequent designers tended to agree.

Cayley wrote of all these matters at a time when steamships and locomotives still lay in the future. He thus was very much ahead of his time, and it didn't help that his *Journal of Natural Philosophy* had only a limited circulation. Indeed, his thinking was so advanced that more than thirty years elapsed before anyone went further, even in speculation. The next developments drew on the science of flight, but particularly addressed its public anticipation.

The poet Alfred, Lord Tennyson captured this anticipation in 1842, with his classic "Locksley Hall":

Men, my brothers, men the workers, ever reaping something
    new:
That which they have done but earnest of the things that they
    shall do:
For I dipt into the future, far as human eye could see,
Saw the Vision of the world, and all the wonder that would
    be;
Saw the heavens fill with commerce, argosies of magic sails,
Pilots of the purple twilight, dropping down with costly bales;
Heard the heavens fill with shouting, and there rain'd a ghast-
    ly dew
From the nations' airy navies grappling in the central blue;
Far along the world-wide whisper of the south-wind rushing
    warm,
With the standards of the peoples plunging thro' the thunder-
    storm;
Till the war-drum throbb'd no longer, and the battle-flags
    were furled
In the Parliament of Man, the Federation of the World.

Just a year later, as if in fulfillment, came what the historian
Charles Gibbs-Smith in time would hail as "one of the most out-
standing and influential aeroplanes in history." This was the Aerial
Steam Carriage, the work of the lacemaker William Henson.

In 1843, working in Somerset, he received a patent for this concept.
His patent document included a fine set of drawings. He also acquired
an active publicist, who supplemented them with vividly imaginative
engravings of his own. These soon appeared in such widely-read publications as the *Illustrated London News* and *L'Illustration* in Paris.
Gibbs-Smith describes the Steam Carriage as "the first design in history for a fixed-wing airscrew-propelled aeroplane of modern configuration." It lacked ailerons for control and would have benefited from
a bigger rudder, but in other respects it was largely correct in its
specifics.

To the modern eye, the most arresting feature is its large mono-

Aerial Steam Carriage concept of 1843.

plane wing that measured 150 feet by 30 feet. Designers of that era did not yet appreciate the merits of the biplane, with wings and struts that could combine to give a very strong yet lightweight structure. Ironically, then, whereas biplane concepts of 1895 or 1910 nowadays look their age, the Steam Carriage seems much more recent. It mounted two propellers at the rear of this wing and included elements that are instantly recognizable as a fuselage, tail, and landing gear. Like a ship at sea, it also flew the Union Jack.

Like the science-fiction movies of a century later, depictions of this airplane encouraged people to believe that it soon might come into existence. At times the illustrations showed uncanny prescience. One presented the Steam Carriage in elegant detail, while a paddle-wheel steamboat and a locomotive with a tall smokestack lay in a junkyard because they could not compete. Jet airliners indeed drove passenger trains and ocean liners into oblivion, but not for another 120 years. Other renderings showed the Steam Carriage in exotic locales such as

Egypt, flying over the banks of the Nile with the pyramids in the background, or soaring over the plains of Hindustan.

Henson was well aware that this publicity might help him mulct investors of cash. He took out full-page advertisements. He planted a rumor that this airplane had already crossed the English Channel. He printed the assertion that his craft could reach China "in twenty-four hours certain." A Boeing 747 flew nonstop from London to Sydney, Australia, in 1989 but Henson was working in an era when not even steamships could carry enough coal for such a voyage. He tried to win support from Parliament, but when he didn't, he went ahead anyway. He set up the Aerial Transit Company and sold shares to the public.

He might as well have been proposing to fly to the moon. The eventual Boeing 747 took off with 200,000 pounds of thrust, the equivalent of 200,000 horsepower when climbing while gaining speed. Henson proposed to fly to China with a steam engine of thirty horsepower. Yet even this lay beyond the state of the art, for during the mid-nineteenth century, the most that anyone managed to do was to fly with three horsepower. This happened in 1852 as a wealthy Parisian, Henri Giffard, set out to build a steam-powered dirigible. His bag had the shape of an elongated football, 144 feet in length and 39 feet across. Filled with hydrogen, it could lift three tons. Its motor, rated at three horses, turned a propeller of eleven-foot diameter.

He took off from the Hippodrome, a racecourse in Paris. Dressed in a top hat and frock coat, he started his engine. A gentle breeze was blowing and he rode with it, while his big propeller whirled as if it was pushing him along. Seventeen miles from his starting point, he decided to turn for home. He swung a large sail that was to serve as his rudder—and made no headway. It didn't matter that the wind was the merest zephyr; it sufficed to defeat him. Instead of inventing controlled flight, all he had was a free balloon with excess baggage.

Giffard's flight followed Henson's publicity by only a few years. Henson's sudden fame drew attention from other inventors, including a fellow lacemaker, John Stringfellow, who was an innovator as well. Stringfellow had started by building carriages (of the horse-driven kind), and developed enough mechanical skill to advance to crafting small steam engines. Working at first with Henson and then on his own, Stringfellow built a model airplane with a 10-foot wingspan. It followed the general layout of the Steam Carriage, mounting two propellers driven by a lightweight engine and boiler in a gondola below the fuselage.

Like Giffard, he needed quiet air. He found it within a local lace mill. His craft ran along an overhead wire, bypassing the need for its wings to carry its weight while also sidestepping all issues of stability in flight. He nevertheless succeeded after a fashion, for in his best flight, the machine lifted from the wire and stayed in the air while covering a distance of over thirty feet before crashing into a canvas screen that stood in its path. This was not flight to China, but it showed that the knowledge was in hand to build a powered model that could fly this distance indoors without stalling or diving into the floor.

Henson's ideas not only inspired Stringfellow but drew Cayley back into aviation. The old gentleman had not contributed to this field since 1809, when he had published his papers, but now he came back strongly. He started in 1843 with a critique of the Steam Car-

Sir George Cayley.

riage. Arguing that its monoplane wing was too weak, he called for several crossbraced wings, stacked "one above the other at a convenient distance." He particularly recommended a "three decker," a triplane. He then adopted triplanes for his own work as he set out to build a man-carrying glider. He made an important advance in 1849, crafting a triplane that could carry a lightweight boy. In a paper of 1853, he wrote that "a boy of about ten years of age was floated off the ground for several yards on descending a hill."

Avoiding publicity, working in the seclusion of his Yorkshire estate, Cayley built a larger glider that also was ready in 1853. However, he now was eighty years old, and his penchant for privacy leaves the historian with only a tantalizing glimpse of what may well have been the first true manned glide. He did not write of it, and what we know of it comes largely from a letter written in 1921 by his daughter Dora:

> I remember in later times hearing of a large machine being started on the high side of the valley behind Brompton Hall where he lived, and the coachman being sent up in it, and it flew across the little valley, about 500 yards at most, and came down with a smash. . . . [The coachman] struggled up and said, "Please, Sir George, I wish to give notice. I was hired to drive and not to fly."[4]

This letter smacks of a statement, heard at second hand and not set down on paper until 1965, of a successful powered flight prior to those of the Wrights. It lacks the clear and convincing character of the written evidence that supports Cayley's other achievements. Moreover, a glide of 1,500 feet would have been well beyond anything that even the Wrights achieved, half a century later, after learning far more aeronautics than Cayley had at his disposal. Still, the story gains credibility from the coachman's quote and from the fact that Cayley indeed crafted a glider that might have been suitable. If this flight actually happened, it gave an appropriate coda to his life, for he established aeronautics as an engineering discipline while still leaving much to accomplish.

Cayley died in 1857. Following his death another Englishman, Francis Wenham, came to the forefront as the next significant investigator. Born in London in 1824, he spent much of his career as a designer of engines, particularly for steamships. He introduced improvements that enabled such vessels to run at higher speeds, outracing Union warships that were blockading Confederate ports during the Civil War. He displayed a broad range of interests, devising improved microscopes and better methods of photography. Late in the 1850s, he became involved with flight.

His friends included James Glaisher, the high-altitude balloonist. These men were among the founders of the Aeronautical Society of Great Britain, the first professional organization to actively pursue the heavier-than-air flying machine. This society encouraged engineers to approach problems of flight using solid technical arguments, while providing a forum for their papers. Wenham himself delivered one of the more significant of these contributions, reading it as a lecture during the Society's first meeting, in 1866.

He began by speaking of propellers. As a marine engineer, he had seen the first steamship to use a screw propeller and had predicted that such screws would supersede paddlewheels. He now declared that propellers would prove to have similar importance in aviation. Drawing on experience with ships, he presented recommendations for the design of airscrews. He thus illustrated how engineers might apply lessons from other fields to address problems in aeronautics.

Wenham then discussed issues that involved wings. Cayley had written that when a wing develops lift, the center of lift "does not coincide with the center of its surface, but is considerably in front of it." To Wenham, this meant that the only important part of a wing was the forward portion, immediately behind the leading edge. Cayley's concept of 1799 had called for a square wing, but Wenham saw that its rearward areas would add weight and drag while contributing little further lift. He wrote that a wing should have the shape of "a narrow plane, with its long edge in the direction of motion."

The Aerial Steam Carriage had proposed to use such a wing, with considerable span, and Cayley had written that it would break for lack of strength. Wenham's argument meant that it was not possible to improve the design by returning to a square shape; he emphasized that "*length of wing is indispensable!*" Still, as Cayley had come to appreciate, Wenham argued that there was no need to build a long wing as a monoplane. A designer could cut it into two or three sections, stacking them to form a biplane or triplane. In Wenham's words, "the surfaces may be superposed, or placed in parallel rows, with an interval between them."

Cayley's gliders had used this approach, late in his life, but again he had been ahead of his time; he had done this work before there was an Aeronautical Society. Wenham's paper outlined the wing design that went on to dominate aviation during its early decades. John Stringfellow set the pace in 1868, presenting a model triplane at the world's first aeronautical exhibition. It was held at London's Crystal Palace, under sponsorship of the Society, and Stringfellow's model, suspended from the ceiling, became a center of attention. Here was Wenham's concept, on display for all to see.

In 1871 Wenham took another important step. Working with a colleague, John Browning, he built the world's first wind tunnel. It was 10 feet long, square in cross section and 18 inches across, with a fan driven by a steam engine. Wenham and Browning revisited Cayley's whirling-arm experiment, testing flat plates set at various angles to the wind. They concluded that at small angles, "the ratio of the lift to the drag was very great," and invited other investigators to go further by using wind tunnels to study curved wings.

Horatio Phillips, another researcher, responded by building his own wind tunnel. He launched the study of airfoils, seeking wing cross sections that could develop the most lift. Some of his shapes were so promising that he had them patented. This launched the wind tunnel on one of its most important applications, and it did more. The best of Phillips's wings gave so much lift and so little drag as to suggest strongly that full-size versions could carry particularly heavy loads. This brought the powered airplane closer, because Phillips's findings gave reason to expect that an airplane with good wings could indeed lift the weight of a powerful steam engine, which might make it fly.

Amid these British advances, people across the Channel were prepared to assert that France still held the spirit of the Montgolfiers. Paris had its own coterie of aeronauts, who followed the example of the Aeronautical Society by setting up a counterpart, the Société Francaise de Navigation Aerienne. Soon after, one of their countrymen made a brilliant advance by building and demonstrating what Cayley had merely envisioned: a fully-stable flying airplane.

He was Alphonse Penaud, the son of an admiral. In 1870, age twenty, he introduced the rubber band as a source of power for small model planes. Generations of hobbyists ever since have had cause to appreciate this, but the models that resulted were more than mere toys. They were serious flying machines that bypassed the need for a steam engine while staying aloft for useful durations.

Penaud started by using two long bands to run a pair of oppositely turning propellers at the ends of a stick. This invention resembled the whirling plaything that had attracted Cayley, with the rubber giving more power and longer times in flight than Cayley's flexible bow with its cords. Penaud called this device his *helicoptère*. Next came his *Planophore,* a true model plane with a long rubber band that spun a pusher propeller at its rear. In August 1871 he flew it at the Tuileries in front of members of the new Société. It stayed in the air for eleven seconds and flew 131 feet, showing a performance that many of today's modelbuilders might envy.

The Planophore was small, only 20 inches in length, but in aeronautics, size didn't matter. Models far smaller in dimensions went on to give useful data in wind tunnels; Penaud's invention gave a concrete demonstration of the feasibility of stability in flight. Stringfellow had tried to do this by making his steam engine fly, but the 30 feet of its free flight had been far too short. What was more, Penaud did it simply by following Cayley's writings closely, as he gave dihedral to the Planophore wing and took care to note the location of its center of lift. These same principles could apply to a full-size craft that could carry a man.

In seeking such designs, though, size did matter. Rubber bands weren't enough; they continued to need steam engines, and such motors still were better suited to small airplanes than to big ones. Felix Du Temple, another naval officer, learned this as he proceeded with his own program. As early as 1858 he achieved what Stringfellow had not, crafting a steam-driven model that took off by using this power, remained briefly in the air, and landed safely. If it had been stable in flight then it might have covered a fair distance, but this achievement still was more than anyone else had attained as of that date.

Working with his brother Louis, Du Temple proceeded to try to invent a steam engine for aircraft. Cayley, in 1809, had hoped for one that could deliver a single horsepower for a weight of 163 pounds. Two-thirds of a century later, the Du Temples built a lightweight boiler weighing as little as forty pounds to the horsepower. They tried to use it in a man-rated craft with a forty-foot wingspan, but came away with nothing worth taking to the Tuileries. One account states that it rolled down a ramp and hopped briefly into the air, and that was that. Apparently it still was too heavy. The American specialist Octave Chanute did not even cite this limited success, for he wrote: "Careful search by the writer through various French and English publications has failed to discover any account of the operation of this machine, save the statement of M. Tissandier that 'notwithstanding the most persevering efforts, no practical results could be obtained in experimenting with this apparatus.'"

Could an Englishman do better? Thomas Moy, an engineer and a patent agent, made the attempt in 1875. He wrote of achieving flight by means more elegant than Giffard's "cumbrous gas-bags and feeble screws rotated by leaky accumulators and a table-cloth for a rudder." Having flown as a balloonist, he added: "We have had 100 years of balloons, and it is quite time that some advance should be made, leaving drifting bladders behind." The advance he sought lay again in his steam engine, which weighed eighty pounds with its boiler and developed three horsepower. This was half the weight of Cayley's imagined motor, with three times its power. Moy's motor ran two large propellers, each with six blades.

He built an unmanned craft called the Aerial Steamer and arranged to fly it at the end of a tether, executing a wide circle around a fountain on the grounds of the Crystal Palace. However, his wing was too small. He tried to get more lift by mounting it at a ten-degree angle, but this merely increased the drag. Six burners heated his boiler, but Chanute wrote that "when running in the open air, the fumes from the three forward lamps extinguished the three after lamps, and thus reduced the power one half." The machine reached twelve miles per hour during its best test, but Moy estimated that it needed to get to 35 miles per hour if it were to rise into the air. He rebuilt it as a helicopter, which also remained stubbornly on the ground, and ran out of funds before he could get further. Gibbs-Smith writes that the Aerial Steamer "was chiefly of propaganda value, and did not advance aviation."

More power certainly would help, and a Russian naval captain, Alexandr Mozhaisky, took this step in 1884. He needed all the assistance he could get, for he built his monoplane wing in the shape of two squares, one on each side of the fuselage. Francis Wenham had argued that this was a good way to add drag without lift, but Mozhaisky apparently was not aware of this. He nevertheless installed power galore, with a twenty-horse steam engine driving a big four-bladed front propeller while a ten-horsepower engine ran a pair of small propellers at the rear. A smokestack mounted amidships added to the arrangement.

His thirty total horsepower matched the rating envisioned for the Aerial Steam Carriage, but although Russia shared a border with China, Mozhaisky never got there. He tried to fly it near St. Petersburg, with one I. N. Golubev as the test pilot. It rolled down a ramp and was airborne momentarily, though it covered no more than a hundred feet before it came down. In proportion to its size, this was only on a par with the thirty-foot indoor flight of Stringfellow's model in 1848. Gibbs-Smith later wrote that Mozhaisky's craft was able "to leave the ground, but not to fly."

If power alone would not suffice, perhaps the missing ingredient was money. France's Clement Ader had it, having earned it as a leader in his country's telephone industry. Like Moy and Mozhaisky, though, he put his emphasis on building good steam engines while paying less heed to problems of wing design and control in flight. His airplane, named Eole, took shape as a monoplane with the form of a bat that mounted his own large four-bladed propeller in front. He made his attempt at a château near Paris in 1890, with the Eole becoming the first piloted airplane to rise into the air from level ground under its own power.

Still, that was not the same as actually flying. He reached an altitude of eight inches, and if this was flight, then a horse could do it as well. Photos made in 1878 by the American photographer Eadweard Muybridge had shown that a galloping steed exhibited moments when all four of its feet were off the ground. As for Ader, his eight-inch rise was enough for Eole to lose control. He had crafted it without a tail and with no means of flight control. It crashed after only a few seconds in the air and covered an estimated distance of only fifty meters, some 165 feet. This was on a par with the circus stunt of being shot out of a cannon.

Perhaps the path to aviation called for a really lavish budget, a steam engine better than any built to date, and a demonstrated record of success by the inventor. Hiram Maxim, an expatriate American living in England, combined all three. He came to aviation by way of a fascination with weaponry, though not because he wanted to build an airplane to carry a machine gun. He had made his fortune by inventing such automatic guns in the first place.

Born in Maine in 1840, he began thinking seriously about the design of machine guns while still in his teens. He discussed his plans with gunsmiths and built models with wooden parts. He followed no fixed trade for a time, learning metalwork from local machinists, building the proverbial better mousetrap as an inventor, while working in turn as a carpenter, building contractor, carriage maker, and painter. He was quite strong physically; he had good fists and competed as a prizefighter. He also spent some time as a bartender. His biographer, Joseph Slade, states that Maxim "was particularly suited to this last occupation because he did not drink and because his great strength could clear a bar of rowdy customers in minutes." He was of prime military age during the Civil War, being twenty-one years old when it broke out in 1861, but he never saw service. He was exempted after two of his brothers had died in battle.

He got married in 1864 and took a job with his uncle, who was active in gas lighting. He developed strong skills as a draftsman and as a smith who could do precision work with wood, copper, and brass. He also fell in love with steam engines and began building components and complete engines of his own design. He entered the field of gas lighting as an independent businessman, crafting a particularly bright gas headlamp for locomotives. Then, realizing that electricity was the coming thing, he switched to this new field and worked to invent an electric light bulb. He soon found himself competing with Thomas Edison, but still he made his mark. He introduced and patented a method for making good filaments for such bulbs, and had the pleasure of seeing Edison purchase the rights to its use.

Maxim was the first to light a building using electricity. He did it in the fall of 1880, at the Equitable Life Assurance Company in New York, two years before Edison's system entered service. However, while Maxim had emphasized his bulbs, Edison offered a complete package that included the power-producing dynamos. A new manager at Maxim's firm, Charles Flint, realized that Edison's position was strong—and that Maxim loathed Edison deeply for having beaten him in competition over other patents. To keep him from causing trouble with this personal vendetta, Flint sent him to Europe.

With this, it was time for another career change. Maxim found his new goal through conversation with a man he met in Vienna, who said, "Hang your chemistry and electricity! If you want to make a pile of money, invent something that will enable these Europeans to cut each other's throats with greater facility." This encouraged him to renew his thoughts of machine guns. Hand-cranked quick-firing weapons were already in service: the American Gatling gun, the French *Mitrailleuse*. But they were heavy, jammed easily, and tended to blow flame from the breech if a round did not fire immediately. Maxim thought he could prevent such blowbacks, while introducing fully automatic operation.

He moved to London and had a prototype working two years later. It used the recoil force of each bullet to eject the spent cartridge and insert the next round. In tests, it fired five hundred shots per minute, giving it the firepower of a hundred breech-loading rifles. He showed it to representatives of the British army in 1885, and began racking up sales. The British adopted it in 1889, with Austria, Germany, Italy, and Russia following during 1890. It first saw action during a British colonial war in Africa in 1893. In one battle, fifty soldiers armed with four Maxim guns fought off a force of five thousand warriors of the Matabele tribe.

This success gave Maxim the wealth and professional achievement he had sought, while giving him the means to try to invent a flying machine. Like other inventors, he put particular emphasis on building good steam engines. The designs of 1890 were not at all like those of 1800; they were far lighter and developed vastly more power. Lightweight boilers contributed strongly, for the boilers that raised steam no longer amounted to big teakettles heated over open fires. They now were built from large numbers of thin tubes, carrying water that might be heated by thousands of small burner flames running on petrol. This greatly increased the effective surface area of a boiler, helping it to raise steam quickly and to provide a copious supply at high pressure.

Markedly increased pressures also characterized the newest designs, with consequent boosts in horsepower. The steam engines of earlier days somewhat resembled a modern automobile motor with badly-worn piston rings. Such a motor loses pressure and develops little power. Steam engines of the late nineteenth century took advantage of the burgeoning machine-tool industry, which could fabricate pistons and other parts to tight and precise tolerances. The engines then could operate routinely at high pressure and with high power. This allowed engineers to develop locomotives and steamships that were unprecedented in size and speed, while also giving life to the hopes of Maxim and his fellow planebuilders.

By working with a pressure of 320 pounds per square inch, Maxim crafted an arrangement of pistons and cylinders that developed 180 horsepower. Yet it was light enough to pick up with his hands. Two such units powered his flying machine, each driving a propeller that was nearly eighteen feet in diameter. The complete twin-engine installation tested at 363 horsepower and weighed little more than a ton, including the boilers with their water, pumps, and gas generators that vaporized the fuel supply before it went into the burners.

Maxim's airplane was a behemoth, with a 107-foot wingspan and a weight of four tons. Like Ader, he faced the issue of flight control. Unlike Ader, he bypassed the need for it by taking good care to prevent his craft from rising into the air. He ran it along a track a third of a mile long; in that heyday of railroads, the track was his runway. Auxiliary rails, elevated on posts and set well to the side, were to engage wheels mounted on long axles that extended to the left and right from his airplane. If it began to lift, the rails would catch the wheels and prevent the machine from flying into an out-of-control crash.

Preparations took several years. One almost hears Maxim's harrumph when he wrote, "I am only able to devote a small fraction of my time to these experiments, as I am and have been for many years, the managing director of a great English company." Finally, on a pleasant summer day in 1894, all was ready. His airscrews could deliver over a ton of thrust, and he wrote a personal account of what happened:

> Careful observers were stationed on each side of the track, and I took two men with me on the machine, the duty of one being to observe the pressure gauges, and that of the other to observe and note the action of the wheels on the upper track. The machine was tied up to a dynamometer, the engines started at a boiler pressure of 310 pounds and with a screw-thrust of a little more than 2100 pounds. Upon liberating the machine it darted forward with great rapidity while the screws rotated at a terrific rate. I turned on slightly more gas and the pressure almost instantly rose to 320 pounds to the square inch and blew off the safety-valve at that pressure. After running a few hundred feet, the machine was completely lifted off the lower rails, and all four of the upper wheels were engaged on the upper or safety rail. After running a few hundred feet in this position, the speed of the machine greatly increased and the lift became so great that the rear axle-trees holding the machine down were doubled up and the wheels broken off. The machine then became liberated, the front end being held down only on one side. This swayed the machine to one side, brought it violently against the

upper rails, and stopped it in the air, the lift breaking the rails and moving them outward about ten feet. Steam was, however, shut off before the machine stopped. The machine then fell to the earth, imbedding the wheels in the turf.[5]

The magazine *Scientific American* hailed this achievement: "On Tuesday, July 31, for the first time in the history of the world, a flying machine actually left the ground, fully equipped with engines, boiler, fuel, water, and a crew of three persons." Actually, it no more had been permitted to fly than a locomotive on railroad tracks could roam freely like a Land Rover. Maxim had shown that it now was entirely possible to build and operate a very large steam-powered airplane, as long as it was prevented from flying.

Though no one in 1894 was ready to build a craft that could actually fly, the art had advanced substantially in the eighty-five years since Jacob Degen had used a balloon to lift his ornithopter. Maxim's steam engines showed that the problem of power was reasonably in hand. Wenham and Phillips had learned much about wings, while introducing the wind tunnel as an instrument whereby inventors could learn more. Cayley had discussed aircraft designs that could be stable in flight, with Penaud's small rubber-powered models actually demonstrating this quality.

Still, something was missing. No one, not even a wealthy man such as Maxim, could truly invent an airplane without first mastering an issue that everyone to date had ignored: control of an airplane in flight. Maxim was well aware of the need for such control, even if his other contemporaries were not, and his failure to address this problem can be taken as showing that he was not truly serious in his quest. As a successful inventor, he was well aware that the path to invention lay in dealing with the difficult parts of a problem. Yet he had contented himself with using his track and rails to slide around it. The first men to pay proper attention to the issue of flight control also became the men who invented the airplane: Wilbur and Orville Wright.

THREE

TEACHERS AND
FIRST LESSONS

IT WAS POSSIBLE TO FLY POWERED model airplanes, even if they didn't go very far. Researchers were at work in their labs; the beginnings of a good technical literature were in libraries. True powered airplanes, with men aboard, still lay beyond the state of the art. Even so, the 1890s saw several inventors build man-carrying gliders, which gave an immediate prelude to the work of the Wright brothers.

In Germany, Otto Lilienthal emerged as another engineer who used his background to address problems of flight. Born in 1848, he developed an early fascination with birds, which he shared with his brother Gustav. He continued to hold this interest as he studied mechanical engineering and then fought in the Franco-Prussian War. His fellow soldiers in the infantry later recalled that he talked often of flying machines. Demobilized in 1871, he went to Berlin and set up a small factory. This gave him his livelihood, while permitting him to pursue studies of aviation on the side.

Otto Lilienthal.

He held the conviction that the proper approach to flight lay in building ornithopters. To do so successfully, he knew he needed the strongest possible background in the observation of birds. He learned that birds propel themselves by using their outer feathers; he developed tables showing the lift provided by wings with various amounts of curvature. He published his findings in 1889 in a book titled *Der Vogelflug als Grundlage der Fliegekunst* (*Bird Flight as the Basis of Aviation*), which quickly became influential within this nascent field.

Soon after, he began building a succession of gliders. He made no attempt to introduce movable controls; instead, he steered them by moving his body and legs. His first two designs didn't work, but he learned from his mistakes and crafted an increasingly successful series, beginning in 1891. He also had a stroke of good fortune when he learned that a canal was to be built near his home. He allowed the contractor to pile the excavated dirt on land that he owned, creating a hill fifty feet tall. He could take off in any direction from its top, depending on how the wind was blowing.

Lilienthal flying one of his hang gliders.

He also flew from hills near Berlin, making a weekly excursion every Sunday. As his designs improved, he achieved ranges as great as 1,150 feet. Most of his craft were monoplanes, with the plane of the wings at chest level. However, his Number 11 of 1894, which he regarded as his standard model, was a true hang glider that placed his entire body below the wing, for greater stability. It had a separate tail with vertical and horizontal stabilizers. He made some 2,500 flights in the course of five years, taking off by running downhill and into the wind. As few as three steps would see him airborne, with a seat supporting his weight. When landing, he pushed the wings to angle them upward, losing speed and dropping lightly to the ground.

Although Number 11 was his best, he remained open to new approaches. He built and flew a biplane. He considered the use of control surfaces: a movable tail, an airbrake at each wingtip to produce drag for steering by making the craft turn in the air. He also built lightweight engines, though he did not fly with them. He did not plan to use a propeller; he continued to think of propulsion using flapping wingtips, an approach that reflected his continuing interest in ornithopters. Nevertheless, his strong base of experience in controlled flight placed him in a good position to become the first to fly under power.

He never lived to make the attempt. One day in August 1896, he was flying his reliable Number 11 when a sudden gust of wind lifted the nose and made him stall. He threw his weight forward to try to bring the nose down, but he did not succeed, falling off on one wing and slamming into the ground. He suffered internal injuries that included a broken back, and died the next day.

Much the same fate befell a Scotsman, Percy Pilcher, who was active at the same time. He had served in the Royal Navy and took a post in naval architecture at Glasgow University. He crafted a glider, spent some time with Lilienthal in Berlin, flew one of Lilienthal's biplanes from the artificial hill, and proceeded to improve his own designs. There were hills aplenty in the Highlands, and Pilcher introduced the use of a towrope to pull him into the air. He learned still more by working as an assistant to Hiram Maxim. His best flight, in June 1897, covered 750 feet.

Like Lilienthal, he built a small engine and tested it in a laboratory. However, he never got to fly with it. During a flight in September 1899, a bamboo rod in the tail broke. The tail assembly collapsed, and his glider dove into the ground. He died two days later.

Despite their progress, neither Lilienthal nor Pilcher came close to inventing a powered airplane. When the Wrights entered the field, they did not merely carry Lilienthal's work to completion, but started afresh with a largely original approach. Even so, Europe lost two key innovators in aviation with the death of these men. Leadership in aeronautics now passed to the United States, where the engineer Octave Chanute had been active and vigorous for some time.

Born in 1832, he was in his sixties during the 1890s. He had had a distinguished career in civil engineering, building a bridge over the Missouri River at Kansas City and serving as chief engineer of the Erie Railroad. Residing in Chicago, his projects also included the Union

Stock Yards. He came to aviation by meeting Wenham in 1875 and by reading an article by France's Alphonse Penaud in 1876. This led him into a careful study of the available literature. His friends included the editor of *Railroad and Engineering Journal,* who invited him to contribute a series of articles on the subject of flight.

The first of them appeared in October 1891, with new ones being published monthly through the end of 1893. The following year the complete series appeared as a book, *Progress in Flying Machines.* Along with Lilienthal's *Vogelflug,* it too became a classic, for it offered an insightful survey of the attempts made to date, showing what had and hadn't worked. Chanute also entered into extensive correspondence with other inventors, including Lilienthal, Maxim, and Lawrence Hargrave, an Australian who invented the box kite.

Then in 1896, he decided that he could build successful gliders of his own. He set up a camp amid sand dunes on the southern shore of Lake Michigan, working initially with a Lilienthal-type glider built by an assistant, Augustus Herring. Chanute felt that he was too old to fly

Octave Chanute.

himself, and encouraged Herring to be a test pilot. A storm blew in and ripped up their tent; Chanute sent for a new one. A reporter from the *Chicago Tribune* learned what they were up to and wrote stories that attracted a steady stream of bothersome visitors. Chanute and his associates nevertheless went ahead.

The Lilienthal glider flew repeatedly but did not work well, finally being damaged beyond repair following a bad landing. Chanute by then had developed ideas of his own, and was ready to nurture a fondness for designs with a large number of wings. His next device, the Katydid, had as many as six pairs. It too was a hang glider, steered through movements of the pilot's body, and he hoped it would show a high degree of inherent stability. He wrote that "the wings should move automatically so as to bring the movable center of pressure back over the center of gravity, which latter would remain fixed. That is to say, that the wings should move instead of the man."

Chanute's biplane gliders introduced the Pratt truss, which had previously been used in railroad bridges.

It flew acceptably, though for shorter distances than the Lilienthal model, and Chanute declared that he had learned more in two weeks of flight test than in years of studying other people's writings. He returned to Chicago with his group and proceeded to build a new glider that was considerably simpler in form. It took shape as a triplane, which he later converted into a biplane by the simple method of removing the bottom wing. He built it as a Pratt truss, a lightweight structure patented in 1844 that he had previously used in railroad bridges. This represented a real contribution, for subsequent biplane designs, including those of the Wrights, used the Pratt truss as well.

Chanute returned to the dunes in August. He picked a location five miles farther down the coast, where the dunes were taller and the site was harder for the casually curious to reach. Photos of subsequent flights with the biplane have a distinctly modern appearance, as we see Herring and others skimming along the face of a dune or lifting into the air for a long glide. The beach and the sandy hills have not changed in the past hundred years, while the biplane design shows a simplicity that suits the mind of today. Herring set the record for this

Samuel Langley.

round of experiments, flying 359 feet in fourteen seconds. The glider also proved to be flyable in winds that topped thirty miles per hour. Some visitors found their way to the secluded camp, and by late September, Chanute had so much confidence in his biplane that he allowed these rank neophytes to fly with it.

Chanute, Pilcher, and Lilienthal together showed that good solutions were in hand for wings and for overall designs, with a pilot achieving control by moving the weight of his body. However, successful powered flight would call for more than scaling up the design and installing an engine. These hang gliders lacked movable control surfaces—ailerons, elevator, rudder—and hence could not grow in size. Already, Maxim had built a large machine that lacked such surfaces and that therefore could do no more than lift itself from a track.

Only a pilot could exercise control in flight, but people knew by then how to build airplanes that would be inherently stable in the air, and advances in steam-engine design brought new opportunities for unpiloted models. The man who did the most in this area was Samuel P. Langley, the director of the Smithsonian Institution in Washington. Like Cayley, he was an aristocrat. He did not trace his background to the Norman Conquest, but his ancestors had come to Massachusetts soon after the arrival of the *Mayflower*. These forebears included the religious leader Cotton Mather as well as Increase Mather, an early president of Harvard College.

He developed a strong early interest in astronomy, and worked with his younger brother to build telescopes with mirrors of his own design. This brought him appointments at Harvard and at the Naval Academy in Annapolis, followed by a permanent position as director of the observatory at the nascent University of Pittsburgh. His work helped to broaden astronomy into the new realms of astrophysics, moving beyond a traditional concern with the positions of stars to embrace their study as physical objects. He specialized in studies of the sun, leading an expedition to the top of California's Mt. Whitney and making observations at high altitude, where more could be seen. He also invented the bolometer, a sensitive instrument for measuring the flow of energy at any wavelength.

However, Pittsburgh was no place for a first-class scientist such as Langley. It was an industrial town, where people with real brains were in short supply, and it didn't help that he was painfully shy. Though tall and commanding in appearance, he was unattractive to women; he never married, and he formed few close friendships. He therefore responded eagerly in 1887, when he received an appointment as Assistant Secretary of the Smithsonian. Later that year he became full Secretary, or director, upon the death of his predecessor.

Already he was nurturing an interest in aviation. This dated to the previous year, when he had attended a meeting of the American Association for the Advancement of Science and read a paper on the flight of soaring birds. With help from William Thaw, a wealthy local philanthropist who had financed the Mt. Whitney expedition, Langley built a large whirling arm driven by a steam engine. He concluded that one horsepower could lift 200 pounds into the air, at a speed of 60 feet per second.

During 1887, with Washington as his new home, he also began experimenting with small models powered by rubber bands, in the fashion of Alphonse Penaud. He had no background in airplane design, but he learned what he could from other people's layouts, and he worked by trial and error as he sought success. It took him four years before one of his models flew well, and he never achieved distances greater than a hundred feet. Nevertheless, by 1892 he was ready to build lightweight steam engines, and he made his first attempts at powered flight.

He called his craft "aerodromes," from the Greek for "air runner," with the first of them being No. 0. Its design was so inadequate that Langley abandoned it before completing its construction. Nos. 1, 2, and 3, which followed, all proved to be so underpowered that they could not fly. Nos. 4 and 5 had better engines, but their wings proved to lack structural strength. By then it was 1895, and Langley had succeeded only with his rubber-band models.

But during that year, he settled on a new configuration that seemed to hold particular promise. It was a tandem-wing monoplane, with wings of equal size set one behind the other. England's D. S. Brown had published this concept some twenty years earlier, and had shown that it was stable in pitch. Langley rebuilt Nos. 4 and 5 to this new design, redesignating the former as No. 6. He continued to work with tandem wings during subsequent years.

He launched his aircraft from a catapult atop a houseboat that he moored in the Potomac near Quantico, Virginia. The remote location gave him privacy; the aerodromes could take off into the wind from any direction and fly over a flat river surface, devoid of trees. He also expected that a rough landing in water would do less damage than a similar crackup on land. In May 1896 he was ready to try again. On the first attempt, with No. 6, a guy wire snagged an obstacle during launch and a wing collapsed. He brought out No. 5 and placed it on the catapult. As for what happened next, we have Langley's own report:

May 6, 1896: Langley successfully flies a steam-powered model airplane.

The signal was given and the aerodrome sprang into the air. I watched it from the shore with hardly a hope that the long series of accidents had come to a close. And yet it had.

For the first time, the aerodrome swept continuously through the air like a living thing. Second after second passed on the face of the stopwatch until a minute had gone by. And it still flew on.

As I heard the cheering of the few spectators, I felt that something had been accomplished at last. For never in any part of the world or in any period had any machine of man's construction sustained itself in the air for even half of this brief time.

Still the aerodrome went on in a rising course until, at the end of a minute and a half (for which time only it was provided with fuel and water), it had accomplished a little over half a mile. Now it settled rather than fell into the river with a gentle descent.[1]

Alexander Graham Bell, inventor of the telephone, was there with Langley, and gave his own description. Bell wrote that the model "rose at first directly into the face of the wind, moving at all times with remarkable steadiness, and subsequently swinging around in large curves of perhaps a hundred yards in diameter, and continually ascending until its steam was exhausted. At a lapse of about a minute and a half, and at a height which I judged to be between eighty and one hundred feet in the air, the wheels ceased turning."[2]

The craft that did this had a wingspan of fourteen feet, with an engine that delivered a single horsepower. It weighed about thirty pounds—and on this first flight, it covered some 3,300 feet. Then, just to show that this was no fluke, Langley fished it from the water and launched it on a second flight, later that afternoon. This time it circled to the left, but it stayed aloft for about the same time and covered the same distance.

Late in November, he was back on the river and ready to try with a repaired No. 6. It did even better, for instead of circling it flew in a long gentle curve that hugged the shoreline, remaining in the air for a minute and 45 seconds while covering over three-fourths of a mile. Here was something new and highly significant, for in contrast to

Ader and Maxim, Langley had done what he set out to do and had achieved true powered flight. Moreover, this accomplishment represented work by the Smithsonian Institution, one of the nation's premier scientific organizations. Both in its prestige and in the extent of accomplishment, Langley's work topped anything done to date.

He had done what he could with models and small steam engines. Piloted flight, in a full-scale airplane, clearly stood as the next goal. However, such a project lay beyond the resources of the Smithsonian. Then in April 1898, the nation declared war on Spain. The Spanish-American War lasted only a few months, but that was long enough for President William McKinley to take an interest in potential military applications of Langley's work. He appointed a committee, which recommended support. In December, Langley accepted an invitation from the War Department to build a man-carrying airplane, with a grant of $50,000. No one had yet flown successfully in a powered aircraft, but already the federal government was ready to get involved.

During the next several years, he worked closely with an assistant, Charles Manly, and placed particular emphasis on engines. He took full advantage of a century of technical advances in this area, but his powered craft, Aerodrome A, was on a par with the Aerial Steam Carriage. He built it as a tandem-wing monoplane, with a movable elevator at the rear to control the pitch. To turn it, he installed a rudder like that of a ship. The wings had dihedral for stability, and he expected that this would keep his airplane on an even keel while the rudder did its work. His emphasis on intrinsic stability followed conventional wisdom, and drew on his experience with Nos. 5 and 6.

Langley's success with steam-driven models, coupled with his War Department support, placed him in the forefront at a time when the Wrights still were in their bicycle shop. The exciting advances of the 1890s largely bypassed them, though here and there a news item or a magazine article did catch their attention. The historian Gibbs-Smith believes that their first introduction to the subject came from an article, "The Flying Man," that appeared in the September 1894 issue of *McClure's Magazine.*

McClure's often appeared within the Wright household. The article went well beyond simple description, for it carried halftone illustrations. Such published reproductions of photos stood as one more recent technical innovation, giving undeniable proof in ways that the simple line drawings of old could never approach. The *McClure's* article discussed the work of Lilienthal, with the halftones showing him taking off, gliding, and landing. Clearly, flight was feasible.

The young Wrights responded in their usual way, by reading pertinent entries in the encyclopedias that were part of their home library, and by checking out the holdings within the Dayton public library. They found little, for aeronautics still was far too new as a field to have developed an extensive published literature. In this respect, the editors at *McClure's* had shown that they were good journalists, getting out front with an interesting story that almost no one else was covering. The Wrights set aside their nascent interest in flight and returned to their bicycles.

Aviation once more was in the news during 1896, with the death of Lilienthal. This might have stirred their interest anew, but for some time during that year, Orville was very sick with typhoid. Indeed, for a time his life was in danger, and all that anyone could do was to wait for his fever to break. Wilbur meanwhile had to take on additional responsibility for the brothers' printing and bicycle ventures, while helping to nurse Orville in the bargain. When he finally recovered there was much work to catch up on. Once more their interest in aviation flickered and died.

But during 1899, changing circumstances once more drew them to this field, this time for good. The bicycle business was running smoothly. The sale of the printshop meant that the brothers could anticipate having some extra money along with some free time. Wilbur was still Wilbur, now in his early thirties but still unmarried and still living at home with his dad. Restless, hoping for something new, he turned again to books and readings, knowing that he might find something to spark his interest.

He read James Pettigrew's *Animal Locomotion,* which included discussions of bird flight. This book complemented one that he had read several years earlier: Etienne Marey's *Animal Mechanism*. Neither of these books gave any useful clues as to how the movement of birds' wings might carry over for use in a flying machine. But Wilbur gained inspiration, if not useful technical knowledge, from *L'Empire de l'Air*, a book by France's Louis Mouillard. It too had much on the subject of birds, but Mouillard had gone further and had built and flown simple hang gliders. He had corresponded with Octave Chanute, who had helped him to secure a patent for a proposed aircraft. Wilbur did not read the book itself, which was in French, whereas his own studies of languages had inclined more to Latin and Greek. But parts of this book appeared in translation within the Smithsonian Institution's *Annual Report* for 1892, which was available in the Dayton library.

Mouillard had written of the lure of flight: "If there be a domineering, tyrant thought, it is the conception that the problem of flight may be solved by man. When once this idea has invaded the brain it possesses it exclusively. It is then a haunting thought, a walking nightmare, impossible to cast off." Wilbur was not about to allow this vision to possess him exclusively, not while he still had a bicycle shop to help run. However, it was clear that he could hope to learn more by writing to the Smithsonian.

On May 30, he sat down with two sheets of Wright Cycle Company letterhead stationery and drafted a handwritten letter:

The Smithsonian Institution
Washington

Dear Sirs:
  I have been interested in the problem of mechanical and
human flight ever since as a boy I constructed a number of bats of
various sizes after the style of Cayley's and Penaud's machines. My
observations since have only convinced me more firmly that
human flight is feasible and practicable. It is only a question of
knowledge and skill just as in all acrobatic feats. Birds are the most
perfectly trained gymnasts in the world and are specially well
fitted for their work, and it may be that man will never equal

them, but no one who has watched a bird chasing an insect or
another bird can doubt that feats are performed which require
three or four times the effort required in ordinary flight. I
believe that simple flight at least is possible to man and that the
experiments and investigations of a large number of independent
workers will result in the accumulation of information
and knowledge and skill which will finally lead to accomplished
flight.

The works on this subject to which I have had access are
Marey's and Jamieson's books published by Appleton's and
various magazine and cyclopedia articles. I am about to begin a
systematic study of the subject in preparation for practical work to
which I expect to devote what time I can spare from my regular
business. I wish to obtain such papers as the Smithsonian
Institution has published on the subject, and if possible a list of
other works in print in the English language. I am an enthusiast,
but not a crank in the sense that I have some pet theories as to the
proper construction of a flying machine. I wish to avail myself of
all that is already known and then if possible add my mite to help
on the future worker who will attain final success. I do not know
the terms on which you send out your publications but if you will
inform me of the cost I will remit the price.[3]

At the Smithsonian, this letter was routed to Richard Rathbun, an
assistant to Langley. Rathbun was accustomed to receiving such
requests, for Langley's work had made the Smithsonian a center for
information on aeronautics. Rathbun responded by sending four
Smithsonian publications, which had been printed as pamphlets. They
included the partial translation of Mouillard's *Empire*, which Wilbur
had seen, along with items written by Lilienthal and by Langley.

Rathbun also included a list of recommended books and docu-
ments. These included Langley's *Experiments in Aerodynamics* (1891),
with Rathbun adding helpfully that this publication was available from
the Smithsonian for a price of one dollar, including postage. Rathbun
also advised Wilbur to read Chanute's *Progress in Flying Machines*
(1894) and to bring himself up to date with *The Aeronautical Annual*

for 1895, 1896, and 1897, published in Boston. Wilbur proceeded to obtain copies of all these publications, and he read them with care.

He was surprised to learn that they offered no clear path to success in aviation. He later wrote that "there was no flying art in the proper sense of the word, but only a flying problem." So-called flying machines "were guilty of almost everything except flying." The existing literature was "mere speculations and probably ninety percent was false. Consequently, those who tried to study the science of aerodynamics knew not what to believe and what not to believe."

Even with Orville joining in the reading and discussion, Wilbur was in no position to separate the wheat from the chaff. However, the brothers at least could organize their reading systematically. They could conceive of a flying machine as an assembly of fundamental elements, and consider each paper or book chapter as germane to one or more of them.

What would it take to build an airplane? Well, it certainly would need an engine. This did not look like a problem. The Wrights were well aware of the internal-combustion motor, more so since they had designed and built one to power the machine tools within their bicycle shop. If they ever got far enough to need motive power, such an engine would be ready for their use.

An airplane would need wings. There was much to learn in this area, but Lilienthal had crafted successful wings, as had Chanute. Their work at least gave a point of departure on which other investigators might build.

An airplane had to have a structure, light in weight but strong enough to carry the weight of a man. Chanute, a civil engineer with expertise in structures, had done particularly outstanding work on this part of the overall problem.

An airplane also needed methods for control in flight.

This last topic particularly drew the Wrights' attention. As they proceeded with their reading, they realized that no one to date had addressed this issue in a proper manner.

Lilienthal and Chanute had built hang gliders. However, their method of steering, by shifting the pilot's weight, certainly did not look like a good way to proceed. It had already killed Lilienthal, even though he had conducted numerous successful glides in the course of several years. Moreover, weight-shifting did not appear feasible even in principle if a flying machine was to carry the added weight of an engine. On this point, the Wrights were entirely correct. True hang gliders used in sport did not emerge until the 1970s. Powered versions, called ultralights, used modern lightweight engines rather than the far heavier motors of the late nineteenth century.

Penaud and Langley had built successful model planes, powering them respectively with rubber bands and with steam. These inventors had built their craft for stability in unpiloted flight, relying on wings that formed Cayley's broad V when seen from the front. This slight upper angle of each wing, measured from side to side, indeed made those aircraft stable when flying. However, the use of this dihedral raised the question of how to achieve a turn. Langley believed that the way to do it was to install a rudder like that of a ship. Use of this rudder then might enable his airplane to make a slow flat turn, with the wings remaining level.

The Wrights had come up as bicycle men, and were well aware that control was the essence of successful rides. A bicyclist executed continual small control movements to keep from falling over. Moreover, a cyclist made banked turns, heeling over with the cycle in the direction of the turn. Wilbur and Orville anticipated that a successful flying machine would resemble a bicycle in this respect; it would also bank while turning.

Their readings disclosed that other investigators had also noted similarities between bicycling and flying. James Means, editor of the *Aeronautical Annual* series, had written in the 1896 edition: "To learn to wheel one must learn to balance. To learn to fly one must learn to balance." Lilienthal had responded with a letter: "I think that your consideration of the development of the flying machine and the bicycle and the analogy between their development is quite excellent. I am sure the flying machine will have a similar development."

The Wrights' readings disclosed no suitable proposed method by which an airplane, particularly a large one with a motor, might make banked turns. Here then was an untreated problem on aeronautics. Here was Wilbur's "mite," the contribution that could potentially help the inventors of the future.

In gaining this insight, the Wrights acted like intelligent graduate students at a university. They read the literature critically and chose a problem for experimental study by relying on a strong general sense of an airplane as a system. Other inventors, from Leonardo to Lilienthal, had conceived of flying machines as wing-flapping ornithopters. The Wrights saw them as bicycles with wings. This point of view proved to be completely correct, although experience showed that only heavier-than-air winged craft had to bank in this fashion. Dirigibles proved indeed to be ships of the air, turning gracefully by using only their rudders. Helicopters dispensed with fixed wings altogether and changed direction without needing specialized controls to achieve a bank. Large rocket vehicles steered by swiveling their engines.

In creating an invention, the difficult part of a problem often consists merely in understanding it properly. Once this perception is in hand, a solution may follow with no more than modest thought. For the Wrights, their selected problem was to devise a concept for a winged flying machine that could execute banked turns, with the core of the challenge involving a way to achieve the bank.

Ailerons on the wings emerged in time as the solution, but in 1899 this concept did not even exist yet. People were trying to craft good wings, but their imagination did not yet extend to wing-mounted control surfaces. The Wrights did not invent the aileron, but they had done a fair amount of reading in ornithology, and had studied published photographs of birds in flight. They also had visited hills in the Dayton area, and had tried to make close observations of buzzards in the air. As Wilbur wrote a year later: "My observation of the flight of buzzards leads me to believe that they regain their lateral balance, when partly overturned by a gust of wind, by a torsion of the tips of the wings. If the rear edge of the right wing tip is twisted upward and the left downward the bird becomes an animated windmill and instantly begins a turn, a line from its head to its tail being the axis."

How could a flying machine be built that could twist its own wingtips in such a fashion? The Wrights' initial thoughts called for building wing extensions that were separate from the wings themselves, being mounted on shafts running to the center of the aircraft. A set of gears then could ensure that when one extension was angled upward, the other would angle downward. In time, ailerons did this; this Wright concept amounted to using movable wingtips as ailerons. However, such an arrangement threatened to be unacceptably heavy, while posing danger if one of these wing extensions were to break off.

A better concept soon emerged, growing out of the Wrights' continuing work at their bicycle shop. One evening a customer came in and purchased an inner tube for a tire. Orville pulled the tube from its cardboard box and started chatting, holding the box and twisting it in his hands. After completing the transaction, he realized that this long box resembled a set of biplane wings. Significantly, the box remained stiff along its length even when the twist was quite considerable. This was it! By twisting the wings of a biplane in opposite directions, he could solve the problem of banking an airplane.

Back at home, Wilbur's mind raced with excitement as he explained this principle to Orville. He demonstrated it by twisting the box in his own hands, then handing it to Orville to see for himself. Orville quickly agreed that this was the way to proceed. The new concept came to be called "wing warping." It did not require heavy onboard equipment such as shafts and gears, but only needed a wing structure that was free to flex. Lightweight cords could then twist this structure appropriately.

The brothers had already been planning to test their concept of control by building it into a large kite. Wilbur now lost himself in details, working with sketches to understand the specific arrangements of cabling that could enable a pilot to warp wings in flight. He also built a small scale model of the kite, crafting it of split bamboo and paper, with strings to achieve the wing warping.

The kite itself had a five-foot wingspan. The Wrights designed its wing structure as a version of Chanute's Pratt truss, with the two wings supported by vertical struts and diagonal wires. To give this kite its necessary flexibility, they avoided diagonal braces running fore and aft, which would have made the structure rigid and unable to warp. Long cords, running from each wing's front corner to a pair of hand-held sticks, enabled an operator on the ground to fly this kite while exercising the wing warping.

In addition to banking, the Wrights also wanted this craft to rise and descend. Again, the cords and sticks made this possible. They warped the wings when pulling in opposite directions, but an operator could also use them to pull in the same direction. When the top cords were both tugged taut, the top wing slid forward. A horizontal stabilizer, or tail surface, also angled upward, and the craft rose. Similarly, pulling both bottom cords made the upper wing slip backward and the stabilizer turn downward. The kite then descended.

Wilbur flew this kite late in July, taking it to a field west of Dayton. He used the sticks and cords to control it in the air, and as he had hoped, the wing warping indeed made it bank as he had wished. He was right! However, when he tried to execute a controlled descent, the kite lost altitude suddenly, nearly colliding with a group of young boys who were there to watch. Clearly, he and Orville had to learn much more before they could hope to succeed. Still, that single day's experiments showed that they were on the right track.

In only a few weeks, during June and July, the Wrights succeeded in gaining several important insights and achievements. They emphasized that full-size airplanes had to be controllable. They appreciated that means for control had to be built in at the outset, rather than being added later. They broadened their understanding of what wings could do, for while inventors had known for centuries that they were to give lift, the Wrights introduced the key concept of wings as organs of control.

Chanute later introduced the term "wing warping," but the Wrights invented it. Though superseded relatively quickly by the use of ailerons, this concept proved sufficiently robust to enable the first true airplanes to take to the air. In addition, the five-foot kite represented a proof-of-principle experiment. Its horizontal stabilizer was not new; Cayley and his successors had similar thoughts, while the overall structure showed the influence of Chanute. But by demonstrating through actual flight that the wing-warping principle was sound, this kite laid important groundwork for the Wrights' subsequent work.

The testing of that kite was as far as the Wright brothers went during 1899. They still had their bike shop to run, and it says much about their strong fascination with aviation that they devoted so much time to it, even though the cycling season was at its peak. Still, the next step was clear: to build a much larger kite and, if possible, to have it carry a man. If all went well, it might fly as a glider.

In preparing a design for this new kite, the Wrights found themselves led deeply into problems of the aerodynamics of wings. They had used wings with gently-curved upper surfaces on their 1899 kite, but bypassed serious attention to the choice of curve because the kite was very low in weight and took to the air with ease. But for a large man-carrying version, proper attention to wing design was essential.

They were particularly concerned with the center of lift, also called the center of pressure. This was a balance point; a wing generated equal amounts of lift ahead of and behind that point. Some ninety years earlier, Cayley had written that this center would lie close to a wing's leading edge.

The Wrights saw that this was particularly true if a wing faced the onrushing air at a modest upward tilt, or angle of attack. This would happen when climbing after takeoff, and when flying slowly, immediately prior to landing. The wing's lower surface then would shield the upper surface from direct contact with the oncoming airflow.

But when the wing leveled off and approached zero angle of attack, as for cruising flight, it might present a substantial amount of upper surface to this airflow. The Wrights were concerned with the forward part of this upper surface. By facing this flow, it would produce a good deal of downward pressure on the front of the wing. The center of pressure then would travel well to the rear of the wing—and this could bring disaster. It would unbalance the aircraft, perhaps causing it to fall from the sky.

Lilienthal and Chanute had used simple arcs of a circle for the curving airfoils of their wings, with these arcs having a good deal of curvature. Following their reasoning, the Wrights decided that such shapes would produce particularly large amounts of center-of-pressure travel. This was because such airfoils presented particularly large amounts of forward upper surface area to the airflow.

A good airfoil, then, had to minimize this presented surface. The Wrights addressed this issue by breaking with Lilienthal and Chanute in two key respects. Rather than use the uniform curve of a circle's arc, they put most of the curvature well to the front. They also made the wing considerably thinner, flattening the rearward curve.

The Wrights' airfoil thus represented an important step toward the elongated teardrop shapes that in time became standard. This airfoil also resembled some of the long curved teardrops of Horatio Phillips, in England. However, whereas Phillips had used a wind tunnel, the Wrights relied principally on physical argument, which showed good understanding of the aerodynamic forces that governed travel of the center of pressure.

This wing promised to reduce that travel considerably, but still the center of pressure would move. To keep an aircraft in steady flight despite such movement, it needed a method for controlling its pitch. This was easy to understand. If travel of this center unbalanced the craft, this unbalance would take the form of a severe movement in pitch, either upward (leading to a stall and consequent loss of lift), or downward (leading to a crash).

To control pitch the obvious solution, again, was a horizontal stabilizer. Wilbur had installed one on the 1899 kite, and had learned during its test flights that this stabilizer could work equally effectively when mounted before or behind the wings. For the new and much larger kite, the brothers decided to mount it at the front, in a configuration later known as a canard.

A prime reason lay in the Wrights' expectation that the craft would drag its tail when landing. If it landed tail-first, it could easily damage that fragile structure. Placing it forward meant that it would stay out of harm's way. In addition, a forward stabilizer would give the pilot a valuable horizontal reference, showing immediately and accurately whether the nose of the aircraft was pointing above or below the horizon. This would encourage close control of pitch.

Within their literature, the brothers had equations and other published data that enabled them to calculate an appropriate size for their
new kite. It was to fly in the breeze, which had to be of a certain velocity. The winds lacked strength near Dayton. For the kite to support its
own weight along with that of Orville or Wilbur, it then would have to
be inconveniently large in size. The five-foot kite of 1899 had been
large enough for the Wrights to apply methods of construction and
control that could carry over to the new one, but still its size had to
stay within bounds.

Swift breezes would permit a substantial reduction in this size, but
this approach could easily get out of hand as well. They knew that stiff
winds generally meant stormy weather, with gusts that could easily
blow a flying machine into the ground. They settled on a reference
wind speed of fifteen miles per hour. With this choice, and with their
equations and data in hand, the new design called for biplane wings
measuring 18 by 5 feet.

These decisions committed them to fly somewhere other than
Dayton, at a location where the winds would be sufficiently strong.
They were aware that Chanute had flown his gliders near Chicago,
and considered that the nearby Lake Michigan dunes might suit them
as well. Chicago, after all, was known as the Windy City, though this
name had derived less from its weather than from the boastfulness of
its politicians. It was readily accessible by rail from Dayton.

During the fall of 1899, Wilbur wrote two letters to the Weather
Bureau in Washington, asking for information on wind speeds near
Chicago. He particularly wanted reports of measurements for the
month of September, a time of the year when bicycle work slacked off
and left the Wrights with time to travel. The chief of the Bureau
responded with current issues of the *Monthly Weather Review*. One of
them gave tables that presented average hourly wind velocities, measured at 120 Weather Bureau stations around the country.

Chicago indeed proved to have the highest average wind speeds,
which approached 17 miles per hour for September. However, further
thought convinced the brothers that they needed more than good

breezes; they needed isolation. News reporters and other visitors had dogged Chanute in the course of his own test flights, and the Wrights wanted privacy. Locations near Chicago therefore were out.

The brothers had plenty to do in their bike shop during that autumn and winter, but with the coming of spring, their thoughts turned anew to aviation. Selection of a test area was still high on their list of things to do. Accordingly, in mid-May of 1900, Wilbur wrote to Chanute. He asked for advice; he also presented his views more generally, and his letter ran to several pages:

> For some years I have been afflicted with the belief that flight is possible to man. My disease has increased in severity and I feel that it will soon cost me an increased amount of money if not my life. I have been trying to arrange my affairs in such a way that I can devote my entire time for a few months to experiment in this field. . . .
>
> I conceive that [Lilienthal's] failure was due chiefly to the inadequacy of his method, and of his apparatus. As to his method, the fact that in five years' time he spent only about five hours, altogether, in actual flight is sufficient to show that his method was inadequate. Even the simplest intellectual or acrobatic feats could never be learned with so short practice. . . . I also conceive Lilienthal's apparatus to be inadequate not only from the fact that he failed, but my observations of the flight of birds convince me that birds use more positive and energetic methods of regaining equilibrium than that of shifting the center of gravity. . . .[4]

Chanute, like Langley and Rathbun at the Smithsonian, was accustomed to receiving such letters. They all were known as leaders in aviation, thereby attracting attention from other people of similar interest. In addition, Chanute took his correspondence seriously. He used exchanges of letters not only to learn what others were doing, but to offer encouragement when he could.

Wilbur's letter presented a plan: "I shall in a suitable locality erect a light tower of about one hundred and fifty feet high. . . . The wind will blow the machine out from the base of the tower and the weight will be sustained partly by the upward pull of the rope and partly by the lift of the wind." In this fashion, it appeared feasible to practice by staying in the air for hours at a time, safely secured by the rope. He hoped in this fashion to "escape accident long enough to acquire skill sufficient to prevent accident." Having set forth his ideas, Wilbur wrote that he would be "particularly thankful for advice as to a suitable locality where I could depend on winds of about fifteen miles per hour without rain or too inclement weather."

Chanute took the view that the Wrights needed sand dunes like those near Lake Michigan, to take off from a height when attempting free flight, with the sand cushioning any rough landing. He replied that he "preferred preliminary learning on a sand hill and trying ambitious feats over water." He noted that locations with good wind included San Diego, California and St. James City, Florida, a village on the Gulf Coast near Fort Myers. Neither of these choices had good sand dunes, but the Wrights might find what they wanted "on the Atlantic coast of South Carolina or Georgia."

This sent them back to their Weather Bureau reports. The Chicago area was already out, despite its high winds, while California and southern Florida were too far away. Several potentially promising sites in the Bureau's tables proved to be too flat or to lack sand or privacy. However, one weather station looked appealing: Kitty Hawk, North Carolina. Its average wind speed of 13.4 miles per hour was the sixth-highest in the tables. In addition, it was located on the Outer Banks, north of Cape Hatteras, in a seaside location that suggested plenty of sand and more than ample isolation.

The brothers' plans took form along with their new kite. They formed ribs for the wings by taking strips of wood, exposing them to steam to make them flexible, and bending them to their proper shape. Sateen fabric was to serve as the covering. The cloth and the ribs would form a compact bundle that might be readily transported for assembly in a remote location. The wings needed 18-foot spars, which were too long and unwieldy to travel by train. However, the brothers were well aware that wooden beams of all descriptions were available at lumberyards across the country. They expected to purchase their spars in a town near the test area, then assemble their kite on the spot once they reached their destination.

"I have fallen in love with American names," wrote the poet Stephen Vincent Benét. Kitty Hawk was one such name, deriving from the local Indian pidgin phrase "Killy Honk," a place where they shot honking geese for food. For centuries it had been close to history, for it lay only a few miles from Roanoke Island. Here Sir Walter Ralegh planted the first English colony in North America, in 1584. Here the baby Virginia Dare came into the world, the first English child to be born on American soil. This colony held an enduring fascination. It had vanished virtually without a trace around 1588, probably because of severe drought, while England was preoccupied with the Spanish Armada.

Four centuries later, the area still was inaccessible either by rail or by road. This raised questions concerning food and accommodations for visitors. Early in August, Wilbur set out to address these issues by writing to the Weather Bureau station at Kitty Hawk. Joseph Dosher, the lone employee at that station, responded with hopeful news: "I will say the beach here is about one mile wide, clear of trees or high hills and extends for nearly sixty miles same condition. . . . I am sorry to say you could not rent a house here, so you will have to bring tents. You could obtain board."

Kitty Hawk was a tiny fishing village where everyone knew everybody else's business. A letter from far-distant Ohio was an event. The local postmaster, Addie Tate, saw its return address even before she had a chance to deliver it. Tongues then wagged even more loudly when it proved to concern the prospects for testing a flying machine. Dosher showed the letter to Addie's husband William, who had been postmaster before his wife took the job, and who was a notary and a Currituck County commissioner. He responded to Wilbur Wright with a warm letter of his own:

Mr. J. J. Dosher of the Weather Bureau here has asked me to answer your letter to him, relative to the fitness of Kitty Hawk as a place to practice or experiment with a flying machine, etc.

In answering I would say that you would find here nearly any type of ground you could wish; you could, for instance, get a stretch of sandy land one mile by five with a bare hill in center 80 feet high, not a tree or bush anywhere to break the evenness of the wind current. This in my opinion would be a fine place; our winds are always steady, generally from 10 to 20 miles velocity per hour.

You can reach here from Elizabeth City, N.C. (35 miles from here) by boat directly from Manteo 12 miles from here by mail boat every Mon., Wed., & Friday. We have Telegraph communication & daily mails. Climate healthy, you could find good place to pitch tents & get board in private family provided there were not too many in your party; would advise you to come any time from September 15 to October 15. Don't wait until November. The autumn generally gets a little rough by November.

If you decide to try your machine here & come I will take pleasure in doing all I can for your convenience & success & pleasure, & I assure you you will find a hospitable people when you come among us.[5]

These letters decided the issue: Kitty Hawk was where the Wrights would try their wings. They decided that Wilbur would go there, set up camp while leaving Orville in the bike shop, and then invite Orville to join him when all was ready.

In contrast to his father Milton, Wilbur had done virtually no traveling during his life. He had attended the great Columbian Exposition in Chicago during 1893, a world's fair that featured the dancer Little Egypt and introduced the first Ferris wheel, but he had spent his life close to home, never venturing far from civilization. It did not take long for him to learn that the journey to Kitty Hawk would broaden his horizons in ways that were more than aeronautical.

He started on September 6, taking an evening train from Dayton. He rode through the night and reached Old Point Comfort near Norfolk, Virginia, the following day. He took a ferry across Hampton Roads to Norfolk and checked into a hotel, then got up the next day and went shopping for the long spars that he needed. He did not dress for the weather, but followed the custom of that era by dressing as a gentleman, in a high starched collar and a dark suit jacket. He thus sought to present himself as a man of consequence rather than a mere mechanic. Dayton had often been hot enough during summer, but in Norfolk the temperature approached a hundred degrees. As Wilbur later wrote, "I nearly collapsed."

He wanted spruce spars, but this type of wood proved to be unavailable. He had to settle for white pine, which was common enough in the local area but was less resilient. Nor could he find the 18-foot lengths he wanted; he had to accept sixteen feet. This meant that the kite would have less wingspan, but he could compensate by flying it in a somewhat stronger breeze. He made the purchase at a sawmill, describing the foreman as "very accommodating" and paying $7.70. Spars in hand, he finished his day by taking a train to Elizabeth City, North Carolina, where again he found a hotel and spent the night.

William Tate's letter had advised him that it was easy to get to Kitty Hawk from the town of Manteo. Manteo was on Roanoke Island, more than forty miles away by water, with weekly boat service from Elizabeth City. However, Wilbur had missed the boat; it had departed the day before. He went down to the waterfront, hoping to find a different passage to Kitty Hawk. He was appalled to find that no one he met knew anything about the place.

He stayed in town, continuing his inquiries. Finally, three days later, he met a waterman named Israel Perry who had lived in Kitty Hawk and was willing to take him there. Wilbur left most of his kite's parts with a freight agent for later delivery, but kept hold of the spars, which were easy to damage and hard to replace. The voyage to Kitty Hawk called for a three-mile trip in Perry's skiff to reach his fishing schooner, named *Curlicue*, which would carry them the rest of the way.

Also onboard was Perry's grown son, as well as Wilbur's luggage. Hence the skiff was heavily overloaded, with water at times coming over the side. It also leaked badly. Still, by bailing continually, the three men reached Perry's schooner. As Wilbur later noted, "I discovered at a glance that it was in worse condition if possible than the skiff. The sails were rotten, the ropes badly worn and the rudder post half rotted off, and the cabin so dirty and vermin-infested that I kept out of it from first to last."

Their route ran down the Pasquotank River and into Albemarle Sound. The winds initially were light, but the water was choppy, which Perry interpreted as a sign of an oncoming storm. Soon the winds indeed became stormy, sending heavy waves against the hull. Perry made little progress; in Wilbur's words, "the leeway was greater than the headway." The boat rolled and pitched, springing a leak, while water came over the bow. Again, the men had to bail.

This storm may well have been part of the backwash of the deadliest hurricane ever to strike the United States. It had come ashore at Galveston, Texas, on September 8, driving walls of water into the town and killing some six thousand people. Hurricanes weaken when over land, but the winds from this one may have reached as far as the North Carolina coast.

As midnight approached, they grew stronger still, and drove the boat uncomfortably close to the north shore. Perry tried to maneuver to safety in the North River, but a powerful gust blew the foresail loose. Wilbur was no seaman, but he worked with Perry's son and managed to take it in. Then the mainsail tore loose as well. With only a jib, a triangular sheet angling upward from the bow, the boat soon turned its stern to the gale. This was dangerous, for waves now broke over that stern. Fortunately, Perry was an experienced sailor. He kept his *Curlicue* under control and reached the North River channel.

The three men slept on board the boat, with Wilbur on the hard wooden deck. There was food aboard, but he didn't touch it, relying instead on a single jar of jelly that his sister Katharine had given him. He woke up in the morning with a sore back from sleeping on deck. They remained at anchor until well past noon, repairing the sails. Late in the afternoon, they returned to Albemarle Sound and resumed their voyage. It was nine p.m. before they finally tied up at the Kitty Hawk dock, too late to go ashore. Once again, then, Wilbur spent the night with the deck for his bed.

The following morning, he asked directions and found his way to the home of William Tate, a large two-story frame house with a wraparound porch. Wilbur described it as having "unplaned siding, not painted, no plaster on the walls, which are ceiled with paint not varnished. He has no carpets at all, very little furniture, no books or pictures," with this house nevertheless being "much above average" for the community. The Tates welcomed him warmly. When Addie learned that Wilbur had eaten nothing more than his sister's jar of jelly during the past two days, she served him a big breakfast of ham and eggs.

This was no small matter, for eggs were in short supply within Kitty Hawk. This village lived by fishing, but little if any of the catch was available locally; most of it went to Baltimore. If anyone wanted fish for dinner, they took their boat and caught it. Seabirds and wild game were available in similar fashion, with no game warden to enforce the law. The soil was sandy and poor in quality, but Wilbur wrote that "they attempt to raise beans, corn, turnips, &c., on it." Their incomes as fishermen were modest, but they bought food and other goods from the mainland, with a store standing near the wharf. Wilbur described the people as "friendly and neighborly," with William Tate adding that they believed in "a good God" and "a hot Hell."

Tate's home had an extra bedroom, which they offered to Wilbur as a guest room. He was glad for its bed, for it gave relief after two nights of sleeping on deck. The family drew its water from an open shallow well near the house, and Wilbur asked Addie for a pitcherful every day, boiled to protect against typhoid. His crates arrived, containing most of the parts for his kite, and he set to work. Borrowing Addie's sewing machine, he cut down the fabric of the wing coverings and proceeded with assembly, working within a large tent that he had brought for that purpose.

Bill Tate introduced him to the community, which proved to be somewhat less than Arcadia on the Outer Banks. The villagers had what they needed, picking up a little extra income by working from time to time at a government lifesaving station that had been built to guard against shipwrecks. Still, many things were unavailable. "No one down here has any regular milk," he wrote in one of his letters home. "The poor cows have such a hard time scraping up a living that they don't have time for making milk. You never saw such poor, pitiful-looking creatures as the horses, hogs, and cows down here. The only things that thrive and grow fat are bedbugs, mosquitoes, and wood ticks."

Kitty Hawk also lacked supplies of coffee, tea, sugar, and blankets for use during cold nights. When Wilbur wrote to Orville and invited him to come to Kitty Hawk, he asked his brother to bring these things, along with cots for sleeping. Orville came within days, timing his connections adroitly and arriving on September 28. He also brought an acetylene lamp for a bicycle, to provide light when camping out in the open.

The brothers stayed at the Tates for an additional week, with Bill Tate continuing to help. He made a trip to the mainland and came back with dishes, a gasoline stove, and a barrel of gasoline. The Wrights then set up camp out on the dunes. Wilbur washed the dishes by scrubbing them with sand. Water still came from the Tate well, but now they had to carry it a thousand feet.

The brothers had brought money and were able to purchase whatever they wanted—as long as it was available. "There is no store in Kitty Hawk," Orville wrote. That is, "not anything you could call a store. Our pantry in its most depleted state would be a mammoth affair compared with our Kitty Hawk stores." The brothers had a taste for eggs, but Orville noted, "Our camp alone exhausts the output of all the henneries within a mile." Still, Bill Tate continued to extend his hospitality: "He invited us up to help dispose of a wild goose which had been killed out of season by one of the neighboring farmers." Orville soon saw that he and his brother were making an impact:

> The economics of this place were so nicely balanced before our arrival that everybody here could live and yet nothing be wasted. Our presence brought disaster to the whole arrangement. We, having more money than the natives, have been able to buy up the whole egg product of the town and about all the canned goods in the store. I fear some of them will have to suffer as a result.[6]

In Kitty Hawk, even a can of evaporated milk was a luxury: "This condensed milk comes in a can and is just like the cream of our homemade chocolate creams. . . . We just eat it out of the can with a spoon. It makes a pretty good but expensive dessert."

They had come for sand and wind, and they had plenty of both. The sand blew into everything they owned, while the wind howled amid the nighttime emptiness. But there was natural beauty as well:

> The sunsets here are the prettiest I have ever seen. The clouds light up in all colors in the background, with deep blue clouds of various shades fringed with gold below. The moon rises in much the same style, and lights up this pile of sand almost like day. I read my watch at all hours of the night on moonless nights without the aid of any other light than that of the stars shining on the canvas of the tent.[7]

The time now was at hand to test their flying machine and see how well its wings and controls would work. The pilot lay prone, in the center of the lower wing, without a seat belt. This position reduced air resistance. His feet pushed against the crosspiece of a T-shaped bar that could swing to left or right to control the wing warping. The horizontal stabilizer was directly in front of the craft, with a hand-held lever to control its tilt.

Bill Tate joined Wilbur and Orville for the first attempts at flight, with Wilbur as the pilot. He stood within an opening in the lower wing, with each hand grasping a rib. The other two men stood at the wingtips, each with a coil of rope that was tied to the kite. They all ran forward into the wind. When it began to lift its own weight, Wilbur climbed up as if emerging from a manhole, assuming the prone position and trusting that his weight would hold him in place. The strong wind now took hold and wafted it into the air. Wilbur was flying! He was not in free flight, for the attached lines were serving as tethers. But his weight was borne entirely by the air.

He did not stay up long before the kite began to oscillate up and down. Wilbur felt danger and yelled, "Let me down!" The other men obliged him by pulling their cords, causing the craft to settle gently on the sand. Wilbur was safely down, but it was clear that they needed much more experience before they could try again with a pilot. They continued by flying the device as an unmanned kite, loading it with chains to add known amounts of weight.

Wilbur had described their enterprise as "scientific kite flying." This meant making measurements of lift, drag, and wind speed. Lift was easy; it was simply the weight of the kite, with or without the chains. To measure drag they used a spring scale, which people in the area used for weighing fish. The airspeed indicator was a hand-held anemometer borrowed from Joe Dosher of the Weather Bureau. The brothers flew the kite with the controls tied down and inoperable, but they also ran lines to the T-bar and the forward elevator, to control it from the ground.

They flew it in this fashion for several hours on each of two successive days, with a windstorm then bringing an interruption. When better weather returned, the Wrights decided to fly it from a tower. Wilbur's 150-foot spire had proven to lie far beyond their grasp, but they had secured some additional lumber and built a framework 12 feet high, resembling an oil derrick. A rope ran through a pulley at the top. Orville wrote to Katharine that "we sent it up about 20 feet, at which height we attempt to keep it by manipulation to the strings." He added, "The greatest difficulty is in keeping it down. It naturally wants to go higher & higher. When it begins to get too high we give it a pretty strong pull on the ducking string, to which it responds by making a terrific dart for the ground."

They had it on the ground and were making adjustments when a sudden gust of wind flipped it out of their hands and set it down with a crash. It was in no condition to fly, for it had sustained a good deal of damage. The brothers were badly startled. They could easily think of the broken struts as a pilot's broken legs; they also were disheartened to see how events could escape their control from one second to the next. They thought of going home, but decided to sleep on it. Next morning, they found that while the kite indeed had been broken in places, it could be fixed. They called their dune the Hill of the Wreck, and in this spirit, they proceeded with repairs. Then, since the trip to

Kitty Hawk had been planned as a vacation as well as a research opportunity, the Wrights took some time off and went hunting.

In making repairs, they also modified the basic design. They had built the wings with dihedral, a broad V-shape recommended by Cayley for stability. However, the upturned wingtips of this configuration had actually brought instability, offering surface area to the wind gust that had nearly brought disaster. They re-rigged the wings as level planes. They also decided that the derrick had brought no advantage, so they elected to dispense with it.

Having modified their craft by removing its dihedral, they now ran anew through their test program, again using the fish scale and Dosher's hand-held anemometer. The results were disappointing, for the wings proved to develop considerably less lift than they had planned. This meant that flight with Wilbur or Orville at the controls was out of the question. Still, they were not at a loss, for they had the company of young Tom Tate, Bill's nephew. This boy was light enough in weight to permit him to fly, with the Wrights keeping a good grip on the control lines.

The next series of experiments exercised the controls, and brought further disappointment. The wing warping worked well, when operated with ropes from the ground. This was important; as in 1899, this showed again that this method of banking had real merit. But problems arose when the brothers tried to work the wing warping and the elevator simultaneously, again from the ground. "We tried it with the tail in front, behind, and every other way," Orville wrote to Katharine. "When we got through, Will was so mixed up that he couldn't even theorize. It has been with considerable effort that I have succeeded in keeping him in the flying business at all."

It was time to take stock. They now had gone as far as they could in flying their craft as an unpiloted kite, loading it with the weight of chains or of young Tom Tate and controlling it from the ground. They had hoped to fly it for hours on end as a piloted kite, perhaps while tethered to the derrick with a rope. But the unanticipated reduction in lift, coupled with the reduction in wing area that resulted from the use of 16-foot spars, made this highly inadvisable. To do this would require unacceptably high winds, which would be gusty and hence unsafe.

Still, they could bypass the long-duration tethered flights and try to glide down the face of a tall dune. Lilienthal had done this repeatedly, and they had used Lilienthal's data in designing their own craft. Such glides would last for only a few seconds at a time. Even so, they would represent free flight with a pilot, which the brothers had not yet achieved.

They carried the kite to a sand hill about a mile away. The wind lost strength as they arrived, but there was enough of a breeze to enable them to check for unfavorable gliding characteristics. Treating it like an enormous model plane, they ran forward while holding its wingtips and launched it into flight. It sailed outward and into the wind, soared upward, then turned and flew downwind to strike the side of the hill. It remained stable while turning, and did not nose upward into a stall or dive into the ground. The sand cushioned the impacts, with the resulting damage being easily repaired. Clearly, they had a flying machine that a pilot could trust.

The next series of flights were to be piloted glides, with Wilbur aboard the craft and at the controls. They needed taller dunes for longer glides, and with help from Bill Tate, they set out on a trek of several miles to the Kill Devil Hills. Like the name Kitty Hawk, these hills had their own story, for it was said that during a storm, sailing conditions in the nearby waters were so severe that it would kill the devil himself if he tried.

The glider—for this is what it was now, with its new assignment— weighed 50 pounds. This was no great burden for three strong men, who lived in an era that accepted physical exertion as a matter of routine. Still it was not easy to make their way through the sand, while the ever-present wind blew at the craft and imposed further demands. They nevertheless reached their destination—and found that the winds were too strong. Fortunately, they were gentler a day later.

They tied down the wing warping to ease the problem of control, leaving only the forward elevator free for control of pitch and altitude. Wilbur expected to stay close to the ground for safety. He didn't know it, but this decision meant that he had additional lift. It came from the "ground effect," which was not properly characterized until half a century later. This involved the layer of air between a low-flying wing and the ground, with this layer not easily flowing out of the way as the wing descended. That reluctance to flow outward was what generated the additional lift.

With Wilbur standing in the manhole amidships, and with the other men at the wingtips, they all ran forward and launched Wilbur into his first glide. It worked! He was airborne, but rather than controlling his glide with crude body movements, in the fashion of Lilienthal and Chanute, Wilbur found that he could achieve good control with up-and-down movements of his elevator. Here too was another important advance, demonstrating the value of this control in actual piloted flight.

Like hang-glider enthusiasts more than seventy years later, the Wrights quickly learned that carrying their craft up a hill, even with wind at their back, was one of the more physically demanding tasks in their work. They nevertheless did this repeatedly, with Wilbur again and again taking the controls. (Orville did not fly in such a fashion until 1902.) As the day progressed, Wilbur gained skill and succeeded in staying aloft longer. The best of his glides ran as long as 15 seconds, which was similar to what Lilienthal and Chanute had achieved, while covering distances of several hundred feet.

These successful tests all used only pitch control, with the wing warping being inactivated. Wilbur tried a few glides while exercising both controls, but again found that this was quite difficult. The brothers might have come back and flown some more, setting this as a new goal, but by now they felt that they had done enough. Nor could they expect to stay, for a letter from Katharine had warned them that they were needed back at the bicycle shop.

They abandoned their glider, leaving it to the wind and sand. However, Addie Tate had her eye on its fabric, a closely-woven white French sateen that was much better in quality than the yard goods she was accustomed to purchasing during trips to the mainland. Her neighbors had remarked that it was a shame to waste such fine material on something as silly as a flying machine, and she agreed. Some weeks later she took a pair of scissors, walked the distance to the glider as it rested on the sand, and helped herself to its wing coverings. Back home, she used her sewing machine to fashion new dresses for her young daughters Pauline and Irene.

For the Wrights, the trip to Kitty Hawk left them with a good deal of food for thought. They had shown that they could fabricate good wings and could build a successful man-carrying glider. They had given it good flying characteristics, while making it easy to repair when damaged in an accident. The wing warping again had worked when controlled from the ground. In gliding flight, Wilbur had controlled the pitch with ease by using his forward elevator.

Even so, something was wrong in the design. It showed considerably less drag than Wilbur had calculated. But it also had only about half the lifting power that he had anticipated.

The Wrights were concerned with the angle of attack: the angle at which wings meet the onrushing air. Wilbur had initially laid out a design for a kite that was to lift its weight plus his own, for a total of 190 pounds, in a wind of 15 miles per hour. He had used data from Lilienthal that was valid for an angle of attack of 10 degrees. His calculations then showed that he needed 205 square feet of lifting area, some of which could be allotted to the forward stabilizer.

This angle of attack proved to be uncomfortably high, compromising the kite's controllability. A lower angle, with the kite being pointed more nearly flat into the wind, meant less lift but better control. In addition, the final wing was shorter, spanning 165 square feet, plus 12 square feet for the stabilizer. Wilbur selected an angle of attack of three degrees, rather than ten. He then calculated that the kite should lift his weight in a breeze of 21 miles per hour.

In tests, however, at that speed and angle of attack, the kite could lift just 75 pounds of chains, plus its own weight, for a total of only 125 pounds. That length of chain had just half of Wilbur's weight. To lift him, the kite needed a windspeed of 25 miles per hour, at an angle of attack of 20 degrees! This angle was far too steep. It brought very high drag, along with loss of effectiveness of the elevator, which could work only at much lower angles of attack.

Wilbur had glided repeatedly from the Kill Devil Hills at low angles of attack and in windspeeds as high as 30 miles per hour. However, he had achieved such windspeeds by adding his kite's forward velocity, in a downhill glide, to that of the ocean breeze. They wanted that same lift without the glide, and it wasn't clear why they didn't have it.

They had crafted their wings with curvature that was considerably shallower than Lilienthal's. Could that account for the loss of lift? They had used the sateen covering without applying varnish as a sealant. Perhaps this fabric was too porous, allowing the air to flow through it. Or—perhaps Lilienthal's data were wrong.

They had done what they could during the year 1900. Late in October, riding home to Dayton on the train, they knew that they would design and build a new glider for 1901, and would try to grapple with the loss of lift.

FOUR

HITTING A WALL

AVIATION HAD BEGUN with the balloons of King Louis XVI, prior to the French Revolution. Hopes for successful heavier-than-air machines had flourished a century later, amid the work of Lilienthal, Pilcher, Penaud, Ader, Moy, and Maxim. Yet at century's end, these hopes lay dying. Faced with a crippling disease, Penaud had committed suicide; Lilienthal and Pilcher had died in crashes of their hang gliders. The well-financed Maxim had accomplished little, while Ader and Moy had withdrawn from attempting further experiments.

Still, while flight in heavier-than-air machines remained out of reach, the advent of new and relatively lightweight engines brought new hope for a different form of flight: dirigibles. The best and most memorable of them took shape as zeppelins. They stand to this day as emblems of Germany's technical prowess, and as one of the most romantic inventions of the twentieth century. Yet their creator, Count Ferdinand von Zeppelin, was very much a man of an earlier time, when kings still ruled and noblemen held sway.

Born in Konstanz in 1838, he spent much of his career in the service of his native Württemburg, which until 1871 was an independent kingdom. He entered its army at age fifteen, and when war broke out, he hastened to the colors. With Europe being at peace, the conflict that attracted him was America's Civil War, in which the colors were the red, white, and blue of the Union. He did not enlist, but accompanied the Army of the Potomac as a foreign military observer. He met briefly with President Lincoln; he then made his way to the headquarters of the commanding general, Joseph Hooker. He remained there during much of June 1863, at a time when Robert E. Lee was preparing to invade the North. Count Zeppelin saw action, fighting a cavalry skirmish with troops of Jeb Stuart, and escaped capture only through the good speed of his horse. Then, only days before the Battle of Gettysburg, he left Hooker and began a lengthy excursion through the Midwest.

In St. Paul, Minnesota, he met the aeronaut John Steiner, an immigrant from Germany who had made flights for the Union army. They made a tethered ascent to an altitude of some 700 feet, and Zeppelin saw a ridge of hills that "forms a very good defensive position against an aggressor marching up through the valley." Steiner told him that balloons would be more useful if they could be made navigable. He also declared that an unpowered balloon might be steerable if it was long and slender and mounted a large rudder. The Count later stated: "While I was above St. Paul I had my first idea of aerial navigation strongly impressed on me and it was there that the first idea of my zeppelins came to me." He did not envision such behemoths as the eponymous *Graf Zeppelin,* not in 1863, but within a decade his thoughts began to take appropriate form.

He returned home and became a cavalry officer, fighting against Prussia in a war of 1866 and then on the side of Prussia in the war against France of 1870. (Such shifts in allegiances were par for the course in that era.) He advanced through the ranks. Then in 1885 he was posted to Berlin as Württemburg's Ambassador Extraordinary and Minister Plenipotentiary. In 1890 he returned to active duty, commanding a Prussian cavalry brigade. He quickly fell into disfavor with the Kaiser, for he resented Prussian domination, writing that the lordly attitudes of the Emperor's fellow Prussians reduced his cherished King of Württemburg to "the role of a mere rubber stamp." This lack of royal favor meant that he would not be promoted to command a division. With this, he left the army and retired to his estates.

He now had the opportunity to pursue his old vision. As early as 1874, his thoughts had been fired anew when he attended a lecture and heard a suggestion that mail might be carried around the world by dirigible. He wrote in his diary, "The craft would have to compare in dimensions with those of a large ship. The gas compartment shall be divided into cells which may be filled and emptied individually." He thus appreciated that a successful airship would require heroic size, to provide enough lift to carry a large engine with enough power to make way against a headwind. Knowing the density of air in comparison to that of water, he already understood the central problem: to design a vessel the size of an ocean liner but of only a thousandth the weight.

After 1890, he set himself up as a full-time inventor. He spent that decade working on his first airship, the LZ-1, and in the course of those years, he found himself facing competition from France. His challenger was a wealthy Brazilian, Alberto Santos-Dumont, the son of one of that country's richest coffee growers. Whereas Zeppelin had been a fighting cavalry commander, Santos was a dandy. He barely topped 5 feet and weighed 110 pounds; to compensate, he sometimes wore inch-high heels.

But he was a man of courage. "Go to Paris," his father had told him, "the most dangerous city in the world for a young man." He eagerly embraced both automobiles and balloons. On his first ascent, he rose over that city and enjoyed a luncheon of roast beef, chicken, ice cream and cake, champagne, and hot coffee. "No dining room is so marvelous in its decoration," he told his friends at the Jockey Club.

He purchased a gasoline-powered motorcycle with three wheels, thus gaining familiarity with the nascent internal-combustion engine. He then set out to combine his two new interests by building a dirigible, powering it with an engine similar to the one that carried him around the city on his cycle. It delivered three and a half horsepower, little more than the steam engine of Henri Giffard in 1852, but it had only one-eighth the weight. Hence his gas bag was much smaller, and was less than a hundred feet in length.

On his first try, in September 1898, the wind blew him into a tree. Two days later he was back in the air, and this time he showed that he could maneuver at will. For the first time, a powered airship responded to its helm! He put his craft into a dive, making people cry out in expectation of a crash. Then he pulled out and climbed anew. He made a circle; he did a figure-eight. He flew over the housetops of Paris, still under complete control, and felt the wind in his face.

Suddenly he saw that his gasbag had lost hydrogen and was contorting in its shape. He still had ballast; he lost altitude, but he expected to come down safely. He flew over an open field where some boys were flying kites, still descending. His long guide rope hit the ground and he called, "Take the rope! Run into the wind!" The breeze gave him extra lift, and he touched down lightly.

Zeppelin's turn came two years later, in July 1900. His LZ-1 was 420 feet long; it was by far the largest dirigible built to date. But its girders bent easily, and while it weighed thirteen tons, its two motors together had less horsepower than a Volkswagen Beetle. On its first flight, it stayed in the air 18 minutes. In that brief time a winch used for control jammed, an engine failed, and the hull sagged at both ends. Two subsequent flights, made with a stiffened frame, showed mainly that the ship lacked the power to fly against even a mild breeze.

For Zeppelin, it was back to the drawing board, amid further news from France. In April 1900, at the Aero Club in Paris, the financier Henri Deutsch de la Meurthe announced that he would award a prize of 100,000 francs. The winner was to fly from the grounds of the club to the Eiffel Tower and back, a total of 7 miles, in half an hour. Santos-Dumont was the popular favorite. Still, while he found it easy to fly downwind and to circle the Tower, it was another matter altogether to return against the wind, and to beat the clock.

On his first try, in July 1901, he flew the course but arrived at the finish line 11 minutes late. Before he could land, the wind took hold of his craft and his motor failed. He wound up in a chestnut tree on the estate of the Baron de Rothschild, where rescuers found him nonchalantly enjoying lunch. On the second attempt, three weeks later, his dirigible plunged onto the Trocadero Hotel, and his gasbag ripped apart. He leaped to safety on a window ledge, and firemen helped him down amid cheers from a crowd. But on the third try, in October, he flew around the Tower and returned with 30 seconds to spare. Once again, he was the toast of Paris.

Successful powered flight thus was a reality while the Wright brothers were still working with gliders. With balloons having flown for over a century, there now was every prospect that motor-driven dirigibles were about to emerge as the next major advance in aeronautics. Still, the Wrights had had a good summer during 1900, and they were ready to move forward with their own approach. On November 16, three weeks after returning from Kitty Hawk, Wilbur outlined their current status in a letter to Chanute.

Wilbur presented details of his structural design. This amounted to repaying Chanute in his own coin, for the 1900 glider had used a variant of the Pratt truss that Chanute himself had introduced. Wilbur showed how single long strands of steel wire strengthened the trusswork; by pulling on one end of the wire, every diagonal wire brace was tightened. Chanute, a civil engineer with much experience in these matters, wrote a note in the margin: "Remarkably good construction." But Chanute was somewhat less sanguine in responding to Wilbur's use of the prone position for a pilot in flight. Wilbur claimed, correctly, that this position reduced drag by diminishing the pilot's frontal area, and had enabled him to lengthen his glides. "This is a magnificent showing," Chanute responded, "providing you do not plow the ground with your noses."

In other areas, the Wrights still had lessons to learn. They had fabricated their wings using long horizontal spars placed fore and aft. The forward spar formed the leading edge, which was quite reasonable. However, the rear spar was mounted above the ribs, a foot in front of the trailing edge. They would have done well to place this spar below the ribs, enclosing it within a flat sheet of fabric that would have formed the wing's lower surface. Such an arrangement would have smoothed the overall airflow. Instead, in Wilbur's words, "an extra piece of cloth ran up over it to lessen resistance." This probably disturbed the airflow over the rearward portion of the wings.

In presenting the important matter of control, Wilbur showed that he and Orville were well ahead of Chanute. Wilbur took care not to disclose too much, for he was quite aware that other inventors were all too ready to take the Wrights' ideas and run with them to the nearest sand dune. He wrote of twisting the wings, raising and lowering the wingtips on opposite sides of the glider. Chanute coined the term "wing warping," but he did not understand its true significance. He viewed it as a means of turning an aircraft by increasing the drag on one side, an approach with which he already was familiar. In fact, wing warping sought to bank a glider by increasing the *lift* on one side, while reducing the lift on the other. By failing to grasp this point, Chanute showed that he no longer was ready to keep up with the latest developments, even when they were presented in a personal letter.

He nevertheless remained a man to reckon with, a leader in engineering who remained ready to disclose the latest aeronautical developments. This led him into a delicate pas de deux with the Wrights, as all three of these men sought to strike a balance that would enable their fellow astronauts to learn something of the Wrights' achievements, without allowing them to learn too much.

On November 23rd, Chanute responded to Wilbur with a letter of his own: "I have been asked to prepare an article for *Cassier's Magazine,* and I should like your permission to allude to your experiments in such brief and guarded way as you may indicate." Wilbur answered with a letter of his own, which stated his stipulations:

> It is not our intention to make a close secret of our machine, but at the same time, inasmuch as we have not yet had opportunity to test the full possibilities of our methods, we wish to be the first to give them such test. We will gladly give you for your own information anything you wish to know, but for the present would not wish any publication in detail of the methods of operation or construction of the machine. . . .
>
> The machine had neither horizontal nor vertical tail. . . . Lateral

balancing and right and left steering were obtained by increasing
the inclination of the wings at one end and decreasing their
inclination at the other. . . .[1]

This discussion of wing warping was so general that it could have
applied to the Wrights' initial 1899 concept of using movable wingtips
mounted on shafts. It was considerably less suggestive than Wilbur's
twisted bicycle-tire box, again of 1899, which had inspired him to try
the idea using his kite of five-foot wingspan.

While keeping the details of control under wraps, the Wrights nevertheless were quite willing to write about another of their innovations: their use of the prone position for a pilot in flight, as a means of
reducing drag. Chanute's letter to Wilbur contained the statement, "I
congratulate you heartily upon your success in diminishing the resistance of the framing and demonstrating that the horizontal position
of the operator is not as unsafe as I believed."

Wilbur also gave an open discussion of the advantages of the prone
position, in a two-page article that appeared in a German aeronautical magazine. He addressed the issue of safety during landings, outlining results from his glides at Kitty Hawk: "We made repeated
landings in wind velocities exceeding 20 miles per hour (9 meters per
second) without incurring any accident to us or the machine." This
brief paper was part of an effort by the Wrights to introduce themselves to the European community of aviators. In a second paper,
"Angle of Incidence," Wilbur defined this quantity as "the angle at
which aeroplane and wind actually meet," or what later became
known as the angle of attack. He proposed that when observing gliders in flight, experimenters could determine values of this important
quantity by using data from tables given by Lilienthal, Langley, and
Chanute. This article appeared in *Aeronautical Journal*, the main publication of Britain's Aeronautical Society.

As the brothers had anticipated, work in the bicycle shop absorbed
most of their attention during the months that followed their return
from Kitty Hawk. The approach of summer gave them more free
time, and once again their thoughts returned to flight. They had every

intention of crafting a new glider and taking it to the North Carolina dunes, and they intended to take a conservative approach. The 1900 glider had produced less drag than expected, but it also had given much less lift. Wilbur had raised these issues in correspondence with Chanute, but had learned little. Chanute attributed the reduced drag to excellence in design. This merited another of his compliments, but when it came to explaining the reduced lift, he too was at a loss. This meant that when the Wrights set out to design wings for their newest glider, they had to turn again to data given by Lilienthal.

Their need for conservatism reflected the fact that not only did they lack understanding of the reduced lift, but also had attained only partial success with their flight controls. In particular, Wilbur had experienced much difficulty in simultaneously working the wing warping and the pitch control, using the forward-mounted elevator. These flight-test results impelled them to stay close to the basic design of the 1900 model, while introducing a minimum of innovations.

They compensated for the reduced lift by the simple method of making the new one larger. The 1900 glider had proved to develop only half the planned lifting power; hence the 1901 version was given twice as much wing area, 290 square feet versus 165. The new wings measured 22 feet by 7 feet, whereas those of 1900 had been 17 feet by 5 feet. This in itself was a significant advance, for it took the 1901 design well beyond the size range of the hang gliders of the day.

Chanute's largest glider had used biplane wings with a total of 134 square feet. Lilienthal's monoplane had 151. The 1900 Wright model, with 165 square feet, was only slightly larger, even though it used an elevator and wing warping rather than allowing the pilot to steer by shifting his weight. But the 1901 version, with its 290 square feet, was in another class entirely. Weighing 98 pounds empty, it took shape as the largest glider built to that date. There was no turning back; this time the controls had to work.

The Wrights also showed conservatism in wing design. They believed that the loss of lift might have resulted from their use of a thin and gently-curved airfoil. In 1901 they returned to the thicker type of airfoil used by Lilienthal, though they kept most of its curvature near the leading edge. Again, this was to reduce the travel of the center of pressure. The choice of airfoil shape was far from obvious. Hence they added arrangements that gave them the option of changing the curvature or depth of the wings, if experience in flight were to show that this was advisable.

During the 1900 excursion to Kitty Hawk, the Wrights had left their bicycle shop in the hands of their sister Katharine and of a young hired man. That arrangement had not worked well, for Katharine had had to dismiss him, thus precipitating the Wrights' return to Dayton. They needed a new hired man for 1901, and they found him in an old friend, Charlie Taylor. He had little formal education, having advanced only as far as the seventh grade. However, he was a first-rate machinist. He had set up his own machine shop, producing parts for the Wrights' custom bicycles; he also had helped with production of their prized oil-retaining hubs. Even so, finding enough work for his shop had proved to be a struggle, and he had abandoned it to work as a machinist with the Dayton Electric Company.

One Saturday evening in June, he dropped in at the Wrights' bicycle shop while on his way home. One of them offered him a job, at $18 per week. This was 30 cents per hour for a 60-hour week, compared with 25 cents per hour at Dayton Electric. "The Wright shop was only six blocks from where I lived," Taylor later wrote, "and I could bicycle home to lunch. Besides, I liked the Wrights." He not only helped them successfully during that summer, but stayed on through subsequent years as an active participant in their adventures.

He started work on June 15, thereby encouraging the Wrights to plan for an early return to Kitty Hawk. Wilbur advised Chanute of his intentions. Chanute responded that he expected to do some traveling of his own, which could enable him to visit the brothers in Dayton. He arrived on June 26, spending the night and staying past lunch on the following day. The Wright family was eager to show respect to so impressive a guest. Milton was present; Katharine had the assistance of Carrie Kayler, a fifteen-year-old girl who was helping her with the housekeeping. They had melons for dessert, and Katharine instructed the girl to make sure to give part of the better one to Chanute. The second melon proved to be unripe and too hard to eat, so she set it aside, cutting the good one into five slices. Chanute, Wilbur, Orville, Katharine, and Milton each had one, but Katharine decided that this wasn't good enough. She upbraided the girl, stating that she should have reserved complete half-melons for Milton and for Chanute, while serving slices of the hard unripe fruit to the younger family members.

Chanute's meeting with the young Wrights was one of those historical moments when the past meets the future. Chanute was approaching the age of seventy, making him a full generation older than the Wrights. As an engineer, he had been accustomed to laying out plans for others to execute, and he had followed this practice in his aeronautical work, relying heavily on the assistance of associates. He hoped to bring the Wrights into his fold as new and highly promising colleagues. The brothers respectfully demurred, preferring to remain independent. Nor were they swayed when Chanute offered to help them with funding. The five Wright children had each received $3,000 from sale of one of the family farms, in Illinois. Moreover, the work of Wilbur and Orville cost little. The glider of 1900 had required only fifteen dollars for the cost of its materials.

Still, if Chanute could not entice the brothers to join him, he hoped to send two men to join them at Kitty Hawk. That era was one in which people trusted a gentleman when he gave his word, and with Chanute vouching for those two associates, the Wrights had good reason to believe that this was an offer made in good faith rather than a ploy to steal their secrets. Chanute's two protégés were Edward Huffaker and George Spratt.

The Wrights already knew the name of Huffaker. He had worked with Langley at the Smithsonian. He also had authored an article, "On Soaring Flight," which had been one of the items that Richard Rathbun had sent to Wilbur back in June 1899. Huffaker had obtained a good education, holding an M.S. in physics from the University of Virginia. However, his work in aeronautics was another matter. Drawing on a proposal from Chanute, Huffaker was building a glider with a framework constructed largely of cardboard tubing. It offered the ultimate in light weight, but Chanute himself agreed that it lacked structural strength. He hoped for little more than to fly it as a kite.

George Spratt had obtained medical training, and Chanute left the Wrights miffed by suggesting that this background could be handy if either of them were to be injured while flying their glider. Spratt had fallen in love with aviation, writing to Chanute in 1899 and subsequently being taken under the old man's wing. He had never built a piloted glider, or even seen one in flight. However, he had made at least a modest contribution by building equipment to measure the lift of a curved wing. If nothing else, at Kitty Hawk he could provide one more strong set of muscles to help wrestle the Wright glider to the top of a tall dune.

The brothers departed for North Carolina on July 7th. They were better prepared than Wilbur had been ten months earlier; they were not about to cast their fates to the wind. This time they brought everything they needed, including the long wing spars. Their shipment of freight included their existing tent, a cooking stove, canned goods and other supplies, bunks for sleeping, and tools. They also brought wood with which to build a hangar. The 1900 glider had fit within their tent, but the 1901 model was larger and needed an enclosure of its own.

The previous September, while crossing Albemarle Sound aboard the *Curlicue*, Wilbur had been caught in what may have been the backwash of the deadly hurricane of 1900. When the brothers arrived for their second visit, they met weather that was no mere backwash, but a brand-new hurricane. One anemometer measured wind speeds of ninety-three miles per hour before it ripped away. Torrential rains accompanied the storm, soaking them thoroughly while dense black clouds scudded overhead. When they reached the village of Kitty Hawk, they found that their old friend Bill Tate was as hospitable as ever. Unfortunately, the guests in his home included bedbugs.

The weather cleared. The Wrights loaded their equipment on a cart and set out for the Kill Devil Hills, their intended site for gliding. The heavy rains had left pools of standing water, which gave ideal breeding grounds for mosquitoes. Orville wrote that they "came in a mighty cloud, almost darkening the sun." He described this as "the beginning of the most miserable existence I have ever passed through":

The agonies of typhoid fever with its attending starvation are as nothing in comparison. But there was no escape. The sand and grass and trees and hills and everything were crawling with them. They chewed us clean through our underwear and socks. Lumps began swelling up all over my body like hen's eggs. We attempted to escape by going to bed, which we did at a little after five o'clock.

The season was summer, which soon brought its own problems:

The wind, which until now had been blowing over twenty miles an hour, dropped off entirely. Our blankets then became unbearable. The perspiration would roll off us in torrents. We would partly uncover and the mosquitoes would swoop down upon us in vast multitudes.[2]

They gained some relief by burning tree stumps to produce smoke, but the only real solution was to wait for those insects to die off. Their lifespan was short, and the weather stayed mild, preventing the formation of pools on the porous sand where new mosquitoes could breed.

The Wrights arrived at their camp on July 12th and spent most of the next two weeks preparing for flight. They built their hangar with tar paper as roofing. It had large doors at both ends, which swung upward and could be propped open with poles. This made it easy to move the glider in and out. The doors also served as awnings, giving shade against the hot sun while allowing them to gain further comfort from the cooling breezes.

Mosquitoes remained a problem through most of that month. They had brought netting but found that it was not of fine enough mesh. Wilbur had invited Chanute to visit them at their camp. When he renewed his invitation with a letter, he warned Chanute to "by all means bring with you from the North eight yards of the finest meshed mosquito bar you can find, as the bar here is too large to keep them off at night."

Huffaker and Spratt arrived during those days of preparation. The Wrights had never met them previously, and soon took their measure.

The historian Fred Howard writes that Huffaker "was given to laying stopwatches and anemometers in the sand and to using the Wrights' box camera as a stool. One of his specialties was delivering lectures on character building for the benefit of the sons of Bishop Wright." His cardboard-tube glider proved to be worthless, as it crumpled into a heap of wreckage. Orville wrote that he was lazy, having "good ideas but little execution." He also proved to be unpleasantly slovenly in his personal appearance. This was a sore point with the Wrights, who faced each new day with fresh linen, clean celluloid collars, and neat ties, even while camping in the wilderness of the Kill Devil Hills.

George Spratt offered a welcome contrast. He had taken up farming; indeed, his arrival at Kitty Hawk was delayed by demands of the harvest. He was a cheerful fellow, not a dour moralist like Huffaker, with amusing stories that made him attractive as a companion. His work with curved wings had given him experience that showed its value in the course of that summer when the Wrights encountered problems. The three men formed a strong friendship, which continued during subsequent years.

The glider was fully assembled and ready for flight on July 27th. The Wrights expected to begin by flying it as a kite, as during 1900, but the breeze that day was too light. Wilbur therefore boldly declared that he would plunge ahead and pilot it as a glider, taking the controls and skimming down the face of a hill. He had had no practice since the previous October, and his craft was completely untested. But he was impatient and did not want to hold back.

Huffaker and Spratt were with the Wrights, along with Bill and Dan Tate, who had given good help during the previous year. Together they manhandled the glider halfway up Big Kill Devil Hill. Wilbur took his position and lay prone on the lower wing. Other men lifted the craft by its wingtips, ran forward, and launched it into the air. But instead of sailing into flight, it nosed downward and settled into the sand.

This was disappointing, but at least it avoided the wearisome task of carrying it upward through soft sand for a long distance. Wilbur had some leeway in choosing his location on the lower wing, and he was aware that the glider had headed downward because it was nose-

*Holding the 1901 glider by the wingtips, Bill and Dan Tate
helped Wilbur Wright to get it into the air.*

heavy. He tried to counter this imbalance by taking a position slightly to the rear. It didn't work, for again his glider pitched downward onto the dune.

There was nothing to do but to keep trying. The ground crew made additional attempts, with Wilbur shifting his weight farther and farther rearward. The results were the same, for time and again the craft lowered its nose, and down it went. This was likely to go on all day, but still they all kept at it.

Then, unexpectedly—success! Wilbur kept his glider in balance, caught the ground effect that gave him extra lift, and skimmed down the hill. He remained two or three feet above the sand, continuing onward for some 300 feet before finally settling onto the slope. Spratt and Huffaker were astonished, particularly because they knew that this was by far the largest such craft ever to fly. Orville was pleased to see that it could do at least as well as the version of 1900.

Wilbur, by contrast, was very unhappy. It had indeed flown successfully, but he had had to execute full deflections of the forward elevator to maintain control of pitch. This showed a sharp difference from his experiences in the previous autumn, for he had controlled the pitch of that model with only one-fourth as much deflection. Something was wrong with the new glider, and the only way to learn about it was to fly some more. Again, he called on his ground crew.

Toiling in the sun, they carried it up the hill for another try. Wilbur took to the air, very quickly finding that his craft showed a strong tendency to rise out of the ground effect and to lift into free flight by gaining altitude. He applied full down elevator to counteract this, hoping to stay close to the ground. Suddenly there came a new surprise, as the glider wafted twenty or more feet upward—and stalled. It lost forward speed and seemed to hang in the air.

Such a stall had killed Lilienthal. Wilbur was at a lower altitude and had soft sand below, but his prone position increased his danger. As Chanute had warned, he was in imminent peril of plowing the ground with his nose, if not with his head. His elevator was already fully down; he pulled himself forward, hoping to use his weight to bring down the front of the glider. It responded! It did not crash, but settled gently into the sand, as if being lowered by a parachute.

Wilbur didn't know it, but the design of the craft had saved him by drawing on an unknown but fortunate feature of the forward-mounted elevator. When an airplane stalls, the forward lifting surface loses lift first, while the rear-mounted surfaces continue to produce lift. For Wilbur, this meant that his forward elevator lost effectiveness while his wings still were holding the craft in the air. When he nosed downward, the elevator regained effectiveness, restoring proper control.

During that same afternoon, a similar incident again placed him in danger as the glider nosed upward into the wind. It came to a stop in midair and actually began to slide backward. Again he used his forward elevator to regain control, averting a damaging nosedive and settling down for a soft landing. The Wrights didn't understand how their elevator gave their craft such forgiving flying qualities, but they knew a good thing when they saw it. They had made an important discovery in observing those stalls and recoveries, and came away with a renewed commitment to the forward mounting of elevators.

Initially they had adopted this arrangement because a tail-mounted elevator faced damage during nose-high landings, and because a forward-mounted elevator gave the pilot an easy way to determine his pitch. (To do this, he merely had to see if the elevator was above or below the horizon.) But the forward mounting now promised safety, in what certainly was a highly risky business. The Wrights stayed with such arrangements until 1910.*

This safety feature encouraged them to proceed with additional glides during that July afternoon. Wilbur showed that he had an increasingly good feel for his controls, for his best flight ran to 19 seconds and covered 315 feet. A single second can be a long time when gliding, and Wilbur's craft now appeared successful indeed. Still, he remained dissatisfied. He had not been able to maintain steadiness in pitch, but had flown in a wavy or undulating manner.

The brothers appreciated that he had been overcontrolling, like a motorist who steers in one direction, turns too sharply, and has to turn in the opposite direction to compensate. They tried to make the elevator less sensitive by reducing its size from 18 to 10 square feet. It didn't work. Further glides with the new elevator showed that the craft was still highly sensitive in pitch, and prone to overcontrol.

With this, everyone had had enough for the day. They came back the next day and returned to their original plans by flying the glider as an unpiloted kite, using a hand-held anemometer to measure wind speeds. The winds were better that day, permitting a good series of experiments, and the Wrights soon encountered more disappointment. They had made the wing thicker in hope of obtaining more lift. However, the new tests showed even less lift than in 1900, with the wings producing as little as one-third as much as they had calculated. To make matters worse, tests with a spring scale showed that the drag was considerably greater than anticipated.

---

*Rear-mounted elevators in time became the norm, as airplanes reached toward higher speeds. For such aircraft, stalls indeed could lead to deadly nosedives, because the forward-mounted surfaces that lost lift first were now the wings themselves. However, faster speeds meant that stalls were far less of a threat. Rear-mounted elevators also gave better control during landings, for they enabled pilots to approach a runway at speeds that were slower and therefore safer.

*The Wright glider of 1901 lacked a tail. The brothers flew it as a kite
as well as in piloted flight.*

That evening, Wilbur wrote down the good and bad points of the
new glider. It had stayed airborne for as long as 19 seconds. Its front
elevator had emerged as an important safety feature, making the craft
forgiving in stall. It was sturdy in construction and had avoided damage. The wing warping had again shown its usefulness by enabling
him to fly straight and avoid turning to the side. In addition, the sheer
size of the wings gave promise of still larger counterparts that could
carry the weight of a motor.

But there were problems as well. There was too much drag, as
shown not only in the spring-scale tests but also by the failure of the
glider to pick up speed while sailing downhill. Pitch control had
brought serious difficulties as well, with the craft requiring large elevator movements and being subject to overcontrol. In addition, the
wings once again showed a major deficiency in lift.

During 1900, the brothers had considered that a similar loss of lift in that year's glider might have been due to a leakage of air through the French sateen wing fabric. Wilbur had responded by visiting a Dayton dry-goods store and purchasing several rolls of a tightly-woven muslin. The brothers now tested the porosity of the new material by fabricating and testing two small wings, one with standard muslin and the other covered with muslin that had been sealed with varnish. The two wings gave the same lift. This meant that while the Wrights still did not understand the reason for the loss of lift, at least they could rule out porosity of wing coverings as a cause.

The problem of elevator effectiveness also remained open. Wilbur and Orville were aware that it might be linked to an unanticipated movement of the center of pressure, associated with changes in pitch or in angle of attack. Still they were reluctant to declare that this was the cause, for they thought they had guarded against such movement by using an airfoil that placed much of its curvature well forward. But Spratt and Huffaker both had conducted experiments with curved wings, and had learned about center-of-pressure travel in their own right. Having had no involvement in the design and construction of the 1901 Wright glider, they unhesitatingly suggested that unplanned excursions of this center were at the root of the pitch-control problem.

The Wrights sought to resolve the issue, not through argument, but by means of experiment. They removed the top wing from the rest of the glider and flew it as a kite, using their anemometer to note the strength of the wind. They regarded the center of pressure as a pivot, like that of a seesaw, with the wing angling upward or downward about this pivot. If there was a pronounced change in the location of the center of pressure, then the wing would display a sharp change in its angle, much as a seesaw can rock downward by changing the position of its own pivot.

In meticulous fashion, they measured the speed of the varying wind and carefully noted the behavior of the kited wing. In a light breeze, the wing angled with its leading edge upward. This meant that the center of pressure was well forward, with most of the wing's weight toward the rear. But when the wind stiffened and blew strongly, the wing flew very differently. It showed a pronounced tendency to dive into the ground, angling downward and requiring a good pull on the tethering lines to keep it in the air.

Clearly, the stiffening breeze had caused the center of pressure to move well to the rear. The tendency to dive then showed that most of the wing's weight was in front of this center, not behind it. Huffaker's good suggestion now brought him a measure of redemption in the eyes of the Wrights, while Spratt's contribution enhanced their mutual friendship. It now was easy for the brothers to understand what probably had been happening.

The glider of 1900, with its thin wing, apparently had lived up to the Wrights' hopes by showing little shift of position in the center of pressure, despite changes in the strength of the winds and in the pitch or angle of attack. This had made it easy to control in pitch; small movements of the forward elevator had sufficed. That glider had resembled a well-balanced seesaw, with the elevator movements corresponding to a light touch that rocks the teeter-totter back and forth.

But in the glider of 1901, the center of pressure evidently had made large excursions. When Wilbur had found that nothing less than full elevator deflections could provide control in pitch, the reason apparently was that he had had to use the elevator to exert additional force to compensate for this travel of the center of pressure. With this center not fixed but easily changing its location, the glider's propensity to overcontrol also became explicable. This too could be understood as a consequence of a center that would not stay put.

Could the brothers test this theory? If they were right, the solution to their pitch-control problems lay in returning to the thin airfoil of 1900. They had built their 1901 glider with wing spars that were mounted fore and aft, running along the entire wingspan. They now mounted a new spar to each wing, midway between the existing ones, and erected kingposts with this spar as a supporting base. They also ran wires from the kingposts to the wing ribs. Those ribs, which defined the wing's curvature, had followed Lilienthal's designs by being well curved for a thick airfoil. The wires now pulled on the ribs, reshaping them to reduce their curvature and make the wings thinner.

It worked! Wilbur again took the controls—and found that the glider now responded smartly to even small movements of the elevator. The change in wing curvature made the center of pressure far more steady in position. The tendency to overcontrol disappeared, while elevator effectiveness was greatly enhanced.

Wilbur later wrote that "after a few trials," he succeeded in making "a glide of 366 feet and soon after one of 389 feet." He made it "almost skim the ground, following the undulations of its surface." He also caused it to "sail out almost on a level with the starting point, and passing high above the foot of the hill, gradually settle down to the ground." The wind soon increased in strength, blowing now at up to 22 miles per hour. Even so, "The control of the machine seemed so good that we then felt no apprehension in sailing boldly forth. And thereafter we made glide after glide, sometimes following the ground closely, and sometimes sailing high in the air."

In this fashion, the Wrights made several new advances. They showed that they knew how to devise airfoils that could minimize the travel of the center of pressure. They also demonstrated a means for experimentally observing such travel, by flying a wing as a kite in winds of varying strength. Their use of a spar, kingposts, and wires to change the airfoil shape opened the prospect of an experimental program that might systematically vary a wing's curvature, to develop a design that could give good lift while maintaining a stable position for that center.

Octave Chanute arrived on August 4th, while the glides were under way, intending to stay for a week. He brought a camera and took a number of photos, some of which showed Wilbur in a glide. With the Wrights now having good command of straight-ahead glides, directly into the wind, they took advantage of Chanute's presence by initiating a new and more demanding effort. The goal now was to execute banked turns.

During 1900, Wilbur had operated a wing-warping mechanism by pushing with his feet. The 1901 glider introduced a different method that used a hip cradle. Wilbur now expected to warp the wings, and to turn, by applying body English. By moving his hips to the left or right as he lay prone on the bottom wing, he expected to turn in the same direction, with the cradle pulling on the appropriate wires. He had used this arrangement to keep his glider flying in a proper straight-ahead manner. But to turn by means of wing warping, he had to warp the wings more strongly, and for considerably longer durations.

He took to the air in his usual fashion, with other people holding the craft by its wingtips and running forward into the wind. Airborne again, he moved his hips to the left. This twisted the wings, with the right one moving its leading edge up and the left one putting its leading edge down. The right wing thus generated more lift. It rose, and as anticipated, the glider began to bank to the left, following the movement of his body.

Suddenly, the craft responded bizarrely. Instead of turning to the left, it reversed direction and began to turn to the right! Wilbur had become accustomed to a steady feel of his glider, but he now felt that something was wrong. He straightened it out, again by using the wing warping, and landed safely. His friends brought the craft back up the hill, and he soon made another attempt, trying again to turn while in flight. Much the same happened. He made a few straight-ahead glides, thereby reassuring himself that the wing warping still worked in this more limited role, then decided to try another turn.

The flight that resulted was the best of the day, at least for range, for the glider covered 335 feet. However, a dropping left wing captured his attention and led him to ignore his elevator for a moment as he shifted his hips to the right. Suddenly this craft darted toward the sand. Wilbur tried to respond with a movement of his elevator, but he was too late. The glider crunched against the dune, throwing him forward. He came away with a black eye and a bruised nose.

The Wrights stayed at the Kill Devil Hills for nearly two additional weeks, repairing the damaged glider and trying again to turn in flight. They made no further progress; indeed, even when Wilbur again took to the air, his glides were considerably shorter than his best. Chanute had no insights to offer concerning this new problem: the lack of control while turning. Nor did he stay long, leaving on August 11th. Huffaker and Spratt left as well, during the following week, substantially reducing the size of the ground crew. Rain came and continued for several days, dampening further both the Wrights' spirits and the prospects for flight while it persisted, and raising anew the prospect that they would soon face further attacks by mosquitoes.

The Wrights could have stayed longer, for the bicycle shop was in good hands back home. They nevertheless saw little reason to continue, breaking camp on August 20th and returning to Dayton by train. They now felt nearly overwhelmed by the task they had taken on, in seeking to invent a fully-controllable glider. Wilbur told Orville that the problems looked hopeless; man would not fly for fifty years.

Their achievements of 1901 were undeniable. They had learned that the forward elevator gave safety during a stall. They had shown that their wings could limit the travel of the center of pressure. They had made repeated long straight-ahead glides in their craft, which was twice as large as any built previously. Even so, there was every reason to believe that they now were up against a wall. They had worked very hard since the previous year, but had done little more than to replicate their 1900 successes with a larger craft. The glides during 1901 had taught them little if anything that was fundamentally new.

The problem of lift from the wings still remained. It had first shown itself during 1900, and the brothers had considered several explanations. They now were in a position to rule out some of them and to see that this problem indeed was difficult. The loss of lift did not result from anything so simple as leakage of air through the wing fabric; they had ruled this out with their varnished and unvarnished wings. Nor did it stem from their choice of a thin airfoil. This same loss of lift had appeared particularly strong with their initial thick wings of 1901—which had been modeled after those of Lilienthal himself.

The only plausible explanation for the loss was that something was wrong either with the equations that they had used in calculating lift and drag, or with the data that had gone into those equations. Yet, again, that data had also come from Lilienthal, an engineer of considerable practical experience. The Wrights might try to make measurements of their own, but if even Lilienthal perhaps had failed to do so correctly, could they?

The problem of wing lift was worrisome, but they had dodged

around it during 1901 by the simple expedient of making their wings large. The loss of lift had not seriously hampered their progress. The second problem was far more severe, for it struck at the heart of their effort. This was their inability to execute controlled turns by means of wing warping.

They had made a few initial attempts with the glider of 1900. Pressed for time, drawn back to Dayton by the needs of their business, they had cut short their stay in Kitty Hawk and had left the problems of turning for 1901. But although they had installed a hip cradle for easier control, with Chanute himself close at hand to serve as a consultant, their new glider had proved to be as uncontrollable as the earlier one. This meant that they had expended two seasons' laborings and had failed to make headway against this problem, which they had recognized and sought to address as early as 1899.

Returning home on August 22nd, Wilbur wrote a letter to Chanute, who had missed the final week of activity. In personal notes, Wilbur had summarized his observations: "Upturned wing seems to fall behind, but at first rises." That is, the craft was tending to turn toward the wing that went up due to the warping, when he had expected it to turn toward the one that went down. In the letter, he wrote, "Our machine does not turn toward the lowest wing under all circumstances, a very unlooked for result and one which completely upsets our theories as to the causes which produce the turning to right or left."

This problem was all the more puzzling because the wing warping worked satisfactorily when executing the small hip movements that maintained straight-ahead flight. The reversal of control, with the craft turning in a direction opposite to that of the hip cradle, appeared only during the large movements of a true change in direction. This control reversal was not only unexplained but was unpredictable. Hence the Wrights could not merely regard it as a quirk of their design, to be lived with, used perhaps to advantage, and understood at some future date.

Chanute still had no technical advice to offer, but he nevertheless saw that he was in a position to help them. The Wrights had failed to make turns, but no one else had done so, or even tried to turn by using aerodynamic controls. Moreover, their work with wings, with pitch control, and with a glider of unprecedented size had brought achievements that certainly would interest Chanute's fellow specialists.

Chanute was president of an important technical organization, the Western Society of Engineers. It was about to hold a meeting in Chicago, and he invited Wilbur to give a paper describing their work. Wilbur was well aware that this invitation represented a large step upward from their bicycle shop in a provincial town. In addition, he had taken photos on glass-plate negatives, which could readily be transformed into lantern slides. With such transparencies illustrating his talk, he could display the drama of flight already accomplished.

The Wrights had made a point of dressing neatly even while on the dunes, but Chanute's invitation called for much more than usual. Orville was the nattier dresser, wearing clothes that were about the same size as Wilbur's. Accordingly, Orville loaned him a shirt, cuffs, cuff links, and overcoat. Katharine wrote, "We discovered that to some extent 'clothes do make the man' for you never saw Will look so 'swell.' "

He took a night train to Chicago, where Chanute had invited him to stay as a house guest. He arrived the next morning, which gave him plenty of time to prepare. Some seventy engineers were in attendance, many of them accompanied by their spouses, and Chanute personally presented him to the group with a warm introduction. Speaking of the joint work of the Wrights, Chanute stated that they "have been bold enough to attempt some things which neither Lilienthal, nor Pilcher, nor myself dared to do. They have used surfaces very much greater in extent than those which hitherto have been deemed safe, and they have accomplished very remarkable results."

The bulk of Wilbur's presentation consisted of a detailed review of the work of the previous two years. He said virtually nothing about turning, but had much to say concerning his straight-ahead glides. Because he was addressing a group of technically capable people, he did not hesitate to give a detailed account of the movement of the center of pressure. He also noted that the forward elevator had contributed to the forgiving flying characteristics of his craft.

He emphasized the importance of hands-on practice in learning to fly, likening his flying machine to a balky stallion:

Now, there are two ways of learning how to ride a fractious horse: One is to get on him and learn by actual practice how each motion and trick may be best met; the other is to sit on a fence and watch the beast a while, and then retire to the house and at leisure figure out the best way of overcoming his jumps and kicks. The latter system is the safest, but the former, on the whole, turns out the larger proportion of good riders. It is very much the same in learning to ride a flying machine; if you are looking for perfect safety, you will do well to sit on a fence and watch the birds; but if you really wish to learn, you must mount a machine and become acquainted with its tricks by actual trial.[3]

He dwelled at length on the control of pitch. Nearly a century earlier, Cayley had written that an aircraft could maintain suitable control by placing its center of gravity below the wings' center of pressure. Wilbur elaborated on this with results born of hard experience:

The balancing of a gliding or flying machine is very simple in theory. It consists in causing the center of gravity to coincide with the center of pressure. But in actual practice there seems to be an almost boundless incompatibility of temper which prevents their remaining peaceably together for a single instant, so that the operator, who in this case acts as peacemaker, often suffers injury to himself while attempting to bring them together.

He was referring to the need to use his forward stabilizer frequently, to maintain steady flight while gliding downhill.

Cayley had proposed that a steam engine of a single horsepower, offering the power of a horse with the weight of a man, might suffice to permit powered flight. Wilbur's colleagues had made careful observations of his own flights, noting wind speed, distance covered, time from takeoff to landing, and angle of the downhill slope. Knowing that the weight of the 1901 glider with its pilot was some 240 pounds, Wilbur had been able to calculate the horsepower needed for flight:

. . . by comparing the distance traveled in gliding with the vertical fall it was easily calculated that at a speed of 24 miles per hour the total horizontal resistance of our machine when bearing the operator amounted to 40 pounds, which is equivalent to about $2^1/_3$ horsepower. It must not be supposed, however, that a motor developing this power would be sufficient to drive a man-bearing machine. The extra weight of the motor would either require a larger machine, higher speed . . . and therefore more power. It is probable, however, that an engine of 6 horsepower, weighing 100 pounds, would answer the purpose. Such an engine is entirely practicable. Indeed, working motors of one-half this weight per horsepower (9 pounds per horsepower) have been constructed by several builders. . . . The probability is that the first flying machines will have a relatively low speed, perhaps not much exceeding 20 miles per hour, . . .

Again Wilbur gave a distant echo of the voice of Cayley, who had written of airplanes flying "with a velocity of from 20 to 100 miles per hour."

With a long lifetime separating Cayley from Wilbur, their conclusions were strongly complementary. Both men had worked with the same laws of physics, with Cayley showing deep insight in his reasoning while Wilbur and Orville showed similar insight in interpreting the results of their attempts at flight.

Wilbur also hinted at his direction for future research by noting the importance of control, both in pitch and while turning: "When this one feature has been worked out, the age of flying machines will have arrived, for all other difficulties are of minor importance."

This paper, clearly written and comprehensive in its treatment, quickly became a classic. Published under the modest title "Some Aeronautical Experiments," it first appeared in the December 1901 *Journal of the Western Society of Engineers*. Other magazines either summarized it or printed it in full. An aeronautical publication, *Flying*, ran it as a serial, in four parts printed over a period of ten months. It was translated into German and appeared in a periodical aimed at airship specialists. Closer to home, the Smithsonian Institution printed it in its entirety in their 1902 *Annual Report.* This represented a fair exchange, for the Wrights had begun their work in 1899 by ordering publications from the Smithsonian for their own use.

Wilbur and Orville did not let this attention turn their heads. They were only too well aware that they had yet to crack the difficult part of the problem, which was to make controlled turns using wing warping. Still, the preparation of the paper had done more for Wilbur than merely flatter his ego. The work had led him to review closely the Wrights' activities during the past two years, giving him a better understanding of what they knew—and didn't know. The meeting in Chicago thus laid further groundwork for research that the brothers expected to conduct in the coming months.

During 1899, Wilbur had hoped for little more than to contribute his "mite" to aeronautics, adding a few bricks to a large structure of technical understanding. His Chicago talk, written up and published, certainly had fulfilled this early hope. Having gone this far, Wilbur and Orville now wanted more. They might have hit a wall that summer, but they intended to break through it. They no longer expected to leave the main problem of powered flight to future investigators. Instead, they anticipated that they would do all they could to win this prize for themselves, by inventing the airplane.

FIVE

"WE NOW HOLD ALL
THE RECORDS!"

WHEN WILBUR GAVE HIS TALK in Chicago, in September 1901, he emphasized what he and Orville had already learned. On returning to Dayton, he turned his attention to what he didn't know. High on the list of things to determine were certain poorly-known numbers that he had been using when calculating lift and drag.

He had found values for these quantities by relying on standard equations that had been published many years earlier. Neither he nor Orville had to derive them; these equations were already in print, in the writings of Lilienthal and in the *Aeronautical Annual*. They called on investigators to find values for lift and drag by multiplying together a set of quantities:

Lift: $L = k C_L S V^2$
Drag: $D = k C_D S V^2$

where

  k = 0.005, a constant.
  C_L = coefficient of lift.
  C_D = coefficient of drag.
  S = surface area of wings and elevator, in square feet.
  V = airspeed, the total of wind speed plus forward speed of the
      glider, in miles per hour.

Lilienthal had given tables that presented values of C_L and C_D, which he had found by experiment. Using these values in the equation for lift, Wilbur had estimated that a kite needed surface area S of 205 square feet to support its weight along with his own weight as the pilot, in a breeze of 15 miles per hour. He had designed the gliders of 1900 and 1901 accordingly, and had been quite disappointed to find that the lift was much less than he expected.

At Kitty Hawk, the work of 1901 had ruled out two plausible reasons for this shortfall. Wilbur had considered that the wings might have lost lift because air had leaked through porous fabric of their coverings, but tests with an airtight wing, sealed with varnish, had demonstrated similarly low values. He also had found that the wings of the 1901 glider did not regain lift when given the strong curvature used by Lilienthal himself. Hence the problem had to lie in the values he had used for k, for C_L, or perhaps for both.

The quantity k was known as Smeaton's coefficient. Modern aerodynamicists no longer use k; instead they use a closely-related quantity, which is equal to one-half the density of air. However, the Wrights and their contemporaries, including Lilienthal, followed a tradition that dated well into the eighteenth century by treating k as a quantity with a value that had been found through experiments using whirling arms. The first such experimental results had been reported in a paper by England's John Smeaton, in 1759. He did not give a value for k, but he presented data from which other scientists subsequently found the value 0.00492, which was usually rounded off to 0.005.

For well over a hundred years, this remained the accepted number.

Lilienthal himself used it. Even so, investigators of the late nineteenth century showed an increasing reluctance to rely unquestioningly upon this value, which was derived from data taken not long after the time of Isaac Newton. Octave Chanute collected a host of recent measurements and found that they ranged all over the map, from 0.0027 to 0.0054. Clearly, there was no reason to prefer the old value based on Smeaton's data—or to select any of the newer ones instead.

The high estimate was twice as large as the low one. This meant that a designer might build a glider by using the value 0.0054, expecting such a craft to lift a weight of 200 pounds. But if the low value of 0.0027 was in fact correct, then the glider would lift only a hundred pounds. To achieve greater lift, it would have to fly in a much stiffer breeze. Wilbur had encountered precisely this problem, and was quite prepared to challenge the accepted value of k.

As early as mid-September, in his Chicago address, he suggested "that the well-known Smeaton coefficient of $0.005 \, V^2$ . . . is probably too great by at least 20 percent." He had continued to keep track of the work of other experimenters, including Langley at the Smithsonian. On September 26, only days after returning home, he wrote to Chanute: "Prof. Langley and also the Weather Bureau officials found that the correct coefficient of pressure was only about .0032 instead of Smeaton's .005."

Other experimenters had used whirling arms, but Wilbur had something better: his glider of 1901. Several of its long glides had been documented with particular care, with the notes giving specific attention to distance flown, time aloft, and windspeed measured by a handheld anemometer. Together this data gave the true airspeed, V. The surface area (S) was known from the glider design: 290 square feet. By working with results from these glides, he succeeded in deriving new and independent values of both C_L and of the all-important k.

Data from six specific glides gave a well-bunched set of estimates for k, ranging from 0.0030 to 0.0034. Writing again to Chanute in early October, Wilbur declared that he saw "no good reason for using a coefficient greater than .0033 instead of .005." In subsequent letters, he reported that with k equaling 0.0033, "we get results corresponding very well with our Kitty Hawk observations. It is evident that in our observations at least the value 0.0033 should be used for indicated speeds from 18 to 22 miles per hour."

This determination of k proved to give an important benchmark. The Wrights continued to use this value as they went forward with the design and construction of other aircraft during subsequent years. Their estimate of 0.0033 differs by about 14 percent from the currently accepted value of 0.00289, published in 1957. Even so, their value of k proved accurate enough for their purposes.

At a stroke, the new value addressed several issues. It was fully one-third smaller than the previously accepted estimate, the classic k = 0.005. The deficiency in lift that the Wrights had experienced now found an immediate explanation. The glider of 1900 also had displayed a puzzlingly low drag. Chanute had attributed this to their skill in design, but now this too could be seen to follow from their use of a too-high value for k. Moreover, the brothers were well aware that Lilienthal had used this value as well. This raised a tantalizing question: If that great German aeronaut had gotten Smeaton's constant wrong, what else might he have missed?

Lilienthal had crafted his airfoils with uniform curvature, having an arc of a circle as their cross section. His values for the lift coefficient, C_L, compared the lift produced by such a wing to the force of air pressure on a flat plate with the same size, and at the same windspeed. If the wing produced lift of half that force, for instance, then $C_L = 0.5$. If the wing was larger, having twice the area of the plate, then the forces produced by the two surfaces were to balance exactly.

The Wrights saw that they could use this concept of balance to test the correctness of Lilienthal's measured values. Using one of their bicycles as a test instrument, they rigged a vertical frame in front of the handlebars and mounted a small bicycle wheel atop this support. This wheel was horizontal and was free to turn on its ball bearings. On one side of its rim, they placed a flat plate that was to face an onrushing wind, serving as a reference. On the other side of the rim, they installed a small Lilienthal wing. If there was an error in Lilienthal's published value of C_L, then the horizontal wheel would turn slightly to establish a new balance.

The winds of Dayton were insufficiently strong to conduct this test with the bike at rest. This made it necessary to actually ride the bike, with the rider maintaining his own balance while trying to watch the wheel. The lift of the model wing increased with its angle of attack, as did its C_L. If Lilienthal's data were right, the flat plate and model wing would produce a balance of forces when the latter had an angle of attack of 5 degrees.

This did not happen. The horizontally-mounted wheel did not show balance until the angle of attack was as large as 18 degrees! Clearly, Lilienthal had seriously overestimated the lift of his wings. Moreover, because the Wrights had relied on Lilienthal's data in crafting their own wings, this simple experiment with the bicycle gave an additional explanation for their shortfalls in lift: Not only had they used an erroneously high value of k, but their values of C_L had been excessively high as well.

The bicycle with its horizontal wheel represented a new proof-of-principle experiment, akin to the original kite of 1899. That early kite had shown that there was real merit in the concept of wing warping for flight control, but had been too small to serve as a piloted glider. The new bicycle experiment demonstrated its own principles, showing both that Lilienthal's data were wrong and that it was possible to obtain new data by balancing wing lift against the force of an airflow on a flat plate. However, riding a bike was no way to obtain the accurate measurements of C_L that clearly were needed. To get them, the Wrights saw that they needed something new: a wind tunnel.

The first such facility dated to the work of Francis Wenham in 1871, but thirty years later, they were only beginning to catch on. Part of the reason was that it was far from easy to build wind tunnels that could give reliable, reproducible results. Wenham's installation had illustrated some of the difficulties. Its fan, driven by a steam engine, gave a top windspeed of 40 miles per hour, but the device lacked vanes for guiding the air to assure a smooth flow. Its test section, where Wenham made his observations, was not within an enclosed duct but was 2 feet downstream of the duct exit. Its airstream was unsteady, making accurate measurements nearly impossible. Wenham certainly deserves credit for having made this invention, but he left it to others to develop into a useful instrument.

His immediate successor, Horatio Phillips, improved the quality of the airflow by dispensing with a motor-driven fan. Instead, he used a steam ejector: a ring of pipe pierced with numerous holes and set within the duct with the holes facing downstream. Pressurized steam from a boiler, bursting through the holes and expanding rapidly, entrained an airflow within the duct that reached speeds matching the 40 miles per hour of Wenham. By adjusting the steam flow, he could vary the speed of the airflow within his installation.

He published his results in 1885, comparing a flat plate with a bird's wing and with each of six different curved airfoils. He mounted each model wing to a pivoted balance that allowed the wing to change its angle of attack so as to "fly" while lifting a standard weight of 9 ounces. Then, by varying the airspeed, he determined the speed of an airflow that produced a standard amount of drag, 0.87 ounces. The "best" airfoil was the one that achieved these values of lift and drag at the lowest airspeed.

His results were of high importance, for he gave the first quantitative data showing that curved wings gave better performance than a flat plate angling upward. However, his test wings were not of the same size. Chanute wrote in 1894 that Phillips had failed to note a critical quantity: observed values of his angles of attack. Phillips also did not suspend his 9-ounce weights from the wings' centers of pressure, and hence failed to accurately measure their true lift. The modern aerodynamicist John Anderson writes, "Phillips produced a series of data points that, for the most part, are not related in a logical fashion." He describes Phillips's data "as simply a random collection, from which we cannot select the 'best' airfoil shape."

Lilienthal and Langley bypassed the use of wind tunnels altogether, becoming the last important pioneers to rely on whirling arms. Nevertheless, the new century brought renewed interest in wind tunnels. At Catholic University in Washington, D.C., the professor Albert Zahm was a friend and colleague of the Smithsonian's Langley. In 1901 he built a particularly large wind tunnel, with a test section 6 feet square. It gave a windspeed of only 27 miles per hour, but much of his work involved studies of dirigibles, which were not to fly at high speeds. He used screens of wire mesh and cheesecloth to produce straight flows with low turbulence, and his instruments were first-rate. He made an important discovery by showing that skin friction was a major contributor to the drag on an airship's hull.

Zahm held a Ph.D. in physics from Johns Hopkins University. His ties to the Smithsonian gave him access to the best work in American science. The Wrights had little more than the facilities of their bicycle shop in Dayton, but they also had ingenuity, along with a considerable talent for precision. Work at the frontiers of technology has been described as "an infinite capacity for taking pains," and the Wrights had this in full measure.

They started with a simple set of experiments, building a small wind tunnel from a box that had held laundry starch. A pane of glass, set into the top, permitted observation of its interior. The wind for this impromptu tunnel came from a hand-carved wooden propeller. The bicycle shop had a homebuilt one-cylinder motor that powered its machine tools, driving them with belts that ran from a rotating overhead shaft. A similar belt drove gears from a grinder and powered the wooden fan, which spun at four thousand revolutions per minute.

The internal instrument resembled a weathervane, with a broad tail that pointed downstream. The top of the vane was a small flat plate, set at an angle. The bottom of the vane was a curved surface of the same size, set at the same angle but tilted in the opposite direction. If the two surfaces generated the same lift, they would cancel each other out and keep the vane pointing straight to the rear. Because the curved bottom portion generated more lift than the top part, the Wrights expected that the vane would tilt slightly about its mount, and would angle off to one side.

It took only a single day's work to garner their results. They verified a claim by Lilienthal that a curved wing could produce lift even when angled downward into the wind, at a negative angle of attack. They also tested a small model of Lilienthal's wing, using his published data to predict an angle for their weathervane and then measuring the actual angle within the starch box. In a letter to Chanute on October 6th, Wilbur displayed new confidence: "I am now absolutely certain that Lilienthal's table is very seriously in error, but that the error is not so great as I had previously estimated."

Using the bicycle with its horizontal wheel, the Wrights first learned that Lilienthal's data lacked accuracy. Their small wind tunnel confirmed this, while reducing the apparent size of the error. The brothers had gained these insights by working with little more than the odds and ends of their bicycle trade, and this raised a tantalizing question: What might they learn if they took the time to do it right?

Doing it right meant building a new wind tunnel that could operate with precision. It took shape as a wooden box, 6 feet long and 16 inches across, again with a glass window set into the top. It was crude in its overall appearance, somewhat resembling a coffin mounted on wooden supports, but the Wrights used their craftsman's touch where it counted.

As before, they relied on their two-bladed wooden propeller and drove it using their shop motor along with its belt and the set of gears they had used previously. This arrangement was prone to vibration, which threatened to spoil the accuracy of their measurements. Hence they did not mount the wooden fan within the tunnel proper, but supported it along with its driving gears on a separate stand. The fan rotated within a circular shroud of sheet metal that surrounded it closely, without allowing it to transmit vibration to the tunnel itself.

"Our greatest trouble was in obtaining a perfectly straight current of wind," Wilbur wrote to Chanute. They improved its quality by having the airflow pass through a "straighter," a crosshatched grid of thin wooden strips that resembled a honeycomb. To avoid disturbing the flow, they took care not to move furniture or other large items within the room. Only Wilbur or Orville was allowed in the room during a test, and when operating the equipment, he always stood in the same spot that he or his brother had used previously.

"We spent nearly a month getting a *straight* wind," Wilbur later wrote. Building the basic installation was not difficult, but the brothers then spent several weeks during October and November in adding necessary refinements, including the straighter. They also gave considerable thought to the design of instruments for use with test models of wings.

Initial thoughts, during October, aimed at a single arrangement that could measure both lift and drag. However, its measurements were subject to errors of around ten percent, which was unacceptably large. In seeking a new approach, the brothers remembered conversations with George Spratt while at Kitty Hawk during the previous summer. Spratt had conducted experiments of his own in Pennsylvania, and had already considered the best way to proceed. He suggested that rather than measure lift and drag separately, as forces, it would be easier and more accurate to measure their ratio. That would give an important quantity, C_L/C_D, equal to the lift-to-drag ratio.

Pursuing consequences of this idea, the Wrights developed two instruments that took shape as balances. The brothers built them from wire for bicycle spokes. They were delicate and fragile, easily coming apart within the wind tunnel and requiring frequent reassembly. Even so, they did the job, while showing anew that the Wrights had a talent for asking the proper questions.

The first balance followed Pratt's proposal by giving a direct measurement of C_L/C_D. It held a test model wing, mounted vertically like a slender pole within its wire framework. The brothers wanted to study wings at various values of angle of attack. To make measurements at a specific value, the operator of the wind tunnel oriented the balance, with its wing, at the desired angle. The airflow caused the wing to produce both lift and drag. Together, these forces caused the balance to swing in position, and to move a pointer set upon a protractor. This protractor measured the pointer angle, and this angle gave a direct determination of C_L/C_D.

The second instrument measured C_L, permitting its determination as a fraction of the drag coefficient for flow directly onto a flat plate. This coefficient was assigned the value 1.0, taken as a standard. This instrument also operated as a balance, with a flat plate, eight square inches in area, set within the airflow. When this plate proved to disturb the airflow, the brothers replaced it with four metal strips that once had been hacksaw blades, and that had the same area.

These blades were mounted to a support that was free to swing in the flow, turning another pointer. A separate support held the test wing, again mounted vertically, though this time the wing itself was mounted with a chosen angle of attack while the balance remained fixed in orientation. Once more, with the fan turned on, this wing produced both lift and drag. These forces combined with the drag on the hacksaw blades, again turning the pointer and yielding a new angle reading. Now, however, the angle measured a new quantity:

$$C_L/(1.0 + C_D)$$

with the quantity $(1.0 + C_D)$ measuring the combined drag of the wing and the hacksaw blades. With C_L/C_D having been determined by using the other instrument, a simple calculation with a slide rule gave a value for C_L. The value of C_D then followed directly.

This experimental arrangement gave a number of advantages. The Wrights might have measured lift and drag, determined as forces. However, such measurements would not have given C_L and C_D; rather, they would have yielded kC_L and kC_D, which would have been corrupted by using a value, such as $k = 0.005$, that proved to be wrong. By contrast, the Wrights indeed determined C_L and C_D for particular wings at specified angles of attack. They not only bypassed a potential source of error in k, but obtained numbers that they could use directly in their equations when designing full-size wings.

Their apparatus generated winds with top speeds of around 30 miles per hour. In contrast to Phillips, who had sought to make measurements at the lowest possible airspeeds, the Wrights' technique enabled them to use their winds' full force. The reason was that they were determining ratios of quantities, which did not change with airspeed. In addition, strong airflows exerted particularly large forces within their balances, which overcame any tendency to stick or to fail to respond fully.

Their experimental technique lent itself to rapid testing of a large number of test wings. Their procedure tested a wing at each of fourteen angles of attack. "We can make a complete chart of lifts of surface from

0° to 45° in about an hour," Wilbur wrote. Chanute found this astonishing: "It is perfectly marvelous to me how quickly you get results with your testing machine. You are evidently better equipped to test the endless variety of curved surfaces than anybody has ever been."

Horatio Phillips had tried to conduct a systematic survey of wing designs, but the Wrights were the first to do it. A wing is a three-dimensional object that has a cross section or airfoil, as well as a shape when seen from above, or planform. The Wrights investigated variants of both. Some of their planforms were square, as Cayley had proposed in 1799. Others were long and narrow, having the shape of a wooden ruler. Still others were pointed at the wingtips, resembling surfboards. Others resembled half of a surfboard that had been split down the middle.

They fabricated their wings by cutting basic shapes from sheet steel. These could be bent to give the desired curve of an airfoil. To thicken the leading edge, it was easy to add wax or to solder a strip of tin into position. "With a pair of tin shears, a hammer, a file, and a soldering iron you can get almost any shape you want," Wilbur wrote. They tested arrangements of wings as well as wing shapes, experimenting with biplanes, triplanes, and Langley's tandem-wing concept that placed one wing behind the other.

They were venturing where no one had ever gone before, and they knew it. No previous investigator, nor even all of them together, had ever done remotely as much, or with comparable accuracy. "Wilbur and I could hardly wait for morning to come," Orville later recalled, "to get at something that interested us. *That's* happiness!"

In the course of their work, they revisited the efforts of several pioneers. Francis Wenham, for one, had emphasized the importance of using wings that were long and narrow, thereby reducing drag. He had recommended the biplane or triplane as a convenient way to make the wing longer still. Horatio Phillips had gone much further, crafting wings with span of 50 feet and width of only 1.5 inches, then stacking fifty of them in an array that closely resembled a venetian blind. In 1893 he had actually used these wings to build a flying machine, with a pusher propeller and a 6-horsepower steam engine. He kept it tethered to a circular track. Like Hiram Maxim's much larger design of

1894, this one lifted its weight but was not permitted to fly freely. Even so, it appeared to show that Phillips's wing had merit.

The Wrights did not go so far as to place a venetian blind within their tunnel. However, they closely examined the lift and drag of square and of rectangular wings that differed in length or wingspan. Their 1900 and 1901 gliders had wings with respective dimensions of 17 feet by 5 feet, and 22 feet by 7 feet. They now found an advantage in making their wings narrower still, and greater in span, for this indeed would reduce the drag. Their results showed clearly that Wenham was right. They designed their wings accordingly when they prepared to build their next glider.

The Wrights also took a fresh look at results published by Langley. That man was a distinguished professor who had access to Albert Zahm's excellent wind tunnel at Catholic University, but the brothers concluded that they had little to learn from him. Langley had worked initially with a whirling arm; he had published his data while also plotting his points to give a curve. This curve was smooth in appearance, but when the Wrights repeated his experiments, their own data showed a strange hump. Returning to Langley's original published numbers, they saw that he had obtained similar measurements, but had ignored them, apparently in the belief that they were erroneous. Indeed, he had marked a particular set of data with an asterisk and the word "Omit." The Wrights were appalled, for Wilbur had written that it was necessary to "let the lines run where they will, instead of running them where I think they ought to go. My conclusion is that it is safest to follow the observations exactly."

Chanute was corresponding with Langley as well as with the Wrights, and had access to some of Langley's newest findings. In November, Langley sent test results to Chanute concerning a wing design that he had tested recently, which Chanute promptly forwarded to Dayton. The Langley wing had a sharply-pointed leading edge, like that of a knife blade, which he believed would reduce drag. The Wrights fabricated and tested a model of this wing, finding results that agreed with Langley's to within two percent. This gave good reason to believe that Langley and the Wrights both were superb experimenters. However, the Langley wing gave a poorer lift-to-drag ratio than wings of the Wrights' own design. The sharp leading edge did not reduce the drag; indeed, it was preferable to use a blunt or rounded leading edge. Wilbur and Orville used blunt leading edges in their subsequent designs, leaving Langley to gain whatever advantage he could from his sharp ones.

Then there was the data of Lilienthal. He had worked at the outset with a whirling arm, publishing results in his book of 1889, the *Vogelflug*. However, as a meticulously-trained German engineer, he was well aware that the whirling arm was not and could not be a precision instrument. He switched to conducting studies of wings in natural wind, within the open air, and found results that indeed differed substantially from those of the whirling arm. He published his findings in 1895, in Germany and in the German language. Chanute brought them to America, having them reprinted in the 1897 *Aeronautical Annual.*

When people spoke of "Lilienthal's tables," these were the data to which they referred. Lilienthal had intended to make them useful to other investigators and inventors, and had prepared them according-ly. Like the Wrights a few years later, he worked with ratios of forces rather than with the forces by themselves, referencing his measurements to the drag on a flat plate. His findings therefore were correct to within his errors of measurement, even though he used an incorrect k. To improve his accuracy, he gave averages of a number of observations. This tended to allow random errors to cancel each other out.

The Wrights greatly admired Lilienthal, who had died while trying to fly. In contrast to Shakespeare's Mark Antony, the brothers had every wish to praise their Caesar rather than bury him. They had relied on his tables in designing their 1900 glider. Later that year, Chanute wrote in a letter, "I tested the Lilienthal coefficients with models, and found them to agree closely." The brothers therefore relied again on that same data in fashioning their glider of 1901.

Although their subsequent experiments pointed to errors, additional work encouraged them to renew their high opinion of Lilienthal's findings. As early as October 6th, Wilbur wrote that "the error is not so great as I had previously estimated." He made this assertion even though he believed, mistakenly, that Lilienthal had determined his recent results with a whirling arm, a known source of inaccuracy.

But in a letter of October 10th, Chanute corrected him: "Lilienthal's coefficients were obtained in natural wind, which he claims to give much greater values" than those of the arm. This encouraged Wilbur, who replied on the 16th: "It would appear that Lilienthal is very much nearer the truth than we have heretofore been disposed to think." Early in December, when their work with the wind tunnel was well under way, he went further: "The Lilienthal table has risen very much in my estimation since we began our present series of experiments for determining lift."

In that same letter to Chanute, Wilbur responded to an invitation to present tables of their own, and in the same German publication that had presented those of Lilienthal. Wilbur wrote that a table by the Wrights "should preferably be of a surface of a markedly different character," to avoid "contradicting Lilienthal." He also described the differences: For angles of attack less than ten degrees, "our measurements run below his (at small angles much below), but at larger angles we are above him."

The analyst Peter Jakab notes that some Wright and Lilienthal values for C_L were in close agreement for angles of attack between 5 and 8 degrees. It would have been quite feasible to build a glider that would have flown at such angles. Moreover, Lilienthal's data certainly applied with some accuracy to Lilienthal's own wing, which the Wrights might have copied. Had they done so, all they would have needed was a correct value of k. They then could have built a craft that would have produced its calculated lift, rather than falling well short.

Lilienthal had developed his data for a wing of specified curvature, planform, and thickness. In publishing the data within the *Aeronautical Annual*, Chanute presented his tables with an accompanying discussion that encouraged readers to treat these coefficients as universal in application, suitable for use with a wide variety of wing designs. The Wrights had used Lilienthal's tables in just this fashion. An important conclusion of their wind-tunnel work was that there was no such universality, that Lilienthal's data—even if correct—applied only to his own type of wing. Every other wing design had its own coefficients, which generally differed markedly.

Now the Wrights could understand why their gliders had shown shortfalls in lift. Their incorrect value of k, 0.005 instead of 0.0033, meant at the outset that their wings would give one-third less lift than expected. Moreover, their planform, airfoil shape, and wing thicknesses differed substantially from those of Lilienthal. The aerodynamicist John Anderson estimates that these changes reduced their C_L to only 0.6 times Lilienthal's value, a reduction that the Wrights might have found themselves by direct measurement in the wind tunnel.

In combination, even with no error in Lilienthal's data, the glider of 1901 would have cut its planned lift to only 40 percent of the Wrights' initially-calculated value. (With a correct k, 0.00289, this would have been 35 percent.) This was close to what Wilbur himself observed. He wrote on July 29th: "Found lift of machine much less than Lilienthal tables would indicate, reaching only $^1\!/_3$ as much."

In sum, this loss of lift did not necessarily arise because Lilienthal's data were wrong. His table therefore indeed merited Wilbur's praise. The problem was that the Wrights had used his numbers uncritically, failing to appreciate that their own wing designs had their own values of C_L and C_D, which differed from Lilienthal's.

Those values had held enormous influence. Chanute himself had used them and had followed Lilienthal's wing design, although he stood in the forefront of American engineering and certainly was well prepared to conduct original work. In critiquing Lilienthal's work, the Wrights now moved well beyond him. Their studies of planform and airfoil-shape effects marked a milestone on the road to successful flight. Moreover, their data was unrivaled both in breadth and accuracy.

Wilbur had written, "we think our machine will now give results within two or three percent of the real truth," while the "comparative lifts of different surfaces will be obtained with almost absolute correctness." They indeed duplicated some Langley results to within two percent, but the formal determination of measurement errors is a technical discipline in its own right. John Anderson thus notes that even today, an accurate estimation of their accuracy would call for a substantial research project. Still, as with their value of k, the brothers now had what they needed. Their values of C_L and C_D were precise enough for use in design, while they now were in a position to fulfill Horatio Phillips's hope by picking the best wing.

Thus, in only a few months during 1901, the Wrights gained results that vaulted them to the vanguard in aeronautical experimentation. They built the world's largest glider and flew it successfully, at least in straight-ahead flight. They introduced wind-tunnel techniques that complemented those of Zahm in Washington, turning the wind tunnel into a precision research instrument. They advanced substantially beyond Lilienthal, gaining an unrivaled understanding of planform and airfoil-shape effects in aerodynamics, while compiling a highly valuable store of data on specific wing candidates.

In mid-December, having done all this, they put aviation back on the shelf and returned to their work as bicycle builders. They had to make a living, after all; their friend Charlie Taylor had proven invaluable in keeping their bike shop during their long absences, but there was only so much they could ask of him. In particular, it was time to begin crafting the custom bikes that they would sell during the spring season.

On December 7th, Katharine wrote a letter to their father: "The boys have finished their tables of the action of the wind on various surfaces, or rather they have finished their experiments. As soon as the results are put into tables, they will begin work for next season's bicycles." A week later, Wilbur sent similar comments to Chanute: "I regret that we did not have time to carry some of these experiments further, but having set a time for the experiments to cease, we stopped when the time was up. At least two thirds of my time in the past six months has been devoted to aeronautical matters. Unless I decide to devote myself to something other than a business career I must give closer attention to my regular work for a while."[1]

The reader might well feel astonished at the thought of the Wrights assembling bicycles just after they had made major strides toward inventing the airplane. Chanute felt this way as well, and responded on December 19th: "If some rich man should give you $10,000 a year to connect his name with progress, would you do so? I happen to know Carnegie. Would you like for me to write to him?"

Andrew Carnegie was a leading philanthropist who had endowed libraries in a host of towns across the country. He also was one of the world's foremost industrialists. During that very year, the financier J. P. Morgan had bought out his holdings for $480 million and had reorganized them to form United States Steel. Even so, Wilbur demurred: "I think it possible that Andrew is too hardheaded a Scotchman to become interested in such a visionary pursuit as flying." In any case, the Wrights were not about to surrender their independence: "I do not think it would be wise for me to accept help in carrying our present investigations further, unless it was with the intention of cutting loose from business entirely and taking up a different line of lifework."

Still, if Chanute found himself rebuffed when he offered to lead the Wrights to Wall Street, he remained ready to help at a much humbler level. "You will need to publish a table for each form of surface and aspect," he wrote to Wilbur. "This will involve considerable figuring, and if I can help you in this respect, I shall be quite at your service."

Any individual calculation of C_L or C_D was straightforward, given the data in hand. The problem was that there were so many such values to calculate. In the course of three weeks, during November and December, the brothers had taken data for 48 test wings on their first balance, which measured C_L/C_D, observing each wing at twelve different values of angle of attack. They also had used the second balance that determined C_L, studying 43 wings, each at 14 different angles. Together this meant a total of 1,178 coefficients to be determined, and then to be presented using 91 plotted curves.

Before the advent of electronic computation, the word "computer" meant a low-ranking member of a research group, typically a woman, who occupied her time by making repetitive and routine calculations. The work somewhat resembled the standardized tasks of a copyist or a bookkeeper, though with less margin for mistakes. Chanute, a dean of American engineers, now volunteered for this role. Leaving soon after on a two-month visit to the West Coast, he took a thick envelope that held a copy of the Wrights' raw data. Wilbur added a cover letter that ended, "I hope you enjoy your sunning in California."

Chanute worked with the data through much of 1902. Also, the question of publication came up. Lilienthal's tables had made a huge impact; similar tables from the Wrights could have been even more influential. Nor did the brothers insist on treating their data as proprietary, for they did not fear disclosure; they were well aware that it took more than good lift and drag coefficients to design successful aircraft. However, they simply never got around to preparing their work in publishable form. Never.

Chanute died in 1910, with the data still unpublished. Wilbur followed in 1912, with no change in this situation. Orville lived for another third of a century and still never wrote up their results for the press. The data finally reached print in 1953, with the posthumous publication of the Wrights' personal papers and correspondence, but by then their coefficients were only of historical interest. The federal National Advisory Committee for Aeronautics had long since taken studies of wings as a specialty, conducting definitive wind-tunnel investigations and publishing the results in readily-accessible reports. Still, during 1902 and afterward, the Wrights had their data immediately at hand, ready for use in carrying through a proper job of wing design.

Only a few months earlier, when they had hit the wall, the brothers had felt that they were lost. Now, following the success of their experiments, their confidence was high indeed. They showed this by not responding to a promotional contest planned for the forthcoming Louisiana Purchase Exposition, which was to be held in St. Louis in 1904. That national fair brought the introduction of the hot dog, and the song "Meet Me in St. Louis." It also featured a competition that offered up to $100,000 for a successful heavier-than-air craft that could fly. In February 1902, in a letter to Chanute, Wilbur dismissed the contestants peremptorily:

> The newspapers are full of accounts of flying machines which have
> been building in cellars, garrets, stables, and other secret places,
> each of which will undoubtably carry off the hundred thousand

dollars at St. Louis. They all have the problem "completely solved," but usually there is some insignificant detail yet to be decided, such as whether to use steam, electricity, or a water motor to drive it. Mule power might give greater *ascensional force if properly applied,* but I fear would be too dangerous unless the mule wore pneumatic shoes. Some of these reports would disgust one, if they were not so irresistibly ludicrous.[2]

This amounted to asserting that other inventors expected to succeed by mounting gossamer wings to a locomotive, or by arranging for a waterfall to fly. It reflected Wilbur's hard-won understanding that people could not invent their way to an airplane by crafting a basic design in the manner of Lilienthal or Chanute and then tweaking it until it gave full success. The effort demanded data that only the Wrights possessed, along with key insights in areas such as control.

The Wrights showed further confidence in working with their data. They had experimented with test wings of different thicknesses—and had found a pronounced improvement in lift-to-drag ratio for one particular wing, which was the thinnest in their series. Without returning to the wind tunnel, they boldly extrapolated their findings and decided, correctly, that this improved performance would become better still if the wing was even thinner. They selected a design that was slender indeed, more so than in either 1900 or 1901, and then added arrangements to adjust its curvature so as to make it thinner yet.

In other respects, the new wings followed their data more closely. Their experiments had pointed up the merits of a wing that was long and narrow, echoing Francis Wenham by showing that it would reduce the drag. Their configuration for 1902 lengthened the wings to 32 feet, 10 feet greater in span than in 1901. The width of these wings was reduced to only 5 feet.

It became a byword in aeronautics that an airplane had to look right to fly right. For several years, gliders based on the Pratt truss, built by Chanute as well as by the Wrights, had shown a simple and elegant appearance. The refined dimensions of the new 1902 glider added a particular touch of gracefulness.

The forward-mounted elevator had shown its uses during 1901 by giving good stall characteristics to that year's glider. In crafting the 1902 model, the Wrights took care not to build its frame in a single unit, as by bolting together its pieces. They understood that such a framework would easily break in a hard landing. Instead, they mounted the wing ribs to the spars loosely, notching the ribs for a close fit and tying the joints with cord. They covered the wings with muslin, which they had used in 1901, applying this fabric on a bias. This helped to hold the wings together, supplementing the knotted cords. It also imparted further strength, while accommodating the twisting of the wings that was essential for wing warping.

In this fashion, they addressed issues of structural design as well as of aerodynamics. Their use of the muslin as a structural or load-bearing element anticipated the "stressed skin" construction of several decades later, which lightened the weight of an airplane's internal framework by arranging for the aluminum skin to carry part of its loads.

There still was the bothersome problem of control during a turn. This had brought the brothers to invent wing warping as early as 1899. It thus was the earliest of their problems, as well as the most elusive. In addition, it fell outside the scope of their wind-tunnel work. Early in 1902, the Wrights directed attention to the issue of turning, not by conducting experiments but by thinking through what Wilbur had experienced in piloting their gliders.

In straight-ahead flight, the biplane wings faced the onrushing air at a small but nonzero angle of attack. When Wilbur warped the wings, for a turn to the left, the cables attached to his hip cradle gave a downward twist to the left wingtips and an upward twist to those on the right. The left tips developed less lift, the right tips gave more lift, and the glider was to bank with its left wing down. This arrangement had worked well when making small corrections to stay on a straight-ahead course, for the necessary warpage had been small.

But when attempting to execute a deliberate turn, the warpage necessarily was larger. The left tips then might face the airflow nearly flat-on, at near-zero angle of attack. The right tips, by contrast, had their angle increase markedly. The low angle of the left tips produced min-imal drag. The high angle of the right tips gave plenty of drag, and this was what led to the control problem. The excess drag on the right was causing that wingtip to slow down, while the left wing continued ahead at full speed. In consequence, although Wilbur had hoped to bank to the left, he found that the drag on the right wing caused him to turn to the right.

Chanute had been unable to help overcome this effect because he did not see it as a problem. He thought that wing-warping indeed had the purpose of creating drag at one wingtip, to swing the glider accordingly, and to turn without banking. He and the Wrights had been unable to reach a mutual understanding, and part of the reason was that the Wrights themselves did not truly grasp just how an attempt at a left turn could produce a swing to the right. But having reasoned it through, they now saw a solution: a vertical tail.

They had built their 1900 and 1901 gliders entirely without tails, believing that all they needed for control was wing warping plus the forward-mounted elevator for use in pitch. The modern mind recoils at the thought of flying without a tail; in war movies such as *Pearl Harbor,* when a fighter pilot shoots off the rear of an enemy aircraft, viewers all know that this plane is doomed. Lilienthal had installed tails on his hang gliders, as had Chanute. In his 1901 address in Chica-go, Wilbur had stated that "tails, both vertical and horizontal, may with safety be eliminated in gliding and other flying experiments." But only a few months later, he and Orville were ready to install one on their next design.

Their vertical tail took shape as a pair of long rectangular surfaces set closely together. They were mounted at the rear, not at the front. They had to be at the rear because they were to function like fins on an arrow. If drag at one wingtip became large and began to swing the craft in the direction of that tip, the tail would bite into the airflow and produce a countering force, halting the incipient turn.

Banking, achieved through wing warping, remained the key ele-ment of a turn. A banked aircraft produced a lifting force from its wings that did not point straight up but tilted to one side, in the direction of the bank. The sideways component of this force then caused the aircraft as a whole to move in that direction. The overall movement of the glider then would result from the combination of this sideways motion together with its straight-ahead motion, due to its flight speed. In consequence, the craft would turn.

The Wrights' new tail surfaces were fixed in position. They were not to move like a ship's rudder, or like the rudder of a modern airplane. Instead, while counteracting improper turning due to drag from the upturned wing, the vertical tail was to keep the craft pointing in the direction of flight.

Investigators as far back as Cayley had envisioned the use of rudders, but the Wright concept was fundamentally new. Their predecessors had envisioned movable rudders like those of ships, to execute flat turns. Such rudders indeed played this role in dirigibles. By contrast, the Wright rudder was immovable, at least initially. One purpose was simply to counteract the excess drag from an upturned wingtip, which could swing the craft in the wrong direction. The banked wings were to execute a banked turn, with the rudder keeping the glider aligned with its changing course.

The brothers planned out the glider of 1902 well before they were able to find the time to build it, for the first half of that year was taken up with bicycles. In addition, Milton once more found himself caught up in an imbroglio that involved his church, and Wilbur took some time to help him. Finally the Wrights were ready to proceed. A letter from Katharine to Milton, on August 20th, gives a picture of their activities shortly before they departed anew for North Carolina:

> They really ought to get away for a while. Will is thin and nervous and so is Orv. They will be all right when they get down on the sand where the salt breezes blow. They insist that if you aren't well enough to stay out on your trip, you must come down with them. They think that life at Kitty Hawk cures all ills, you know.
>
> The flying machine is in the process of making. Will spins the sewing machine around by the hour while Orv squats around, marking places to sew. There is no place in the house to live but

I'll be lonesome this time next week and wish that I could have some of their racket around.[3]

The brothers left Dayton by train five days later. One pictures them as travelers, in an age before air conditioning, dressed as usual in a manner that was quite dapper and therefore very hot. We see them riding in a day coach toward the summer heat and humidity of the Carolinas. If their fellow passengers kept the windows closed, then the coach became hotter still. If they opened the windows, coal smoke from the locomotive could blow in. The Wrights' invention led in time to snarled airport traffic and unpleasant delays in terminals, but travel in their day presented discomforts of its own.

Their route followed its now-familiar course to Elizabeth City by way of Norfolk, with the brothers arriving on the following evening. The town wharf stood close to the railroad station. To their delight, they found a schooner named *Lou Willis* whose captain, Frank Midgett, was from Kitty Hawk. Better still, he intended to depart for this home port before dawn of the next morning. No hurricanes were in view, and this vessel was far less foul than the *Curlicue* of 1900. However, to make their sailing they had to bustle around quickly and get what they needed before the stores shut down for the night.

Their trunks, camping equipment, and crates full of glider parts were already in storage at the railroad freight depot. They ran to the baggage room and got there just as it was about to close. Then they purchased a barrel of gasoline at the Standard Oil warehouse, just as its workers were about to leave for the day. Orville also found a hardware store. It was already closed, but he got the merchant to unlock the door and sell him a portable stove. He found a grocery store that was still open and purchased some cans of baking powder. They hauled their treasures to the schooner and made ready to depart.

Having hurried up, they now had to wait, for Midgett took several hours before embarking. The winds then proved to be very light, while at times they blew from the wrong direction. Finally, well into afternoon two days later, they reached Kitty Hawk and tied up at the dock. Dan Tate, the brother of their old friend Bill, met them and used his small spritsail boat to carry their belongings to their base at the Kill Devil Hills, several miles down the shore.

They had built a wooden shed the previous year, which had served as a hangar. Wilbur wrote that during the intervening ten months, "the winds blew all the foundation, which consisted of sand, out from under the building and let the ends drop down two feet, thus giving the roof a shape like that of a dromedary's back." Dan Tate helped them as they strengthened the foundations with wooden posts, then prepared to enlarge it to provide living quarters.

This time they were determined to live in comfort. They had brought a bicycle with wide-tread tires; it navigated the sandy route to Kitty Hawk without sinking into a dune. They drove a well for fresh water. They installed a dining table covered with oilcloth over thicknesses of burlap, along with chairs upholstered using excelsior and burlap. Instead of sleeping on cots, they built beds by mounting heavy burlap on wooden frames, placing these beds amid the rafters with a ladder to reach them.

The local people, living on fish and home-grown vegetables, might well have envied the Wrights' pantry. A photo shows cups, pans, and crockery stacked neatly on a shelf or hanging from unpainted wallboards. They had a dishpan along with pans for bread and for biscuits. (Orville was chief cook; the latter was his specialty.) Other shelves held eggs, apples, and canned goods galore: cling peaches, pineapple, plums, coffee, sugar, cornstarch, salt, pepper, spices, flour, cornmeal, tea, cooking oil, as well as the Royal Baking Powder that Orville had picked up on arriving in Elizabeth City.

On September 16th, Wilbur wrote a letter to their friend George Spratt, inviting him to come down and share their delights:

> Everything is so much more favorable this year than last that it would be a pity to have your ideas of camp life here based on your experience of one year ago. First, we have not seen a dozen mosquitoes in the two weeks and a half we have been here. . . . Second, we fitted up our living arrangements much more comfortably than last year. Our kitchen is immensely improved,

and then we have made beds on the second floor and now sleep aloft. It is an improvement over cots. We have put battens on the cracks of the whole building including the addition, so it is much tighter and waterproof than before as well as more sandproof. Our new well goes down six or eight feet on the ocean . . . and we now have good water. We also have a bicycle which runs much better over the sand than we hoped, so that it only takes about an hour to make the round trip to Kitty Hawk instead of three hours as before. . . . We are having a splendid time.[4]

Following their arrival at Kitty Hawk on August 28th, it took some three weeks of preparation before they were ready for flight. They spent about half of these days building their new home and workshop. In the course of this work, they faced such challenges as hungry razorback hogs, descendants of local stock that had reverted to living in the wild, which they drove away. Work on the glider then began. They recovered wing struts from the glider of 1901, which no longer was of any use, and assembled their new craft from the parts they had brought.

They began this assembly on the afternoon of September 8th. Two days later, they were far enough along to fly the upper wing as a kite. They were highly encouraged to find that it easily rose into the air in a breeze of 12 miles per hour. Their two earlier designs had shown disappointing shortfalls in lift when kited, but the new wing proved to be much closer to the mark. A week later, the complete biplane wings were ready. They also performed well when flown together as a kite.

The finished glider was assembled a few days later and also made its first ascents in this fashion. The brothers were convinced that it had such a high lift-to-drag ratio that it would soar, with its restraining cords standing vertically as if the craft was levitating into the air. They demonstrated this by taking it to a dune of gentle slope, where the wind angled upward at a shallow pitch as it followed the terrain. In this breeze, the glider soared with grace.

Piloted glides followed, initially with Wilbur again at the controls, as during the previous two years. The historian Peter Jakab describes his experience:

> As the breeze flows over the wings and generates lift, there is a sense of the machine stirring to life. It becomes lighter in the handler's grasp as the wings begin to support it and starts to fly on its own as the forces of lift and drag take effect. It is as if the glider develops a mind and a personality. In flight, the operator merely directs its energies according to his or her will, in much the same way as a rider masters a spirited horse. Through this inanimate machine, the human pilot is able, to a degree, to embrace and transcend the forces of nature. There is a distinct feeling of power and control over the glider, yet at the same time there is a clear demand of respect by the machine for the forces it is harnessing. This interaction between pilot, aircraft, and environment is an experience that rarely fails to impress.[5]

Wilbur flies the 1902 glider, which mounted a tail for better stability in flight.

The new glider weighed 116½ pounds empty, noticeably more than the 98 pounds of the 1901 model. The brothers thus needed all the help they could get, both when carrying it up a hill and when holding it by the wingtips while running forward to launch it. They got this help from Dan Tate, who did not fly himself but who had the pleasure of seeing first Wilbur and then Orville do so repeatedly.

The Wrights had changed the leverlike arrangement that worked the elevators. The movements that would have turned this surface upward a year ago now turned it down. In addition, the new glider had quirks that were all its own, as Wilbur soon discovered. This happened on September 20th, while he was making the longest glide of the day. While airborne, a gust of wind struck it from the side and lifted the left wing. Wilbur tried to compensate by shifting his hips to the left to activate the wing warping, intending at the same time to protect his flying speed by turning the elevator down so as to descend. However, in his preoccupation with the wings he forgot the proper way to move the elevator, and he turned it up instead. Orville wrote that this caused the craft "to 'pierce the ethereal' to all appearances at an angle of over 45º," and then to make "a fast downward plunge directly toward the right wing." Wilbur's subsequent description was similarly colorful:

> Almost instantly it reared up as though bent on a mad attempt to pierce the heavens. But after a moment it seemed to perceive the folly of such an undertaking and gradually slowed up till it came almost to a stop with the front of the machine still pointing heavenward. By this time I had recovered myself and reversed the [elevator] to its full extent, at the same time climbing upward toward the front so as to bring my weight to bear on the part that was too high. Under this heroic treatment the machine turned downward and soon began to gather headway again.[6]

Wilbur had climbed into a stall, but once again the forgiving flight characteristics of the craft had enabled him to recover.

What had happened? The answer lay in the unusually long wings of this year's design, which made the glider particularly susceptible to sidewinds. The Wrights responded by retrussing the wings, causing them to bend downward with a shallow curve along the length of the wingspan so that the tips drooped. This solved the problem.

This mishap had left the craft undamaged, but their next flights nevertheless were delayed by two days of heavy rain. When clear weather returned, the brothers decided that it was time for Orville to take his turn as the pilot. He had not flown either in 1900 or in 1901; the entire store of flight experience within the Wright family belonged to Wilbur. But now, although Orville by comparison was the rankest of neophytes, he was to have his chance.

Like Wilbur, he started with a lengthy series of simplified glides, with either the hip cradle or the elevator immobilized. This enabled him to practice straight-ahead flight, first with one control and then with the other. The craft flew so well that it easily remained aloft while the terrain sloped rapidly downward. The new fixed rudders seemed to have tamed the wing-warping control problems of the previous two years. Following those practice flights, Orville advanced to using both the wing warping and the elevator simultaneously.

He made a few successful glides. He then was in the air for one more when he saw that one wing was too high. He quickly became absorbed with using the hip cradle to bring his wings level—and forgot to use his elevator to pitch downward to maintain flight speed. Again the craft reared upward sharply, and stalled. Orville now was 30 feet high, but he lacked the experience that might have made it possible to fly out of trouble. For a moment his craft came to a dead stop in mid-air, supported only by the wind. Then the glider began to slide backward, like a car facing uphill whose engine has failed. As Wilbur put it: "From the height of nearly thirty feet the machine sailed diagonally backward till it struck the ground. The unlucky aeronaut had time for one hasty glance behind him and the next instant found himself the center of a mass of fluttering wreckage. How he escaped injury I do not know, but afterward he was unable to show a scratch or bruise anywhere, though his clothes were torn in one place."[7] Orville wrote similarly of "flying machine, cloth, and sticks in a heap, with me in the center without a bruise or scratch."

This mishap showed that the glider was not only forgiving of mistakes while in the air, but could spare its pilot during a crash by coming apart on impact so as to absorb energy when it struck the ground. Racing-car designs later used this principle, being built to break into pieces in a crash rather than to transmit the shock to the driver. This meant that when spectators saw wreckage fly dramatically in all directions at the Indy 500, the driver was probably safe. The Wrights worked more than a decade prior to the first such race at Indianapolis, but the loosely assembled construction of 1902 incorporated the same approach.

Orville thus avoided a hospital, but the glider was definitely sick and needed several days for repair. This was done, and the refurbished craft soon was back in the air. As usual, this meant repeated and frequent requirements for carrying it up the side of a dune, the hot September sun blazing, feet sinking into loose sand. Wilbur again:

> Whenever the breeze fell below six miles an hour, very hard running was required to get the machine started, and the task of carrying it back up the hill was real labor. A relative speed of at least 18 miles an hour was required for gliding, while to obtain a speed of 12 miles by running required very severe exertion. Consequently unless the wind blew in our faces with a speed of at least six miles we did not usually attempt to practice; but when the wind rose to 20 miles an hour, gliding was real sport, for starting was easy and the labor of carrying the machine back uphill was performed by the wind.[8]

The brothers' skill improved as September shaded into October, as did their distances. Wilbur wrote in a letter, "Yesterday I tried three glides from the top of the hill and made 506 ft., 504½ ft. and 550 ft. respectively."

Still, not all was well. The flights took place at airspeeds that were modest, rarely giving much margin over stalling speed. At times this caused a peculiar type of mishap. A pilot would use the wing warping to execute a bank, preparatory to turning. The glider would begin to sideslip, sliding downward in the direction of the low wing. Meanwhile, the fixed tail was doing its job, keeping the craft on course. But the low wing could stall, ceasing to produce useful lift, while the high wing still was giving lift as usual.

When that happened, the sideslip produced an airflow that pressed on the fixed tail, turning the craft toward the low wing. This rotary motion slowed that wing further, making its stall worse, while causing the high wing to increase its speed and therefore its lift. The pilot could not return to normal flight by warping the wings in the opposite direction. That increased the drag on the lower wing, further promoting its stall. This sequence of events changed a well-controlled turn into an out-of-control spin. Wilbur and Orville both experienced such events, with the sideslip continuing until the low wing struck the sand. The rest of the craft followed quickly, coming down hard on the ground and pivoting to a stop.

The Wrights called this "well digging," because the wingtip dug a shallow pit when it struck the sand, as if it were a shovel. Later aeronauts called it a tailspin, a highly dangerous condition whereby an aircraft could plunge out of control. The low altitudes of the Wrights' glides gave room only for the beginning of such out-of-control falls. Nor did they happen often; on most occasions the fixed tail worked well, enabling Wilbur or Orville to turn as intended. Still, it stood as a problem that had to be overcome.

By early October, both George Spratt and the Wrights' older brother Lorin had joined the camp. This made their discussions particularly lively. On October 2nd, shortly after Wilbur made his glides of over 500 feet, the group stayed up late and Orville drank a good deal of coffee. This left him awake after the others had gone to sleep. He used his solitude to think about well-digging. Next morning, as the conversations resumed, he presented his solution.

At the onset of such a spin, a pilot had a natural tendency to counteract this motion by swinging the hip cradle hard in the opposite direction. Usually this was effective; sometimes it wasn't. Orville therefore declared that it was necessary to give a pilot a means to apply an opposing control force that could restore normal flight even if the countering wing warping failed to work. An aviator could do this if the fixed tail was converted into a movable rudder. By swinging this rudder in a direction opposite to the incipient spin, it could indeed exert a force that would counter the spin and restore straight-ahead flight. Wing warping then would level the wings. In sum, the movable rudder would enable the airman to fly out of the difficulty.

Wilbur was receptive, but he had words of caution. He and Orville both knew only too well that it could be rather difficult for a pilot to make proper use of the existing controls, moving the elevator with the arms while simultaneously activating a wing warp with the hip cradle. If they were to install a moving rudder as a third control, operated perhaps with the feet, then this aerial dance could become complex indeed.

As they discussed this issue, though, the brothers saw a way out. Reasoning through the aerodynamic issues, they decided that a moving rudder would also be useful in a normal turn, for it could help to swing the craft in the direction of that turn. In addition, when countering a failure of wing warping at the onset of well-digging, a given amount of rudder action could replace an equivalent amount of attempted control through such warping. That is, a certain movement of the hip cradle could be viewed as tantamount to a proportionate movement of the rudder.

Wilbur therefore asked: Why not link the hip cradle to the new rudder as well as to the wing warping? A sideways movement of that cradle then would turn the rudder as well. The brothers agreed that this was the way to proceed. They replaced the twin vertical fins of the fixed tail with a single vertical rudder, then rigged the appropriate cables.

It worked. Further flights not only showed that the craft retained good characteristics during a turn, but that the well-digging went away. With this, they solved their problems of control. They now truly possessed the aerial bicycle of Wilbur's 1899 vision: an unstable airplane that could be controlled effectively in all circumstances, while executing well-behaved turns reliably. For the first time, a glider could be flown under a pilot's total command.

The Wrights did not have the definitive controls that subsequently took shape. In time they went over to a fully independent rudder, operated separately from the wing warping. Moreover, wing warping gave way to ailerons for control during a bank or turn. In this respect, wing warping became no more than a halfway technology, adequate for use with aircraft that were too large to fly as hang gliders, but unsuited for the larger craft of the future with wings that could not be made flexible. Even so, with their elevator, rudder, and hip cradle, the Wrights now had the means to fly at will.

Meanwhile, Chanute showed up for another visit, accompanied by an assistant, Augustus Herring. The Wrights soon saw that whereas Chanute had given willingly of his own time in reducing their tables of data to finished lists of coefficients, they now were to return the favor by helping Chanute with some experiments of his own. He and Herring had two new craft: a refurbished version of their triplane hang glider of 1896 and a design with movable wings that somewhat resembled the *Katydid*. The triplane was already at hand, packed within a crate. The movable-wing glider arrived in its own crate a few days later.

Neither design showed anything like the Wrights' mastery of control, but either of them might have acquitted itself decently if it at least had been able to fly well in straight-ahead glides. Herring had flown as far as 359 feet a few years earlier, while Lilienthal had achieved distances as great as 1,150 feet. However, flight experience now showed that Chanute was well past the peak of his inventiveness.

Herring flew the triplane on October 6th. In Orville's words, "After leaving the ground he alighted about 20 feet distant on the right wing and broke the main cross-span to the lower surface." Repairs ensued, but a return to the air did not. The glider failed to fly at all, even in a 20-mile-per-hour wind and with a slope as steep as 15 degrees. Within days, Herring gave it up as hopeless.

Why did it fail? Herring himself seemed to hold the blame, for, with Chanute's assent, he had lightened the glider in ways that proved to reduce its structural strength. It was essential that the wings were not to bend or deviate from their designed shapes. But as Orville wrote on the 11th, "I think that a great deal of the trouble with it came from its structural weakness, as I noticed that in winds which were not even enough for support, the surfaces were badly distorted, twisting so that, while the wind at one end was on the under side, often at the other extreme it was on top."

The hopes of Chanute and Herring now rested on the movable-wing glider. It flew no better than the triplane, and was quickly abandoned as well. Then, like the King of Siam who showed favor to visitors by presenting them with a white elephant, Chanute made a gift to the Wrights of his two gliders.

These men had radically different approaches to flight. The Wrights saw an airplane as a vehicle that was inherently unstable, particularly because of changes in location of the center of pressure. They sought active control of this instability, with wing warping, elevator, and rudder. By contrast, Chanute remained wedded to the idea of using movable wings to achieve automatic stability, with these wings changing position of their own accord in response to the moving center of pressure. The Wrights had absolutely no confidence in this approach. Still, they were men of tact and good manners, and Chanute misinterpreted their politeness as serious interest. The brothers left those gifts in their hangar when they returned to Dayton, fending off Chanute's subsequent inquiries until both craft were destroyed in a windstorm.

Their work now continued during 1902, as Chanute and Herring departed in mid-October. With this, their schedule now was once again their own, while their glider was at its peak of performance. Both in their hearts and with their wings, they were free to soar.

They ran off hundreds of flights during their final weeks on the dunes. Crosswinds proved not to be a problem, while their craft also maintained good stall-recovery characteristics. Orville wrote of a flight wherein Wilbur "came to a stop high in the air, turned with one wing up, and landed with the wind blowing directly from the side of the machine." On another occasion, he wrote that "Will had no trouble in the control of the machine and made a difficult glide from the top of the second hill over a course of about 280 feet, in which the wind came at great angles from one side and then the other."

With help from George Spratt and then from Dan Tate, the

Wrights stepped up their pace as the days proceeded. When the winds were strong and steady, it was easy for this ground crew to carry the craft up a hill. Wilbur wrote that on one such day "we made more than a hundred glides with much less physical exertion than resulted from twenty or thirty glides on days when the wind was light."

They continued onward with their flights through late October, with the days growing cooler. The hours of daylight also became shorter, but the brothers flew from dawn to dusk. Orville wrote a letter to Katharine back home, boasting that in only two days:

> [W]e made over 250 glides, or more than we had made all together up to the time Lorin left. We have gained considerable proficiency in the handling of the machine now, so that we are able to take it out in any kind of weather. Day before yesterday we had a wind of 16 meters per second or about 30 miles per hour, and glided in it without any trouble. That was the highest wind a gliding machine was ever in, so that we now hold all the records! The largest machine that we handled in any kind, made the longest distance glide (American), the longest time in the air, the smallest angle of descent, and the highest wind!!! Well, I'll leave the rest of the "blow" till we get home.[9]

Their parenthetical (American) was appropriate, for Lilienthal, with a glide of 1,150 feet, still held the world record. Perhaps he flew that distance with help from an updraft as a headwind struck his hill, pushing him to higher altitude. Still, the Wrights' achievements were spectacular. Their speed of 16 meters per second, measured by anemometer, was nearly 36 miles per hour. In Wilbur's words, "The longest glide was 622½ feet, and the time 26 seconds."

A photo from those days, taken on October 24th, presents a view from the rear as Wilbur banks his craft to the right while maintaining exquisite control. He is only a few feet above the ground—a shadow on the sand makes this clear—but that was altitude enough for his maneuver. On that same day, a passing coastal steamer drew in close enough to give its passengers a good look at the brothers' flights.

The Wrights ended their season four days later. They would have

Gliding down the face of a tall sand dune, Wilbur executes a banked turn.

willingly stayed longer, but Dan Tate was about to leave them to take command of a fishing boat, and they had relied extensively on his help. In addition, they held excursion-fare railroad tickets that expired at the end of the month.

The weather was chilly and drizzly as they broke camp. Nevertheless, their spirits were high. They not only had tamed the quirks of their glider, but had flown it enough times to build up a base of genuine experience in the air. Their work was also becoming known in Europe. In addition, they already were looking ahead to a new design for 1903—which was to mount an engine. They knew that in building it, they were about to challenge Samuel Langley himself.

SIX

AMBIGUOUS SUCCESS

IN EUROPE, INTEREST in heavier-than-air flight virtually died when Lilienthal and Percy Pilcher went to their graves. For a time, the only active experimenter was a Frenchman, Ferdinand Ferber. He was an artillery captain who commanded a battery, but the nation was at peace and he saw little prospect of martial glory. Bored with military routine, he developed a strong interest in flight.

He started by writing letters, corresponding with Lilienthal's brother Gustav and with Clement Ader, builder of the *Eole*. He went forward by constructing a series of homebuilt craft, starting with a kite and proceeding to develop a version of Lilienthal's monoplane glider. His readings and correspondence led him to Octave Chanute, who welcomed him as one more of aviation's acolytes. Chanute sent him a copy of the 1901 paper by Wilbur Wright, "Some Aeronautical Experiments," which discussed the Wright glider of that year.

Ferber found it fascinating, and used it as a guide when he began to build his next glider. Right at the outset, however, he faced difficulties. Wilbur had taken care not to describe the wing-warping arrangements. Hence, as Ferber wrote several years later, "I judged it useless to begin with." The historian Tom Crouch writes that Ferber's craft "was so crudely constructed that the fabric literally flapped in the wind. The wings were flimsy, the elevator control ineffective, and Ferber did not even attempt to install the wing-warping system." Another historian describes it as resembling "clothes on a washing line."

It nevertheless flew after a fashion, covering distances of up to 150 feet. Late in 1902, he decided to take the next step by crafting a much larger glider and installing a 6-horsepower engine. At once, he faced the issues of stability and control. He bypassed all these matters quite easily by suspending his airplane from the long arm of a crane, with this arm being free to pivot. This avoided all need for flight controls. It also eliminated any requirement for the wings to carry the weight of the craft, or even to attain any significant speed in the air.

Ferber now demonstrated better workmanship, stretching fabric tightly on his wings and squaring his corners neatly. His propeller resembled an enormous four-leaf clover that was larger than a man. However, propeller design is a specialized field in its own right, and his version failed to make effective use of its motor. As he reported in a letter to Chanute, his best speed when dangling from the boom of his crane was a little over 2 miles per hour.

French inventors displayed considerably greater prowess in pursuing lighter-than-air flight. The flight of Germany's Count Zeppelin, in his dirigible of 1900, stirred the French government to action as it funded work by two brothers of Nantes, Paul and Pierre Lebaudy. Their airship had a length of 187 feet, making it considerably smaller than Zeppelin's 420-foot dirigible, the LZ-1. Even so, the Lebaudy craft was far more successful. On its first flight, in November 1902, it flew at 25 miles per hour, which meant it could buck a headwind. In June 1903 it set a distance record of 61 miles.

Pilots thus were covering long distances while the Wrights still were working with their 1902 glider. Wilbur and Orville also faced a well-funded government effort in their own country, led by the redoubtable Samuel Langley. Well into 1903, one could argue plausibly that he had gone farther toward true heavier-than-air flight than anyone else, the Wrights included. His aircraft had no means of active control. However, he built in a large measure of inherent stability. This made them capable of success in unpiloted powered flight, which he achieved with model aircraft as early as 1896.

Langley's concept of an airplane differed markedly from that of the Wrights. Langley, again, believed in built-in stability. He mounted his wings with notable dihedral, to form a broad letter V when seen from the front. Investigators as early as Cayley had advocated such an arrangement for stability in roll. Langley also used a tandem wing, with one set of monoplane wings set behind the other. This assembly was stable in pitch. He installed a tail that followed a design of France's Alphonse Penaud. It had vertical and horizontal fins, like those of an arrow, and kept the craft pointing straight ahead.

The Wrights, by contrast, scorned all thoughts of inherent stability. They had no need for dihedral; indeed, they trussed their 1902 glider with its wingtips down, to guard against crosswinds. Wing warping gave active control of roll, with no need for Langley's passive use of upward-tilting wingspan. The Wrights used their forward-mounted elevator for active control of pitch. Only their vertical rudder had any similarity to the Langley tail.

Langley's unpiloted aircraft of 1896 had already been substantial in size, with wingspans as great as 14 feet. Their paired monoplane wings, mounted fore and aft, gave them the appearance of enormous dragonflies. Langley was quite prepared to believe that those flight tests had validated his approach to aerodynamics, for he had covered distances as great as three-quarters of a mile. He therefore anticipated that he could build a piloted craft simply by scaling up his basic layout to a size capable of carrying a man. The airplane that resulted came to be known as the Great Aerodrome.

Engines represented another matter. His 1896 models had flown with small and highly specialized steam engines of one horsepower, but he saw no future in this approach. The design of internal-combustion motors was making great strides, and he anticipated that an engine of this type would prove suitable. With his basic design of the wings and airframe in hand, he therefore gave particular attention to sponsoring the development of new gasoline-powered motors.

Langley was no engineer. He was a scientist, a good one who had already gained renown for his studies of the sun. Still, this was not a background that could help him build a good aeronautical engine, and he knew it. In May 1898 he wrote to an old friend, Robert Thurston, who headed the College of Engineering at Cornell University. Could Thurston recommend a good young man as an assistant?

Thurston replied by suggesting a senior in his college: Charles Manly, who had studied both mechanical and electrical engineering. The combination was ideal, for Manly was to work on motors, for which electrical ignition using magnetos was essential. Langley was so eager to hire him that Thurston allowed him to leave Cornell a month prior to his scheduled graduation, receiving his bachelor's degree in absentia.

In June, with Manly on hand, Langley sent letters to several inventors who were building internal-combustion engines for use in automobiles. Langley's planned airplane was to have two propellers, and he expected to power each with its own engine. He wanted 12 horsepower—with a total weight of less than 60 pounds, a demanding specification indeed for that day. It was to run for three hours without overheating, with the cost for the research and development being under $2,100.

No one responded. The Smithsonian was certainly prestigious as a prospective client, but Langley's requirements were well beyond the state of the art. He eased the weight limit to 100 pounds, well above his earlier allowance, and set out again in search of a contractor. His attention soon focused on Stephen Balzer, who in 1894 had built the first automobile in New York City. It had used an air-cooled engine, an approach that promised light weight. Langley's contract, issued in mid-December, gave Balzer less than three months to develop a new version that was to be capable of flight.

Balzer's auto engine had used three cylinders. The new one was to have five. Balzer promised to deliver it in as little as ten weeks for a fee of $1,500, but before long it was clear that he was experiencing overruns on this government project, along with schedule delays. Even so, Langley had other things to keep him busy.

During 1896, his Aerodromes Nos. 5 and 6 had made history as the world's first heavier-than-air craft to achieve successful powered flight over substantial distances. They still were available for further use, and during the summer of 1899, Langley flew them anew. He tested a new launch mechanism; he also achieved ranges of up to 2,500 feet, which compared well with those of three years earlier. These flying models also served as testbeds for biplane wings, as alternatives to the monoplanes. The monoplanes proved more difficult to brace than the biplanes, which provided a strong truss. However, the monoplanes gave better performance in flight, and were adopted for the full-size Great Aerodrome.

Meanwhile, work on that airplane's wings was under way within a workshop adjoining the main building of the Smithsonian itself. The design called for four wings, each measuring 24 feet by 11 feet, to be mounted in pairs. Initial tests loaded prototype wings with sandbags, imposing a weight that simulated the estimated loads in flight. The first such tests led to structural failure, showing the wings needed strengthening. A redesign led to new tests with sand. When braced appropriately with wire, the new wing supported a weight of 231 pounds without undue deformation. This version was in hand by the end of 1899, complementing the encouraging results from the flight tests.

Balzer's engine continued to face delay, largely due to problems with the ignition system and with arrangements for lubrication. Langley now had more time on his hands than he had anticipated. He responded by setting forth plans for a new model airplane that was to be a one-fourth scale version of the Great Aerodrome. It needed its own engine, so he and Manly turned again to Balzer, seeking a gasoline-fueled internal combustion motor of $1\frac{1}{2}$ horsepower.

The new year of 1900 brought new difficulty. In March, a full year after Balzer's initially-promised delivery date, Manly wrote him a letter that expressed Langley's impatience: "You must realize that there is a limit to the number of times that a man of the Secretary's experience will allow himself to be given assurance that everything is progressing as well as possible, and then after waiting several months, things are in practically no better shape than they were before. . . ." Balzer responded by testing his engine for power. In May it delivered 8 horsepower, whereas the contract—now nearly a year and a half old—had called for 12. Balzer tried to boost this output, but in August it produced only 6 horsepower.

With this, Langley had had it with Balzer. Manly took personal charge of engine development, starting with a significant change in its basic design. Balzer had built it intending to mount the propeller to the engine itself, with both the propeller and the cylinders rotating around a fixed crankshaft. The cylinders were to cool themselves by spinning rapidly within the open air, thus eliminating the need for a cooling system that would add weight.

Manly now decided that rather than having the crankshaft fixed with the cylinders turning, he would let the cylinders remain stationary and allow the shaft to rotate, with the propeller attached. At a stroke, this would eliminate problems that Balzer had encountered in trying to inject fuel amid the intense centrifugal force of the spinning cylinders. The new arrangement could not rely on air cooling, of course; it would be necessary to install a water-filled cooling jacket that Balzer had tried to avoid, and which would add weight. But Manly was convinced that this new arrangement would enable the engine to deliver far more power, offsetting this weight.

Initial tests showed that this approach was promising indeed. In September, only weeks after Manly had taken the project out of Balzer's hands, the motor delivered "horsepower varying between twelve and sixteen." This was as much as twice the power that Balzer had demonstrated, easily meeting the contract specification.

The initial design of the Great Aerodrome had called for each propeller to be driven by its own engine. Manly now took the view that a new motor of his preferred type could put out so much power as to allow a single such engine to run both propellers. He obtained permission from Langley to fabricate new and larger cylinders for the basic Balzer version, which he had modified with his cooling jacket. This improved motor stood as a key initiative for 1901.

An important event came in June of that year, when the one-fourth-scale model flew with some success. Though similar in size to the earlier Aerodromes Nos. 5 and 6, it had new features, including a rectangular rudder set amidships that was to serve as the model's keel. Fitted with the 1.5-horsepower engine (which Manly had taken from Balzer as well), the model flew four times, covering distances of up to 350 feet.

This was disappointing, for both Manly and Langley had hoped for more. However, the model weighed 58 pounds. More power would certainly help it to fly better, and Manly saw ways to increase its power to two horse. Though short, its flights appeared to have demonstrated its basic stability, which complemented that of Nos. 5 and 6. Moreover, the new flights achieved a milestone, for they were the first wherein a heavier-than-air machine flew with power from an internal combustion engine. All other flights to date, including Langley's in 1899, had used lightweight steam engines.

Work on the full-size motor also advanced during 1901. In June, still fitted with the old cylinders, it tested at 22 horsepower. This resulted from the installation of lightweight pistons and a new ignition system that led to smoother running. This new success, occurring less than two weeks after the test flights of the one-fourth-scale model, seemed to show that the overall program was moving forward nicely.

The new and larger cylinders were in place on the big engine by early October, along with water-filled cooling jackets of suitable size. The jackets leaked water, as did some of the cylinder heads, and it was clear that the motor would demand an extensive rebuilding, with new cast parts. Manly wrote to Langley, "The general condition of the work may be summed up by saying that everything now awaits the completion of the engine." The castings for the motor arrived with the new year of 1902 and soon showed their merits. In April, Manly produced 41 horsepower, raising this further to 45 horsepower a year later. No single breakthrough brought these improvements. Rather, it was a matter of painstaking advances involving the ignition, carburetor, and other components. The finished engine weighed 187 pounds. Nearly a century earlier, Cayley had dreamed of a steam engine of that weight that might deliver a single horsepower. Manly's motor put out over forty times as much.

The Great Aerodrome and its engine both were largely complete by the end of 1902, setting up a race wherein both Langley and the Wrights, working independently, were ready to sprint to victory by achieving the first piloted powered flight. The two efforts had followed markedly different approaches, with Langley's work standing as a monument to the presumed virtues of inherent stability. He had learned most of his aerodynamics prior to the successful flights of 1896, and thereafter had emphasized the development of engines. Manly's version was outstanding indeed.

The Wrights had worked with their wind tunnel and knew far more about aerodynamics, particularly as applied to wing design. They had used this knowledge in crafting their innovative glider of 1902. They also had developed and flown an ingenious set of controls that made it possible to fly this glider successfully under a wide variety of wind conditions. In turn, their gliders of 1901 and 1902 were by far the largest ever built to that time. They had only begun to think about engines, but in most other respects they too were ready for powered flight.

One sees a certain complementarity between those two independent programs. Though the Wrights were masters of the design of wings, structures, and flight controls, they certainly would have benefited if they had had Manly's powerful and relatively lightweight engine. In addition, Langley had favored built-in stability over methods for flight control, and might profitably have consulted the Wrights (who, of course, would have proffered no more than vague hints for fear of disclosure). Even so, both approaches to flight held considerable merit, and it is highly plausible that both might have succeeded during 1903.

But Langley's work held a flaw. Seeking to diminish his risks, he followed a policy of introducing as few innovations as possible. This applied particularly to his method for launching the Great Aerodrome into flight. His models had taken wing from a catapult mounted atop a houseboat—and he intended to do the same with this full-size aircraft. This did not lessen the risks; it increased them.

Manly urged him not to do it, but to have this airplane take off under its own power, perhaps from the surface of the Potomac while floating on pontoons. Such an approach would have enabled him to ease it into flight in small steps, beginning by taxiing it on the water and advancing toward an initial liftoff. Langley insisted that it was to use a new catapult, which was far more dangerous.

Langley and the Wrights both followed conservative approaches. Early in their efforts, both adopted a standardized layout for an airplane and then worked to enlarge it, while testing refinements. This made it possible to learn the characteristics of their designs in considerable detail. It contrasted sharply with the work of Chanute, who experimented with a number of different gliders without getting to know any of them really well. This conservatism also showed its merit when Langley and the Wrights pursued innovation. The Wrights worked with flight controls, starting with the concept of wing warping in 1899. It then took them three years and three gliders before their controls evolved into a fully workable form. For Langley, the new technology was engines—and it took Manly four years, from 1898 to 1902, to build a good one.

Langley therefore was quite prudent when he sought to rest his developmental efforts on what he already knew and to limit the scope of novel invention. Yet to install pontoons on the Great Aerodrome was hardly the stuff of a multi-year engineering program. As it was, his insistence on the catapult meant that his airplane would have to withstand the stress of a sudden acceleration at takeoff, a force considerably stronger than the craft was to encounter in flight. If his Aerodrome could do this, he would have his success. If it couldn't, it was likely to break apart before it ever left the houseboat.

Langley was approaching flight readiness late in 1902, though Manly still was working to coax more power from the engine. By contrast, the Wrights were starting afresh with a clean sheet of paper. This was not the strong white vellum of an engineering office, for as the writers Harry Combs and Martin Caidin note, the brothers continued to work with whatever came to hand. They made the original three-view drawing of their 1903 powered craft on brown wrapping paper. They also made important calculations on scraps of wallpaper. Nor did they give their new craft an orotund name such as "Great Aero-drome," which might have been chosen in anticipation of eventual display in Langley's own Smithsonian Institution. Wilbur and Orville called it simply the Flyer.

It was to fly with power from a motor, which made it necessary to calculate a required amount of horsepower. Their gliders of 1901 and 1902 had used wings with a total area close to 300 square feet. The Flyer was to be larger, to carry an engine with a weight estimated at 200 pounds. Additional weight was necessary for structural bracing. With a pilot on board, the total for this craft came to 625 pounds. This meant a wing area of around 500 square feet. Knowing the coefficient of lift, C_L, for the type of wing they planned to use, they determined that an airplane with this weight and wing area would fly at an air-speed of 23 miles per hour.

Next, they estimated the drag. Their tables of data from their wind tunnel experiments gave the drag coefficient, C_D. They also took account of drag from the struts, the engine, and the pilot. Together, wind resistance from all these sources totaled 90 pounds of drag, again at 23 miles per hour. To overcome this drag, the propellers therefore were to produce 90 pounds of thrust. To obtain such thrust at that speed, the engine was to drive them with 5.5 horsepower.

However, this referred to the horsepower delivered through the action of the propellers themselves, when whirling within the airstream. The power of the engine had to be substantially larger, for two reasons. It had to overcome losses within the transmission or drive train, which would transmit its power to the propellers. More important, those airscrews themselves would operate amid ineffi-ciencies. Like an aircraft that produces drag as well as lift, a propeller would generate losses as well as thrust, for part of its power would simply stir the air uselessly. There was no avoiding this; the brothers could hope for no more than to reduce these losses to a minimum. To provide a suitable reserve of power, leaving 5.5 horsepower for useful thrust, the motor was to put out 8 to 9 horsepower.

Even in 1902, such performance did not seem difficult to attain. Accordingly, the Wrights sent letters to a number of engine manufacturers, presenting their request. They wanted considerably less power than Langley's specification of 12 horses, four years earlier, with the Wrights being willing to accept twice the weight. Even so, no one had a stock engine that was ready for sale.

The brothers had faced such a situation a year earlier, drawing on their own resourcefulness in building their wind tunnel and carrying through their studies of wings. Now, faced with their need for an engine, they decided that they could assemble it in-house. They turned to their old friend, the machinist Charlie Taylor, who proved willing to take on this motor as a custom job. He later described how he did it:

While the boys were handy with tools, they had never done much machinework and anyway they were busy on the air frame. It was up to me. My only experience with a gasoline engine was an attempt to repair one in an automobile in 1901.

We didn't make any drawings. One of us would sketch out the part we were talking about on a sheet of scratch paper and I'd spike the sketch over my bench.

It took me six weeks to make that engine. The only metalworking machines we had were a lathe and a drill press, run by belts from the stationary gas engine.

The crankshaft was made out of a block of machine steel 6 inches wide by 31 inches long and 1⅝ inches thick. I traced the outline on the slab, then drilled through with the drill press until I could knock out the surplus pieces with a hammer and chisel. Then I put it in the lathe and turned it down to size and smoothness. It weighed 19 pounds finished and she balanced up perfectly, too. . . .

The body of the first engine was of cast aluminum, and was bored out on the lathe for independent cylinders. The pistons were cast iron, and these were turned down and grooved for piston rings. The rings were cast iron, too. . . .

The fuel system was simple. A one-gallon fuel tank was suspended from a wing strut, and the gasoline fed by gravity down a tube to the engine. The fuel valve was an ordinary gaslight petcock. There was no carburetor as we know it today. The fuel was fed into a shallow chamber in the manifold. Raw gas blended with air in this chamber, which was next to the cylinders and heated up rather quickly, thus helping to vaporize the mixture. The engine was started by priming each cylinder with a few drops of raw gas.

The ignition was the make-and-break type. No spark plugs. The spark was made by the opening and closing of two contact points inside the combustion chamber. These were operated by shafts and cams geared to the main camshaft. The ignition switch was an ordinary single-throw knife switch we bought at the hardware store. Dry batteries were used for starting the engine and then we switched onto a magneto bought from the Dayton Electric Company. There was no battery on the plane. . . .

We block-tested the motor before crating it for shipment to Kitty Hawk. We rigged up a resistance fan with blades an inch and a half wide and five feet two inches long. The boys figured out the horsepower by counting the revolutions per minute. These two sure knew their physics. I guess that's why they always knew what they were doing and hardly ever guessed at anything.[1]

The motor was ready for test in mid-February of 1903. It lasted only briefly, for on the next day, dripping gasoline caused a bearing to seize. The crankcase broke under the sudden shock as the engine stopped without warning. This was more than Charlie could handle, for that crankcase had been cast in a foundry. There was nothing to do but order a new one, and it took two months before this casting was ready for installation.

When testing finally resumed, the Wrights found that they indeed had a serviceable engine. It weighed 170 pounds and delivered close to 16 horsepower, at least for the first fifteen seconds or so—until it warmed up. Its hot metal then heated the air, causing it to expand so as to burn less fuel and produce less power. Even then, though, the motor still tested at nearly 12 horse, which was more than they had expected. This meant that they had leeway to add equipment to their airplane, increasing its weight, without compromising its ability to fly.

Twelve horse nevertheless was a long way from Langley's embarrassment of riches, and the brothers were well aware that they needed a good propeller to turn their motor into an effective propulsion system. At first glance they believed that this problem would not loom large, for ships had been navigating with screw propellers for much of the previous century. The Dayton public library had material on the design of marine propellers—and once again the Wrights learned that existing literature was of no use to them. No well-founded formulas existed for use in designing these screws. It was a matter of experience and sometimes of cut-and-try. Even then, maritime propellers lacked efficiency. That was not a problem for shipowners, whose vessels typically had power to spare. But it was indeed a problem for Wilbur and Orville, who knew that they had to use every one of their horses or they would never get off the ground.

Once more, then, they were thrown back on their own resources, compelled to apply their ingenuity and to invent anew. As with the wing-warping control system, which had grown out of a twisted cardboard box, it was a matter of gaining a suitable insight and then making it work. The new insight, which again was original, was that a propeller for an airplane could be viewed as a wing tracing a spiral trajectory rather than flying straight ahead. A wing generates pressure on its lower surface, constituting lift that holds the craft in the air. A rotating propeller having the form of an airfoil could generate pressure in similar fashion to propel the craft forward.

To develop this approach was not easy. In Orville's subsequent words:

> At first glance this does not appear difficult, but on further consideration it is hard to find even a point from which to make a start; for nothing about a propeller, or the medium in which it acts, stands still for a moment. The thrust depends upon the speed and the angle at which the blade strikes the air; the angle at which the blade strikes the air depends on the speed at which the propeller is turning, the speed the machine is traveling forward, and the speed at which the air is slipping backward; the slip of the air backward depends upon the thrust exerted by the propeller, and the amount of air acted upon. When any one of these changes, it changes all the rest, as they are all interdependent upon one another. But these are only a few of

the many factors that must be considered and determined in calculating and designing propellers. Our minds became so obsessed with
it that we could do little other work. We engaged in innumerable
discussions, and often after an hour or so of heated argument, we
would discover that we were as far from agreement as when we
started, but that both had changed to the other's original position in
the discussion. After a couple of months of this study and discussion, we were able to follow the various reactions in their intricate
relations long enough to begin to understand them.[2]

The data from their wind-tunnel tests of wings now found a new use
as the brothers sought to choose the best possible airfoil for application
in propeller design. This was airfoil number 9; it had provided the highest lift-to-drag ratio for different values of angle of attack. Selection of
this candidate promised high efficiency at various speeds of the headwind and the airplane. The propeller itself was to have greater speed
near the tip than near the hub, as it rotated in the air. The choice of
number 9 eased the problem of physically fabricating the blades, because
this same airfoil could define the shape along their entire length.

Even so, this choice of airfoil addressed only one of a number of
issues. With the engine whirling at more than a thousand revolutions
per minute, it would have been easy to fashion a propeller of modest
size that could spin very rapidly to produce a propulsive jet of air. The
brothers appreciated that such a jet would be ineffective as a source of
thrust. It was important to try to match the speed of the slipstream
from the propeller to the forward speed of their craft through the air.
Ship propellers did this; that is why they were called screws. Such a
propeller gave the best efficiency when it bored its way through the
water like a screw being driven into wood, while producing no high-
speed wake astern. The Wrights hoped to do the same.

Hence, rather than use a single propeller that would accelerate a
modest airflow to a high rearward speed, it was highly preferable to
accelerate a far greater airflow to a much lower rearward speed. If this
was done properly, the Wright propeller might act again as a screw,
boring through air while producing no jet at all. This dictated the use

of two propellers rather than one, with both being as large as possible. The two-propeller approach offered a further advantage, for a single propeller would act as a gyroscope, making the airplane hard to turn. By arranging for the twin props to spin in opposite directions, the plane could fly with no net gyroscopic effect.

The brothers' experience with wings carried over to the new problem of blade design. The Wrights had learned that long narrow wings worked best, for they diminished the drag produced by excessive chord, or distance from front to rear. Clearly, this meant that a propeller blade should be long and narrow. If it was too wide, it too would produce drag, reducing the efficiency. But if the blade was too narrow, it would resemble a wing that was too small. Such a wing would not produce enough lift, while an overly narrow propeller would fail to produce adequate thrust.

Wilbur and Orville filled five notebooks with formulas, sketches, tables of data, and calculations as they wrestled with their technical issues. They used mathematics where they could, addressing one set of problems by reducing them to quadratic equations in algebra. They fabricated their propellers by roughing out their shapes using a hatchet and then trimming them to final form with a spokeshave. Their main engine still was inoperable, but a two-horsepower motor was available for ground testing, and Wilbur made a key observation: Under some circumstances, a propeller could produce greater thrust by spinning somewhat slowly rather than rapidly. This happened because the slower rotation improved the blades' efficiency, enabling them to convert less power into mere stirring of the air.

This new finding shaped the design of their chain drive. That part of the system at least was familiar, with the motor driving both propellers like a bicyclist using pedals along with a bicycle chain. Even so, the 12 horse of the engine far exceeded the power of a cyclist's legs, so the brothers turned to the Diamond Chain Company in Indianapolis for chains that were being used in automobiles of the day. The final arrangement enclosed the Wright chains within metal tubes to keep them from slapping.

They installed gears that caused the propellers to make one turn for about every three of the motor. Bench tests led to a prediction that their system could deliver 100 pounds of thrust when spinning at 305 rpm. Subsequent measurement showed that the rotation rate for this thrust was actually 302 rpm, which was within one percent of the prediction. In June, with months of hard work now behind them, Orville boasted of what they had done in a letter to their friend George Spratt:

> During the time the engine was building we were engaged in some very heated discussions on the principles of screw propellers, to which we had access, so that we worked out a theory of our own on the subject, and soon discovered, as we usually do, that all propellers built heretofore are *all wrong,* and then built a pair of propellers 8⅛ ft. in diameter based on our theory, which are *all right!* (till we have a chance to test them down at Kitty Hawk and find out differently.) Isn't it astonishing that all these secrets have been preserved for so many years just so that we could discover them!! Well, our propellers are so different from any that have been used before that they will have to either be a good deal better, or a good deal worse.[3]

They proved to be considerably better. They showed an efficiency of 66 percent, which was far higher than anyone else had ever achieved.

The propellers and the engine were central to their preparations for the flying season of 1903, but there were several items left over from 1902. They had not used a motor, but the glider of that year had literally raised the art of flight to new heights. Their work with the wind tunnel, along with their advances in the design of wings and airfoils, represented accomplishments that certainly would attract considerable interest among engineers. Moreover, their improved control system stood as an invention of the greatest importance. By skillfully combining wing warping with a movable rudder, the gliding flights of 1902 had demonstrated successful control in roll, pitch, and yaw, along with the ability to make effective turns.

With Octave Chanute continuing his friendship and support, the Wrights were in a position to win broad-based patents that would give legal protection to their inventions, and to garner acclaim within the world of engineering. Chanute indeed was glad to help. However, he maintained a basic misunderstanding as to what they had accomplished. As this persisted, he made indiscreet disclosures that threatened to compromise their patent rights, while helping to originate a legend that the brothers were merely clever bicycle mechanics who had learned the trade of aviation at his knee.

Wing warping—the phrase was Chanute's—increased the lift on one side of an airplane while reducing it on the other side, enabling the craft to make banked turns like those of a bicycle. Chanute continued not to understand this. He viewed the Wright control system as a variant of one invented by France's Louis-Pierre Mouillard, for which he had helped Mouillard obtain a patent. This arrangement proposed to turn an aircraft by increasing the drag on one side, not the lift, while diminishing the drag on the other side. Chanute didn't appreciate that this approach could not work, for it did not lead to banking, which was essential to turning. In his mind, the Wrights' use of a rudder was simply a way to make Mouillard's approach more effective.

Building on this misunderstanding, Chanute proceeded to expand his own role in the Wrights' work while reducing them merely to protégés. The brothers had started by adopting Chanute's Pratt truss for their biplane wings; this was undeniable. They then had seemed to devise a variation of the basic Mouillard control system that Chanute had sponsored and advocated. They had improved their wing designs by using their wind tunnel, a British invention, with Chanute helping to reduce their raw data to tables and charts. It was easy to downplay their originality in devising precision balances and methods for taking the data, which had enabled Chanute to help with the calculations in the first place.

During the early months of 1903, Chanute sailed to Europe for an extended visit. In April he addressed the prestigious Aero Club, a Paris-based association of rich and fashionable people who had taken up the sport of ballooning. This talk had three consequences. By making it clear that the Wrights' 1902 achievements had placed them on the threshold of complete success, Chanute helped to stir a strong new interest in heavier-than-air flight. The Count of La Vaulx, an attendee, later wrote that his country's inventors "had been resting on the laurels of their predecessors too long, and that it was time to get seriously to work if they did not wish to be left behind." Ernest Archdeacon, a wealthy attorney, was more vivid in his reaction:

> Will the homeland of the Montgolfier suffer the shame of allowing this ultimate discovery of aerial science—which is certainly imminent, and which will constitute the greatest scientific revolution since the beginning of the world—to be realized abroad? Gentlemen scholars, to your compasses! You, the Maecenases [wealthy philanthropists]; and you, too, of the Government, put your hands deep into your pockets—else we are beaten![4]

Archdeacon then quoted Chanute to suggest strongly that the Wrights were merely his apt students: "Admitting that he was no longer young, [Chanute] took pains to train young, intelligent, and daring pupils, capable of carrying on his researches. . . . Principal among them, certainly, is Mr. Wilbur Wright of Dayton, Ohio." The Wrights had not pursued "his researches"; they had gone forward with their own. This subtle denigration later bedeviled them as they struggled to establish that they and they alone were the true inventors of the airplane.

Chanute's talk had a third consequence. Outlining their method of control, he asserted, "To achieve transverse equilibrium, the operator works two cords, which warp the right and left wings and at the same time adjust the vertical rear rudder." He could hardly describe what he did not understand, and no French inventor ever drew guidance from those few words. However, they raised the prospect of "prior disclosure," which offered solid grounds for denial of a patent. A decade later, a German appellate court cited Chanute's statement as cause to restrict the scope of the Wrights' patent in that country.

In a single presentation, then, Chanute depicted the brothers as the men to beat, while simultaneously diminishing both their claims to originality and their position in upholding later patents. He went on to underscore this threefold impact with an article that appeared in the August 1903 issue of *L'Aerophile,* an aviation magazine. Again he described the Wrights' method for executing turns: "The aviator controls direction in the horizontal plane by operating two cords which act by warping the right or left side of the wing and by deflecting at the same time the rear vertical rudder." Chanute also damned with faint praise by describing his own work of 1896 and 1897 in detail, then adding: "The invitation to amateurs to repeat these experiments remained unacted upon till 1900, when Messrs. Wilbur and Orville Wright of Dayton, Ohio, took up the question." These Messrs. had not sought to "repeat these experiments"; from the outset they had pursued wing warping as an original approach. Even so, both this article and Archdeacon's added insult to injury by presenting photos of the Wrights' 1902 glider with the caption, *"L'appareil Chanute."*

The Wrights had already covered their patent position in Washington by filing an application in March—less than two weeks before Chanute gave his talk in Paris. Still, while this solved the problem of prior disclosure within the U.S., it certainly did not guarantee that this application would succeed. For over fifty years the Patent Office had been receiving claims for the invention of flying machines. None had actually flown, and this led in time to a new policy that had been in force since the early 1890s. Patent officials now treated such alleged inventions as if they were perpetual motion machines. They rejected the applications outright unless the inventor actually succeeded in flying.

Working without help from a lawyer, the Wrights submitted drawings and a written description. A patent examiner responded in a matter of weeks with a curt dismissal. The drawings were inadequate; the claims were "vague and indefinite." The airplane overall was "a device that is inoperative or incapable of performing its intended function." What was worse, the Wright claims were covered by six previous patents. The brothers replied with a letter typed on Wright Cycle Company stationery that disagreed with this conclusion, requesting "that the particular claims in the patents cited which anticipate our claims be specified," and attempting to clarify the concept of wing warping. They sent a "little square tube of cardboard," a long box like that of 1899, and explained how it could demonstrate the idea of a warped wing. This letter brought a further rejection, with the examiner in Washington stating that the "card board exhibit" was "of no assistance." He concluded: "The applicants are advised in case of further proceedings to employ an attorney skilled in patent practice."

The original application, dated March 23, 1903, proved in time to be a vital foot in the Patent Office door, but just then the brothers had to put this matter aside while they gave attention to their bicycle business and went on with the work of crafting their Flyer. They continued to show meticulous attention to detail. For instance, conventional wisdom held that the vertical wing struts should have a cross section in the shape of a teardrop, to reduce drag. The Wrights set up their wind tunnel once again, ran tests—and concluded that it was preferable to use struts of rectangular cross section, with the corners rounded.

The wings had a span of forty feet and a chord of six and a half feet, which maintained the proportions of the 1902 glider while substantially increasing the area. Again they used unvarnished Pride of the West muslin, as in 1901 as well as 1902, but this time they covered the bottom of the wings as well as the top for a smoother lifting surface. As usual, they crafted this newest design in a workroom behind their bicycle shop, but even when only part of it was assembled, it blocked the passage to the front. When someone came in from the street, one of the brothers had to go out the side door and around to the front.

That workshop was the focus of their lives. Redolent of wood shavings and of the smell of glue from a sticky pot, it was the place where they were turning hopes into hardware. Yet they were not recluses; they continued to welcome visitors, with Chanute coming around to see them once more early in June, following his return from Europe. He questioned the Wrights' decision to use rounded rectangular struts, but Wilbur and Orville held their ground. They had learned to trust no one's experimental data but their own. In the same letter to George Spratt in which he boasted of his propellers, Orville similarly dismissed criticism of the struts: "We have also made some experiments on the best shapes for the uprights of our machine, and again found out that everybody but ourselves is very badly mistaken!!!"

Such an attitude might have brought disaster, but at least during 1903 the Wrights indeed knew more than any of their contemporaries.

While Chanute was with them as a visitor, he also agreed to invite Wilbur to give another presentation in Chicago, again at a meeting of the Western Society of Engineers. This event took place late in the month, at a time when their motor and propellers were in hand and the preparations for powered flight were well under way. Wilbur did not speak of these matters, of course; everything about their current work was closely held. Orville had shared the news with a handful of close friends such as Pratt, but he had been properly cautious. In his letter to Pratt, he had closed with a P.S.: "Please do not mention the fact of our building a power machine to anybody. The newspapers would take great delight in following us in order to record our *troubles.*"

Wilbur's talk in Chicago covered the activities of 1902, but he still displayed caution. He spoke freely of what they had done, using lantern slides again for illustration, but he said little if anything about how they did it. His title, "Experiments and Observations in Soaring Flight," clearly pertained to gliders, with Wilbur explaining that soaring was not the same as downhill gliding but resembled the flight of large birds that hang motionless in midair by riding an updraft. He noted that they had set a record for America by covering 622 feet in 26 seconds. The Wrights' rudder was clearly visible in some photos of their craft, but he took care not to discuss its wing warping or its method of control, even in generalities.

Chanute might flatter himself that the Wrights were merely executing a program that he had laid out, but the presentation to the engineers in Chicago made it very clear that the brothers indeed were plowing new ground. In Washington, Samuel Langley was moving forward as well. He had completed construction of the Great Aerodrome, installing its powerful motor and proceeding with preparations for flight. If he achieved nothing more than to have his Aerodrome fly as well as his unpiloted models of 1896, which had covered distances of up to three-quarters of a mile, then he would stand as the first to fly and would relegate the Wrights to also-rans.

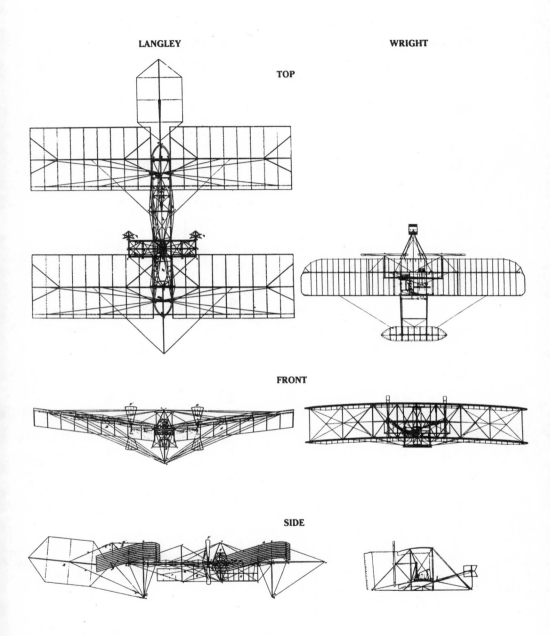

LANGLEY   WRIGHT

TOP

FRONT

SIDE

Langley's "Great Aerodrome" and the Wright "Flyer," at the same scale.
The Wrights used sophisticated design to compensate for
the smaller size and lesser power of their craft.

Langley did not personally attend to the preparations, for as Secretary of the Smithsonian Institution, he indeed was a busy man. He left the project in the hands of Manly, who had volunteered as the pilot and whose weight of 125 pounds counted as a strong qualification. He took the houseboat down the Potomac to a site near Quantico where Langley had flown his powered models. The catapult was on the roof, while its interior held work space along with the wings and other components of the Aerodrome. The quarter-scale model was also at hand.

The houseboat was on station midway through July of 1903. Eight men formed the launch crew, along with a soldier who served as a military guard, with their boat providing sleeping accommodations along with the work area. News reporters set up camp on shore, living on sandwiches and slapping at mosquitoes while they waited for something to happen. For three weeks all they saw was the departure and return of a launch that carried the crew to nearby Chopawamsic Island, where there were cooking facilities. Then on August 8th, they saw a flight.

It was not the full-size Aerodrome; it was the quarter-scale model. It seemed to flutter through the air, rising and falling while covering a thousand feet before it came down in the water. This was nowhere near a record, but at least now something had flown. Still it took two months to get the Aerodrome ready. An attempt in early September was aborted when batteries failed to start the motor. Close inspection showed that glue in the wings had softened, necessitating extensive repairs. Finally, on October 7th, all was ready, and Manly later wrote a description of what happened:

> I felt no jar when the machine was released. But with lightning-like rapidity it gathered speed as it rushed down the track, reaching the end of it in three seconds. As it did, I felt a sudden shock, immediately followed by the sensation of being free in the air.
>
> Hardly had I sensed this, when I realized that the aerodrome was plunging downward at a very steep angle. Instinctively I grabbed the wheel which controlled the setting of the Penaud tail. I threw it "full

up" to depress the rear of the machine and reduce the sharp angle of descent. The craft failed to respond. I immediately recognized that a crash was unavoidable and braced myself for the shock.

The front wings were completely demolished as they struck the surface. Almost instantaneously I found myself and the machine under water. Instinctively I reached upward and grabbed hold of the guy wires above my head. I pulled myself through them, freed myself from the wreckage, and swam upstream as fast as I was able. When I reached the surface, I saw part of the aircraft projecting from the water. I swam over and rested on it until a boat arrived to pick me up.[5]

A photo taken at the moment of launch shows it angling steeply downward, barely clear of the catapult but already heading for the drink. It nevertheless appears to have been intact or largely so, surviving the rapid acceleration of launch but failing to gain flight speed. Fortunately, the wreckage proved to be salvageable, with the motor in particular needing little more than a good cleaning.

Langley in effect had invented the naval aircraft that failed to take off from a carrier flight deck. Still he remained hopeful, issuing a statement: "A part of the aerodrome had been caught or snagged in the catapult launch car and had failed to be released. The accident was due wholly to the launching mechanism. The machinery was working perfectly and giving every reason to anticipate a successful flight." He was in a position to rebuild his craft; then he would try again.

On the day that Manly took his unplanned swim in the Potomac, the Wrights were back near Kitty Hawk. They had left Dayton two weeks earlier, accompanied by substantial shipments of crated supplies. To stay warm during cold autumn nights, and to sleep comfortably, they brought ample amounts of bedding along with mosquito netting and burlap for new beds. Pots, pans, and other items of kitchenware were in their boxes, along with enough canned food to hold them until they could begin to purchase more in the local area. They had a number of instruments: stopwatches, revolution counters for measuring rpm, and a new French anemometer that was a recent gift from Chanute. Anticipating that bad weather could lead to long periods of little work, the brothers packed binoculars for birdwatching, rifles for hunting, and French and German grammars along with reading material in those languages that included articles on aviation. With an eye to future meetings of engineers—and perhaps on history—they brought a camera with a tripod and a supply of glass-plate negatives.

They shipped these supplies by rail freight, with the Flyer in its own crates. They left the Dayton train station on the morning of September 23rd, with their father Milton wishing them well by giving them an extra dollar to send a telegram announcing success. They proceeded to Elizabeth City, as usual—and found that the freight depot had burned down a few days earlier. So far as they knew their precious shipments and perhaps even the Flyer itself had gone up in smoke. Still there was nothing to do but to press onward, catching the steamer *Okracoke* to Manteo on Roanoke Island and then hiring a launch to take them to the Kill Devil Hills. Once there, they saw to their vast relief that all their belongings were safe. The main shipment had been sent onward from Elizabeth City prior to the fire, while the Flyer was still en route from Dayton.

Their wooden shack had been home during the 1902 season, and they had left it to shelter that year's glider. Heavy storms a few months later had damaged this shed, but it still was usable, as was the glider. They nevertheless needed a new hangar that could house the Flyer, and they had ordered a supply of lumber that was waiting for them when they arrived. They hired Dan Tate to help with the construction, but the wind and the weather proved so inviting that the brothers turned instead to making glides. In a letter to Chanute, Wilbur wrote that this was "the finest day we ever had in practice. We made about 75 glides, nearly all of more than 20 seconds' duration. The longest was 30 2/5 seconds which beats our former records. We did some practicing at soaring and found it was easier than we expected."

All too soon, stormy weather blew in. The wind reached 75 miles per hour, which is hurricane strength, and a corner of the big hangar's roof gave way. With the entire roof and hence the hangar itself in danger, Orville put on a heavy overcoat and climbed a ladder with a hammer and nails. The wind caught his coat and blew it over his head. Wilbur, wearing a jacket that was too light for the chill, followed him up to the roof and struggled with Orville's coat while rain drenched them both. Orville managed to drive in the necessary nails, pounding his fingers as he hammered them home, and both men rushed for cover. The gales blew for four days amid continuing heavy rains, blowing five vessels ashore along the stretch of coast from Kitty Hawk to Norfolk. In a letter to their sister Katharine, Wilbur wrote that they nevertheless had taken heart from the advice of a coach at Oberlin: "Cheer up, boys, there is no hope."

The crated Flyer was already at hand, having arrived on October 8th aboard Captain Midgett's sailboat, the *Lou Willis*. The brothers continued to fly in the glider, staying aloft for as long as a minute and setting a world record at nearly 72 seconds. These glides were important, for in addition to honing the skills of Wilbur and Orville, they tested their ability to judge good flying conditions by using their anemometer. For a day or so they had reason to believe that the instrument lacked accuracy, and Orville mentioned the matter in a letter to Charlie Taylor. With day-to-day events making their hopes rise and fall like the stock market, they indeed adopted Wall Street trading as a metaphor:

> Flying machine market has been very unsteady the past two days. Opened yesterday at about 208 (100% means even chance of success) but by noon had dropped to 110. These fluctuations would have produced a panic, I think, in Wall Street, but in this quiet place it only put us to thinking and figuring a little. It gradually improved during the rest of yesterday and today and is now almost back to its old mark.[6]

As they began tests of the engine with its propellers, they soon found themselves wrestling with new problems. Taylor had shown considerable skill in fabricating the motor, but it was not a very good one. Its use of breaker points rather than spark plugs meant that its ignition was unreliable. It lacked a proper carburetor; hence the flow of fuel-air mix to the cylinders also was uncertain. Moreover, the drive train coupled the engine directly to the propeller shafts, without a clutch and with no means to disengage the motor from the two chain drives.

When started, it ran rough and repeatedly misfired, jerking the chains. They got it to run reasonably smoothly—when again it misfired. The shafts were robust enough to withstand a steady torque considerably stronger than what was needed to turn the propellers smoothly, but the sudden jolt pulled the shafts from their supports and left one of them badly twisted. The brothers had hand tools but nothing suitable for such an emergency, and no machine shop was nearby. The only thing to do was to remove the shafts and send them back to Charlie to have them repaired and strengthened. That took two weeks, and until the shafts returned with a freight delivery, hopes for flight were on hold.

The ordinary details of life on the dunes continued to concern them. In a letter to home, Wilbur noted that keeping warm at night was a continual preoccupation:

> The pine we bought of Mr. Baum was hardly worth putting in the stove, it burned up so quickly. We get fourfold value from the live oak. It warms us once to chop it down, second to carry it to camp, third to split it up, and last, but not least, when we burn it in our patent carbide stove.
>
> We can hold fire all night easily. The weather is warm most of the time and we go about in our shirt sleeves, but after each Norther it is rather cold. However, we are entirely comfortable, and have no trouble keeping warm at nights. In addition to the classifications of last year, to-wit: 1, 2, 3 and 4-blanket nights, we now have 5 blanket nights, and 5 blanket and 2 quilt. Next comes 5-blanket, 2-quilt and fire; then 5-2-fire and hot water jug. This is as far as we have got so far. Next come the addition of sleeping without undressing; then shoes and hats, and finally overcoats. We intend to be comfortable while we are here.[7]

They continued to spend time with local people. They hired Dan Tate for general handiwork at seven dollars a week, a very high wage on the Outer Banks even though it meant a seven-day week of ten-hour days. However, Tate and the Wrights had a falling-out when Wilbur told him to collect driftwood for the fire and he replied that they could buy all the wood they wanted from Jesse Baum, at three dollars a cord. This was the pine that Wilbur had found unsuitable. Then when Tate's work proved unsatisfactory in other respects, the Wrights let him go.

They also had visitors from the outside world. George Spratt made the long journey to Kitty Hawk, hoping to see a powered flight. He was on hand when the propeller shaft twisted, but he made himself useful by taking the shafts with him and departing in the company of another local man who was heading for Manteo. Then Chanute himself showed up and stayed for several days, with the shafts being away for repair and the Flyer in no condition to fly. He warned the brothers that they were cutting it very close to the margin on engine power, with little in reserve and possibly less power than they needed. This gave them one more thing to worry about, but they could not run further tests until the shafts returned by rail freight.

Frank Midgett's schooner, the *Lou Willis,* became their lifeline to their sources of supply in Elizabeth City. They had hoped to secure regular supplies of provisions, but when Midgett was delayed one day, the brothers found themselves with nothing but condensed milk and crackers for dinner. Fortunately, Midgett arrived the next day, bringing not only a fresh supply of groceries but the eagerly awaited shafts. Once more, then, the Wrights could resume their preparations for flight.

In Dayton they had estimated the weight of the complete Flyer at 625 pounds. In mid-November, however, Orville wrote, "The weight of our machine complete with a man will be a little over 700 lbs., and we are now quite in doubt as to whether the engine will be able to pull it at all with the present gears." He added an entry in his diary: "After figuring a while, stock in flying machine began dropping rapidly till it was worth very little!"

The only way to halt this bear market was to try to gain reassurance by measuring the thrust. The brothers worked to tune their motor for more speed. To determine propeller effectiveness, they put the Flyer on rollers so it could pull freely against a restraint. By rigging a pulley, they arranged that a force equal to only half the thrust would hold the airplane steady. They applied most of the necessary force using a 50-pound load of sand; a grocer's spring balance gave a direct reading of the additional pull required.

Before they could measure performance, however, they first had to make sure that the shafts would actually turn their propellers. On each side of the Flyer, a chain-driven sprocket drove a prop, with the sprocket mounted to its shaft using screws and nuts. The engine continued to misfire, causing the sprockets to work loose, and no amount of tightening could prevent this. "We kept that up all Friday afternoon," Orville wrote to Charlie Taylor, "and by evening stock had gone still lower, in fact just about as low as it could get, about 100 percent below par."

But by morning they were ready to try something new. Orville later wrote: "While in the bicycle business we had become well acquainted with the use of hard tire cement for fastening tires on rims. We had once used it successfully in repairing a stop watch after several watchsmiths had told us it could not be repaired. If tire cement was good for fastening the hands on a stop watch, why should it not be good for fastening the sprockets on the propeller shaft of a flying machine? We decided to try it. We heated the shafts and sprockets, melted cement into the threads, and screwed them together again. The trouble was over. The sprockets stayed fast."[8] In his letter to Charlie, Orville wrote that "thanks to Arnstein's hard cement, which will fix anything from a stop watch to a thrashing machine, we stuck those sprockets so tight I doubt whether they will ever come loose again."

A test of thrust followed quickly. With the propellers whirling at 351 rpm, the Wrights measured a thrust of 132 pounds. This was far more than they needed for a successful takeoff, even with the Flyer being heavy, and the brothers had the satisfaction of clearing a critical hurdle. In Orville's words, "Stock went up like a sky rocket and is now at the highest level in its history."

The road appeared open to the achievement of powered flight, perhaps within days. But the shafts, which had caused trouble all through November, now caused further difficulty as one of them developed a hairline crack. This was one problem too many; it was clear that they lacked the strength or resiliency to stand up to the uneven running of the motor, and the brothers decided to abandon them and to install new ones. The existing shafts were of tubular steel; the new ones would be solid tool-grade steel. Time was increasingly of the essence, for winter was at hand. On the last day of that month, Orville left for Dayton to secure the new shafts, knowing that passenger railroads were faster than freight. While he was away on this errand, Langley and Manly were in Washington and were about to try again.

The failure of the October attempt might have convinced Langley that catapult launch was not the way to proceed and that he was well advised to prevent a recurrence by fitting the Great Aerodrome with pontoons for takeoff from the surface of the Potomac. However, he had invested substantial sums in his houseboat with its catapult, and he continued to believe that his approach was sound. Having rebuilt his airplane, he did not take it to the remoteness of Quantico. Late autumn brought a sharp falloff in river traffic near Washington, and Langley decided that he would make his second attempt near the city, close to the confluence of the Anacostia and Potomac rivers.

The new test flight took place on December 8th. Preparations continued into late afternoon, for no tugboat was at hand, and it took time to find one. Gusty winds then set in, and twilight was upon the city before they eased. Finally the moment was right, and Manly again gave a description:

> I was facing forward, my attention on the performance of the engine. I therefore did not see anything that occurred at the rear of the machine.
>
> Just before it was freed from the launching car, however, I felt an extreme swaying motion. This was immediately followed by a tremendous jerk which caused the aerodrome to quiver all over.
>
> Almost immediately I found the machine dashing ahead with its bow rising at a very rapid rate. I swung the wheel controlling the Penaud tail as far down as possible. This had absolutely no effect.
>
> By this time, the craft had passed its vertical position and was beginning to fall over on its back. I swung myself around so that, in

striking the water with the machine on top of me, I would be sure to hit feet-first.

Suddenly I found myself underwater with the aircraft on top of me. My cork-lined canvas jacket was caught in the fittings of the framework so that I could not dive deeper and get away. At the same time, the floor of the aviator's car was pressing against my head, pre-

December 8, 1903: Langley's Great Aerodrome is torn to pieces during an attempted takeoff.

venting me from rising to the surface. I knew that if I was to get out alive, I would have to do so immediately.

Exerting all the strength I could muster, I succeeded in ripping the jacket entirely in two, thus freeing myself from the fastenings which had held me.

I dove under the machine and swam under the water for some distance until I thought I was out from beneath it. Upon rising to the surface, I hit my head upon a block of ice. This necessitated another dive to get free of the ice.[9]

One of the workmen jumped into the river to try to help him. Both men were pulled to safety aboard the houseboat. A doctor cut away Manly's soaked clothing, wrapped him in blankets, and gave him half a glass of whiskey. He responded with what another staff member described as "the most voluble series of blasphemies that I have ever heard in my life."

This fiasco was even worse than the one in October. During that earlier attempt, the Aerodrome at least had held together during its swan dive, but this time it was well along in breaking up even before it hit the water. No motion-picture film was made, but still photography showed that the rear wings and Penaud tail crumpled first. This may have resulted from inadequate repair during the rebuilding that followed the October launch, with sudden and severe distortion of these rear surfaces producing the uncontrolled nose-up.

Langley, an esteemed professor and scientist, saw his own prospects crash with his airplane. Overnight he became a national laughingstock. One writer suggested that he might have succeeded if he had hitched his craft to the rising cost of beef. Another reporter noted that the Aerodrome was "pointed straight toward the roofs and towers of the Government Hospital for the Insane." The October mishap had set him back, and this new accident marked the end of his pursuit of flight. During the remaining years of his life, he never tried again.

On the evening of that chilly December day, these consequences lay in the future. At that moment, within the entire world, the Wrights were the only inventors who were actively working toward powered flight. Orville was still in Dayton, but his new propeller shafts were in hand, and he took the train for North Carolina the following morning. He was back with Wilbur by afternoon of the 11th, having spent only two days en route. The shafts were installed and the Flyer was ready on the next day, but the winds were too light. There was a fine breeze on the 13th, but that was Sunday, and they honored the day by letting the opportunity pass. They had promised their father not to work on that day of the week.

The Flyer had skids for landing, but these produced too much friction for takeoff. The craft was also too heavy for the procedure of the previous three years, whereby two men picked up a glider by the wingtips and ran forward to sail it into the air. Bicycle wheels might have served for landing gear, but they would have bogged down in the soft sand, so the brothers used two-by-fours that they could lay to form a launch track. They called it the Grand Junction Railroad. The skids of the Flyer rested on a wheeled dolly that rode this track, with the dolly falling away at takeoff. This arrangement gave them flexibility in choosing a launch site.

Visitors were welcome, not only as witnesses but because they could help in physically carrying the unwieldy craft. Early on Monday afternoon, the Wrights set out a flag as a signal of their intent to fly. It was visible at the Kill Devil Hills Life Saving Station, a mile away, and five men soon arrived, accompanied by two boys and a dog. The wind again was light, so Wilbur and Orville decided to place their track on one of the sand hills, pointing downward. Their impromptu ground crew did not physically carry the Flyer to the takeoff site, a quarter mile away. Instead they pushed it along the rail, moving each fifteen-foot section of track from the rear to the front as they went along. By re-laying this track over and over, their airplane ran on its dolly for the entire distance.

The brothers tossed a coin to see who would be the pilot, and Wilbur won. The motor was started and ran for a few minutes to warm up; then Wilbur took his place within a padded hip cradle that controlled the wing warping. In Orville's subsequent account:

I took a position at one of the wings, intending to help balance the machine as it ran down the track. But when the restraining wire was slipped, the machine started off so quickly I could stay with it only a few feet. After a 35- to 40-foot run, it lifted from the rail.

But it was allowed to turn up too much. It climbed a few feet, stalled, and then settled to the ground near the foot of the hill, 105 feet below. My stopwatch showed that it had been in the air just 3½ seconds.[10]

This certainly was no flight, with the craft having stalled and come down so quickly, but at least the method for launching had worked—which was more than Langley could say. The Flyer had been damaged slightly and would need repair, but this would not take long. Wilbur went to the Kitty Hawk telegraph station on the next day and sent a message to the family in Dayton: MISJUDGMENT AT START REDUCED FLIGHT ONE HUNDRED TWELVE POWER AND CONTROL AMPLE RUDDER ONLY INJURED SUCCESS ASSURED KEEP QUIET. They had covered only 112 feet on that aborted attempt, and wanted more.

They were ready again for flight on the 16th, and the wind at first was good. They laid the track in the sand near the hangar and brought out the Flyer, but the breezes died down before they put out the flag to alert their friends at the Life Saving Station. They waited through the afternoon, but the weather did not cooperate and they decided to see if they might have better luck the following day.

The sky was overcast on the morning of Thursday, December 17th. A stiff gale was blowing, a chilly wind from the north that reached 27 miles per hour as measured by their anemometer. Their airplane could potentially fly as well in a strong breeze as in a calm, for the airspeed in both cases would be the same, but the high windspeed raised the prospect of gusts that might blow the Flyer out of control. They had never flown it as a glider. Years later, Orville wrote, "I would hardly think today of making my first flight upon a strange machine in a twenty-seven-mile wind, even if I knew that the machine had already been flown and was safe." Bill Tate, who had helped the Wrights from their earliest days in Kitty Hawk, declared that "no one but a crazy man would attempt to fly in such a wind." He stayed home, thereby missing his chance to see that day's flights.

But although the gale might turn gusty, it certainly promised to help get the plane into the air. At midmorning they put out the flag to attract their helpers, then laid the track on flat ground nearby. Orville placed his camera on a tripod, aiming it at the end of the track. This time it was Orville's turn to take the controls. John Daniels, one of the lifesavers, took his place at the camera, ready to squeeze the bulb that would snap the photo. Orville writes what happened next:

> After running the motor a few minutes to heat it up, I released the wire that held the machine to the track, and the machine started forward into the wind. Wilbur ran at the side of the machine, holding the wing to balance it on the track. Unlike the start on the 14th, made in a calm, the machine, facing a 27-mile wind, started very slowly. Wilbur was able to stay with it till it lifted from the track after a forty-foot run. One of the Life Saving men snapped the camera for us, taking a picture just as the machine had reached the end of the track and had risen to a height of about two feet. The slow forward speed of the machine over the ground is clearly shown in the picture by Wilbur's attitude. He stayed along beside the machine without any effort.

Daniels's photo—one of the most famous in the history of aviation—shows Wilbur as a featureless black shape, while Orville lies prone within the airplane, displaying neatly polished shoes. As usual, both men dressed nattily that day, being smartly shaved, wearing business suits, and sporting ties and starched collars. This time it suited the occasion, which indeed was historic.

> The course of the flight up and down was exceedingly erratic, partly due to the irregularity of the air and partly to lack of experience in handling this machine. The control of the front [stabilizer] was difficult on account of its being balanced too near the center. This gave it a tendency to turn itself when started, so that it turned too far

*December 17, 1903: the perfect moment, with Orville at the controls
and Wilbur running alongside.*

on one side and then too far on the other. As a result, the machine
would rise suddenly to about ten feet, and then as suddenly dart for
the ground. A sudden dart when a little over a hundred feet from the
end of the track, or a little over 120 feet from the point at which it
rose into the air, ended the flight. . . .

This flight lasted only 12 seconds, but it was nevertheless the first
in the history of the world in which a machine carrying a man had
raised itself by its own power into the air in full flight, had sailed forward without reduction of speed, and had finally landed at a point
as high as that from which it started.[11]

The 12-second duration would be cited many times during the
subsequent hundred years, but it was an estimate rather than a measured duration. In the excitement of the moment, Wilbur forgot to
click his stopwatch at the moment of takeoff. Orville had his own
stopwatch on board the flyer, but the shock of his sudden landing
reset it to zero.

Orville had flown—and yet he hadn't, at least not yet. His airspeed, some 45 feet per second, gave him the equivalent of 540 feet traveled in calm air, but 12 seconds of barely-controlled flight was too little to count. Moreover, his problem with the forward stabilizer echoed that of Wilbur during his attempt of the 14th, for Wilbur had also found the craft to be unpleasantly sensitive in pitch, heading for the sky and stalling in little more than three seconds.

But the Flyer survived the new landing, which meant that Wilbur would try next. This didn't happen immediately, for everyone was cold from the strong chilly wind, so they went inside to warm up. Wilbur soon took his place within the hip cradle, and the launch proceeded. "The course of this flight was much like that of the first," Orville wrote, "very much up and down. The speed over the ground was somewhat faster than that of the first flight, due to the lesser wind. The duration of the flight was less than a second longer than the first, but the distance covered was about seventy-five feet greater."

Certainly this was no way to run a railroad, not even the Grand Junction, but if the brothers could maintain this pace, they both would fly repeatedly that day and might yet make headway in taming their bucking bronco. Once again it was Orville's turn:

> Twenty minutes later, the third flight started. This one was steadier than the first one an hour before. I was proceeding along pretty well when a sudden gust from the right lifted the machine up twelve to fifteen feet and turned it up sideways in an alarming manner. It began a lively sidling off to the left. I warped the wings to try to recover the lateral balance and at the same time pointed the machine down to reach the ground as quickly as possible. . . . The time of this flight was fifteen seconds and the distance over the ground a little over 200 feet.[12]

Was this what they had, then? Could they hope merely for 12 to 15 seconds in the air, while covering distances less than the length of a football field? By now it was noon, with plenty of daylight and ample wind. Once again it was Wilbur's turn.

He again took to the air, barely avoiding another early return to earth as the Flyer lurched downward, and managed to pull it out only a foot above the sand. Then, getting the hang of it, he kept it under good control as he flew onward. He flew! Tens of seconds ticked by, then more tens of seconds, while hundreds of feet of beach unrolled behind him. Onward, onward, and still he stayed in the air, every second adding to his experience and making it plausible that he could continue to stay aloft. A low hummock of sand lay ahead. Wilbur eased his nose upward and cleared it, but then the instability in pitch set in once more. He tried to maintain control, but darted into the ground. Even so, the Wrights finally had something impressive to show for the day. Wilbur had stayed in the air for 59 seconds and had covered 852 feet.

The craft had sustained damage to the front elevator, which meant that once again it would need repair before it could fly. Confident now, Wilbur and Orville discussed the prospect of a truly long flight, perhaps from the Kill Devil Hills to the Kitty Hawk weather station, some four miles away.

Suddenly a fierce gust of wind took hold of the craft and flipped it across the sand. Several people tried to grab hold but only Daniels managed to hold on, and the Flyer threw him about within its interior as it continued to tumble in the turbulence. Daniels came away with bruises, but he was not badly injured. The plane was not so fortunate. When it finally came to rest it had many broken wing ribs, with a spar and several struts also having snapped. The chain guides were badly bent; the motor supports had fractured as well. The craft was salvageable, but not with the limited resources of the base near Kitty Hawk, and the brothers knew that this was it for the year.

Their fourth flight was the one that counted. If that gust had blown up only a few minutes earlier, then all they would have had were the earlier short flights, and they would have had to start again the following year with a rebuilt Flyer. Yet even with that final flight in hand, they had gained no more than an ambiguous success. If Langley had built an aircraft that could not be launched with its catapult, ending in the Potomac as a mass of wreckage, the Wrights' achievement was only modestly more propitious—and had brought its own mass of wreckage.

The Flyer's extreme sensitivity in pitch showed that the Wrights still had much further work in the area of control. This topic had concerned them as early as 1899, amid their earliest thoughts of wing warping. During the glider years, pitch control had not loomed as a serious problem. It now held that status, placing the Wrights in the position of mountaineers who reach the top of a peak only to see other mountains still to climb. Langley's Great Aerodrome had failed to take off, but the Flyer had major defects of its own, for it possessed such poor handling qualities as to be virtually unflyable. The brothers indeed had crafted a flying machine. However, they had far more to accomplish before they could claim to have invented an airplane.

SEVEN

RETURN TO DAYTON

I T WAS TIME TO PACK UP. The brothers had spent part of four years working at Kitty Hawk, but the cost and inconvenience were increasing, while the need for this remote location was at an end. They had come there initially, in 1900, because its winds and sand dunes were useful for gliding. Using the 1902 glider, they had continued to hone their skills as recently as the previous three months. Now, though, they had a powered airplane. It was important to fly it from level ground and in calm air; indeed, the gales of the Outer Banks had shown that they could destroy the Flyer as readily as they could help it rise from the track. They would continue their flights near Dayton.

They had left the 1902 glider in a shed a year earlier. Having no further need for it, they expected to abandon it once more, leaving it to the area's storms and torrential rains. The Flyer was another matter. Though damaged, it could be repaired and restored to use, perhaps to be modified so as to overcome the worrisome pitch problem. Hence it was worth repackaging in its crates for shipment home. This decision did not hold for long; after returning to Dayton, the Wrights turned to crafting an entirely new airplane and stored the Flyer's wooden boxes within a shed, not returning to them for a number of years. Still, by salvaging the Flyer, they ensured that its fate could improve on that of the 1902 glider, which vanished except for a single wingtip.

They intended to work full-time as inventors. They expected to keep the bicycle business as a going concern, personally completing work on several bikes that they had begun to assemble. However, they planned to place new work in the hands of Charlie Taylor. Money now was not a problem, for in 1902, their father had sold a 320-acre farm that he owned in Iowa and had divided the proceeds among his four sons. Wilbur and Orville thus held $4,900 in two local savings and loan associations, which was enough to hold them for several years.

They had built their better mousetrap, but they now were about to learn that the world would beat a path to their door in its own good time and way. On the afternoon of December 17th, they walked down the beach into Kitty Hawk to send a telegram home. Joe Dosher, who had been the first to welcome them more than three years earlier, was on duty. He proceeded to transmit their message to Norfolk for forwarding to Dayton:

> Success four flights Thursday morning all against twenty-one-mile wind started from level with engine power alone average speed through air thirty-one miles longest 59 seconds inform press home Christmas. Orville Wright.

The Norfolk operator responded with a message to Dosher: might he pass this item to a friend who was a news reporter? Absolutely not, replied the Wrights, thereby forfeiting an opportunity to shape this story to their liking. The operator leaked the news to the *Virginian-Pilot*, where it drew quick interest. Someone wired Kitty Hawk and tried to learn more, but the brothers had departed for their camp and were nowhere in view. This did not trouble that newswriter, who exercised a time-honored journalistic prerogative by not allowing his imagination to be constrained by the meager facts that were available.

On December 18th, the *Pilot* front page blossomed with a headline whose format might have been appropriate for a declaration of war:

FLYING MACHINE SOARS 3 MILES IN TEETH OF HIGH WIND OVER SAND
HILLS AND WAVES AT KITTY HAWK ON CAROLINA COAST
NO BALLOON ATTACHED TO AID IT
Three Years of Hard, Secret Work by
Two Ohio Brothers Crowned with Success
ACCOMPLISHED WHAT LANGLEY FAILED AT
With Man as Passenger Huge Machine
Flew Like Bird Under Perfect Control
BOX KITE PRINCIPLE WITH TWO PROPELLERS

The problem of aerial navigation without the use of a balloon has been solved at last.

Over the sand hills of the North Carolina coast yesterday, near Kitty Hawk, two Ohio men proved that they could soar through the air in a flying machine of their own construction, with the power to steer it and speed it at will.

Like a monster bird the invention hovered above the breakers and circled over the rolling sand hills at the command of the navigator and, after soaring for three miles, it gracefully descended to earth again and rested lightly upon the spot selected by the man in the car as a suitable landing place.

While the United States government has been spending thousands of dollars in an effort to make practicable the ideas of Professor Langley, of the Smithsonian Institute, Wilbur and Orville Wright, two brothers, natives of Dayton, O., have quietly, even secretly, perfected their invention, and put it to a successful test.

They are not yet ready that the world should know the methods they have adopted in conquering the air, but the Virginian-Pilot is able to state authentically the nature of their invention, its principle and its chief dimensions.[1]

The craft supposedly had flown with help from an "underwheel," a propeller that had served as a helicopter rotor, with a second airscrew pushing it forward. It had flown from a platform atop a dune, descending a slope and then climbing to an altitude of sixty feet. The motor was suspended beneath a "navigator's car," while a "huge fan-shaped rudder of canvas" provided control.

Meanwhile, the brothers' telegram had arrived in Dayton on the evening of the 17th. It had been slightly garbled in transmission, with the duration of the longest flight being reduced to 57 seconds. Their father had prepared a press release, while brother Lorin had agreed to act as the family's press agent. Katharine came home from work soon after the cable had been delivered. Without waiting for dinner, she walked across the neighborhood and gave it to Lorin, along with the release. Lorin finished his own dinner and then went downtown to the *Dayton Journal,* where he soon met Frank Tunison, a local representative of the Associated Press. Tunison was well aware that French aviators had covered considerably greater distances, and failed to appreciate that a heavier-than-air machine stood as something new. "Fifty-seven seconds, hey?" he responded. "If it had been fifty-seven minutes then it might have been a news item."

Some local news coverage did develop. The story from Norfolk went on the wires and the *Cincinnati Enquirer* picked it up, running it on the front page under its own flaming headlines. The Dayton *Evening Herald* was only slightly more subdued. The town's *Daily News* declared: DAYTON BOYS EMULATE GREAT SANTOS-DUMONT. The Associated Press also offered a shortened version to subscribers, giving it further play. The Wrights understood that in physics, nature tries to fill a vacuum; they now saw that this applied to journalism as well. Lacking information, newswriters had simply gone forward to invent their own airplane.

As they had promised, Wilbur and Orville arrived home before Christmas. The housekeeper, Carrie Kayler, greeted them with porterhouse steaks for dinner along with a tasty dessert, while assuring them that there was more of everything in the kitchen. Orville took her at her word and asked for glass after glass of milk, which he had not had in months, until she had to stretch the supply by diluting it with water. He detected the ruse, thus adding one more item to the family trove of memories. Christmas dinner was at Lorin's, with gifts that included silver forks and steak knives for Katharine along with a two-inch micrometer for Charlie Taylor. Then the new year of 1904 arrived, and it was time for work.

News coverage was high on the agenda, as the brothers sought to correct the misstatements of December. On January 5th they issued a new release to the Associated Press:

> It had not been our intention to make any detailed public statement concerning the private trials of our power "Flyer" on the 17th of December last; but since the contents of a private telegram, announcing to our folks at home the success of our trials, was dishonestly communicated to the newspapermen at the Norfolk office, and led to the imposition upon the public, by persons who never saw the "Flyer" or its flights, of a fictitious story incorrect in almost every detail, and since this story together with several pretended interviews or statements, which were fakes pure and simple, have been very widely disseminated, we feel impelled to make some correction.

The statement continued with their account of the flights, an account that they might have given directly to the *Virginian-Pilot* if they had seized their opportunity. They closed with a summary:

> From the beginning we have employed entirely new principles of control; and as all the experiments have been conducted at our own expense without assistance from any individual or institution, we do not feel ready at present to give out any pictures or detailed descriptions of the machine.[2]

The AP took this story and sent it out—but deleted the first paragraph, thereby upholding the credibility of the press. Octave Chanute read it in Chicago, and decided that he did not like the final paragraph.

He had spent several days with them at Kitty Hawk during November, and had maintained their relationship following the flights of the following month. Katharine had sent a cable while they were still on the dunes, telling him of their success, and he had responded with a warm telegram of his own. On returning home to Dayton, Wilbur sent him a letter that described their recent achievements. But when Chanute invited them to present their accomplishments at a conference of the prestigious American Association for the Advancement of Science, the brothers demurred. They still were not ready to go public. Chanute came away feeling miffed, grumbling that the Wrights were retreating into secrecy.

After reading the Wrights' news item, he asked Wilbur to "please write me just what you had in mind concerning myself when you framed that sentence in that way." He might have run up a signal flag to post a gale warning on the Outer Banks, for close friends are not easily led to such an attitude of suspicion. Wilbur replied tactfully that the statement was a comment on Langley, not Chanute. Langley had worked with federal funds and hence had been obligated to present his results openly, but the Wrights had worked entirely with their own money. As Wilbur put it, "We had paid the freight and had a right to do so as we pleased." Without saying it in ways that could rupture their association, Wilbur also was emphasizing that the Wrights had worked independently of Chanute and were not his kept children.

Problems with the press continued. Early in February an article appeared in a magazine, *The Independent,* under the name of Wilbur Wright. The actual author, one D. A. Willey, was a plagiarist who specialized in writing forgeries in the name of well-known persons. He had helped himself to extracts from Wilbur's copyrighted addresses to the Western Society of Engineers, filling out his "essay" with material from the vividly imaginative *Virginian-Pilot.* Wilbur responded with vitriol: "On page 242 an article was published under my name which I did not write and which I had never seen. . . . I have never given to any person permission or encouragement to palm off as an original article extracts from these copyrighted addresses. . . . Neither have I given to the *Independent . . .* the least permission or excuse for using my name in the furtherance of such attempted fraud." He thought of filing a lawsuit, but decided that Willey lacked funds that he could try to seize, and let the matter drop.

While newsmen were doing their best to show that freedom of the press was the last resort of a scoundrel, the Wrights also found themselves on the receiving end of a most curious proposal from Augustus Herring, a would-be aviator of prior years. After learning of the Wrights' success, he had suddenly discovered that he, not they, was the true inventor of the airplane. He had tried without success for a U.S. patent, and while he had won a patent in London, it had expired because he had failed to pay a renewal fee. Now, though, he offered to set up a company in which he, Orville, and Wilbur would all have equal shares. The Wrights saw that he was merely trying to steal their thunder, and they ignored him.

Yet if the United States appeared to be awash in aeronautical flimflam, in France there were people who were prepared to take them seriously indeed. Members of the Aero Club were getting the real story through correspondence with Chanute, and by early February of 1904, some of these people again were calling, "*Aux armes!*" Victor Tatin, for one, asked whether "aviation, born in France, only became successful thanks to the Americans, and that the French only obtained results by carefully copying them? The first flying machine journey must be made in France. We need only the determination. So let us go to work!" But Ernest Archdeacon, who certainly had been second to none in waving the *tricouleur,* warned that it might already be too late:

> Despite various contradictions, and a fair number of exaggerated reports published in the newspapers, it seems unquestionably true that the Wrights have succeeded in making a flight of 266 meters. . . . It is certain, gentlemen, that the results obtained are considerable, and—I do not cease to repeat—we must hurry if we wish to catch up with the enormous advance made over us by the Americans.[3]

Back in Dayton, the Wrights appreciated that they now were well positioned to seek definitive patent protection for their work. Early in the new year, they learned that Henry Toulmin, an experienced patent attorney, was practicing in the nearby town of Springfield. When Wilbur met with him, the two men hit it off splendidly. Toulmin declared that the original patent application of March 1903 indeed could stand as a point of departure, thereby avoiding problems due to disclosures made during subsequent months. He agreed that they were doing the right thing by maintaining secrecy, particularly as to their technical specifics, and asserted that he could obtain a patent that would not only be broad but that would stand if challenged. A key point was that he would seek patent protection for the Wrights' control system but not for its application to a powered airplane. The reason was that any claims concerning powered flight would require actual demonstration, whereas application to unpowered gliders might bypass this requirement.

A new flying machine was high on their agenda for 1904, and they needed a local field or cow pasture for flight test. They found what they needed at a place called Huffman Prairie, which in time became part of Wright-Patterson Air Force Base. Located eight miles from downtown Dayton, it was close to a station stop on an interurban trolley that ran to Springfield. This meant that the brothers could live at home and commute.

Measuring some one-fourth by one-half mile, this field was bordered with trees and telephone lines. Fortunately, there was an extensive central expanse in which a single tree stood as the only obstacle, and it appeared easy to avoid. Wilbur later described this domain in a letter to Chanute:

> We are in a large meadow of about 100 acres. It is skirted on the
> west and north by trees. . . . The greater troubles are the facts that
> in addition to the cattle there have been a dozen or more horses
> in the pasture and as it is surrounded by barbwire fencing we have
> been at much trouble to get them safely away before making any
> trials. Also, the ground is an old swamp and is filled with
> grassy hummocks some six inches high, so that it resembles a
> prairie dog town.[4]

Torrence Huffman, president of the Fourth National Bank of Dayton, was the landowner. He held it as part of a dairy farm, and while he had little hope for the Wrights' prospects in aviation, he knew the Wright family and respected them. He agreed to let Wilbur and Orville use his field, as long as they took care to shoo the cows and horses out of the way.

The brothers built a wooden shed within this grassy expanse, to serve as their hangar. Their new airplane, the Flyer II, was closely similar in dimensions and general appearance to the Flyer of the previous year, but the differences were sufficiently substantial as to preclude simple repair and modification of the 1903 machine. The new one had greater structural strength, which added weight. To cope with this, they installed a new motor that developed up to 16 horsepower. They had used spruce for the wing spars of 1903, but white pine was more readily available and proved to be just as strong, so they used this wood for the new spars instead.

Kitty Hawk had been pleasantly remote, affording plenty of privacy. Huffman Prairie was also somewhat isolated, for although it lay within easy reach of both Dayton and Springfield, there was no particular reason for anyone to want to go there. The brothers nevertheless were well aware that they might attract onlookers in droves if they began to win success in their flights, with these spectators arriving on the same trolley that made the site convenient for their use. The streetcars followed a schedule and the Wrights hoped to conduct their flights at times when nothing on the line was nearby. Still they knew that it would certainly help if they could avoid attracting the attention of newsmen, whose stories might readily turn their flying field into a magnet for the curious. By then they had learned something of the world of journalism, and they believed they knew what to do.

They wrote letters to the newspapers of both Dayton and Cincinnati, declaring that they intended to attempt to fly on Monday, May 23rd, and that they would be glad to have members of the press in attendance. The only restrictions were that no pictures were to be taken, and the news reports were not to be sensational. Word got around and some forty people showed up, including family friends and neighbors as well as a dozen newsmen.

The brothers expected the Flyer II to lift off by rolling down a new version of the Grand Junction Railway, with this launching track lengthened to a hundred feet. A 60-foot rail, assembled from two-by-fours, had sufficed amid the stiff breezes of Kitty Hawk, but the winds in southwestern Ohio were considerably lighter, which meant the airplane needed a longer takeoff run. Indeed, the wind that day was so light that it couldn't lift from the track at all. Time passed; the air remained nearly calm, and the spectators, who had also been calm, now began to grow impatient. One of the Wrights started the motor, hoping at least to get the craft to run down the track, but this engine began to skip. The aircraft slid off the end of the rail without ever having risen from it.

Clearly, the reporters had come to Huffman Prairie for no particular reason, and with no stories in hand they were reluctant to return. This suited the Wrights' desire for privacy, but they were not about to leave it at that, so they declared that if they could get the motor to run properly, they would try again the next day. Anyone who cared to show up would be welcome.

The problem with the motor proved to have resulted from faulty airflow at the intake pipe, and was easily fixed. Nevertheless, rainy weather set in and made flying impossible for the next two days. Rain continued intermittently on Thursday morning, but the weather cleared during the afternoon and the brothers decided to give it a try. A few reporters had returned, hoping not to be disappointed, but again the Wrights' motor malfunctioned. This time the problem was with the spark ignition in one of the cylinders, which left the engine running on only three of its four pistons. Still there was no time to lose, for everyone could see that another storm was bearing down on them.

It is possible to use an airplane's elevator to force it into the air for a short hop even when it lacks flying speed. This is what Orville did as he lay within the hip cradle. The motor popped, and as Wilbur ran alongside to steady their craft, it ran down the track and jumped upward momentarily. It reached a height of about six feet and then dropped suddenly to the ground. Estimates of the distance of the "flight" ranged from 30 to 60 feet, and it was clear that the newsmen once again would have to use their imaginations if they wanted a story. The man from the *Cincinnati Enquirer* wrote that the Flyer II "is more substantially constructed than other machines of its kind," not appreciating that the only other such aircraft were Langley's wrecked Great Aerodrome and the Wrights' Flyer of 1903 that was packed within its crates. Everyone could see that the brothers had not built anything worth demonstrating, and the news reporters subsequently left them alone.

Wilbur and Orville certainly were willing to use their developmental problems to make newsmen go away empty-handed, but they truly did want to fly, and as the months proceeded, they found that it was surprisingly hard to get off the ground. The authors Harry Combs and Martin Caidin propose that part of the reason was that the air in summer at Dayton was noticeably thinner than in winter at Kitty Hawk. This reflected a rise in altitude from sea level on the Outer Banks to 815 feet at Huffman Prairie, while the warm weather of southwestern Ohio also made the air less dense. Indeed, on a hot day the air near Dayton could have as little as five-sixths the density of the atmosphere at North Carolina's seacoast. The Flyer II therefore developed only five-sixths as much lift as the Flyer of 1903. With the overall enterprise still being marginal, this difference could have been quite sufficient to prevent the 1904 airplane from leaving the ground.

A longer takeoff run could help the craft get airborne, and the brothers lengthened their track to as much as 240 feet. However, it was not easy to maintain a straight and level course across the field's hummocky ground. Even with this long a rail, the airplane still needed some wind to take off, but calm air was all too frequent. The Wrights responded by laying out their launching track in what they hoped would be an appropriate direction, then waiting amid calm air or very light breezes until they saw a wind ruffling the grass in the distance. They would fire up the engine, then prepare to run their Flyer down the track once this gust was upon them. If they had guessed right in setting the track, a successful if brief flight was not out of the question. If the direction was off, they attempted a flight at their peril, for this airplane did not respond well to a crosswind.

They had considerable incentive for success, not only because they wanted badly to build on the achievements of 1903, but because the Louisiana Purchase Exposition in St. Louis offered a prize of $100,000 for a successful flying machine. In February, prior to the opening of the fair on May 1st, Wilbur and Orville had visited the site and had seen that the planned airfield lay amid trees and buildings, making it unsuitable for an airplane. They protested to fair officials and won a change in the rules that allowed them to land well away from such hazards—if they could fly in the first place.

For a time, it seemed that they might compete with no less than Alberto Santos-Dumont, the darling of Paris, who was drawing international acclaim with the success of his airships. He arrived in New York in mid-June, with his dirigible and its engine packed in crates. He met President Theodore Roosevelt at the White House, then went to the Naval Academy at Annapolis to talk with military leaders that included Admiral George Dewey, who had sunk the Spanish fleet at Manila during the war of 1898. Once in St. Louis, he prevailed upon the rules committee to shape the course to his liking, laying it out as a 6-mile round trip between two markers.

Santos-Dumont's airship featured a large hydrogen-filled gasbag, along with a keel that carried the motor, propeller, and pilot. Its crates were opened in the presence of customs inspectors, with the covers being left off. A guard stood watch during the following night, but he took a couple of breaks for coffee, and while the crates were left unattended, someone used a knife and cut four long slashes through the folded fabric. Recriminations and countercharges soon were flying, though the dirigible wasn't, and Santos-Dumont soon left in a huff to return to the more civilized environs of France.

The deadline for entry was September 30th, and with three months ahead of them, the Wrights might have been well positioned. But they still couldn't count on getting into the air, as they continued to wrestle with balky wind conditions in their pasture near Dayton. Early in June, Wilbur made enough of a flight to give him leeway for a mistake in manipulating the front elevator. The craft nosed into the ground, and while he was unhurt, this accident cost the brothers two weeks of their Ohio summer as they made repairs.

Here was the same pitch instability that they had faced during the previous December at Kitty Hawk. Concluding that their airplane's center of gravity was too far forward, they moved the engine and the pilot's position farther to the rear. When they got the plane into the air, it quickly showed that it now was tail-heavy, as it nosed upward into a stall. The brothers spent the month of July making further changes, as they sought to achieve a proper balance.

They found that the only way to fly at all was to keep the elevator turned down slightly, to counter a continuing tail-heaviness. This use of the elevator created drag, which brought a demand for more power, particularly because they still were flying in the hot and less dense air of the season. They finally balanced their craft by adding 50 pounds of cast-iron bars to the nose. The extra weight was unwelcome, but it brought less of a problem than the continued need to apply down elevator.

With the problem of balance now under control, at least in a fashion, long flights now reappeared as a prospect. On August 6th, Wilbur flew for 600 feet. A week later, nearly three months after the first attempts at flight during May, Wilbur topped the Kitty Hawk mark of 852 feet as he sailed across the field for over 1,000 feet. Within days, Orville matched this distance.

They now were taking to the air with some semblance of predictability, but still not all was well. They had not yet learned to turn the airplane in flight; these extended excursions proceeded in something of a straight line. Indeed, they might have gone farther except that the brothers wanted to remain within the confines of Huffman Prairie. In addition, the Wrights faced the toilsome task of retrieving the craft and returning it to the takeoff track. At Kitty Hawk the wind had helped, enabling them to make numerous glider flights in the course of a single day by using the ocean breezes to assist them in carrying a craft up one of the sand hills. Near Dayton there still was no reliable wind to speak of, while their Flyer was considerably heavier than any of the gliders of earlier years. The best they could do was to use a wheeled dolly to transport it over the hummocks. On a good day they could make four flights, but this was no more than they had made on that single morning of December 17th, eight months earlier.

Accidents persisted. Orville was at the controls on August 24th, rising into the air as the wind suddenly died. Lacking flight speed, the airplane plunged downward. The upper wing spar crashed down on his back; it might have delivered a crippling injury, but this spar had already broken in two, enabling him to escape with no more than bumps and bruises. The aircraft underwent repair and the flights continued, for the brothers were well aware that they could not truly fly until they accumulated a great deal of practice. They had followed this procedure with their gliders. It was even more important to do this with their powered airplane, which might stay aloft for a long time while executing turns and other maneuvers.

The August 24th accident drove home the need for a means to take off by accelerating to flight speed while still on the ground. Their motor still lacked enough power for an unassisted takeoff, but the brothers found what they needed by using a weight to pull the plane forward along its track. The weight—800 pounds initially, increasing in stages to 1,600—dangled at the apex of a pyramid-shaped framework formed from four 30-foot poles that met at the top. It might have served for the frame of an Indian tepee; it looked like a smallish version of an oil derrick. The weight exerted its force through a pulley, dropping through 16$\frac{1}{2}$ feet while pulling the flyer through a distance of nearly 50 feet. The arrangement placed the weight and derrick at the head of the launching track with the Flyer accelerating away from them, for unobstructed motion.

This device amounted to a catapult. Langley had used one in attempting to launch his Great Aerodrome from atop his houseboat, with his version using a powerful spring. The Wrights had not designed the Flyer II to withstand the stresses of catapult launch, but they used the force of gravity in a way that imposed considerably gentler loads. Moreover, use of this new arrangement enabled them to shorten the takeoff track to as little as 60 feet, matching the minimal length of the Grand Trunk Railroad at Kitty Hawk. The first catapult-assisted takeoff took place on September 7th, with Wilbur as the pilot. The wind was very light, but he set a distance record with a flight of nearly 1,400 feet, well beyond their best achievement on the Outer Banks.

Flights of such length meant that the brothers were about to run out of room within their pasture, making it all the more important to practice how to turn. An important issue involved learning how much banking was needed. This was easy to learn when beginning to ride a bicycle; a balance of forces readily provided the proper bank. In an airplane, though, excessive bank was possible. At the Wrights' low altitudes it might cause their aircraft to sideslip into the ground. Alternately, the airplane might enter a bank and resist recovering into level flight.

Wilbur made the first attempts on September 15th, trying from the start to turn a full circle. He flew toward the northern boundary of the field, then veered to the left. Trees lay ahead, and he landed to avoid them. Much the same happened later that day, during a second attempt. Wilbur noted that his aircraft had a tendency to slide to the outside of its curving flight path as he proceeded with his turn. Still he came away with the conviction that further practice would win full success.

The next attempts came five days later, and the brothers had a visitor. He was Amos Root, whose business was bees; he sold honey as well as supplies for beekeepers. He owned one of the first automobiles in Ohio, and while he had been entranced with the Wrights ever since reading of their work in the early news reports, he had done something equally marvelous by driving his flivver a distance of some 200 miles from his home in Medina, near Akron. He also published a magazine, *Gleanings in Bee Culture*. His presence suited the Wrights' purposes. He could stand as an independent witness to verify their achievements, but *Gleanings* was sufficiently obscure that it would not lead to a flood of inquiries from major newspapers.

The day began amid dark clouds that carried an imminent threat of rain. The rain held off, and Wilbur made his takeoff with help from the catapult. He covered 1,000 feet, approached a barbwire fence, and shifted his body within the hip cradle to initiate the turn. The craft banked, with the left wing dipping while the right wing rose, and Wilbur flew into the wind while keeping his distance from the lone tree that stood amid open ground. However, he was unable to hold his banked position, as the aircraft again seemed to slide outward. He leveled his wings, dipped the one on the right, and changed his turn into an S-shaped curve. Trees again lay ahead, blocking his path, while he lacked the altitude to fly over them. He came down and landed safely. He had not completed his turn, but even so, he had added to the brothers' store of accomplishments. He had topped the one-minute mark, staying aloft longer than the 59 seconds of Kitty Hawk.

He talked about the flight with Orville. In addition to sliding outward, the plane's tail had failed to assist the turn and seemed to have contributed to an instability. Drawing on their experience and their technical knowledge, the brothers tried to come up with a solution, but it eluded them. Heavy rain began to fall, and although they had to hasten to put the craft back in its shed, at least they had more time for discussion. The skies cleared during the afternoon, with the wind coming now from a different direction, and Wilbur mounted his airplane as he prepared to try again.

He began by following the course of the morning flight, heading north toward the fence. As before, he shifted his hips, banked, veered left, and cleared the tree. Perhaps this time the wind direction made the difference; perhaps Wilbur had a better feel for his controls. He continued to turn, proceeding toward the field's southern limit, then succeeded in banking toward the north. He stayed in the air, flew past the shed, took care to cross his takeoff point, and then landed. For the first time, a heavier-than-air machine had flown a complete circle.

Back on the ground, Wilbur explained how he did it. This feat indeed had demanded a sure touch, for the plane had tended to increase its angle of bank as it continued through a curve. Wilbur had countered this with a slight shift of his hip cradle to the right, which held the bank steady without returning to flight with the wings level. A stopwatch showed that he had remained aloft for over a minute and a half. By tracing the course and counting the revolutions as they rolled a wheel of known circumference, they measured the distance: 4,080 feet, nearly three-fourths of a mile.

Amos Root proceeded to write a florid account in *Gleanings*:

Dear friends, I have a wonderful story to tell you—a story that, in some respects, outrivals the Arabian Nights. . . . God in His great mercy has permitted me to be, at least somewhat, instrumental in ushering in and introducing to the great wide world an invention that may outrank electric cars, the automobiles, and all other methods of travel, and one which may fairly take a place beside the telephone and wireless telegraphy. . . .

He explained why the work of the Wrights might be pertinent to beekeepers:

They not only studied nature, but they procured the best books. . . . When I first became acquainted with them, and expressed a wish to read up all there was on the subject, they showed me a library that astonished me. . . . Now let me draw a contrast. During the years that are past, quite a number of men have come to me with their patented hives. A good many of these men had never seen a bee-journal. Some of them who had paid out their hard earnings to the Patent Office had almost never seen a book on bee culture. . . . We have inventors at the present time who are giving their lives and money to the four winds in the same poor foolish way. If you wish to make a success of any thing . . . find out what the great and good men have done in this special line before you.

Root recalled how he had learned to ride a bicycle by practicing in the privacy of a large open room, and noted that the Wrights had conducted their work amid the privacy of Kitty Hawk and Huffman Prairie. Through much effort, the Flyer II "was finally cured of its foolish tricks, and was made to go like a steady old horse," after they had "cured it of bobbing up and down" by adding the iron weights. Root concluded with his eyewitness account:

The operator takes his place lying flat on his face. This position offers less resistance to the wind. The engine is started and got up to speed. The machine is held until ready to start by a sort of trap to be sprung when all is ready; then with a tremendous flapping and snapping of the four-cylinder engine, the huge machine springs aloft. When it first turned that circle, and came near the starting-point, I was right in front of it; and I said then, and I believe still, it was one of the grandest sights, if not the grandest sight, of my life. Imagine a locomotive that has left its track, and is climbing up in the air right toward you—a locomotive without any wheels, we will say, but with white wings instead, we will *further* say—a locomotive made of aluminum. Well, now, imagine this white locomotive, with wings that spread 20 feet each way, coming right toward you with a tremendous flap of its propellers, and you will have something like what I saw. The younger brother bade me move to one side for fear it might come down suddenly; but I tell you friends, the sensation that one feels in such a crisis is something hard to describe. The attendant at one time, when a rope came off that started it, said he was shaking from head to foot as if he had a fit of ague. His shaking was uncalled for, however, for the intrepid manager succeeded in righting up his craft, and she made one of her very best flights.[5]

During the fall of 1905, long flights at Huffman Prairie showed that the Wrights had indeed invented the airplane.

When Root compared the lightweight Flyer to a locomotive, even one of aluminum, he certainly was stretching his point. The simile would better have suited the large aircraft of World War II, four decades later. One of Root's contemporaries was more apt in his description, writing that the airplane's biplane wings looked like a streetcar with its side panels missing. A photo from the summer of 1904 shows clearly that the Wrights' aircraft closely resembled the Flyer of 1903, not only in its wings but in its propellers, sprockets, and twin tail. That photograph was printed in black and white from a glass-plate negative, but it still evokes a bygone time that lives in national memory as an era of innocence. It takes little imagination to think of damp grass underfoot or to appreciate the warm and mellow freshness in the air of a rural morning.

Within that air, the brothers still had much to do. The successful circling flight had demanded a touch that was deft indeed, which showed that the plane's handling qualities continued to call for improvement. As an interim measure, the brothers installed a short length of string to a crossbar beneath the elevator. When the airplane was properly aligned in its flight, pointing straight ahead in the direction of motion, the string streamed rearward. If it executed a sideslip, the string shifted to one side or the other, informing the pilot as he made corrections.

With Wilbur having flown his circle, Orville wanted to try as well, but it took time before he succeeded. For several days he found that even with help from the catapult, he was unable to rise into the air for a flight having any duration. On October 1st he finally flew a smooth curve that covered half a mile. He then flew another such curve and appeared to be well on his way toward completing his circle. He turned toward the south—and at low altitude, flying in ground effect, he saw some cows directly ahead. He gave his craft a little up elevator, eased his way upward, lost the extra lift from ground effect, and came down hard. Instead of duplicating Wilbur's feat, he had little more for his effort than a rough landing.

A dozen subsequent tries brought no success, but two weeks later came a day to remember. Orville indeed flew his circle, though the curve of his flight path was shallower than Wilbur's. Believing that he could turn more tightly, he went up again and fell short of completing his circle by no more than a few feet. Wilbur then took over, setting a new mark as he rounded the field and stayed aloft for more than a mile.

There still was time to enter the St. Louis exposition. Few if any serious competitors had sent in the $250 entry fees to qualify, and officials had responded by extending the deadline for an additional month, to October 31st. The Wrights were still far from achieving the 6-mile length of the course, but this no longer seemed to be out of reach. Indeed, there already had been flights that had terminated not because of problems while airborne, but simply because the plane was running low on gasoline.

But only a day later, on the 15th, the brothers found that they still had lessons to learn. Orville launched into the air and started to turn, quickly observing that the bank of his craft was sharper than he wanted. He shifted his hips to diminish the bank, but the wings failed to respond. Meanwhile, a strong crosswind was blowing under the raised right wing, tending to push it more steeply upward. Facing the prospect of an uncontrolled turn, he applied down elevator and dropped to a landing that was particularly rough. He came down with his nose high and his propellers still whirling. Both of his airscrews struck the ground, with blades splintering and snapping off.

The deadline passed and the Wrights did not send their $250. It was just as well; the fair ran in the red, and officials impounded the prize money—including the $100,000 that had lured Santos-Dumont to cross the Atlantic. November arrived, bringing cooler weather that made the air more dense and enhanced the brothers' ability to fly. On the ninth Wilbur made a flight of 5 minutes, covering over three miles and flying four times around the field. This was as close as the brothers had yet come to truly practical flight, belatedly fulfilling the claim of the *Virginian-Pilot* headline of the previous December. Wilbur found that this prolonged duration brought new problems. He had enough gas to stay up longer, but his motor overheated. In addition, pilot workload brought fatigue, more so because he still had to lie prone to reduce drag.

He later stated that "control of the equilibrium, the vertical steering, the horizontal steering" brought a "strain upon the human system" that "kept the mind and body under continuous stress."

The flights continued as autumn settled in. Three weeks after Wilbur made that 5-minute flight, Orville matched him with one of his own. By then winter was approaching, and the brothers ended their season on December 9th. They had accomplished much, advancing from a nearly complete inability to get off the ground to repeated flights that executed multiple turns around the field and covered miles. They continued to face problems of pitch instability; they had achieved their long flights in part by trimming the balance with an additional 20 pounds of iron, which was not quite the same as finding a fundamental solution. They nevertheless had accumulated a total of 45 minutes in the air, which gave them a good background for the coming year of 1905.

They already were beginning to view their airplane as a product to sell, with governments as their intended customers. Patent protection had remained on their minds; midway through 1904, they won a patent in France. They also attracted attention in Great Britain, which had used balloons for reconnaissance in the recent Boer War in South Africa. The British Balloon Factory had come into existence, a forerunner of the renowned Royal Aircraft Establishment. Officers of the Factory included Lieutenant Colonel John Capper of the Royal Engineers.

In June 1904 the War Office in London arranged for him to attend the aeronautical displays at the St. Louis exposition. He talked with British specialists who knew aviation and learned that Americans who were worth visiting included Octave Chanute and the Wrights. He saw little of interest in St. Louis, but had a long meeting with Chanute in Chicago. Then it was on to Dayton, where the Wrights greeted him on October 24th. He caught them just as they were in the middle of their flights for distance, for while their five-minute three-mile excursions still lay ahead, Wilbur had recently broken the one-mile mark.

Capper asked for a demonstration flight. The brothers demurred, knowing both that such an attempt might not get far off the ground—they still were not able to make good flights at will—and that even if it did, it might disclose secrets of design that they were eager to continue to protect. The brothers nevertheless had photos, which showed that while they had risen no more than a few feet off the ground at Huffman Prairie, they indeed had flown. An impressed Colonel Capper invited them to prepare a written proposal for sale of a flying machine to the British government.

The Wrights let the matter sit for the rest of the year, but they had encountered enough problems in dealing with the Patent Office within their own country, and they appreciated that they needed advice before they could approach an officer of the Crown. Early in January 1905, they visited their congressman, Robert Nevin, at his home in Dayton. Nevin had good cause to meet these constituents, for their father still was a bishop in the United Brethren Church and hence was a man of influence. Moreover, Nevin and the Wrights were all Republicans.

Nevin listened to them with interest and suggested that they use his good offices to seek support from the U.S. Army. He asked them to send a letter to his address on Capitol Hill, presenting all appropriate information. He promised to forward the letter to the Secretary of War, William Howard Taft, who by coincidence was also a Republican from Ohio. Nevin then stated that he could open doors for the Wrights in Washington and could arrange a productive visit.

In the wake of the meeting with Nevin, the Wrights made a mistake. They would have been well advised to have their attorney Henry Toulmin draft the pertinent correspondence, sending it under his letterhead. Instead the brothers relied on their own devices, using stationery of the Wright Cycle Company. On January 10, Wilbur wrote to Colonel Capper in England, stating that flights accomplished following his visit had been "so satisfactory that we now regard the practicability of flying as fully established." They stated that they could provide a vehicle capable of carrying two men at thirty miles per hour for a distance of fifty miles.

A week later, they sent their letter to Congressman Nevin:

The series of aeronautical experiments upon which we have been engaged for the past five years has ended in the production of a flying machine of a type fitted for practical use. It not only flies through the air at high speed, but it also lands without being wrecked. During the year 1904 one hundred and five flights were made at our experimenting station, on the Huffman prairie, east of the city; and though our experience in handling the machine has been too short to give any high degree of skill, we nevertheless succeeded, toward the end of the season, in making two flights of five minutes each, in which we sailed round and round the field until a distance of about three miles had been covered, at a speed of thirty-five miles per hour. The first of these record flights was made on November 9th, in celebration of the phenomenal political victory the preceding day, and the second on December 1st, in honor of the one hundredth flight of the season.

The numerous flights in straight lines, in circles, and over S-shaped courses, in calms and in winds, have made it quite certain that flying has been brought to a point where it can be made of great practical use in various ways, one of which is that of scouting and carrying messages in time of war. If the latter features are of interest to our own government, we shall be pleased to take up the matter either on the basis of providing machines of agreed specification, at a contract price, or of furnishing all the scientific and practical information we have accumulated in these years of experimenting, together with a license to use our patents; thus putting the government in a position to operate on its own account.

If you can find it convenient to ascertain whether this is a subject of interest to our own government, it would oblige us greatly, as early information on this point will aid us in making our own plans for the future.[6]

This was not the sort of missive that was likely to draw serious attention. If five years of work had led to a machine with a range of only three miles, one could just imagine how long it might take before they could offer real performance. Personal support from Congressman Nevin might nevertheless have helped, but he was ill when the letter arrived at his office, and a clerk sent it onward to the War

Department as a matter of routine. It then went to the U.S. Army Board of Ordnance and Fortification.

That military office had put up $50,000 to support Langley's work and had been badly burned by the experience. Federal support for research and development lay well in the future; the Board's allocation had been a one-of-a-kind arrangement, and the money had sunk into the waters of the Potomac. This had drawn a good deal of mockery, not only from newspapers and magazines, but from members of Congress. The Board certainly was not eager to repeat this experience, particularly since Langley's failure had brought a steady stream of similar letters from would-be inventors who were certain that they could succeed, if only the Board would treat them as generously as Langley. Like the Patent Office, the Board therefore adopted the practice of demanding a demonstration of successful powered flight, with anything less leading merely to a form letter of rejection. Such a letter, sent to Nevin for forwarding to the Wrights, went out over the signature of Major General G. L. Gillispie, president of the Board:

> I have the honor to inform you that, as many requests have been made for financial assistance in the development of designs for flying machines, the Board has found it necessary to decline to make allotments for the experimental development of devices for mechanical flight, and has determined that, before suggestions with that object in view will be considered, the device must have been brought to the stage of practical operation without expense to the United States.
>
> It appears from the letter of Messrs. Wilbur and Orville Wright that their machine has not yet been brought to the stage of practical operation, but as soon as it shall have been perfected, this Board would be pleased to receive further representations from them in regard to it.[7]

Clearly, lack of direct help from Nevin had brought the brothers nothing more than a brush-off. They might have won at least a minimal expression of interest if the letter had come from Toulmin, if it had enclosed a photo of their craft in flight, and if they had noted that they had increased the range from a thousand feet to three miles in only three months. As it was, all they had was another lesson in the ways of Washington.

Exchanges with the British were more promising, at least for a time, largely because they had personal support from Colonel Capper. He forwarded Wilbur's letter to his superiors, adding a note requesting "very special attention" and stating, "I have every confidence in their uprightness and in the correctness of their statements. Taking their letter for granted, it is a fact that they have flown and operated a flying machine for a distance of over three miles at a speed of thirty miles per hour."

Capper's immediate manager, Richard Ruck, responded with a letter to the Wrights that invited them to describe the performance of their proposed craft and to state terms for a possible sale. The brothers responded early in March with a long letter that showed a fair amount of thought. "We are ready to enter into a contract with the British Government to construct and deliver to it an aerial scouting machine of the aeroplane type," they declared. They recommended that such a contract "be based upon a single machine and necessary instruction in its use," but added that they were willing "to insert in the contract an option on the purchase of all that we know concerning the subject of aviation." This included the material on methods of control in flight that was covered by their application for a U.S. patent, which had not yet been granted.

They stated that their proposed craft was to carry two men for a distance of at least 50 miles, at a speed in still air of at least 30 miles per hour. The purchase price was to be determined by the maximum distance covered during a series of trial flights, and was to be £500, some $2,500, per mile. If they indeed achieved a range of 50 miles during these test flights, their fee would be $125,000 in American currency, which was more than twice what the Army's Board of Ordnance and Fortifications had spent in support of Langley.

The letter from London, requesting their proposal, had come from the Director of Fortifications and Works. The Wrights' response went to that same official, who was no more prepared to part with such sums than was General Gillispie. He sent the Wrights' letter through channels to the Royal Engineer Committee, which responded during April that the proposed airplane was too uncertain in its prospects to warrant immediate acceptance. However, the Committee decided to try to learn more by sending the British Embassy's military attaché in Washington to witness test flights in Dayton.

In mid-May the Wrights received an official letter from the Assistant to the Secretary of the War Office, advising them to expect to hear from this attaché, Colonel Hubert Foster. With this, matters slowed markedly. Foster was accredited in Mexico City as well as in Washington, and he spent much of 1905 in Mexico. He did not contact the Wrights until November. With their British connection dangling, and with the War Department in Washington having rebuffed them, they could only hope for better fortune in the future.

The return of spring brought a new flying season, and a new airplane. At the outset, the Wrights intended to fly with wings of greater curvature, to take off more readily in light wind. This change by itself would have necessitated a complete rebuilding of the wings, with ribs formed to the new shape. The brothers also wanted to strengthen the framework in its weak spots. In addition, the Flyer of 1904 had accumulated a number of dings and dents during its numerous accidents. Extensive damage, such as broken spars or struts, had brought outright replacement of these structural members, but much of the craft nevertheless was a patchwork of repair. The brothers removed the engine and the chain-and-sprocket drive trains for re-use, but burned what was left. This made room in their shed for the new flying machine.

The flight controls received their first significant modification since 1902. That year, while at Kitty Hawk, the brothers had introduced a movable rudder and had linked it to the wing-warping mechanism. The hip cradle thus turned the rudder as well as warping the wings. The Wrights now disconnected these control surfaces, installing separate hand-operated levers for the rudder and the forward-mounted elevator, while continuing to rely on the hip cradle for wing warping. A pilot's aerial dance now could be intricate indeed, for to get out of a tight situation, he might have to move his hips simultaneously with his left and right arms to work all three of his controls.

The brothers improved the effectiveness of the rudder by mounting "blinkers" on the forward elevator. A horse's blinkers were small slats placed near the eyes, blocking vision to the sides to keep him looking straight ahead. The Wrights' blinkers were semicircular vanes that amounted to a small double vertical rudder, set within the frame of the biplane elevator. They helped to keep the nose pointing in the proper direction during a turn. This gave better control, for the blinkers diminished the danger of having the turn tighten and cause the airplane to plunge to the ground.

It took a month to build the Flyer of 1905, with the work beginning late in May and continuing through much of June. They had left their bicycle business in the hands of Charlie Taylor during earlier flying seasons, but now he too abandoned it as he joined them in the work at Huffman Prairie. His physical strength helped them in manhandling the heavy aircraft onto its launching rail, in hoisting the catapult weights, and in retrieving this airplane by pulling it over rough ground when it landed in the distance. A continuing succession of accidents brought recurring damage, as during 1904, which meant that his skills as a mechanic were useful as well. He indeed spent some time back at the bicycle shop, but mostly it was to use the shop's tools to fabricate new parts as replacements when making repairs.

Because the 1905 Flyer was a new aircraft, it took time for the Wrights to learn how to fly it. They could not simply pick up where they had left off, by repeating the 3-mile circling flights of the previous autumn. Orville made the first attempt of the season, on June 23rd, and failed to achieve flying speed. He lurched briefly into the air, came down with the airplane tilting to the left, and cracked four wing ribs. Wilbur had a similar problem on the next day, for while he indeed reached an altitude of 8 or 9 feet, his craft again banked to the left and came down hard, damaging the wing tip even more severely.

The brothers decided to proceed cautiously and to restore the Flyer more nearly to the configuration of the previous year, by removing the blinkers. They quickly found that with the rudder now operated independently, the problem of control was more difficult than before. Pilot inexperience therefore limited the flights to no more than 700 feet in distance, but worse difficulties lay ahead. Wilbur, working the rudder lever, brushed against the shutoff valve of the engine's fuel supply and cut the power from the motor. He might have glided to a safe landing, but the unexpected distraction led him to make an improper move with the elevator. The vehicle nosed up into a stall and came down hard, again taking a fair amount of damage. Wilbur was unhurt, but once more the craft was down for extensive repair.

This took several days. Rainy weather then set in, turning Huffman Prairie into a marsh. It was mid-July before a combination of good weather and a dryer field permitted resumption of flight. Very quickly the old problem of pitch instability set in again, this time causing the most serious accident that they had experienced in some time.

Orville was at the controls, sailing along on what promised to be that year's first really good flight. Preparing to turn, he began to work the hip cradle and the rudder lever. Suddenly his craft began to bob up and down in its flight, then headed downward. He tried to restore steady flight with his elevator, but it was too late. The airplane hit the ground at higher speed than in previous accidents, sustaining an unusual amount of damage while hurling Orville bodily through a broken section of the top wing. He avoided serious injury, probably because the still-damp field cushioned his impact, but it now was clear that their Flyer would need more than simple repair.

This accident led them to extensive modifications. They enlarged the elevator surface area from 53 to 83 square feet, while moving it forward by 50 inches. This gave the elevator greater control authority, with the longer mount increasing its effectiveness. Rain continued through much of August, again turning their pasture into a shallow lake, and it was August 24th—two months after the first attempt of the season—before they were back in the air.

Very quickly, though, the modified elevator showed its merit. On the first flight of that day, Orville covered more than a quarter-mile. Later that day, Wilbur extended this to nearly a half-mile. On the 28th, he stayed in the air for well over a minute and flew for a measured distance of 4,257 feet, showing that the one-mile mark lay within reach. Nine days later, it was Orville's turn. He started by covering just over 2,000 feet, which would have been a splendid accomplishment only three weeks earlier but now was merely a warmup. On his second flight of the day, he matched the best achievements of the previous year as he remained aloft for nearly 5 minutes, circling the field four times and attaining a range of 3 miles.

During 1904, it had taken months of effort to recognize and address the need for catapulted takeoffs, and to gain skill through practice in flight. The decoupling of the rudder and the wing-warping had given the new Flyer an entirely different set of handling characteristics, which they had to learn anew, while sharply limiting the value of the previous year's experience. During 1905 it again took months to recognize and deal with a key problem, the need for a redesigned elevator, while the long downtimes enforced by weather and by the need for repairs had brought additional delays.

However, the maneuverability of the craft now came to the forefront. A day after making that 3-mile flight, Orville did it again. This was an important step toward a goal of being able to make long flights at will. Those three-mile flights had shown that their Flyer could handle repeated turns. Hence, on the following day Orville flew a figure-eight. It was the first ever flown in a heavier-than-air machine. The new elevator also enhanced safety, for the flights of August and early September proceeded without a serious accident.

The rains returned, forcing another standdown. However, the brothers used this time to good advantage. Because the enlarged elevator had worked so well, they had reason to expect that they would obtain good results if they also made the rudders larger. They therefore increased their surface area from 20 to 35 square feet. Propeller research also drew attention. Their blades were wide and thin, but the performance of these propellers had failed to agree with calculations. The brothers considered that the thin blades might be twisting under the forces of flight. To see if this was true, they fastened vanes called "little jokers" to the rear of the blades, to set up forces that would counteract such distortion. They were right; the little jokers cured the problem. However, they did not keep these attachments as standard equipment. Instead they fabricated new propellers, redesigned to prevent the unwanted twist.

Late in September, both the weather and the Flyer were suitable for a return to flight. Long excursions now were at the top of the agenda, with Wilbur setting the pace on the 26th by making 16 circuits of the field and staying aloft for more than 18 minutes. He would have flown even longer except that he ran out of gas. Two days later it again was Orville's turn. Eight minutes into his own attempt at a record, he flew past the shed and headed toward the lone tree that had become a turning point. He banked left, saw that he was about to head for the tree (which had branches that were full of sharp thorns), and tried to correct his course by shifting the hip cradle to ease toward the right.

The aircraft failed to respond. It continued in a tight turn, still heading for the thorns. Orville saw that his only recourse was to apply down elevator and try to land before the situation became, well, thorny. He pushed the elevator lever to its full down position—and suddenly recovered control! The left wing rose; the craft picked up speed and veered to the right. It did not run full tilt into the tree but merely brushed it, tearing away part of a branch, and Orville saw that he was in the clear. He even saw a decent chance to avoid a sudden landing. He gave the plane full up elevator, skimmed the grass, returned to normal flight, and landed safely in front of the shed. The thorn branch had pierced one of the struts and remained lodged in place, as a souvenir.

As he and Wilbur talked it over, they appreciated that entirely by happenstance, Orville had come upon the solution to another important control problem. They had found during 1904 that when entering a tight turn, the craft sometimes failed to respond to movements of the hip cradle that were meant to bring the wings more nearly level. Instead, the plane increased the bank on its own and made the turn still tighter. As it continued onward it dropped the nose, requiring full up elevator to maintain altitude. The blinkers and the decoupling of rudder and elevator had been attempts to deal with this. The Wrights also made tight turns for practice, trying to find a means to address this issue more effectively, but had made no headway.

They understood that in a tight turn, the craft in effect was pivoting about a center that lay near the inboard wing. With flight speed being only modestly greater than stalling speed, the turning motion caused the inboard wing to advance through the air more slowly, producing less lift. The outer portion of that wing, which was closer to the turning center, might actually stall and lose lift entirely. Meanwhile, the outboard wing was traveling through the air more rapidly and generating still more lift. This imbalance was what had caused the turn to tighten on its own, with the inboard wing dropping farther and the outboard wing rising. The overall effect was to steepen the bank, with the wings generating forces on their own that wing warping could not counter.

With the vehicle banking, the lift of the wings was no longer directed upward, but tilted well toward the turning center. The craft then tended to nose downward because there was less lift in the upward direction, as a consequence of the tilt. With the plane heading toward the ground, it was natural to pull back on the elevator in an attempt to stay in the air. However, during the encounter with the thorn tree, Orville had saved the situation by pushing the elevator downward, rather than up!

How had this helped? The brothers understood that the real problem in a tight turn was lack of overall speed. That was why the inboard wing could lose lift. Orville's brief dive, which he had produced by applying down elevator, had increased the speed—and had made it possible for his left or inboard wing to regain normal lift. The craft now no longer flew within the realm of conditions where wing warping lost effectiveness. With this effectiveness regained, the airplane had responded to Orville's hip movement to the right, and had gone from a steep left bank into a moderate right bank. This increase in speed thus restored overall control, enabling him to fly back to a safe landing.

In addition to winning a good measure of mastery over the troublesome pitch instability, the Wrights now knew what to do in tight turns: push the elevator down to restore flying speed. It went against their instincts, but it was an easy rule to keep in mind, and it solved the last important problem in flight control. Nor did it call for physical modifications to that year's Flyer. The solution was elegant because it called merely for greater skill as a pilot.

During 1904 the Wrights had cultivated Huffman Prairie as if they were farmers, toiling through the spring and summer to reap a harvest of good flights during the fall. They were ready to garner a new bumper crop as a reward for their labors of 1905, and they were willing to invite witnesses. Charlie Taylor had been watching them fly all year; when Wilbur made his 18-minute flight on September 26th, Charlie had tried to keep track of the number of times he circled the field, but admitted that he had lost count. For the new flights, guests included family neighbors, who drove out to Huffman Prairie in their automobile and brought their three-year-old son. For weeks afterward, the young boy ran through his house with arms outstretched, making the sound of its motor.

The brothers were well aware that such witnesses could give them credibility. Among the invitees were tradesmen with whom the Wright family did business, as well as people of standing. The latter included officials of the city of Dayton and of local banks. Torrence Huffman, a bank president, came to see what the brothers were doing within the field that he owned. Orville was the pilot on many of the witnessed flights, while Wilbur kept watch to make sure that no one brought a camera. The brothers remained very cautious concerning disclosures, for they were well aware that a small leak might sink a great ship.

Wilbur's 18-minute flight quickly proved to be merely a prelude to more impressive achievements. A day after Orville's encounter with the thorn tree, he was back in the air and flew for 20 minutes. Again, he would have stayed aloft longer but he ran out of fuel. He flew again on the following day but landed after only 17 minutes. Only a week earlier that would have counted as a record flight, but now it was nothing of the sort, for he had come down while he still had gas in his tank. The rear crankshaft bearing had overheated, forcing him to terminate the flight prematurely.

A larger fuel tank was clearly appropriate, and the brothers installed one with capacity of three gallons. On October 3rd, Orville covered 15 miles in 26 minutes, setting new records, but again the rear bearing became hot and led him to come down early. The faulty bearing was given an oil cup, which helped Orville set new marks of 33 minutes and 20 miles on the following day. Yet this flight fell short as well, for this time the front bearing overheated. It received its own oil cup, and with this, the brothers had every reason to look ahead to a true record.

However, the long flights had taken a toll on Orville as well as on the bearings. He had continued to lie in the standard position: prone, with his head raised and his arms outstretched. He might have been a rifleman shooting from cover, and he found this position to be highly uncomfortable. As he later told the biographer Fred Kelly, "I used to think the back of my neck would break if I endured one more turn around the field." Having done his part to extend the frontiers of flight, he turned the airplane over to Wilbur for the following day of activity.

It began in standard fashion, by hauling the Flyer's wings from the shed, lengthwise. The tail and forward elevator were bolted on, for the shed was too small to hold the complete airplane. Men hoisted heavy weights to the top of the catapult and then pushed the assembled craft, which also was heavy, onto the launching track. Wilbur climbed into the cradle and tested the controls: rudder, elevator, wing warping. Someone approached the engine with an electric coil and attached leads to it; two other men swung the propellers to force the motor to turn over. It came to life with a roar.

The weight fell. Wilbur took off but landed only moments later, for he had failed to gain altitude and had seen a fence immediately ahead. This brought a delay in the action while the Flyer was trundled back to its starting point. Wilbur again took it into the air, gained altitude, and soon showed that this flight indeed was the one to watch. Fifteen minutes passed, twenty, half an hour. Still he remained aloft, executing wide turns and displaying his control by swinging into tight ones. The motor kept on running, working evenly and continuing to produce its welcome sound, while the propellers spun rapidly amid their own swishing. Finally, after thirty circuits of the field—24 miles—Wilbur ran the tank dry. He glided in to a smooth landing, skimming across the grass until he stopped. His time in the air, measured by stopwatch, was just over 38 minutes. His own neck now needed a rest. Still, he had the pleasure of knowing that with only a little more gasoline, this single flight might have lasted longer than the 45 minutes in the air that the brothers had accumulated through the whole of 1904.

This record flight was the last important one of the season, and stood as the culmination of two years of effort near Dayton. At Kitty Hawk in 1903, their airplane had required strong winds to take off, and was so tricky to fly that it needed considerable skill merely to remain aloft for a single minute. The subsequent two years had brought the catapult for reliable takeoffs even in a dead calm. Redesign of the rudder and elevator cured the dangerous pitch instability. Even the engine cooperated, for that faithful old horse of 1904 remained in use through 1905 as well. Its parts wore together so well that its internal friction diminished, enabling it to put out more power as time went along.

During 1903, the Wright brothers had invented a flying machine. By late 1905, they owned something far more valuable: a finished airplane, capable of flying long distances and of staying aloft for considerable durations—and of doing these things day by day as matters of routine. The Wrights also had honed their skills as pilots and now stood ready to teach these skills to others. Having succeeded where Langley failed, they had well and truly invented the airplane. As a consequence, they now faced a different task: to sell it.

EIGHT

INTO THE WORLD

THE WRIGHTS HAD WAYS of dealing with the press. In May 1904, their invited exhibition successfully promoted an impression that they were no more than a couple of local hopefuls with nothing to display. After that, they resorted to hiding in plain sight. Huffman Prairie was not like the secret Air Force test centers of a much later day; it was accessible by trolley. Anyone could visit simply by climbing over a fence. Still, few people had reason to take the trouble; so far as most of them were concerned, it was just another cow pasture. Nearby farmers often saw them in the air but thought little of it. It was only those fellows from town, flying again.

The brothers' acquaintances included Luther Beard, managing editor of the *Dayton Journal*. He taught school in Fairfield, about two miles from Huffman's acres, and sometimes rode with the Wrights on the same streetcar. "I used to chat with them in a friendly way and was always polite to them," he later recalled. "I sort of felt sorry for them. They seemed like well-meaning, decent enough young men. Yet there they were, neglecting their business to waste their time day after day on that ridiculous flying machine. I had an idea that it must worry their father."

Beard nevertheless was aware that someday the brothers might do something interesting, so he stayed in touch. They answered inquiries in a casual fashion and then changed the subject. For instance, in response to one such question, Orville said that yes, they'd made a 5-minute flight just that day, but all they did was go around the field. Beard was well aware that Santos-Dumont had done far more in his airships, and made no attempt to follow it up. It helped the Wrights that at the *Journal,* Beard's boss was Frank Tunison. He had turned down the story of the Kitty Hawk flights, asserting that they had been too short.

Their long flights of September and October 1905, to which they invited witnesses, might have compromised their security. Some of these people might have told their stories to newsmen. Beard himself was a spectator when Wilbur made his flight of 38 minutes on October 5th. He nevertheless found himself scooped, for already on that day the rival *Daily News* ran a story reporting "sensational flights" being made every day. The article stated that "according to reliable witnesses the machine soared gracefully for some 25 minutes, responding to all demands of the rudder." This was a reference to the long flight of two days earlier. The *Cincinnati Post* then ran its own item, and it was not long before other newsmen were making their way to Huffman Prairie. But they found only cows, horses, grass, and trees. The Wrights had closed up their activities for the season.

Even so, they were willing to show something of what they had to professional colleagues, if not to the press at large. They hoped to extend Wilbur's time and distance records by remaining aloft for a full hour, with Chanute as a witness. They invited him to Dayton; he arrived on November 1st, but heavy rain fell and the brothers did not fly. This exchange nevertheless demonstrated that they still were prepared to share their work with others whom they trusted. In mid-November they sent letters to three such men, describing their recent successes.

One went to Britain's Patrick Alexander, an ardent balloonist. He had learned about the Wrights through sources that traced back to Chanute, and had visited them in Dayton as early as December 1902. Alexander later spoke of them to Colonel Capper, giving him a letter of introduction. After receiving the Wrights' newest correspondence, Alexander read it at a meeting in mid-December of the Aeronautical Society in London. This was a novel and significant report for these British aeronauts, but it had no larger consequence.

The Wrights also sent a letter to Carl Dienstbach, the New York correspondent for Germany's *Illustrierte Aeronautische Mitteilungen.* It too had little consequence. It appeared in translation in that magazine's February 1906 issue, but an accompanying editorial cast doubt on the brothers' claims. More than aeronautics was involved, for in a separate letter to France's Ferdinand Ferber, the Wrights had written that the Emperor of Germany was "in a truculent mood." Ferber leaked this letter to *L'Aerophile*; the editor of the *Mitteilungen* then let his readers know that those fellows in Dayton had insulted the nation's beloved Kaiser Wilhelm. Their credibility might be judged accordingly.

Yet while the letters to Alexander and to Dienstbach had little lasting effect, a third letter set off a sequence of events that gave a considerable boost to their credibility. This one went to Georges Besançon, editor of *L'Aerophile.* To achieve early publication, Besançon had it translated for *L'Auto,* a Paris daily for sports fans, where it appeared in the November 30th issue. It raised a considerable stir among such chauvinists as Ernest Archdeacon, who had participated in offering a prize of 50,000 francs, some $10,000, for a closed-circuit flight of a single kilometer. If the Wrights indeed had flown for forty kilometers, as Wilbur claimed he had done on October 5th, then the game was up and France was completely out of the running.

Frank Lahm, a wealthy American in Paris, also read the news. In mid-October he had heard of the Wrights from Patrick Alexander. Lahm was originally from Ohio and had stayed in touch with people back home. He had a brother-in-law, Henry Weaver, who lived in the town of Mansfield. A succession of cablegrams led Weaver to Dayton, where he received a warm welcome. The brothers had dismantled their Flyer of 1905, but Orville could introduce him to witnesses who had seen the flights. These included the farmer Amos Stauffer, who had been working in a cornfield when Wilbur made his long flight of October 5th. "I just kept on shucking corn," he told Weaver, "until I got down to the fence, and the durned thing was still going round. I thought it would never stop."

Particularly telling support for the Wrights came from Charlie Billman, the three-year-old son of neighbors who had taken to running through the house with his arms outstretched. The Billmans were a large family and were friends of the Wrights; nearly all of them had seen the activity at Huffman Prairie. Weaver asked young Charlie, "Son, have you ever seen a flying machine?" The boy responded by doing his imitation as he ran around the room. "I'm about convinced," Weaver laughingly told Orville. "That boy couldn't be a bribed witness." That evening, he sent a cable to Lahm in Paris: "Claims fully verified, results by mail." He followed with a detailed letter describing what he had learned in Dayton.

The Wright letter in *L'Auto* also led Robert Coquelle, one of its correspondents, to make his own journey to Dayton. He had been attending a six-day bicycle race in New York; Ohio was not far away. He soon sent his own cable to Paris: "The Wright brothers refuse to show their machine, but I have interviewed the witnesses, and it is impossible to doubt the success of their experiments." His four-part series, "Conquete de l'Air par Deux Marchands de Cycles," appeared late in December in four daily installments. Coquelle was not above stretching the truth for the sake of a good narrative. The series owed more to his imagination than to his interviews, but it too supported the brothers. Moreover, just to set the record straight, the Wrights responded to a letter from Besançon of *L'Aerophile* by giving further details of their recent flights.

Meanwhile, Weaver had sent his letter to Lahm, who prepared a translation into French and arranged to read it at a meeting of the Aero Club on the evening of December 29th. The gathering was stormy. A handful of members—Lahm, Ferber, Besançon, Coquelle—had the advantage of personal visits to Dayton or of past correspondence with the Wrights, and were prepared to believe their claims. The majority, led by Archdeacon, had not pursued such exchanges and preferred to view them as *bluffeurs.*

These skeptics soon made themselves heard, for members raised a hubbub while Archdeacon rapped a table with a flat metal ruler as he called for order. Why had the Wrights' flights not been covered in American newspapers? They were men of modest means; who had financed them? Why had they shown no interest in the 50,000-franc prize? Lahm repeatedly rose to their defense, arguing particularly that the brothers had paid for the work from their own pockets. Still, he too found it hard to understand the lack of press coverage.

That lack, at least, was about to be redressed. On December 31st, *L'Auto* printed the full text of Weaver's letter to Lahm. It soon appeared as well in the Paris edition of the *New York Herald* and in *Les Sports,* a rival of *L'Auto.* In turn, this continuing coverage in Paris raised questions in New York, home of *Scientific American.* That publication also was linked to the aeronautical grapevine, though only in a fashion. Midway through December it stated, "The most promising results to date were those obtained last year by the Wright brothers, one of whom made a flight of over half a mile in a power-propelled machine." In October, Wilbur had flown to fifty times that distance.

In January 1906, *Scientific American* returned to this topic with an article titled "The Wright Aeroplane and Its Fabled Performances." Citing a letter to Ferber as a source, the magazine accurately summarized the long recent flights—and dismissed them as "alleged experiments." The magazine then wondered out loud how those men of Dayton could have won attention in Paris while bypassing Manhattan:

Unfortunately, the Wright brothers are hardly disposed to publish any substantiation or to make public experiments, for reasons best known to themselves. If such sensational and tremendously important experiments are being conducted in a not very remote part of the country, on a subject in which almost everybody feels the most profound interest, is it possible to believe that the enterprising American reporter, who, it is well known, comes down the chimney when the door is locked in his face—even if he has to scale a fifteen-story sky-scraper to do so—would not have ascertained all about them and published them broadcast long ago?[1]

Scientific American understood that an airplane was not an airship, buoyed by a bag full of hydrogen. Most other newsmen did not. They didn't have to scale a sky-scraper; they merely had to climb the steps of the Wrights' family home. They did no such thing because the view continued to prevail that the brothers were little more than followers of Santos-Dumont, whose flights had been both earlier and longer.

With the Wrights indeed living in a not very remote part of the country, *Scientific American* would have been well advised to check with them before going to press. Instead, that publication followed the all-too-common practice of shooting first and asking questions later. The brothers did not appreciate the notion that their Flyer's performances were "fabled"; the flights had been documented and witnessed. When an editor of that magazine sent a clipping to the Wrights and asked for more information, the brothers responded by referring him back to the press coverage in Paris.

The Wrights had been exchanging correspondence and visits with Chanute since 1900, but he shared their reticence with the press. In 1906, however, there was a technically knowledgeable group in New York called the Aero Club of America. In March 1906 the Wrights sent them a letter that summarized their work. It contained technical detail: "The lengths of the flights were measured by a Richard anemometer which was attached to the machine. The records were found to agree closely with the distances measured over the ground when the flights were made in calm air over a straight course." It included a table summarizing six of the best flights of 1905: date, distance, and time in the air. The letter also listed seventeen witnesses. These included Torrence Huffman, Amos Stauffer, and C. S. Billman, father of young Charlie.

The Aero Club published this letter as a circular, which quickly reached *Scientific American*. Its editor dispatched letters to the witnesses, asking them to describe specifically what they had seen. Eleven of them responded, giving answers that supported the Wrights. The magazine recanted, running a new article on April 7th that left out the word "fabled" as it carried the title, "The Wright Aeroplane and Its Performances." The text now stated, "There is no doubt whatever that these able experimenters deserve the highest credit for having perfected the first flying machine of the heavier-than-air type which has ever flown successfully and at the same time carried a man." The article included a supportive response written by the Wright Cycle Company's landlord. The magazine also reprinted the Wrights' letter to the Aero Club.

A few weeks later, the brothers obtained their U.S. patent, No. 821,393. It had not come easily. Their open flight demonstrations and published correspondence had raised issues of prior disclosure, which could be avoided only by continuing to work within the frame of their initial and somewhat amateurish application of March 1903. This led them to avoid all reference to powered flight. Much delay also resulted because the patent examiner in Washington did not understand how the Wrights' control system was supposed to work. As late as May 1905, well over a year after the attorney Henry Toulmin had taken the Wrights as clients, that examiner held that the application contained "ambiguities, inaccuracies, and imperfections" that were sufficient "to preclude intelligent action upon the merits of the claims." Toulmin responded with a personal meeting with the examiner, which broke the logjam and opened the door to subsequent approval.

The final patent included a diagram of a Wright biplane that lacked an engine or propellers. However, the patent had the subject of "flying machines," which was a choice of words that differed from an alternative, "gliders," and covered powered flight. It contemplated application to trussed biplanes with flexible wings that could be warped. It did not stand as a guide to aircraft construction, presenting diagrams and descriptions that would enable other planebuilders to copy the Flyers of the past three years, as by following directions. Rather, in technical and legal language it presented eighteen claims, with Claim 14 being typical:

A flying-machine comprising superposed connected aeroplanes [wings], means for moving the opposite lateral portions of said aeroplanes to different angles to the normal plane thereof, a vertical rudder, means for moving said vertical rudder toward that side of the machine presenting the smaller angle of incidence and the least resistance to the atmosphere, and a horizontal rudder [elevator] provided with means for presenting its upper or under surface to the resistance of the atmosphere, substantially as described.[2]

The Wrights subsequently asserted that the concept of "opposite lateral portions of aeroplanes" that could be moved "to different angles" applied to ailerons. These rigid movable surfaces, mounted near wingtips, supplanted wing warping and became essential for the control of large aircraft that had rigid rather than flexible wings. In this manner, the Wright patent showed brilliant originality. Though framed in an era when literally no one else properly understood the control of a heavier-than-air machine, it embraced technical advances that the brothers had not initially contemplated. Indeed, it covered many aspects of flight control that are familiar to designers to this day.

Hence, in the spring of 1906 the achievements of the Wrights were recognized at the Patent Office, the Aeronautical Society, and by technically knowledgeable publications in both Paris and New York. Wilbur's presentations to the Western Society of Engineers, delivered through support from Chanute, also had won attention from the engineering profession within the United States. What the brothers lacked was the prospect of making a sale.

They had had further exchanges with the U.S. Army during the previous autumn. Chanute had encouraged them to renew their approach, which they did in a letter to Secretary of War William Howard Taft on October 9, 1905:

Some months ago we made an informal offer to furnish to the War Department practical flying-machines suitable for scouting purposes. The matter was referred to the Board of Ordnance and Fortification, which seems to have given it scant consideration. We do not wish to take this invention abroad, unless we find it necessary to do so, and therefore write again, renewing the offer.

We are prepared to furnish a machine on contract, to be accepted only after field trips in which the conditions of the contract have been fulfilled; the machine is to carry an operator and supplies of fuel, etc., sufficient for a flight of one hundred miles; the price of the machine to be regulated according to a sliding scale based on the performance of the machine in the trial trips; the minimum performance to be a flight of at least twenty-five miles at a speed of not less than thirty miles an hour.

We are also willing to take contracts to build machines carrying more than one man.[3]

Such a letter might have served the brothers if their recent achievements had been widely publicized, and if they already had a close working relationship with the Army that left no doubt as to delivering what they promised. Instead, this letter added nothing to the minimal information they had presented in January. It made no mention of the 24-mile flight of only four days earlier. There were no affidavits from witnesses. Press coverage was still scanty. Within the Wrights' correspondence, the lack of new information made it easy to conclude that they had made no progress since the previous year.

In accordance with standard procedure, the letter went from Secretary Taft's office to the Board. Its formal reply carried the standard first paragraph, but additional text opened a door:

I have the honor to inform you that, as many requests have been made for financial assistance in the development of designs for flying-machines, the Board has found it necessary to decline to make allotments for the experimental development of devices for mechanical flight, and has determined that, before suggestions with that object in view will be considered, the device must have been brought to the stage of practical operation without expense to the United States.

Before the question of making a contract with you for the furnishing of a flying-machine is considered it will be necessary for you to furnish this Board with the approximate cost of the completed machine, the date upon which it would be delivered, and with such drawings and descriptions thereof as are necessary to enable its construction to be understood and a definite conclusion as to its practicability to be arrived at. Upon receipt of this information, the matter will receive the careful consideration of the Board.[4]

The author John Evangelist Walsh notes that an important reason for requesting "drawings and descriptions thereof" was to determine whether the proposed aircraft was delicate and fragile, or was rugged enough for use in the field. However, the Wrights had no such documentation. Like skilled makers of furniture, they had not worked from engineering drawings but from a clear sense of what they wanted to build. Their first three-view drawing of the Flyer of 1903 had been outlined on wallpaper. Even their mechanic Charlie Taylor had fabricated engine parts from nothing more than rough sketches on paper that served their purpose and then were discarded.

This exchange of letters took little more than a week. Very quickly, the Wrights responded and raised the point that truly concerned them:

We have no thought of asking financial assistance from the government. We propose to sell the results of experiments finished at our own expense.

In order that we may submit a proposition conforming as nearly as possible to the ideas of your board, it is desirable that we be informed what conditions you would wish to lay down as to the performance of the machine in the official trials, prior to the acceptance of the machine. We cannot well fix a price, nor a time for delivery, till we have your idea of the qualifications necessary to such a machine. We ought also to know whether you would wish to reserve a monopoly on the use of the invention, or whether you would permit us to accept orders for similar machines from other governments, and give public exhibitions, etc.

Proof of our ability to execute an undertaking of the nature proposed will be furnished whenever desired.

The Board was not free to issue contracts at will, and lost little time in letting the Wrights know it. Previous letters to Dayton had been signed by major generals, but this one came from a mere captain:

> The Board of Ordnance and Fortification at its meeting October 24, 1905, took the following action:
> The Board then considered a letter, dated October 19, 1905, from Wilbur and Orville Wright requesting the requirements prescribed by the Board that a flying-machine would have to fulfill before it would be accepted.
> It is recommended the Messrs. Wright be informed that the Board does not care to formulate any requirement for the performance of a flying-machine or take any further action on the subject until a machine is produced which by actual operation is shown to be able to produce horizontal flight and to carry an operator.[5]

The ball was back in the brothers' court, but they declined to pursue the matter further. They were no closer than before to a sale, but at least the Army had not made mention of seizing their invention or of prohibiting its purchase by other nations. Indeed, further discussions with overseas governments soon were under way.

In England, during that same October, someone noticed that the report on the Wrights from the military attaché Hubert Foster was overdue. Prodded by the home office, he wrote to the Wrights on November 18th and requested a visit. As their exchanges proceeded, Foster and his colleagues quickly learned that the Wrights had some rather peculiar ideas as to how to sell what they were offering.

Two points of view, strongly held and somewhat contradictory, framed the brothers' dealings with the world. The first was that they were so far ahead of potential competitors that they could easily sit back and let people come to them. They made this attitude clear in a letter to Chanute:

> If it were indeed true that others will be flying within a year or two, there would be reason in selling at any price but we are

convinced that no one will be able to develop a practical flyer
within five years. This opinion is based upon cold calculation. It
takes into consideration practical and scientific difficulties whose
existence is unknown to all but ourselves. Even you, Mr. Chanute,
have little idea how difficult the flying problem really is. When we
see men laboring year after year on points we overcame in a few
weeks, without ever getting far enough along to meet the worse
points beyond, we know that their rivalry and competition are not
to be feared.[6]

This attitude shaped their approaches to the Army, which amounted to a bald assertion: "We know how to build a flying machine; come
buy it." It also showed in their reticence when dealing with the press.
They were willing to share their achievements with the technically
knowledgeable: Georges Besançon of *L'Aerophile,* the Aero Club in
New York, and, of course, Chanute. But ordinary newsmen, unable to
tell an airplane from an airship, got the back of the hand.

Yet while the Wrights expected to rest on their laurels, they also
nurtured a strong concern that their lead was fragile. Incautious disclosures might enable competitors to catch up quickly. Therefore, it
was out of the question for the Wrights to conduct exhibition flights
in front of people who knew about airplanes, as distinct from friends
and neighbors. Examination by specialists of the Flyer on the ground
was also out of the question, with even photos being prohibited if they
threatened to show too much detail. The brothers made their legally-
required disclosures within patent applications, and events showed
that these indeed did not compromise their secrets. But that was as far
as they would go.

In dealing with governments, these attitudes put them in the position of an auto salesman who will not allow a buyer to take a test
drive, to kick the tires, or even to see the car. The customer is to commit to a purchase sight unseen, basing his decision entirely on testi-
monial endorsements and on the honesty of the dealer. Moreover, the
Wrights took the view that government officials were only too likely to
steal their innovations, like unscrupulous mechanics building a flying

machine in a barn. The brothers were willing to show photos of a Flyer in the air, taken at a distance, and stood ready to introduce such officials to witnesses such as Torrence Huffman. On this basis, they expected to win a commitment to purchase their wares, including a price and terms for delivery. Then, and only then, would they undertake demonstration flights and permit the customer to take a close look at the product. No money was to change hands until the purchaser agreed that the Wrights were indeed offering what they had promised. However, success in the demonstrations was to trigger full acceptance and execution of the contract.

The Wrights were unwilling to accept that this was not how the world did business. They were sons of Bishop Milton Wright; they had no doubt either as to their own honesty or to their reputation for probity, at least in Dayton. Moreover, their religious background encouraged them to view the wide world as a nest of sin and corruption. It did not readily occur to them that the sinners with whom they hoped to negotiate might take the view that skillful liars and professional con artists were far more common than men who could invent a successful airplane.

Foster's letter reached the Wrights on November 22nd. He wanted to come to Dayton to see a flight. The brothers responded that they had finished their work for the year, but would be glad to have him meet with their witnesses. Foster didn't like that, replying a week later that the War Office in London had numerous eyewitness accounts concerning flying machines, and didn't care for more. He asked again to see a flight; the Wrights refused. He then wrote, "The fact seems to me that the War Office cannot commit itself to negotiations with a view to purchasing unless sure that your invention gives the flight it claims, while you do not wish to show its flight until the War Office has made some arrangement with you. Thus there is a deadlock." Discussions among officials back home produced no resolution, and, early in 1906, the Wrights received official notification that their terms were unacceptable.

By then they were actively pursuing a possible sale to France. Across the Rhine, the Kaiser had indeed been truculent, challenging

French control of Morocco during 1905 and raising the threat of war. If armies were to fight in the African desert for control of that colony, scouting aircraft might help to find the enemy and to carry messages across the trackless wastes. Santos-Dumont had his dirigibles, but they could not be counted on to make headway against desert winds, while the Wrights had already flown at nearly forty miles per hour.

The French sale had its start in a letter to the Wrights from Ferdinand Ferber, sent the previous May. The Morocco crisis had broken out only a few weeks earlier, and Ferber, a captain in the French army, wanted to know if the brothers would sell a powered airplane and on what terms. Here indeed was reason to believe that the world indeed would rush to their door, if only they cared to let it in. They did not reply until October 9th, four days after Wilbur flew for 24 miles, with their letter stating that they indeed could build aircraft that could cover up to four times that distance. In a subsequent exchange, the Dayton planebuilders quoted a price of a million francs, some $200,000.

Events soon showed that amid the pressure of Morocco, the French were willing not only to use that price as a basis for negotiation, but to do business on the Wrights' terms. An emissary, Arnold Fordyce, visited the brothers shortly after Christmas. They introduced him to some of their witnesses; like Henry Weaver, Fordyce came away convinced. He had the authority to negotiate an agreement, and quickly did so.

It was not a contract that bound the parties, but an option. The French were to put up earnest money of $5,000. If they then wished to proceed, they were to do so by placing the rest of the $200,000 into escrow by a deadline of April 5th. If the French indeed did this, the Wrights then would travel to France and make demonstration flights. If these flight tests met French expectations, the option would turn into a contract and would go into force, with the brothers being paid in full.

The $5,000 went into a New York bank early in February. Six weeks later, a group of French commissioners came to Dayton to discuss arrangements for the test flights. In addition to Fordyce, its members included the French military attaché in Washington as well as the French ambassador's attorney. The Wrights did not fly for them, but the visitors saw photos and interviewed witnesses, who left them persuaded as well. The leader of the group, Henri Bonel, headed the army's corps of engineers and was a member of the General Staff. He had come in a spirit of skepticism, but now he not only became a believer, he was enthusiastic.

Back in Europe, however, the war clouds were dissipating. An international commission, meeting at Algeciras in Spain, had undertaken to resolve the Moroccan issue through diplomacy and was about to agree to give France a free hand. In Paris, this greatly lessened the urgency of having to deal with the *Americains* in Ohio. The contract had been negotiated but was not yet in force, and at the Ministry of War, officials considered that they could cancel the deal by asking the Wrights for greater performance. They particularly wanted an altitude of a thousand feet, to avoid enemy fire, at a time when Wilbur and Orville had rarely flown much higher than a hundred feet.

By presenting the brothers with demands for more than they could deliver, the War Ministry succeeded in wriggling out of the agreement. The prospect of $200,000 went glimmering. Still there was that $5,000 being held in escrow, and it indeed went to the Wrights as a consolation prize for their trouble. Here was a new lesson in the working of governments. For the first time, the brothers had made money from their invention. That sum was more than enough to cover all their expenses since 1899, but in the words of the biographer Fred Howard, the brothers earned this money "not by selling, but by not selling a flying machine."

As the French connection faded, the prospect of a British arrangement flickered anew. Their old friend Patrick Alexander came to Dayton late in April, giving them reason to believe that His Majesty's Government might be amenable to a new approach. A letter to the War Office, early in May, launched a new round of exchanges. Late in July these led the brothers to write to a new military attaché in Washington—Lieutenant Colonel Edward Gleichen, who had succeeded Colonel Foster—and to invite him to Dayton. Gleichen arrived a week later. He too came away impressed, describing the Wrights as "intelligent looking, not 'cranks,' apparently honest—their venerable father being a bishop of some hazy denomination—and with little or none of the usual braggadocio of the Yankee inventor." Again they wanted

$200,000, for which they were prepared to sell an airplane, patent rights, along with exclusive use of "knowledge and discoveries together with formulae and tables which make the designing of flyers of other sizes and speeds a science as exact as that of marine engineering."

Their old friend Colonel Capper also was very much in the picture and remained confident that the Wrights could deliver what they were promising. Moreover, he had recently won a promotion and now headed the British Balloon Factory. In this position, he was authorized to participate in all decisions affecting the development of British aeronautics. However, he had lately become convinced that there was no need to purchase rights or flying machines from Dayton. He now was directing a heavier-than-air program of his own, and took the view that British inventors could solve the problem of flight through their own ingenuity. They did no such thing; the focus of his hopes, Lieutenant John Dunne, built a glider that Capper himself tried to pilot, only to crash it into a stone wall. But just then, in 1906, Capper's reluctance to work with the Wrights spelled doom for their latest attempt. He advised the War Office not to respond to their offer, arguing not only that the price was too high but that Dunne was likely to come up with a heavier-than-air machine that was equally capable. Wilbur and Orville learned the bad news in December.

The Wrights now had gone zero for five in their approaches, thus gaining the dubious distinction of failing to score with governments in Washington, London, and Paris. The French opportunity had been particularly promising, but it did not escape attention that this country's interested parties were to place $200,000 in escrow to purchase not merely a flying machine, a questionable invention indeed, but one that no Frenchman had ever seen. The British took a similar attitude: In comparing the unseen from America with the nonexistent at home, the latter easily won preference.

As these failures multiplied, the Wrights added a prickly defensiveness to their inexperience. This brought quick death to a potentially promising initiative that had the support of Senator Henry Cabot Lodge. It stemmed not from the brothers but from a wealthy Bostonian, Godfrey Lowell Cabot, whose very name made him a

Brahmin of the first order. He had learned of the Wrights as early as December 1903 from the press coverage. Early in 1906 he read the Aero Club bulletin that reported the flights of the previous fall, which sparked his interest anew.

He wrote to the brothers in April, inviting them to send him a prospectus if they wished to set up a company. They responded a month later with the sad tale of their dealings with the War Department. Senator Lodge was Cabot's relative; Cabot wrote to him to plead the cause of the Wrights. Lodge added a cover letter and sent it along with Cabot's to Secretary of War Taft, who again forwarded this correspondence to the same Board that had conducted the previous exchanges. Its president, Brigadier General William Crozier, responded to Lodge that "if those in control of the flying-machine invented by the Wright brothers will place themselves in communication with the Board of Ordnance and Fortification, War Department, Washington, D.C., any proposition that they may have to make will be given consideration by the Board."

This response was sufficiently encouraging to bring Cabot to Washington on a personal visit. He met with General Crozier, showing him the Aero Club publication that described the flights to distances as great as 24 miles. Here was strong evidence that the Wrights indeed had not only succeeded but had accomplished more than they had disclosed to the Board in their own letters. Crozier responded by advising Cabot that he and his colleagues would welcome a new letter from Dayton, and might even send an emissary to that city.

Cabot reported these events to Wilbur and Orville, who replied to him with something less than eager readiness:

> If General Crozier should decide to send a representative to Dayton we would be glad to furnish him convincing proof that a machine has been produced which by actual operation has been shown to be able to produce horizontal flight and to carry an operator.
>
> We are ready to negotiate whenever the Board is ready, but as the former correspondence closed with a strong intimation that the Board did not wish to be bothered with our offers, we naturally have no intention of taking the initiative again.[7]

The Board, after all, had committed the unpardonable sin of asking the brothers for detailed information, including—gasp!—the observation of actual *flights*! The Wrights thus responded to an initiative from the Board itself by claiming to be hurt and offended because the Army had not hastened to accept their unsupported words. (In their innocence, they may not have known that exaggerated sensitivity in response to demands for proof—"what, don't you trust me?"—is a ploy widely used by professional scam artists.) Crozier did not send a man to Dayton. The initiative died by the Wrights' own hand.

At the end of 1906, the letter of rejection from the British War Office amounted to an unwelcome Christmas gift within a year that had largely been wasted. The brothers had built no new airplane. The 1905 Flyer remained safely crated and ready for further adventures, but had made no flights since the fall of that year. None of the brothers' contacts had panned out, while such promising potential supporters as Godfrey Lowell Cabot had slipped through their fingers. In addition, while they were busily clutching their secrets to their bosoms, Alberto Santos-Dumont had been active in France.

During 1906 he built an airplane that newsmen called the Bird of Prey. He crafted its wings with plenty of dihedral, for stability in roll. Those wings resembled large boxkites. A single boxkite, set well forward at the end of a long fuselage, could be tilted up or down to serve as an elevator. It also could swing from side to side to act perhaps as a rudder. The fuselage made it look like a duck or goose in flight with its neck thrust forward. People called this arrangement a *canard*, which translates as both "duck" and "hoax."

He first tested it late in August, within the Bois de Boulogne. It hopped briefly into the air but proved to lack power and broke its propeller when it landed. Santos-Dumont replaced its 24-horsepower motor with one of 50 horsepower, and tried again three weeks later. Trailing smoke, it stayed airborne for less distance than its length, then once more broke its propeller while collapsing his undercarriage. His next attempt came on October 23rd. He began with trial runs, in which a propeller blade flew off and a landing wheel came loose. Then—success! What was more, he did it in public.

Ferdinand Ferber was on the scene as an observer. "At 4:45 in the afternoon, his airplane left the ground smoothly and without a shock," he wrote. "The crowd watched, spellbound, as though witnessing a miracle; it remained mute with astonishment, but immediately afterward, at the moment of landing, gave vent to a roar of enthusiasm and carried the aviator shoulder high in triumph." Once again the landing gear collapsed and the propeller shattered, but the man had *flown*.

Initial details in the press were confusing, but Chanute wrote to Wilbur, "I fancy that he is now very nearly where you were in 1904." Wilbur replied, "This report gives such an excellent opportunity for exercising our powers as prophets that I cannot resist making a forecast before the details arrive. From our knowledge of the degree of progress that Santos has attained, we predict that his flight covered less than 1/10 of a kilometer. If he has gone more than 300 feet, he has really done something; less than this is nothing." The actual distance came to no more than two hundred feet. Chanute conceded the Wrights' continuing advantage, admitting that "Santos is not now as far along as you were in 1903."

But the dapper little Brazilian added new surfaces to his wings to redress a loss of balance in flight, and was ready for more on November 12th. A *New York Herald* reporter wrote of "a vast hush as the motor began to turn, and then a shout of satisfaction as the Bird of Prey bounded off like a flash and was tearing through the air at nearly forty kilometers per hour." The wheels collapsed again on landing, as usual, but that didn't matter. He had stayed in the air for over twenty seconds while covering 726 feet.

The Wrights had published their letters in Paris newspapers, supported by the one from Henry Weaver to Frank Lahm, but no one had seen them fly and nothing new had been heard of them in nearly a year. As far as anyone could see by direct observation, the airplane was indeed being invented in France, home of the Montgolfiers, and by everyone's favorite aviator. Wilbur himself was impressed, calling this flight "the first real indication of progress that has been displayed in France in five years."

It drew press coverage from many newspapers in addition to the *Herald,* with some of the writers adding comments about the Wrights. The readers of these articles included one Ulysses Eddy, a New York businessman who specialized in putting deals together. He took a train to Dayton, met the brothers, found himself impressed, and came away convinced that he could play an important role in helping them to arrange a sale.

Eddy had close ties to Charles Flint, who had worked with Hiram Maxim decades earlier and now was one of America's leading financiers. Flint's personal circle included the Rothschilds and J. P. Morgan, who had founded U.S. Steel. President Theodore Roosevelt was another of Flint's acquaintances; he also had met Octave Chanute. He was one of the world's top merchants in the international arms trade, having purchased ships for Japan and Russia while selling an entire squadron to Brazil. He also had established a number of companies of substantial size, including United States Rubber.

Eddy's initial meeting with the Wrights took place on November 30th. His visit raised new hope, with Wilbur writing, "It seems the favorable conditions we have been awaiting for six months have now arrived." The brothers departed for New York a few days later, having planned for some time to attend an exhibition sponsored by the Aero Club of America. *Scientific American* added further hope with its own coverage of that show, running an item, "Genesis of the First Successful Aeroplane." "In all the history of invention," the magazine declared, "there is probably no parallel to the unostentatious manner in which the Wright brothers, of Dayton, Ohio, ushered into the world their epoch-making invention of the first successful aeroplane flying machine."

The meeting at Flint and Company went well. Charles Flint himself was out of town, but Eddy had arranged for them to meet one of his senior associates, who agreed that a deal was well worth pursuing. Flint himself returned a few days later and summoned the brothers to return to Manhattan for further discussion, with his telegram arriving in Dayton on the auspicious date of December 17th. Orville made the trip alone, thereby assuring that nothing definite could be decided immediately, and heard Flint suggest a price of $500,000 for all overseas rights. This was by far the largest sum they had ever heard mentioned to that date, and brought an encouraging note at the end of a year in which such moments of hope had been all too few.

The new year of 1907 brought new negotiations, with both brothers traveling again to New York in January. The parties now agreed that half a million was not enough; the Wrights' invention potentially would be worth millions. Flint now proposed that his company would serve as the Wrights' business agent in Europe, covering all expenses while taking a hefty commission: 20 percent on all transactions up to $500,000 and 40 percent thereafter. This was close to what the brothers were willing to accept, more so because it left them free to continue to hold all sales rights in the United States. Flint and the Wrights did not wrap up the deal at that meeting, but Flint's new terms gave a good basis for the discussions that ensued.

During their visits to Manhattan, the brothers developed an acquaintance with Cortlandt Bishop, president of the Aero Club. While Wilbur was in New York in March, Bishop introduced him to a brother-in-law, Congressman Herbert Parsons, who was a Republican and hence was in a position to get things done. Parsons listened with interest as Wilbur told of the brothers' dealings with the U.S. Army, and came away believing that he could help. Early in April he wrote to them in Dayton, requesting copies of their correspondence during 1905 with the Board of Ordnance and Fortification. He put together a collection of news articles that included some of the coverage in *Scientific American,* and sent it over to the White House. Roosevelt himself read it and sent this material to Secretary Taft with a note that recommended action. Taft added a note of his own and sent the package, as usual, to the Board. This brought a letter from the Board to the Wrights, dated May 11th, and signed this time by a major:

> I am directed by the President of the Board to enclose copies
> of two letters referring to your aeroplane, for your information,
> and to say that the Board has before it several propositions for
> the construction and test of aeroplanes, and if you desire to take

any action in the matter, will be glad to hear from you on the subject.[8]

This was not quite the same as the provisional offers from Flint, but the "copies of two letters" came from Roosevelt and from Taft, indicating possible interest at levels far higher than they had dealt with to date.

This letter arrived a day after the brothers received a cable from Flint. He had a senior agent in Europe, Hart Berg, who held responsibility for overseas negotiations but was skeptical of the Wrights' claims and wanted to talk with one of them before proceeding further. Flint now invited Wilbur or Orville to travel to Europe, at his expense, to meet with Berg and to strengthen the groundwork.

Just then, in Dayton, the brothers were at work on a new airplane and a new engine. With their activities ramifying, for the first time each of them was to take separate responsibility, and Wilbur elected to make the overseas trip. He embarked for Liverpool on the Cunard liner *Carmania,* taking a week for the crossing, then took a train to London's Euston Station. Berg was there to greet him. "I knew him the minute he stepped from the train," Berg later recalled. "To begin with, it is always easy to spot an American among Englishmen, and I saw no other American coming down the platform. There was a modest self-assuredness about him that tallied with his character as I had heard about it." Wilbur had brought only a single suitcase, expecting to stay no more than a week or two, but Berg knew that he would be in Europe for months. Berg therefore took him to a tailor on the Strand and had him measured for a dinner jacket and dress suit.

In Dayton, Orville took on the task of responding to the War Department letter and initiating negotiations. He settled on a price of $100,000 for the first airplane, half what the French had offered but twice what the Board had given to Langley. Exchanges of letters ensued, with Orville preparing his offer as a formal proposal. This was more money than the Board could dispense, and, during June, Orville learned that this sum could not be obtained until appropriated by Congress during its next session. This was a polite way of inviting

Orville to cut his request, but he declined to do this, and the matter was left to languish. One more approach to the Board appeared to have ended with the Wrights still dangling.

In Paris, Wilbur and Berg quickly won support from Henri Deutsch de la Meurthe, a wealthy industrialist who had made a fortune in oil and who had a strong interest in aviation. Deutsch soon made it clear that he was ready to take the lead in setting up a company based on the work of the Wrights. Seeking military support, he met with the Minister of War, General Georges Picquart. Picquart spoke with Commandant Henri Bonel, who had headed the commission that visited Dayton during 1906. Bonel's reports had supported the Wrights. His work now left Picquart persuaded that the Ministry indeed could do business with Deutsch, whose new company could provide airplanes for purchase by the army. For Wilbur, bright success again appeared imminent.

But Bonel had also worked closely with Arnold Fordyce, who was secretary to another wealthy man, Henri Letellier. Letellier had served as a broker during the 1906 negotiations with the Ministry. Now, as he learned about Deutsch's new initiative, he became highly displeased at being left out. Nor did he enjoy thinking that Deutsch might succeed where he had failed. He lost little time in finding his own way to Picquart. His aeronautical arrangements had collapsed over a year earlier and no longer held legal force, but Picquart was a political appointee, while Letellier's family owned one of Paris's major newspapers. Purchase of flying machines was likely to prove controversial even in the best circumstances, more so if ridiculed in the press. Picquart decided that the safe way to proceed was to reaffirm Letellier's rights as a broker, and to decline any further approaches from Deutsch.

Deutsch didn't like that, especially because he viewed Letellier as a rival. He also was well aware that Letellier's rights had lapsed, leaving him with no further standing to speak for Wilbur and Orville at the Ministry. Deutsch concluded that he was being treated badly in the present matter and dropped it in a huff. This was bad, for events soon showed that no one else—in particular, not Letellier—had the clout to take Deutsch's place. Letellier could approach Picquart, but that was not the same thing as setting up a company and closing a deal. With this, Wilbur too was left dangling.

He went to plenty of meetings, but none of them resulted in signatures on the bottom line of a contract. He tried to play the American tourist in Paris, but his souring mood made it difficult for him to take pleasure from the sights. As a boy, he had read Victor Hugo's *Hunchback of Notre Dame*. Now he remarked in a letter to Katharine that the cathedral "was rather disappointing as most sights are to me. The nave is seemingly not much wider than a store room and the windows of the clerestory are so awfully high up that the building is very dark." He visited the Louvre and saw the world-renowned art but complained, "The Mona Lisa is no better than the prints in black and white."

Even aviation failed to give enchantment. He saw a Lebaudy airship in flight, a behemoth with length of two hundred feet that made people stop where they were and look upward. His main impression was that it would lose headway in even a mild wind. He joined three other men and rode in a balloon, reaching an altitude of three thousand feet, which gave him far more of a view than he had ever before enjoyed. Still he wrote that "a few glorious hours in the air are usually followed by a tiresome walk to some village, an uncomfortable night at a poor hotel, and a return home by slow local trains."

He nevertheless showed that he was no innocent abroad. He still wanted a million francs for a sale to the army, the same price as during the previous year, and found himself dealing with one of Letellier's political associates. That worthy wanted an additional quarter of a million as a commission—that is, a bribe. Wilbur coolly responded that the price could indeed be revised upward—provided that the contract named the person to receive the additional sum, and specified his services.

In Dayton, Orville was ready with the first of the new models of 1907. In design it closely resembled the successful Flyer of two years earlier, but it mounted a more powerful motor. In addition, it now allowed the pilot to ride in a seat rather than lie prone, thus avoiding the painful discomforts of that position. The controls had been modified accordingly, while the extra power served in part to overcome the drag of the pilot.

Wilbur tried to keep his brother informed concerning progress and its lack, but this proved difficult. Exchanges of mailed letters took as much as three weeks, far too long for the sudden if evanescent flashes of hope that reappeared from time to time. Cable service was considerably faster, but such messages were necessarily very cursory, and at times were so cryptic as to be confusing. Clearly, Orville had excellent reason to come to Europe and join the discussions. He reached Paris late in July.

He brought one of his new Flyers, with its parts stored in crates, in hope that negotiations might reach a point where demonstration flights would be appropriate. Therefore their mechanic, Charlie Taylor, came as well, arriving two weeks after Orville. This could have easily led to a public display of the Wrights' aerial prowess, which would have produced a sensation. Santos-Dumont had not repeated his long flight of the previous November, while no other European aviator was anywhere close. The Wrights would have made headlines merely by taking off, to say nothing of their ability to stay in the air for as much as an hour and to maneuver at will. Such exhibitions would have stirred excitement, sharply improving the prospects for a deal. They also could have placed Charles Flint in a position to make sales to Germany as well as France, and to play these bitter enemies against each other, for the Wrights had been holding discussions in Berlin as well as Paris. These things did not happen. Wilbur and Orville remained intent on preserving the security of their secrets, and the Flyer remained in crates within a customs shed at Le Havre.

The endless meetings nevertheless gave the brothers excellent opportunities to talk to members of the Paris aeronautical community. These included Ferdinand Ferber, Georges Besançon, the Count de La Vaulx, Frank Lahm, Gabriel Voisin, who had worked with Santos-Dumont, and Robert Esnault-Pelterie, who had experimented with gliders. Lahm's son had recently graduated from West Point, and showed his own support by writing a letter to his commanding general. Nevertheless, not everyone agreed that the Wrights even were in the game, with Ernest Archdeacon remaining as a leader of the skeptics. Even after meeting Wilbur, he wrote that their claimed distance record of 24 miles "will, I am sure, be beaten by us" before the brothers "will have decided to show their phantom machine."

Yet by mid-1907, it was quite evident that the age of powered flight was at hand. Santos-Dumont, if not Wilbur and Orville, had already made this clear for all to see. Even so, no observer could truly overlook the brothers from Dayton, for their work had garnered plaudits from both *Scientific American* and the Aero Club of America. Further advances appeared close at hand, for the Aero Club exhibition in New York, early that year, had emphasized displays of engines suitable for use in aviation.

Important new developments also were under way in the realm of dirigibles. In France, Santos-Dumont and the Lebaudy brothers had remained active, while there was stirring in Germany as well. Count Ferdinand von Zeppelin had failed in 1900 with his LZ-1 and then took five years before failing again with the LZ-2, which made only one flight before being wrecked in a storm. But his LZ-3 of 1906 gained full success, vindicating his belief that enormous size would be a key feature of proper design. It carried eleven people for over two hours on its first flight, and flew again the following day. A flight for distance during 1907 covered 220 miles and lasted eight hours. The LZ-3 also carried the German crown prince, son of Kaiser Wilhelm, as a passenger. General Helmuth von Moltke, chief of the General Staff, declared that such an airship could be superior to anything built by the French.

Within the U.S. Army, the Signal Corps had handled a highly limited involvement with observation balloons that dated to the Civil War. On August 1st, an Aeronautical Division came into existence within that organization. During the subsequent four decades it grew into the Army Air Service, the Army Air Corps, the Army Air Forces, and then the United States Air Force. Still, as early as 1907, the advent of this new division greatly strengthened the prospect that the Army indeed would begin to acquire its own airplanes. The Board of Ordnance and Fortification continued to hold responsibility for procurement of such aircraft. The Chief Signal Officer, Brigadier General James Allen, was a member of this group. Hence the Signal Corps was directly involved in its deliberations.

Its last letter to the Wrights had gone out on June 8th, raising questions concerning terms of their offer and noting that a congressional appropriation would be needed to meet their price of $100,000. The brothers had responded a week later, answering the questions. The matter then rested for several months, until taken up again at a meeting of the Board on October 3rd. Two days later, a new letter went out to Wilbur and Orville, again stating a need for congressional action. However, it raised no further concerns, and invited them to meet with Army officials. Just then Orville was in Paris while Wilbur was in Germany. The letter made its way overseas via Dayton, and did not reach Orville until late in the month. He replied by mail on October 30th, stating that he and Wilbur were prepared to be forthcoming in order to reach an agreement, and that one of them was ready to return immediately for a meeting in Washington.

Soon after, Wilbur decided that there was little further reason to remain in Europe. He embarked for New York on November 14th with Charlie Taylor in tow, leaving Orville in France to wrap up some arrangements concerning engines. Arriving eight days later in Manhattan, Wilbur checked in at the offices of Charles Flint and then caught a train for Washington. He needn't have hurried; it was Friday and the weather was rainy, leaving him once more to spend a weekend in a hotel with little to do. On Monday he went to the War Department, a block from the White House on Pennsylvania Avenue, which was in today's Old Executive Office Building along with the State and Navy departments.

He and Orville had decided to cut their asking price from $100,000 to $25,000. He met with two brigadier generals, William Crozier and James Allen, and learned that the Army indeed was ready to show a serious interest. The issue of price soon arose, with even $25,000 being high enough to demand a congressional appropriation, and this could not be in hand at least until March. The full Board met on December 5th, with Wilbur again making an appearance, but again he came away with no reason to believe that action was imminent. However, the Board had a small fund left over from the Spanish-American War, nearly a decade earlier, which sufficed to yield the full $25,000. After two years of effort on two continents, the Wrights finally had a customer.

This still was not quite the same as a sale, for the Army was barred by law from simply purchasing one of their airplanes. Instead it was necessary to seek competitive bids. On December 23, General Allen issued a solicitation titled "Advertisement and Specification for a Heavier-Than-Air Flying Machine." This document, Signal Corps Specification No. 486, called for a two-seater airplane that could serve as a trainer with a pilot and student, or as a reconnaissance aircraft carrying an observer.

The flying machine was to be "supported entirely by the dynamic reaction of the atmosphere and having no gas bag." It was to be "quickly and easily assembled and taken apart and packed for transportation in army wagons" while being capable of operation "in any country which may be encountered in field service." A range of 125 miles was required, along with "a speed of at least forty miles per hour in still air." The vehicle was to make a demonstration flight "of at least one hour during which time the flying machine must remain continuously in the air without landing. It shall return to the starting point and land without any damage that would prevent it immediately starting another flight. During this trial flight of one hour it must be steered in all directions without difficulty and at all times under perfect control and equilibrium."[9]

Sealed bids were due by February 1, 1908. The Wrights put theirs in at $25,000—and found that they were being underbid by the ever-present Augustus Herring, who quoted a price of $20,000. He hoped to take a fee for his professional services and subcontract construction of his airplane to the Wrights. The Army went through the motion of accepting his bid, for he had to fly his craft before he could receive money, but accepted the Wright proposal as well. On February 10th the Signal Corps issued a form to be sent to Wilbur and Orville. It carried the words they wanted: "I am directed by the Chief Signal Officer of the Army to place order with you for the articles listed below. . . ." The document continued:

ITEM:
One (1) heavier-than-air flying machine, in accordance with Signal Corps Specification No. 486, dated December 23, 1907, at $25,000.00————————————————$25,000.00

Meanwhile, French aviators were beginning to show that they too knew how to fly. Late in 1906 Gabriel Voisin set out to build airplanes, brought in his brother Charles as a partner, and offered to take orders from paying customers. The first of them was Leon Delagrange, a Parisian artist and sculptor. Next came Henri Farman, who was widely known as a racer of bicycles and automobiles. He soon showed similar talent in the air, for on October 15, 1907 he covered nearly a thousand feet, breaking Santos-Dumont's record that had stood for almost a year. Later that month Farman did it again, flying for 2,350 feet. Delagrange made his own mark in November, at half a kilometer.

Farman took it from there. He set out to win a prize of fifty thousand francs, $10,000, for being the first to fly a full circle while achieving a range of a full kilometer, 3,280 feet. As early as 1904 that would have been little more than a warmup for the Wrights, but they were not about to fly publicly and compromise their secrets for so trifling a sum. Farman made his try three years later, on November 18. He covered a kilometer and a half and came close to success, but the judges ruled that he had fallen short of completing the circuit and that his wheels had touched the ground during the flight. No matter; he tried again in mid-January, and this time his minute and a half in the air enabled him to gain the prize. With the name of Farman in every newspaper, Paris had a new idol.

The War Ministry had continued to drag its feet, but Farman's enormous public adulation made it clear that plenty of other sportsmen were likely to fly as well. Only a few weeks later, word came from

Washington that the U.S. Army had ordered a Wright airplane with far greater range. Hart Berg, still representing Flint, had tried without success to win his own military order, but now turned to the civilian market. Deutsch de la Meurthe returned to the fold, though not as the lead investor. That position went to Lazare Weiller, another wealthy man who controlled the taxicabs of Paris. Along with additional capitalists, they organized the Compagnie Generale de Navigation Aerienne. Its business plan envisioned purchase of the Wrights' French patents and manufacture of their designs under license. Wilbur and Orville were to receive half a million francs on delivery of their first airplane, along with 20,000 francs for each of four subsequent deliveries. They also would get half of the founders' shares in the new firm.

Since their initial meeting with Congressman Nevin three years earlier, the brothers had endured a succession of please-go-aways from the Army along with outright rebuffs from France. Now, within a brief and dazzling season, the rising promise of aviation had given weight to their words and had brought sales in both nations. The Washington order was less lucrative, but was likely to lead to others. Flight demonstrations now lay ahead on both sides of the Atlantic. For the first time since 1905, the Wrights could return to the trade of building and flying airplanes.

They had not flown since that year, and knew that it was wise not only to refresh their skills but to practice with the new controls that had been adapted for use with upright seating. They still hoped to protect their privacy, which meant that Huffman Prairie was out. As a test site, it now was a little too public. However, the Outer Banks still had the good breezes that had attracted them in days when their world was young, and still was difficult for newsmen to reach. The brothers therefore decided to return to Kitty Hawk.

This proved to be no exercise in nostalgia, for there was too much work. Wilbur went on ahead to prepare the camp, arriving in Elizabeth City early in April. He quickly ran into John Daniels, who had taken the famous photo of the first flight in 1903, and learned that the storms of several seasons had reduced their old wooden buildings to ruins. Wilbur had purchased lumber in Norfolk; now he bought more, along with a barrel of gasoline, and waited for transportation. His old friend Captain Frank Midgett arrived in a motor-powered launch, while Midgett's son came along in the family's old sailboat *Lou Willis*. Construction work followed, but the weather was unhealthful and Wilbur caught an illness that left him sick with diarrhea.

Orville came from Dayton, bringing the airplane. It was the Flyer of 1905, modified with upright seats and new controls. Newsmen followed as well, soon showing that they had lost nothing in their talent for imagination. The first flights covered about a thousand feet, but the *Virginian-Pilot,* which had reported a three-mile flight in December 1903, now wrote of a sensational ten-mile excursion over the Atlantic.

More newsmen found their way to the dunes; the Wrights ignored them. A mechanic from Dayton also arrived, a friend of Charlie Taylor named Charles Furnas, who made himself useful as a passenger in early two-man flights. The brothers advanced by stages to flights of several minutes, and again the soft sand served them well. One day Wilbur pushed the elevator control forward when he meant to pull it back. Flying with a tailwind, his craft went into the ground at 50 miles per hour. He came away dazed and bruised, but with no serious injury.

In mid-May an urgent telegram came from Flint and Company, declaring that one of the brothers must leave for France promptly. Wilbur elected to go, leaving Orville to remain in the States and to prepare for demonstration flights of the Army's airplane. Wilbur traveled directly from the Outer Banks to New York and embarked for Le Havre on May 21st. It was a season when the achievements of French aviators were advancing triumphantly.

During the spring and early summer of 1908, Delagrange and Farman took turns in pushing European records for time and distance to Wright-like levels. The game began on March 21st, when Farman covered two kilometers in three and a half minutes. Delagrange doubled these marks three weeks later, then decamped to Rome and remained in the air for over fifteen minutes, performing for a crowd that included the king and queen of Italy. Late in June he topped this performance as well, but Farman by then was ready for a comeback. On July

6th he pushed the record for duration to just over 20 minutes. This represented a sixtyfold improvement on the record set by Santos-Dumont in November 1906, barely a year and a half earlier.

A Wright airplane had spent much of that time packed in crates at Le Havre, and the stakes for its success now had risen sharply. In mid-1907 it would have stirred excitement merely by getting into the air. Now, with Farman and Delagrange chasing each other furiously, even the best demonstrated performances, such as the 38-minute flight of October 1905, might appear merely as yesterday's news if those men of France could only stay up a bit longer.

Yet in important respects, the Voisin biplanes flown by those champions were aircraft of the past, while the Wright designs point-ed to the future. Gabriel and Charles Voisin certainly had learned what they could from the Wrights, particularly after a pirated drawing of the 1905 Flyer was published. Ferdinand Ferber later commented that "this drawing had great importance; it showed us the last details of which we were ignorant; and it was this drawing which caused the first aeroplanes of Delagrange and Farman—February and June of 1907—to have a forward [biplane elevator]." Yet there still was much that the Voisins did not know, for that 1905 rendering had failed to disclose the use of wing warping for control.

The Voisin designs looked to the past because they continued to lack adequate means for control. Following a tradition that dated to Sir George Cayley, a full century earlier, these craft continued to rely on wing dihedral for built-in stability in roll, with turns to be accomplished by swinging a rudder. Banked turns were unknown to the Voisins, and it showed. When Farman executed his circles and won the prize, he did it with a succession of wide skidding arcs. The dihedral kept the wings more or less level. The rudder, mounted at the end of an open framework, pushed the rear of the aircraft to one side. The overall effect was somewhat like trying to steer a car by using movable tailfins.

The Wrights had never pursued such arrangements. Rather than attempting to rely on built-in stability, they had deliberately built their craft with a slight instability, requiring active control by the pilot. This reflected their experience with bicycles, which were also unstable. In the air, it made their Flyers more responsive. Moreover, banked turns were tight turns, and could be controlled with precision. The Wright aircraft thus were vastly more maneuverable than those of Voisin. The historian Fred Culick has noted that these flying machines had other advantages:

> As late as 1908, when the Wrights first flew publicly, no one else yet understood the need for lateral control, much less the function of the vertical tail. Therefore no one else could execute proper turns. No one else knew how to make propellers correctly. Above all, no one else had pursued a comparable program: doing the necessary research, constructing his own aircraft and doing his own flying, so that he understood the entire problem.[10]

Wilbur arrived in Paris at the end of May. He needed work space along with a field for flight, and found both with help from a friend, the automobile manufacturer Leon Bollee. Bollee allowed him to use part of a factory that he owned near the town of Le Mans, which also had a large racecourse that was suitable for an airplane. Orville had packed the parts of the aircraft in wooden crates, but when Wilbur opened them, he was thoroughly dismayed. He quickly wrote a letter to let his brother know about it:

> I opened the boxes yesterday and have been puzzled ever since how you could have wasted two whole days packing them. I am sure that with a scoop shovel I could have put things in within two or three minutes and made fully as good a job of it. I never saw such evidences of idiocy in my life. Did you tell Charley not to separate anything lest it get lonesome? Ten or a dozen ribs were broken. . . . The cloth is torn in almost numberless places and the [paint] has rubbed off of the skid sticks and dirtied the cloth very badly. The radiators are badly mashed; the seat is broken; the magneto has the oil cap broken off, the coils badly torn up, and I suspect the axle is bent a little; the tubes of the screw support are mashed and bent. . . . Please bear in mind hereafter that everything must be packed in

such a way that the box can be dropped from a height of five feet ten times, once on each side and the other times on the corners.[11]

The idiocy was French, as was the scoop shovel. Customs inspectors had inspected the boxes' contents and then dumped them back in. Santos-Dumont had retreated from America over nothing more than slashed cloth, but Wilbur knew that failure to fly would destroy the new Compagnie Generale. He accepted that he needed time to cope with the damage, and set to work.

Within the auto factory, the workmen found him most intriguing. He had come from far-off America; clearly he was a man of means. He also had the backing of wealthy and powerful men in Paris. Mechanics and workers were his to hire at will. Yet he came in day after day and did the work himself, wearing overalls and using wrenches as if he was one of them. Nor did he hold himself aloof; he brought a lunch bucket and broke bread as they did when the noon whistle sounded. The name "Wilbur Wright," pronounced in French, sounds much like the phrase *vieille burette,* "old oilcan." The men adopted this as his nickname. He had paid the compliment of working as they did; they returned the favor with this name that reflected his skill.

He was testing a new engine early in July when a hose in its cooling system broke loose, scalding him with boiling water. Bollee rushed to apply picric acid as a salve, while a doctor swathed the injuries with oil. Even so, he was left with second-degree burns. "The blister on my arm was about a foot long and extended about two-thirds of the way around my arm," he wrote to his father. "That on my side was about as large as my hand." For a time he could not move his left arm, and even after he began to regain its use, his burns healed slowly. He nevertheless pushed ahead with his work, playing over pain like a football quarterback.

The long-awaited public flights began on August 8th at the Le Mans racetrack. Spectators began to arrive during the morning but found themselves waiting through a long afternoon, for Wilbur was not about to fly until everything was in order. His arm still had not healed, while his airplane was of the new type that he had flown during only a few days at Kitty Hawk, three months earlier. He therefore waited for the wind to approach a dead calm, knowing that it might be hard to tell the effect of a sudden gust from that of an error in using the new controls. Finally, around six-thirty, he felt ready to proceed.

The catapult weight fell and within seconds, Wilbur was in the air. This by itself was surprising, for French airplanes customarily required a long lumbering roll over the ground to take off, if they took off. This quick rise from the launching rail testified to the high efficiency of the Wrights' propellers. French airscrews more nearly resembled rotating paddles, and while that nation's aviators made up for their poor performance by mounting engines of greater power, this added weight. The Wright machine with its motor came in at around 800 pounds, which was light enough for superb nimbleness when airborne.

Poplar trees lay ahead, and Wilbur lacked the altitude to clear them. He warped his wings and entered a bank. Cries of alarm came from the grandstand, for the observers had seen uncontrolled banks by their country's aircraft and feared that the visiting *Americain* was about to sideslip into the ground. The cries quickly turned to cheers as he turned his rudder and swept through a banked turn, an astonishing maneuver that no one in France had ever seen. Here was no wide flat turn like those of Farman and Delagrange. Here was flight with a precision and agility that no one had even imagined.

Wilbur swept past the trees and flew down the backstretch of the racetrack, maintaining an altitude of about 35 feet. Everyone watched this man as he sat within his airplane, his hands on the controls. More woods lay in his path, and he avoided them again with another banked turn. He made a second circuit of the field, then used his elevator to come down for a safe landing. He had been in the air for less than two minutes.

In that brief moment he laid to rest the continuing accusations of *bluffeur,* showed for all to see that the Wrights possessed methods of control that were vastly superior to those of Voisin, and gave a telling display of what aviation could be. He did these things while in no way attempting to fly Farman-like distances; his two laps around the course sufficed to make his points.

Onlookers cheer as Wilbur flies at Le Mans in 1908.

As his aircraft came to a stop, people rushed onto the field, shouting, cheering, pushing toward him to touch or embrace him or to place their hands on the fabric of his wings. Paul Zens, who had recently built his first airplane, had been at the racecourse since morning but told a reporter, "I would have waited ten times as long. Mr. Wright has us all in his hands." Another neophyte aviator, the balloonist René Gasnier, declared that "the whole concept of the machine—its execution and its practical worth—is wonderful. We are as children compared to the Wrights." Louis Bleriot, one of the country's top pilots, was aware that he had witnessed history. He said to a newsman, "I consider that for us in France and everywhere, a new era of mechanical flight has commenced." Groping for more, he confessed, "I am not sufficiently calm after the event to thoroughly express my opinion."

Ernest Archdeacon, leader of the French skeptics, acknowledged that he was wrong with a statement that appeared the following day in *L'Auto*: "For a long time, for too long a time, the Wright brothers have been accused in Europe of bluff—even perhaps in the land of their birth. They are today hallowed in France, and I feel an intense pleasure in counting myself among the first to make amends for that flagrant injustice."

Wilbur, for his part, kept his feet on the ground. He still needed experience with his airplane, and his arm still bothered him. He answered a reporter's question with the reply, "While in the air I made no less than ten mistakes owing to the fact that I have been laying off so long, but I corrected them all rapidly so I don't suppose anyone watching really knew I had made mistakes at all."

The next day was Sunday. Wilbur, the son of a bishop, took the day off, while Paris newspapers resounded with his praises. *Le Figaro* wrote: "It was not merely a success but a triumph; a conclusive trial and a decisive victory for aviation, the news of which will revolutionize scientific circles throughout the world." *Le Journal* added: "It was the first trial of the Wright airplane, whose qualities have long been regarded with doubt, and it was perfect."

Le Mans lay only a few hours from Paris by train, and the press coverage swelled attendance substantially as Wilbur prepared to return to the air on Monday. He again took off with help from his catapult, and again saw trees lying directly in his path. He couldn't fly over them and was too close for a safe landing, so once more he relied on his craft's maneuverability. Pushing hard on his controls, he swung into a steep bank that again left the spectators shouting in surprise, then made an unusually tight turn. He flew through a large part of a circle, leveled his wings, and landed. He did not care to turn so sharply, for it put considerable strain on his wings, and with his ears he detected a possible problem with the engine. Once more, then, everyone had to wait until he was satisfied.

He again flew through a banked turn and straightened out. He did not complete the circle; instead he banked in the opposite direction and executed a new turn. Together those maneuvers produced a figure-eight, the first ever flown in Europe. Leon Delagrange was present, having come up from Italy to see how a brief flight like that of two days earlier could overshadow his own record time in the air. After seeing what Wilbur could do, his response unconsciously echoed a warning from Archdeacon five years earlier: "Well, we are beaten! We just don't exist!"

Wilbur had further surprises in store. He approached the unprecedented altitude of a hundred feet, while lengthening the duration of his flights. Afterward he remained imperturbable, for his upbringing had left him convinced that fame was mere vainglory. In a letter to Orville he wrote of French aviators who "were so excited they could scarcely speak" or "could only gasp and could not talk at all. You would have almost died of laughter if you could have seen them. The French newspapers, *Matin, Journal, Figaro, L'Auto, Petit Journal, Petit Parisien,* &c., &c., gave reports fully as favorable as the *Herald*. You never saw anything like the complete reversal of opinion that took place after two or three little flights of less than two minutes each."

As the adulation grew more heated, he kept his cool. Later in August he wrote again to Orville: "The excitement aroused by the short flights I have made is almost beyond comprehension. The French have simply become wild. Instead of doubting that we could do anything they are ready to believe that we can do everything. So the present situation is almost as troublesome as the former one."[12]

He willingly accepted the honors and awards that streamed in, but although he had given excellent prepared talks at the Western Society of Engineers, he was not about to become an after-dinner speaker. When an influential baron called on him to make a speech at a banquet in Paris, he demurred: "I know of only one bird, the parrot, that talks, and it can't fly very high."

Remaining near Le Mans, he switched his base to a military field a few miles away that was considerably larger. As winter set in, he decamped to a resort far to the south, near the Pyrenees. He now was willing to talk to news reporters, but he made them earn their interviews by assisting him in the hangar, handing him a wrench or using physical strength to hoist the catapult weight. They counted such chores as honors: "I helped Wilbur Wright launch his airplane today."

The French ambassador, Jules Jusserand, took ship to New York and stated upon his arrival that Wilbur was the most famous man in France. Meanwhile, he continued his flights. Members of the nobility came to watch, and got the same treatment as the newsmen. Lord Arthur Balfour, who had recently been Britain's prime minister, willingly took off his coat and hauled on the catapult. The historians Harry Combs and Martin Caidin present an exchange between Wilbur and Lord Northcliffe, owner of London's *Daily Mail*, who pointed out another well-born nobleman: "He is the Duke of Northumberland. A very high station indeed. And this particular endeavour in which he is now engaged, namely, pulling on that catapult rope, is probably the only worthwhile thing that he has ever done in his life."

While Wilbur was taking France by storm, Orville made his way to the Army's Fort Myer, near Washington, to prepare for test flights of the military Flyer. He packed it in wooden crates at the workshop in Dayton, using the same care he had applied to Wilbur's machine, and was very pleased to see that with no customs inspectors opening this domestic shipment, it arrived in good shape. Charlie Taylor arrived as well, accompanied by his friend Charles Furnas of the recent Kitty Hawk flights. Orville found lodging at the prestigious Cosmos Club in downtown Washington, from where he commuted to Fort Myer by streetcar. The Army gave him work space within a large balloon hangar on that base, where they assembled the craft and prepared its motor.

Orville did not intend to try immediately for the performance goals set forth in Specification No. 486. He couldn't; they called for a duration in flight of one hour with a passenger, which no one in the world had yet achieved. He also knew that he needed more practice with the new controls. He therefore shaped a plan that called for his early flights to be short. He was to fly from the fort's parade ground, which measured only about 700 feet by 1,000 feet. This was small for an airfield, and he appreciated that he had to learn to maneuver within this limited space.

He first took to the air on September 3rd, staying aloft for little more than a minute while circling the field one and a half times. Only a few hundred people were present, but the spectators included Theodore Roosevelt, Jr., the son of the president, who later recalled that "when the plane first rose, the crowd's gasp of astonishment was not alone at the wonder of it, but because it was so unexpected. I'll never forget the impression the sound from the crowd made on me. It was a sound of complete surprise." Some newsmen who were present were similarly stirred, but Orville had the pleasure of finding that he did not become an overnight celebrity. American news reporters were well aware of the records set in Europe by Farman and Delagrange, and took the view that a one-minute flight was not worth front-page headlines. This suited Orville, for it gave him more opportunity to work.

The crowds grew larger as the initial flight tests grew longer, but Fort Myer was a military base and its commanders could control the flow of visitors at will. Orville topped the eleven-minute mark on September 8th. A day later he went for duration and distance, setting a new world record of 57 minutes in the air. This was the time aloft that the Dayton editor Frank Tunison had suggested in 1903 as suitable for a news item, but now it merely showed that a full hour—a Wright goal since 1905—at last was in reach. Orville topped that mark later that same day, then extended his solo records well past an hour during the subsequent week.

He also began to take passengers on short flights that ran for no more than a few minutes. A five-man Army panel was to certify his compliance with the Signal Corps requirements. He began taking its members up one by one, with his companion for September 17th being Lieutenant Thomas Selfridge. Orville made three circuits of the field—one pictures him as seen from a distance, swinging back and forth with his motor buzzing—and then began a wide excursion that proceeded toward Arlington Cemetery. He became aware of a light tapping at the rear. A quick glance showed nothing wrong, but he decided to cut the motor and glide to a landing as soon as he could do so safely.

Suddenly the taps turned into what he described as "two big

Orville flies successfully at Fort Myer near Washington.

thumps, which gave the machine a terrible shaking." Clearly something had broken. The Flyer veered to the right. He responded by shutting down the engine. Then he found that his control levers brought no response, "which produced a most peculiar feeling of helplessness." He kept pushing on the levers and executed a bank, turning his craft toward the parade ground. He leveled the wings— and instead of gliding, his craft dropped its nose and plunged downward! He pulled upward on the elevator control, jiggling it in case it might be caught, and began to recover from this dive as he approached the ground. The airplane nevertheless did not pull out, striking the earth with great force and raising a cloud of dust.

Investigation traced the cause of the accident to the propellers, which were new and had blades that were six inches longer than usual. One blade split while in flight, flattening out and losing much of its push. The undamaged propeller made the vehicle veer. The damaged propeller, with one good blade and one faulty, set up a powerful vibration that forced its shaft out of position. It broke a wire that braced the tail, rendering the rudder inoperative. The rudder fell over on its side. Being horizontal, it now acted as a rear-mounted elevator, and it had an angle that drove the aircraft sharply downward. Orville still had the opportunity to fight this action by using maximum up elevator at the front, and with another twenty or so feet of altitude, he might have made it. As it was, the bad propeller now brought the most serious accident to date in powered flight.

Army medics rushed both men to the hospital. Orville remained conscious; examination disclosed a fractured left leg and four broken ribs. Selfridge might have come away with similar survivable injuries, but he had sustained a serious skull fracture when his head struck one of the wing struts. The blow knocked him unconscious and left him with a bleeding gash. Surgeons operated and tried to save him, but he died shortly after they had finished their work. He was the first man to lose his life in the crash of an airplane.

When the news reached Dayton, Orville's sister Katharine was starting a new school year. She took indefinite leave of absence and

The crash that killed Lieutenant Tom Selfridge.

hastened to Washington to serve as his personal nurse. Within weeks he was able to get around on crutches and then with help from a cane, but he was left with a back injury that at times brought excruciating pain during the rest of his life. Not until 1920 did he learn that his wounds had been more severe than anyone suspected. They included three fractures in the hip bones, with one of them being dislocated.

In France, Wilbur was devastated when a telegram outlined what had happened. He blamed himself, believing that the accident would not have occurred if he had been there to help. His mood improved as he learned that the fault lay with a propeller and not with Orville, and that his brother some day would fly again. Signal Corps officials called off the test flights, granting a nine-month postponement. Orville was still shaky and in considerable pain, but he anticipated that when the tests resumed, he again would be the man at the controls.

NINE

NOON INTO TWILIGHT

THE YEAR 1908 BROUGHT dramatic new life to aviation. In January the Wrights had not flown for over two years. The big news came from Paris, where Henri Farman stayed in the air for less than two minutes, though he did fly a complete circle. In September Wilbur shattered all records as he flew before a cheering crowd of ten thousand people for an hour and a half. He was ready for more, for his upright seating meant that he could fly at will without straining his neck. He could install a larger gas tank and stay up until his fuel ran out.

André Michelin, a wealthy industrialist, had offered a prize of 20,000 francs for the longest flight of the year. Farman was hardly in the running, holding a personal record of only forty-five minutes, but Wilbur was sure that he could fly for over two hours. He came close to that mark on December 18 and then on December 30, wearing a coat, cap, and gloves to stay warm. A day later, with the new year only hours away, he spent the afternoon repeatedly circling a marked course as he flew through a freezing drizzle. He landed just before sunset, having pushed the record to 2 hours and 20 minutes while covering 77 miles.

Early 1909 brought a welcome pleasure, as Orville and Katharine arrived for an extended visit. He needed a cane to walk, but was back on his feet. Soon afterward, Wilbur transferred his operations to the town of Pau in the south of France, where the visitors now included royalty. King Edward VII was spending the winter at nearby Biarritz and came over to see what was happening. The king of Spain, Alfonso XIII, made his own appearance. He had promised the queen and cabinet that he would not fly, but he sat with Wilbur in the airplane and listened with fascination as he learned how it worked.

As before, the Wrights stayed cool amid this new wave of attention. Wilbur spent much time training student pilots. He acquired a French cook but avoided the area's resort hotels, preferring instead to camp out within his hangar. Katharine told a reporter, "Kings are just like other nice, well-bred people." In one of her letters, she wrote, "We had J. Pierpont Morgan, his sister, daughter and a friend out to visit the camp yesterday afternoon. They were very pleasant people." Lord Northcliffe found a similar straightforwardness. "I never knew more simple, unaffected people than Wilbur, Orville, and Katharine," he later wrote. "After the Wrights had been in Europe a few weeks they became world heroes, and when they went to Pau their demonstrations were visited by thousands of people from all parts of Europe— by kings and lesser men, but I don't think the excitement and interest produced by their extraordinary feat had any effect on them at all."[1]

In April they left France to conduct further flights near Rome. King Victor Emmanuel granted an audience and later followed the earlier monarchs by making his own visit to watch Wilbur take to the air. Again, though, Wilbur continued to emphasize the training of pilots. His students included Umberto Savoia, who later became head of the firm of Savoia-Marchetti, one of Italy's foremost planebuilders.

Europe continued to offer its delights, but Orville was well aware that he still had to complete the Army trials at Fort Myer. The Wrights therefore departed for New York, arriving on May 11th. The brothers were eager to return to their work in Dayton, but first they had to run the gauntlet of a new wave of honors, which began literally as their liner entered port. Other ships dipped their flags while their passengers cheered; small craft sounded whistles and bells. A huge crowd watched them walk down the gangplank. Customs inspectors gave their luggage no more than a cursory search, thereby showing that celebrity indeed had its rewards. A waiting cab then took them into Manhattan for a formal luncheon at the Waldorf.

They did not linger in New York, but took a train for Dayton,

Wilbur, left, and Orville on the steps of their home in Dayton.

where more of the same awaited them. The festivities started 10 miles from home in the town of Xenia, where several of their friends boarded the coach and presented a bouquet of roses to Katharine. Eleven carriages met them at the Dayton depot, with four horses pulling the one reserved for Wilbur and Orville. Cannon boomed a salute; factory whistles tooted a greeting, while a marching band played "Home, Sweet Home." During the evening, ten thousand people gathered to cheer their return. Flags, Chinese lanterns, and fireworks completed the celebration.

Several weeks of peace and quiet ensued, as the brothers worked on the new Army airplane. Orville's strength had returned; he had been able to walk aboard ship without a cane, and he looked forward to resuming his activity as a pilot. First, though, the Wrights had to face another round of honors, this time at the hands of William Howard Taft. A few years earlier, as secretary of war, he had forwarded letters to the Board of Ordnance and Fortification, but the election of 1908 had made him President of the United States.

He welcomed them within the East Room of the White House and gave a speech: "You made this discovery by a course that we of America like to feel is distinctly American—by keeping your nose right at the job until you had accomplished what you had determined to do." Katharine was there as well; the *New York Times* wrote that "Miss Wright blushed as she shook the President's hand, but her eyes were alight with pleasure." Taft then handed a gold medal in a box to each brother.

In Dayton, the general view was that their welcome a month earlier had been only half-hearted and deserved improvement. Accordingly, they were invited to endure two additional days of congratulations. They were working one morning in the bicycle shop, which still was the center of their activities, when suddenly they heard every factory whistle and church bell in town, all sounding together. Bands played in the distance while cannon boomed. After about ten minutes the cacophony died down, but it was not long before a carriage came for them. Escorted by marching bands, they proceeded to opening ceremonies in Van Cleve Park, where actors in costume were ready. One of them held

the role of Jonathan Dayton, for whom the town had been named following its founding in 1796:

DAYTON: Methinks I see two great objects like gigantic birds coming
    from the eastward as if riding on the winds of the morning! What
    manner of birds can this be?
ANOTHER PERFORMER: They are no other than two of Dayton's illus-
    trious sons coming home from foreign triumphs with the greatest
    invention of the age.[2]

The fire department held a parade during the afternoon, at which
the brothers were presented with a key to the city. Evening brought a
reception at the YMCA, followed by fireworks at the riverfront. The
pyrotechnic display reached a high point by presenting 8-foot-tall
portraits of Wilbur and Orville flanking an American flag.

Their father, old Bishop Wright, was in his eighties but still had
enough strength to deliver the invocation that heralded the ceremonies of the second day. The brothers, dressed in morning coats and
top hats, were awarded gold medals. General James Allen of the Signal
Corps presented the first of them, in accordance with an act of Congress. The governor of Ohio followed with medals from the state leg-
islature, while the mayor of Dayton added his own. Some 2,500
schoolchildren were at hand, dressed in red, white, and blue to form
an enormous flag while they sang patriotic songs. More parades followed. One had floats depicting the history of transportation, from
oxcart to covered wagon and locomotive and onward to the Wright
Flyer. Another parade, later that evening, featured a cavalcade of automobiles. One of them, driven by a family friend, was aglow with electric decorations.

With their new medals that complemented similar awards received
in London as well as at the White House, the brothers now had
enough gold to draw attention at Fort Knox. Wilbur nevertheless
found ways to be his taciturn self. At a point in a program marked
"Responses by the Wrights," he said, "Thank you, gentlemen"—and
sat down. He then made his feelings known in a letter to Chanute:

"The Dayton presentation has been made the excuse for an elaborate carnival and advertisement of the city under the guise of being an honor to us. As it was done in spite of our known wishes, we are not as appreciative as we might be." Chanute responded, "I know that the reception of such honors becomes oppressive to modest men and they would avoid them if they could, but in this case you have brought the trouble upon yourselves by your completing the solution to a world-old problem. . . . I hope that when the present shouting is over you will continue to achieve further success."[3]

The opportunity for such success lay immediately ahead, at Fort Myer. Orville's new Army warplane continued to follow closely the designs that had proved themselves as early as 1905. It maintained a strong similarity to the Flyer of 1903 but had markedly longer front and rear supports for the forward elevator and the rudder. These improved the effectiveness of those controls, overcoming the worrisome pitch instability of earlier years. Orville initiated his new series of flight tests late in June 1909, continuing with further flights through July.

While in Washington a year earlier, he had stayed at the Cosmos Club. He did not care to return, for its social life was too distracting, so the brothers roomed instead at the less fashionable Raleigh Hotel. They needed all the time they could spare for their airplane, as it proved balky during early attempts at flight. In three days Orville experienced three aborted takeoffs and two minor accidents. He then made what would have been a successful flight except that the motor stopped in mid-air. He glided on down—and snagged a small tree that left his wing fabric badly ripped. There was nothing to do but return to Dayton to prepare a new covering for the lower wing.

But the flights went better after the middle of July. Orville flew for seventeen minutes, then three days later set a new U.S. record as he raised his mark to an hour and twenty minutes. In turn, this attracted the crowds. Members of Congress had flocked to Fort Myer for his first attempt, but he had to disappoint them because the wind was too strong for him to fly. Now his visitors included President Taft. Alice Roosevelt Longworth, daughter of the recent president and doyenne of Washington society, arrived in an electric automobile and served tea to friends.

Orville had topped the one-hour mark in a solo flight, but he also had to do this while carrying a passenger, so he resumed his practice of flying with members of the Army review board. Wilbur had flown with a passenger for over an hour on two occasions during the previous October while in France, which gave Orville incentive to beat his brother's record while meeting the Army's requirements. He did this on July 27th. His passenger was Lieutenant Frank Lahm, whose father, Frank Sr., had done much to help the Wrights in Paris.

It took time before the weather was right. At first there were heavy clouds that threatened rain, along with a strong and gusty wind. Rain indeed fell, but it soon died down and the sky cleared. The brothers knew that the wind often approached a calm early in the evening, and they were not disappointed. Orville took off shortly after six-thirty p.m., with Lahm at his side, and proceeded with a monotonous circling of the Fort Myer parade ground as he racked up miles and minutes. As he approached his brother's mark of an hour and ten minutes, people in the crowd began to shout and honk the horns of their cars. Orville flew on, made one more circuit of the field, then descended through the summer twilight for a smooth landing.

Next and most critical was the speed trial. The Army contract required forty miles per hour, with a passenger. To increase the speed of their craft, the brothers had reduced its wing area, which lowered the weight. To diminish the weight still further, Orville selected a companion who stood five feet one inch and weighed 126 pounds. He was Lieutenant Benjamin Foulois, who in time became a major general and who headed the Army Air Corps during part of the 1930s.

The rules called for a round-trip flight to and from a turning point five miles away, for a total run of ten miles. The airplane thus was to fly both with the wind and against it. Orville once more waited for calm, being aware that he would lose more time from a headwind than he would gain from a tailwind. He set the turning point as a hill near the town of Alexandria. The Army marked this spot with a captive balloon and stationed observers to report the times of entering and leaving the five-mile course.

The wind continued, but finally died down in the early evening. Then, accompanied by Foulois, Orville rolled into the air as the catapult weight dropped. He circled the field twice to gain altitude and crossed the starting line amid a clicking of stopwatches. Onlookers knew that this was no ordinary flight, for in addition to being a test of speed, it was the nation's first cross-country excursion. The airplane was to vanish from sight for several minutes before it reappeared—if it reappeared.

It did not. People became concerned as they watched for it, while the sky remained empty. Then came cries of "There it is!" Orville had misjudged his approach to the marker balloon and had taken additional time to round this turning point. That did not detract from his measured speed, which was determined by his performance along the straight-line portions of the course. This speed came out as 42.583 miles per hour. In accordance with the contract, this qualified the Wrights for a bonus of $5,000, for a total price of $30,000.

The success of these Fort Myer trials drew notice in Berlin, where the Kaiser headed a government that was militarist to the core. The Wrights now had business interests in Germany as well as in France, but had yet to fly in that country. In the wake of the Army flights, the brothers once more divided their forces. Wilbur had conquered France during the previous year; now he agreed to remain in the States while Orville set out to add Germany to their domains. Katharine accompanied him as he crossed the Atlantic during August.

In heavier-than-air aviation the Germans had no one to compare with Voisin, Delagrange, or Farman, let alone with Wilbur and Orville. That country nevertheless had its own inventor in Count Zeppelin. Late that month he undertook to fly his latest dirigible, the LZ-6, on a nonstop cruise from his base at Lake Constance, near the Swiss border, to Berlin. This was flying indeed; the distance was nearly 400 miles. He broke a propeller en route and had to land for repairs, but continued onward to a successful arrival.

An early dirigible of Count Zeppelin.

Heavier-than-air flights brought astonishment, but Zeppelin brought awe. His vessels were true ships of the sky, with length and size suitable for ocean liners. They flew low, looming in the air like fantasies, while their slow majestic advance, accompanied by the rumble of their motors, would have suited a novel by Jules Verne. As the LZ-6 flew over the city, every church bell pealed out a greeting. A crowd of a hundred thousand welcomed it as it landed on the Tegel parade ground, where the hosts included members of the royal family. The Count came down from his control car and paid his respects to the Kaiser, who introduced him to Orville.

Orville proved quite willing to see what Zeppelin had to offer, accompanying him on a 40-mile flight from Frankfurt to Mannheim. However, Orville had come to show his own wares, and he did this in a series of brilliant demonstrations that attracted as many as two hundred thousand people. Repeatedly remaining aloft for an hour and longer, he showed that his airplane was considerably speedier than a dirigible, and vastly more maneuverable. By flying to an altitude record of 1,600 feet, he showed that he could match Zeppelin and that an airship could not escape by attempting to fly to greater heights.

He and Katharine were lodged in luxurious rooms at the Esplanade, one of Berlin's finest hotels, where a young German woman helped them as an interpreter. She was in their suite one day when the telephone rang. It was the Crown Prince, Friedrich Wilhelm, who wanted to fly with Orville and who had simply picked up the phone to let his royal wish be known. The woman was so overcome that she dropped the receiver and nearly fainted. Orville was quite willing to serve as pilot to the *Kronprinz*, but felt that he needed permission from the Kaiser. Nor could Orville simply respond with a phone call of his own to the palace in Potsdam; he lacked the necessary social connection. Still, as he continued his public flights, he found himself meeting a continuing stream of lesser princes, princesses, as well as the Kaiser's queen. He took these occasions to remark that he expected to fly soon with Friedrich Wilhelm himself. When these family members raised no objection, he extended an invitation and set a date. The flight that ensued, on October 2nd, was the first in which a member of royalty flew in an airplane.

Aviation had been a sport for kings ever since the Montgolfiers entertained King Louis XVI at Versailles in 1783. The Wrights now had performed for the crowned heads of Great Britain, Germany, and Italy, as well as for President Taft. Additional exhibitions also lay ahead, for New York City was about to embark on a two-week celebration. The theme was the Hudson River, which Henry Hudson had navigated in his ship *Half Moon* in 1609, and which Robert Fulton had used as a route to Albany in his steamboat *Clermont* in 1807. The year 1909 was close enough to the centenaries of these events to give opportunity to commemorate both. A highlight was to be a naval review, with warships of the U.S. and of six other powers following the route of Hudson and Fulton with the whole of Manhattan as an audience.

For a fee of $15,000, Wilbur agreed to fly from a base on Governor's Island, a mile from the Statue of Liberty, on a 20-mile round trip to Grant's Tomb. Few aviators had attempted similar long-distance flights, while variable winds over the river made such an attempt more

*Wilbur flies past Manhattan in 1909. Note the canoe
mounted below his airplane.*

dangerous. Having no wish to be buried like General Grant in his own tomb, Wilbur fitted a canoe to the bottom of his airplane. He expected that if he came down in the water, he could stay afloat while he waited for a rescue.

The presence of the canoe brought a need for practice, and Wilbur addressed this with considerable panache. Taking off with help from his catapult, he caught the attention of dozens of vessels in the harbor, whose captains saluted him with a chorus of shrill whistles and blaring horns. He veered to the left, headed for Lady Liberty, then banked and circled her waist while passing under the arm that carried the torch. Meanwhile the liner *Lusitania,* one of the world's largest, was making its own way downriver. He cut in front, close enough to see its throngs of cheering passengers. The ship's commander responded with a deep booming roar from his foghorn.

Unfavorable weather kept Wilbur on the ground for the next few days, but the sky was clear and the winds were mild on October 4th. Once more he flew amid a cacophony of ships' horns, though none were as powerful as that of the mighty *Lusitania*. A gust of wind knocked his aircraft to the side as he flew past 23rd Street, but he maintained control. The whole city seemed to have turned out to hail his flight as he proceeded northward toward Columbia University. Two British cruisers, HMS *Drake* and *Argyll*, stood in the channel and gave him a convenient turning point. He banked left, approached the Palisades, then banked again for the southward run. Flying over battleships that lay at anchor, he returned to Governor's Island.

There was more than showmanship to this flight. Like the others, it gave clear and vivid demonstration that man indeed was ready to conquer the air and that an age of flight truly was at hand. Wilbur now returned to the ongoing work of transforming vision into reality, as he spent the rest of October training Army pilots. He used the very aircraft that he and Orville had recently sold to the Signal Corps. Escaping the limited confines of the Fort Myer parade ground, he conducted these flights in College Park, Maryland, which had a field that was substantially larger.

As success with the Army complemented the cheers in New York, an uncomfortable fact lay in the background: there still was no Wright company within the United States. The brothers' ongoing relationship with Charles Flint had brought the formation of such companies in Germany and France, but on the soil of their own country they held their Army contract and continued to operate their bicycle shop, and that was it. Yet while it had taken three years to arrange the sale to the Army and two and a half years to win a commitment in Paris, the fame of the Wrights and their demonstrated success enabled similar arrangements in New York to go forward in a matter of weeks.

The transaction began early in October, while Wilbur was still in Manhattan for his Hudson River flights. Clinton Peterkin, a young associate at J. P. Morgan & Company, met Wilbur at his suite in the Park Avenue Hotel and offered to attract a group of investors for an American company. Peterkin started at the top by talking with Morgan himself, who was the nation's leading financier. He agreed not only to invest for himself but to bring in his friend Elbert Gary, head of U.S. Steel.

Peterkin then spread the word within his circle of acquaintances. These included DeLancey Nicoll, a senior partner in a Wall Street law firm, whose list of personal associates rivaled Morgan's. By making phone calls, Nicoll quickly expanded the list of supporters to include the railroad magnate Cornelius Vanderbilt, the chairman of Southern Express, a director of Bethlehem Steel, the president of a major coal company, and the head of New York's Interborough Rapid Transit subway. Wilbur added his friend Robert Collier of the magazine *Collier's Weekly* as well as two leading stockholders in the Packard Automobile Company. So much investment capital was available from non-Morgan sources that old J. P. was likely to stand as no more than a minority investor. Even so, the others knew that Morgan's immense clout was likely to give him effective leadership, and they didn't want that. Someone phoned Morgan and told him that the stock was oversubscribed. Amid further objections from other sources, Morgan and Gary voluntarily withdrew.

The new Wright Company was formally incorporated on November 22nd, with an office on Fifth Avenue in Manhattan. Wilbur took its presidency, with Orville serving as a vice president, and the board of directors included Vanderbilt. A new factory in Dayton lay immediately ahead, replacing the bicycle shop. Public exhibitions of flying aircraft represented the most attractive market, for people willingly would pay admission to see a flight—and perhaps a crash. With Wilbur in the front office, Orville began training new pilots as aerial showmen.

The irony is inescapable: After laboring for ten years to solve the mysteries of flight and to invent a practical airplane, the Wrights now were ready to offer merely a new type of sensational entertainment. The 1909 sale to the Army proved to be the only one for two years; the Signal Corps used the first airplane until it needed an extensive refit and purchased one more as a replacement, and that was that. That year marked high noon in the brothers' lives, a year of adulation when doors opened for them at the highest levels of government and business. Now they faced the new task of building airplanes that could do their share of the world's work. They had led all competitors in design as recently as 1908, but after the demonstrations at Le Mans it took only a year before France surged into the lead.

While the brothers protected their secrets, Frenchmen went forward on their own. Planebuilders such as Gabriel Voisin garnered no more than a partial understanding of the Wrights' methods, but still managed to build true airplanes that Farman and Delagrange kept in the air for large portions of an hour. With this background, these designers lost little time in learning from Wilbur's public flights during 1908, which enabled them to build Wright-type controls into their own new aircraft.

Louis Bleriot was in the forefront, achieving success by a somewhat roundabout route. He was an affluent manufacturer of acetylene headlamps for cars, which gave him the money that he used to pursue his fancy. As early as 1901 he had built a wing-flapping machine, which failed to take off. He joined the Aero Club; he met Ferdinand Ferber, who introduced him to Voisin. Just then, in 1905, Voisin was building gliders. He crafted one for Bleriot; it went out of control and crashed. No matter; the two men became partners and set to work on powered machines.

The partnership did not go well, for the two men had radically different ideas about airplane design, but for a time it appeared possible to combine their approaches. One such craft united biplane wings with a tail that looked like a big barrel, flattened into an ellipse. It failed to take off. A similar concept came apart on the ground while taxiing. Bleriot continued with a monoplane that featured wings shaped like a bird's, a rear-mounted motor, and a long forward fuselage that placed both rudder and horizontal stabilizer at the front. This vehicle hopped but did not fly. Voisin responded by breaking with Bleriot, who continued to work on his own.

Bleriot was designing his craft by guess and by golly. He lacked the Wrights' data on wings and propellers, but during 1907 he decided that monoplanes were the designs of the future. He was not prescient; biplanes were lighter and had greater structural strength. Still this decision allowed him to seek improvement within a fixed approach. He also appreciated that with enough power, he could make a barn door fly. He had a motor of 24 horsepower, and he intended to use it.

In July he introduced a craft that had plenty of dihedral for stability, a large aft-mounted tail, and a sliding seat that enabled him to shift his weight as if it were a hang glider. He flew as far as 460 feet and came away convinced that all he needed was a bigger engine. Two months later he raised his record to 600 feet, which approached the mark set by Santos-Dumont the previous November, but his airplane went out of control and crashed. Uninjured, he built a similar version and flew it twice to 1,500 feet before it too was smashed in a crackup.

Even so, he was getting the knack, and during 1908 he approached full success with a new monoplane. Harsh experience had convinced him that he needed better control, and he tried to achieve it with movable wingtips that were to serve as ailerons. They worked, after a fashion, and he covered 6 miles in 8 minutes early in July. Farman quickly upstaged him by remaining aloft for 20 minutes, on the same day and at the same field near Paris. Moreover, Bleriot wrecked this airplane as well, later that month. Still, he now had truly flown.

Then came August 8th, with Wilbur making his first flight near Le Mans. Bleriot had been wrestling with problems of control through several aircraft and a number of crashes, and the work of the Wrights came to him as a revelation. Finally, here was the solution! In the words of a colleague, "We met Mr. Wright, and Bleriot was all excited. He looked over the machine and he felt the wings. Mr. Wright showed him how the wing warping worked. . . . Bleriot was just tickled to death. He said, 'I'm going to use a warped wing. To hell with the aileron.'"

Farman came away with lessons of his own. For the first time, he saw that built-in stability was not enough, that he needed control of roll if he was to turn and maneuver with skill. He did not adopt the warped wing, but instead mounted a set of down-only flaps to the trailing edges of his Voisin biplane. By lowering the flaps on one side while keeping the other ones level, he now could bank at will.

Within months, Farman and Bleriot initiated a succession of cross-country flights. These were new; not even the Wrights had yet attempted such feats, preferring to set their records for duration by circling marked courses that gave opportunity to land immediately if the engine quit. Farman qualified his motor with two such flights during October that kept him aloft for up to 44 minutes. He then covered 16 miles from Chalons to Reims, crossing forests, hills, and a river.

During that same month, Lord Northcliffe announced a prize of 500 pounds—later raised to 1,000 pounds, some $5,000—for the first heavier-than-air flight across the English Channel. Wilbur was in France and might have gone for it, but Orville warned him not to try: "I do not like the idea of your attempting a channel flight when I am not present. I haven't much faith in your motor running." Wilbur was well aware that if he came down in the water he would lose his only airplane, with no replacement available in Dayton and with Orville still recovering from his recent injuries at Fort Myer. He decided not to make an attempt.

Bleriot felt differently. He entered the long-distance derby with his own cross-country flight, one day after Farman's, as he made an eighteen-mile round trip between two small towns. As his preparations continued for a flight from Calais to Dover, he paid particular attention to his engine. His mechanic later declared that it "spit oil out of the holes at the end of every stroke, smearing the pilot with an oily film, so that an aviator had to be heroic as well as long-suffering to keep on flying these miserable mechanisms." It could spit flaming gasoline as well, which burned Bleriot's foot severely during a flight in July 1909. He had to hobble on crutches, but he was not about to delay more than he had to. A competing aviator, Hubert Latham, was also near Calais preparing for his own attempt. Bleriot nevertheless expected to win, for he knew that despite its faults his motor was reliable, whereas Latham's already had failed in flight and had dunked him in the Channel. Bleriot anticipated that his own engine would give him an edge.

He started his final preparations on July 25th, well before the sun was up. Northcliffe's rules allowed him to fly at sunrise, which he did. He carried no compass and soon found himself surrounded by morning mist, with only the sun, low on the horizon, to indicate direction. He flew onward; the mist cleared, and in the distance he saw the coast of England. However, he saw no landmarks and for several minutes he flew in the general direction of the North Sea. Then he saw three small vessels heading for a port, which he presumed was Dover. He altered course to follow them and soon found himself approaching the famous White Cliffs.

He turned left and flew along their faces. Flat areas suitable for landing lay at the top, but those scarps stood 300 feet tall, which was higher than he could climb. Still, he was ready for this. A French newsman had found an open meadow near Dover Castle that was considerably lower, and now was waiting there as he waved a large *tricouleur*. Bleriot saw his country's flag, but the wind had freshened and blew him about when he tried a landing approach. He cut his motor and glided on in. Once again he damaged his craft, but he had done it. He had flown the Channel.

During that same week, Orville made his own cross-country flight at Fort Myer and successfully conducted the Army's speed trial. Yet of those two flights, few people could doubt which was the more portentous. The Channel had been England's moat, protecting the country from invasion by the Spanish with their Armada and then by Napoleon. With his 37 minutes in the air, Bleriot raised the prospect that Great Britain one day might no longer be an island.

Only a month later, an event of similar drama showed anew that France now led the world in flight. This was a week-long *Grande Semaine d'Aviation,* a competition of fliers held near the city of Reims. Champagne country lay close by; major houses such as Veuve Cliquot and Heidsieck put up 200,000 francs in prize money, with their bubbly drinks flowing freely for the spectators. Workers erected ornate grandstands. Lithographed color posters showed aircraft flying near the famous cathedral, while a slender demoiselle, wearing a fashionable hat, waved to her sweetheart as he roared overhead in his biplane.

Filling the last week of August, this air show demonstrated that France had more than individual inventors. It now had an aircraft industry, and the entrants made this clear. They included half a dozen Wright craft, built under license by their French company, along with nine Voisins, four Bleriots, four Farmans, and four aircraft built by a former artist, Leon Levavasseur. He made engines as well as airplanes, naming them all Antoinette in honor of the teenage daughter of his business partner.

Germany had nothing remotely comparable, and it showed. There was not a single entrant from the Fatherland. Count Zeppelin flew his LZ-6 from Lake Constance to Berlin during that week; this was by order of the Kaiser, in an attempt to distract attention. Orville Wright also avoided Reims. He might have flown there but he elected to stay east of the Rhine, for the competition was formidable. Seven aviators topped 60 miles as they flew around a marked course, with Farman covering 112 miles and remaining aloft for over 3 hours. Bleriot, in turn, increased the speed record to nearly 48 miles per hour.

The *Grande Semaine* truly proved to mark a milestone. Charles Gibbs-Smith, the leading chronicler of early aviation, recognized this in 1965 when he titled one of his books *The Invention of the Airplane (1799–1909)*. The first date referred to the initial thoughts of Sir George Cayley. The second covered, among other events of that year, the *Grande Semaine*.

The Wrights were well aware that they could no more hold back the surging French than King Canute could have restrained the tide. In addition, they also found themselves facing an unwelcome challenge within their own country. It came from a man who was on his way toward establishing himself as their greatest rival and most serious competitor: Glenn Curtiss.

The Wrights were closely linked to Dayton; Curtiss had a similarly strong connection to the small town of Hammondsport, located on Lake Keuka within the Finger Lakes of upstate New York. Born in 1878, he dropped out of school following eighth grade and took a job at the company that became Eastman Kodak. His work was sheer drudgery: for $4 per week, he stenciled numbers on rolls of film. He responded by showing natural inventiveness. He built a rack with a movable brush that enabled him to stencil a hundred rolls at once, sharply raising both his production and his wages.

He saved his money and bought a bicycle, then left Kodak and took a new job as a Western Union delivery boy. This led him to form friendships with other young bicyclists, whom he soon engaged in impromptu races. He now showed strong competitiveness, entering local races that were somewhat more formal, and sometimes winning prizes. A local pharmacist had been selling bicycles as a sideline; in 1900 he brought Curtiss in as a partner. Curtiss sold major brands of bikes, then decided he could develop a line of his own. He contracted with a local machine shop and soon had his Hercules brand for sale.

As a background for aviation, his involvement with bicycles paralleled that of the Wrights. However, his personal road to flight went by way of an intimate involvement with motors. He started with a one-cylinder version that he purchased by mail order and installed in one of his bikes. That converted it into a motorcycle. He soon decided that he could build an engine of greater power and lighter weight, and did so. Before long he expanded his line of bicycles to include motorcycles. He entered motocross races and often won, thereby garnering excellent publicity. Attracting capital from merchants in Hammondsport, he built a factory and enlarged it until it had forty employees.

Because his engines were light in weight, he might have proceeded to use one in a flying machine. Instead, he entered aviation when a builder of such a machine needed a motor. He was Thomas Baldwin, an inventor of dirigibles who lived in San Francisco. Curtiss's reputation had reached the West Coast, and Baldwin ordered a used two-cylinder motor midway through 1904. He later visited Curtiss in Hammondsport and further business developed, but for a time Curtiss viewed him merely as a lucrative customer: "I get twice as much money for my motors from those aviation cranks."

But during 1906, Curtiss turned his thoughts increasingly to flight. He attended the first aeronautical show of the Aero Club of America, held in Manhattan that January as an adjunct to a major auto exhibition. There he met Alexander Graham Bell, inventor of the telephone, who held a longstanding interest in aviation and who had been present in 1896 when Langley successfully flew his steam-powered model aircraft. Bell ordered a Curtiss motor. Then in April, the great San Francisco earthquake touched off a citywide fire that reduced Baldwin's office and plant to ashes. He responded by moving his operation to Hammondsport, far from California's tremors and close to his source of engines. In a trice, Curtiss found that an important center for aviation was virtually in his backyard.

Amid these flirtations, he remained very much a motorcycle man. His factory was working both day and night shifts; activity in aviation merely drew him closer to his first love. Other would-be aeronauts placed orders for an 8-cylinder motor, which developed 40 horsepower. Curtiss proceeded to install it in a custom-built motorcycle, with an enlarged frame and a pair of very long handlebars that made it nearly unsteerable. He didn't mind; he intended to try it out at Ormond Beach, Florida, where hard sand provided one of the world's best natural straightaways. Taking two miles to get up to speed, he zoomed through a measured mile, head down and body flattened against his machine, and set a record of 136.3 miles per hour. "It satisfied my speed-craving," he declared.

Even so, events kept returning him to aviation. He attended the second Aero Club exhibition in New York, where Bell sought him out and ordered another motor. The two met again at Bell's home in Washington a few weeks later, where their discussions were more extended. In June 1907, Curtiss finally took to the air in a Baldwin dirigible. This was no flight of fancy; it was a warmup for a visit to Bell at his summer estate in Nova Scotia, where he was assembling a group of enthusiasts to pursue his own aeronautical thoughts. He needed an engine man, and brought Curtiss into his team for a fee of $25 per day.

Bell believed that the way to proceed was to develop man-carrying kites that possessed built-in stability when airborne. His first full-size model, named *Cygnet,* made its only manned flight on a Nova Scotia lake in December. A steamboat pulled it into the air, where it sailed steadily along for several minutes. The wind shifted; the kite settled gently onto the water, so gently that the pilot failed to realize that he was down and did not drop the towrope. Smoke from the vessel's stack hid *Cygnet* from view. The skipper kept chugging along, ripping the craft to pieces as he continued to pull it through the water. A motorboat quickly rescued the pilot, but *Cygnet* was a total loss.

This did not discourage Bell. He was pleased to have seen his kite lift a man and fly with stability, and he was ready to proceed with

Cygnet II. However, he relied on a mode of construction that required thousands of individual cells, making its assembly quite laborious. Members of the group had been reading literature on both gliders and heavier-than-air machines, and decided that they would build and test such aircraft while they awaited Bell's replacement for *Cygnet*.

To escape the harsh Canadian winter they moved to Hammondsport at Curtiss's invitation, where flights with a biplane glider, modeled after Chanute's, were soon under way. A powered biplane followed quickly, with Curtiss providing one of his 8-cylinder motors. It weighed 145 pounds and tested at 40 horsepower, which meant that if raw power alone could permit flight, success was surely at hand. Using red fabric left over from *Cygnet* for the wing coverings, they christened it *Red Wing*.

With sledlike runners for landing gear, it flew from the ice of frozen Lake Keuka on March 12, 1908. It took off, but because it had been built without control of roll, it sideslipped back onto the lake. No matter; it had been airborne, and careful measurement of tracks in a snow cover showed that it had flown for 318 feet, 11 inches. Everyone was jubilant and hoped for even better results on a second flight, but the machine flew for only 120 feet before coming down on the left wing. This time it sustained considerable damage.

Clearly, these inventors needed better control. They were aware of the Wrights' patent, but they were eager to use a method of control that they could claim as their own. Bell agreed that it was necessary "to improve the lateral stability to prevent sliding off to one side." He suggested installing "moveable surfaces at the extremities of the wing piece," which came to be called ailerons. He handed the idea to Casey Baldwin (no relation to Thomas), a member of the group who had piloted both flights of *Red Wing*. Baldwin crafted a set of triangular hinged flaps, sharply pointed, that extended beyond the tips of both the top and bottom wings. The group had run out of red fabric but white stock was available, so they named their creation *White Wing*.

Spring thaw had melted Lake Keuka, so they moved to a flat field. Following two preliminary trials, Curtiss took the controls on May 21st. He covered 615 feet, touched the ground momentarily, then continued in the air for a total distance of 1,017 feet. Bell was famous; anything about him certainly was news, so a telegram to the Associated Press announced this feat to the world. The Wrights still had not flown openly, making this the longest public flight in America to date.

Eight months earlier, *Scientific American* had offered a trophy for the first publicly-observed flight of a kilometer. The Wrights might have walked away with such an award as early as 1904, but they still were holding their secrets, and this prize was available for anyone who could qualify. Curtiss believed that he could win it, for *White Wing* had already covered nearly a third of this distance. Bell's group proceeded with an extensive rebuild, retaining the triangular ailerons in the design while reusing the engines and propeller. They even salvaged the cotton fabric of *White Wing* for reuse. Bell had studied entomology; he discerned a resemblance between its mode of flight and that of a common flying beetle. Accordingly, the new craft took the name *June Bug*.

Curtiss took its controls and made three flights on June 21st, covering 1,266 feet on his best one. Four days later he was back in the air, stretching his record to 3,420 feet, which topped the one-kilometer mark. The Aero Club had sent an observer, who notified the magazine that Curtiss was ready to try for the trophy and intended to do so on the Fourth of July. He waited until early evening when the wind died down, then made an attempt. The *Bug* flew well but rose to an altitude of 40 feet, leading his wife to cry, "Oh, why does he go so high?" His tail had been installed improperly, which produced the climb, and Curtiss responded by chopping the ignition. He settled to the ground a thousand feet short of his goal. There still was enough daylight for a second try, and with his tail reinstalled, he flew for a full mile. The trophy was his, and there was more. Late in August he demonstrated maneuverability by executing a complete circle, while a colleague flew a figure-eight.

Anticipating rapid advances in the art of flight, *Scientific American* had stipulated that the same trophy was to go to the first aviator to achieve a distance of 25 kilometers, some 16 miles. Curtiss was back in July 1909 to try for this feat as well, with a new craft painted with yel-

Glenn Curtiss.

low varnish and named *Gold Bug*. He installed better ailerons, breaking with Casey Baldwin's movable wingtips and fabricating these control surfaces as hinged rectangles set midway between his two biplane
wings. Thus accoutered, he flew nineteen circuits of a marked course,
covered nearly 25 miles, and won the award a second time.

By then his eye was on the *Grande Semaine* at Reims, which was
held a month later. The news publisher James Gordon Bennett, owner
of the *New York Herald*, was sponsoring a speed race with a purse of
$5,000 as the prize, accompanied by a silver sculpture called the Gor-
don Bennett Cup. On arriving in France, Curtiss learned that he was
the only American present for competition. Elimination trials soon
made it clear that he faced only one opponent: Louis Bleriot.

The rules of the competition called for each man to fly two laps for a total of 20 kilometers, and to do so at different times. Curtiss flew this distance in 15 minutes and 50 seconds, for a speed of 47.1 miles per hour. With Bleriot still to fly, he said that he felt "like a prisoner awaiting the decision of the jury."

The Frenchman took to the air and flew his first lap. He beat Curtiss's time by 4 seconds. He flew the second lap, landed, and ran over to the judges' stand. A friend of Curtiss was there as well, erupting in a shout of joy as he ran toward him. "You win! You win!" he cried. "Bleriot is beaten by six seconds!" Curtiss had gone where neither of the Wrights had cared to fly, and had outraced the best that France had to offer.

In the face of this triumph came unwelcome news. Wilbur had filed a lawsuit against Curtiss on grounds of patent infringement. The Wright patent specifically discussed flexible wings that could be warped, whereas the Curtiss wings were rigid with ailerons that were mounted as separate surfaces. The Wrights nevertheless took the view that their patent was broad enough to cover these improvements.

Glenn Curtiss, with ailerons mounted at his wingtips,
flies to victory at Reims in 1909.

Accordingly, the suit sought a court order prohibiting Curtiss from manufacturing, selling, or exhibiting his airplanes.

Relations between these inventors had been friendly enough at the outset, with Curtiss approaching them during 1906 and trying to sell them an engine. Patent law gave Curtiss free rein in using their protected innovations as long as he restricted himself to aeronautical research, but competition for prizes stepped over the line. *Scientific American* gave good coverage of the *June Bug* during 1908, and after Curtiss won that magazine's trophy, he received a letter from Orville that amounted to a shot across his bow:

> I learn from the *Scientific American* that your *June Bug* has movable surfaces at the tips of the wings, adjustable to different angles on the right and left sides for maintaining the lateral balance. . . . We did not intend, of course, to give permission to use the patented features of our machine for exhibitions or in a commercial way.
>
> This patent broadly covers the combination of sustaining surfaces to the right and left of the center of a flying machine adjustable to different angles. . . . Claim 14 of our Patent No. 821,393, specifically covers the combination which we are informed you are using. We believe it will be very difficult to develop a successful machine without the use of some of the features covered in this patent. . . .
>
> If it is your desire to enter the exhibition business, we would be glad to take up the matter of a license to operate under our patents for that purpose.[4]

Curtiss responded with his *Gold Bug*. Its redesigned ailerons gave better effectiveness, while offering hope that they would be less likely to infringe on Patent No. 821,393. He then flew it in front of ticket-buying crowds, sold it for $5,000, and flew it for its new owners to win the *Scientific American* trophy a second time. The Wrights viewed the new ailerons as nothing more than fig leaves, and their attorney took action accordingly.

The request for an injunction went before a federal judge, John Hazel. A decade earlier he had tried a case involving the nascent auto industry, and had shown that he was willing to take a broad view of patent claims. Early in 1910 he gave the Wrights what they wanted by issuing the injunction. This was legal heavy artillery; coming only months after the filing of the suit, it amounted to accepting already that the brothers were likely to prevail on the merits of their case. Curtiss posted a bond of $10,000, for which Hazel suspended his injunction while Curtiss sought an appellate ruling that could overturn it. His appeal succeeded; in June a separate panel of judges dissolved the injunction. Curtiss now was free to continue in business while litigating the matter of patent infringement, which was still at issue before Hazel. This was the main lawsuit, which went forward on its own.

Meanwhile, the Wrights had a company to run, and at the start of the same year they began work on two new designs at their plant in Dayton. The versions of 1907–1909 had amounted to Model A (though they did not use the name), so one of their 1910 craft was designated Model B. It was a two-seater with a 40-horsepower motor, and their grasp of propeller and wing design meant that it would be speedy indeed. The brothers therefore moved the horizontal elevator from the front to the rear, creating a true tail. This helped to give the craft the stability of an arrow, whereas a front-mounted elevator at high speed was likely to flip the aircraft violently up or down. The engine also had enough horses to dispense with the catapult for takeoff. Model R, a small single-seat racing plane, filled out their new offerings.

While legal action continued, Curtiss and the Wrights also competed in the air. Long-distance flights now became their chosen arena, with Curtiss firing the first round by announcing an intention to fly from Albany to Governor's Island, off the tip of Manhattan. The *New York World* had offered a $10,000 prize for this feat during the Hudson River celebrations of the previous year, when distances on this scale lay well beyond the state of the art. The 152 miles separating those locations ran through hilly country that offered few good landing areas, making the venture doubly difficult.

He knew he would need intermediate landing fields; he had no intention of attempting a nonstop flight. He found one on the broad lawns of a wealthy man's estate at the northern tip of Manhattan.

Reconnoitering the Hudson Valley during a riverboat trip, he picked Poughkeepsie as his main intermediate stop. That town held the State Hospital for the Insane, where the director welcomed him: "Certainly, Mr. Curtiss; here's where all the flying machine inventors land." A meadow across town looked even more inviting, and he arranged to have supplies of gasoline, water, and oil ready for his arrival.

He took off late in May, accompanied by a special train with newsmen and photographers on board. The weather was fine; he flew the 87 miles to Poughkeepsie with ease, which set a new record for cross-country distance. Continuing southward, he ran into gusty winds near Storm King Mountain but flew successfully through the downdrafts. He carried a gallon and a half of oil but a leak developed; at Bear Mountain his oil gauge was worrisomely low. The gauge showed further bad news as he passed the wide Tappan Zee, and he decided to make an unplanned landing on those sloping lawns. His surprised host greeted him like a gentleman and helped Curtiss replenish his gas and oil. The cruise to Governor's Island was like a victory lap, for he wrote, "I could see crowds everywhere. New York can turn out a million people probably quicker than any other place on earth, and it certainly looked as though half of the population was along Riverside Drive or on top of the thousands of apartment houses that stretch for miles along the river. Every craft on the river turned on its siren."

This success swiftly brought demands for more, as newspapers in New York and Philadelphia announced a $10,000 award for the first round-trip flight between those cities. That prize went to Charles Hamilton, who flew for Curtiss and who made that two-way trip midway through June. He did not break Curtiss's distance record, but his outbound leg was nonstop. Then the Wrights got into the game. In September one of their own fliers, Walter Brookins, covered 192 miles from Chicago to the state fairgrounds in Springfield with two intermediate stops, while Wilbur followed in a special car attached to a train of the Illinois Central.

Such flights carried the first faint hints of aviation as the world would come to know it. Farman in France had already stayed aloft for three hours; now Curtiss, Hamilton, and Brookins were connecting major cities. There was no similarity with the present day, of course; pilots sat in the open air, and the only comparable modern experience is flight in an ultralight, a powered hang glider. This didn't stop the aviators of that era. In October 1910 the news baron William Randolph Hearst offered $50,000 for a flight from coast to coast in less than thirty days, and it was not long before there were takers.

Harry Atwood, trained by the Wrights, flew a Model B from St. Louis to New York in August 1911. He took twelve days to cover the 1,300 miles. This was the first really long connected series of hops, as distinct from a flight, and Atwood hoped to try for the Hearst prize. He failed to come up with the necessary backing, and the attempt fell to another Wright-trained airman, Calbraith Rodgers. He came from a distinguished naval family; his forebears included Oliver Hazard Perry who defeated the British on Lake Erie in 1812, and Commodore Matthew Perry who opened Japan to the West in 1854. Now Rodgers had the opportunity to make some history of his own.

The Vin Fiz, *en route to its next crash.*

He found the financial support he needed at Chicago's Armour Meat-Packing Company, which now was offering a beverage, a carbonated grape drink called Vin Fiz. Armour promised to pay five dollars for every mile that Rodgers could cover, with the understanding that he would turn his airplane into a flying billboard. He met with Orville, ordered a custom-built version of the Model B, and arranged for Charlie Taylor to come along as a mechanic. Armour also provided a special train with a Pullman sleeping car, a day coach, and a freight car that was loaded with spare parts along with gasoline and oil. Its sides read, "VIN FIZ 5¢ Sold Everywhere," illustrated with a bunch of grapes.

Rodgers started from New York on September 17th, with a bottle of the purple soda serving to christen his airplane. As it rose into the air, people could read the large letters on the underwing: "VIN FIZ The Ideal Grape Drink." Atwood had crossed nearly half the country without serious mishap, and as Rodgers flew on with a cigar in his teeth, he hoped to do likewise. But during takeoff next morning, he failed to clear a tree and rammed into a chicken coop. He came away bleeding at the temple but still holding on to his cigar. Taylor arrived and rebuilt the damaged craft, which took to the air two days later.

A spark plug worked loose. It took two hands to fly a Wright biplane, but he held the plug in place with one hand while operating the controls with the other. He lost his way and wandered into Pennsylvania, where a friendly crowd tried to grab pieces of his flying machine as souvenirs. Shooing away a man who had hoped to chisel off a valve, he continued onward. He snagged a barbwire fence while trying to take off near Buffalo, crashing to the ground amid further serious damage. He was not yet west of New York state, but already had wrecked the *Vin Fiz* twice.

New repairs ensued, and as Rodgers crossed the Midwest, he took off one day amid bad weather. Soon he found himself flying amid a thunderstorm. He quickly became the first man to steer an airplane through such a storm's electrical discharges and blinding rain while living to tell about it, but he saw land through mist and came down safely. Then, trying to take off amid a gusty crosswind, he failed to gain altitude and cartwheeled into a hillside. *Vin Fiz* carried a bottle of that drink as a good-luck charm, which showed its value as it came through unscathed. But this luck did not extend to the airplane, which was badly smashed.

More repairs ensued. Rodgers limped into Chicago on October 8th, three weeks into his journey and only two days prior to a deadline when Hearst was to withdraw the $50,000. Having come this far, he vowed to press onward. The weather cooperated and he ran off a string of good flights during the following two weeks, covering as much as 234 miles as he flew into Missouri two days later. At Armour, accountants trimmed his flight pay to four dollars per mile. He responded by raising his mark to 315 miles in a day as he flew into Texas.

He was outward bound from Austin when he heard a loud bang. The engine shook violently as if to tear itself loose, and Rodgers shut it down before pancaking into a field. Damage to the aircraft was modest; that to his nerves was more severe. Charlie Taylor soothed the situation by installing a replacement engine. Bad weather gave him a chance to rest and to renew his courage, but when he tried to take off from a bumpy road, one of his propellers struck the ground and sent him skidding into a cactus as well as another barbwire fence. Once more his plane needed major surgery, but at least its talismanic bottle of the grape drink remained in good shape.

Rodgers reached the Colorado River on November 3rd, amid gorgeous weather. "I thought it must be a state ordinance," he later told his wife. "No clouds permitted beyond this line." He was thinking of Los Angeles, perhaps only a few hours away, when a cylinder blew out and demolished the engine, spraying hot oil into his goggles and driving shrapnel into his shoulder. He needed a doctor, but by the time one arrived he again was puffing on a cigar.

His earlier engine had been rebuilt to a degree, and although it gave him further trouble in the air, it saw him through to Pasadena two days later. He landed in Tournament Park amid a wildly ecstatic crowd. Yet while he had reached the West Coast, he felt that he could not be satisfied until he actually could touch the Pacific Ocean, 27 miles away at Long Beach.

Vin Fiz by then was on its last legs and was so badly worn that it could hardly be trusted to cover 27 feet. Mechanics did what they could during the next several days, but it wasn't enough. Rodgers took off again on November 12th, ran into more engine trouble over Compton, and came down hard while banking to land. This time he indeed was badly injured, spending three weeks in a hospital, while his airplane had to be rebuilt once more, using plenty of spare parts. He nevertheless was back in the air on December 10th, as he reached the end of his odyssey. Of the original airplane, all that was left was the rudder, the oil pan, and the trusty bottle of Vin Fiz, still intact.

This coast-to-coast journey showed that Wright aircraft were all but indestructible, but it also drove home the fact that there was no such thing as a safe airplane. Lack of safety had not been much of a problem at Kitty Hawk and for some time after, for with airplanes flying at vanishingly low altitudes and speeds, even a serious crash was scarcely more injurious than a bad spill on a bicycle. But when aircraft began to gain altitude, the risks went up as well. The Army's Tom Selfridge had been the first fatality, in September 1908, at a time when no more than ten men had flown for as long as a single minute. The worldwide death toll reached 35 at the end of 1910 and topped a hundred only ten months later.

The most basic forms of safety were entirely absent. Pilots flew without seat belts, believing that it was better to be thrown from an airplane on impact than to be trapped in the wreckage. This brought the death of such flyers as Harriet Quimby, one of the world's earliest women aviators, who fell from her craft when it lost control and plunged downward. Loss of control indeed was an ever-present hazard; it killed Calbraith Rodgers at Long Beach, only four months after his transcontinental flight, when he made a sudden dive to avoid a flock of seagulls. Other people died when their machines came apart in mid-air. This happened early in 1910 to Leon Delagrange, who made too sharp a turn at an air show and lost his life when the wings of his Bleriot monoplane collapsed. Six months later it was the turn of Charles Rolls, a founder of Rolls-Royce, who was flying before a large crowd when an improperly modified tail broke off from his biplane.

The toll might have been lower, but by 1910 aviation was beginning to resemble bullfighting, with the pilots seeking greater thrills for spectators (and bigger turnouts) as they tempted fate. One man advertised his Dive of Death, from which he planned to pull out just in time. Lincoln Beachey, one of the best, learned that a French aviator had looped the loop following such a dive, and promptly incorporated such loops into his show. Walter Brookins, who had flown from Chicago to Springfield, made a specialty of tight turns close to the ground with his craft banked at angles up to eighty degrees.

For planebuilders such as Curtiss and the Wrights, there really were only two ways to make money: by selling airplanes to daredevils and by sponsoring their performances. Both put together teams of flyers, with Curtiss's including Beachey. Wilbur wrote this activity meant that the brothers would "compete with mountebanks for a chance to earn money in the mountebank business," but they did it nonetheless. However, the risks of the venture soon brought it to an end. The Wrights assembled a team on which nine men were members at one time or another, but five of them died within only a year and a half. By then the brothers had dissolved the group, though they continued to sell flying lessons as well as airplanes.

It was quite a turnaround. Only a few years earlier, they had bent every effort to fly in privacy. Now aviation was a series of spectacles performed before grandstands filled with shouting people. In the words of the satirist Tom Lehrer, many of them were hoping that death would brighten an otherwise dull afternoon. Yet there was real prospect for growth in this field, and once again Curtiss was in the forefront, with naval aviation as his new activity.

The first thoughts came from the *New York World*, which had put up the $10,000 prize for Curtiss's flight from Albany to New York. This newspaper showed a continuing interest in that aviator, and proposed that he might fly from the deck of an ocean liner to land, delivering airmail before the ship reached port. This suggestion stirred interest in the Navy. No one at the time was thinking seriously of sending bombers to sink a battleship, but a sea-based airplane might readily fly ahead of a battle fleet and find an enemy, then return to report its position and strength. This role had traditionally been reserved for frigates, small fast vessels with enough speed to outrun a pursuer. Aircraft, serving as eyes of the fleet, could cover wider areas and promised to be far less costly.

In October 1910 a Navy engineer, Captain Washington Chambers, received orders to attend a week-long air show to be held that month outside Manhattan. He met Curtiss, who assigned Eugene Ely, one of his stunt pilots, to be the first naval aviator. Chambers then went to the Norfolk Navy Yard, where the cruiser USS *Birmingham* was at his disposal. He ordered construction of a wooden platform over its bows, with length of 83 feet and a modest downward slope. This was not much room for a takeoff. It would have helped if the cruiser could have steamed full tilt into a stiff wind; Ely's lightweight airplane then might virtually have levitated off the deck. Instead he insisted that the ship remain dead in the water, and he made his takeoff only after the wind had died down. He still had the advantage of the platform's downward slope and of its elevation above sea level, and he made full use of both. His aircraft dropped like a rock after clearing the bows, but picked up speed as it fell. Its propeller tips nipped the water, drenching Ely and blinding him with spray on his goggles, but he kept from ditching and quickly was airborne. He headed out to sea, ran into fog, turned for shore, and landed at the first opportunity.

It was a fine act for a stunt pilot, but to the Navy it looked like another Dive of Death. An observer wrote, "No such narrow margin of safety as this flight showed would be permissible." Still there was an alternative: the seaplane, fitted with pontoons. The observer recognized this, as he wrote, "Means for rising from the water must be devised and means of hoisting the machine aboard ship in case it should land in the water."

The problem of pontoons was trickier than it looked. The thrust from propellers necessarily exerted its force several feet above the water line, exerting an off-balance push. This tended to make the aircraft rotate downward, driving the tip of a pontoon into the water. This turned the pontoon into a major source of drag from the water, while robbing the wings of lift from the air. The Wrights in Dayton had exper-

imented with pontoons during 1907, but did not pursue them seriously. Curtiss conducted experiments and quickly appreciated that a pontoon should not resemble a canoe with a sharp prow. It needed a
rectangular prow with an upward curve on its underside, like the front
end of a ski. Such a device, mounted well forward, could use its buoy-
ancy to keep its nose above the water, with the curved underside generating a force during takeoff to counteract that from the propeller.

In January 1911, while Curtiss was still working on his pontoon,
Ely became the first man to fly from land onto a ship's deck. The Navy
provided the vessel, the cruiser USS *Pennsylvania,* with Curtiss and
Ely directing construction of a 150-foot platform at the stern. They
faced the problem of stopping their airplane after it touched down
and solved it with an arrangement that all naval airmen came to
know. They installed twenty-two arresting ropes, stretched in parallel
across the deck with a sandbag at each end, and placed grabhooks
under the plane's belly to snag those cables.

Ely took off from a parade ground at the Presidio, an old Spanish
fort in San Francisco, and flew out to sea. A lookout aboard ship spotted him; the cruiser's horn blared a welcome. He came in low,
approached the stern, and stopped within sixty feet as his hooks
caught the ropes. It was a performance that certainly called for his
skill, for if he misjudged his altitude he could easily have crashed into
the vessel's superstructure. Still, he had added one more arrow to the
quiver of a nascent naval air force.

Later that month, Curtiss flew with his new pontoon. "I had not
expected to make a flight," he wrote, "only try it on the water to see
how the new float acted. It ploughed through the water deeply at first,
but gathered speed and rose higher and higher in the water and
skipped more and more lightly until the float barely skimmed the surface of the bay. So intent was I in watching the water that I did not
notice that I was approaching the shore, and to avoid running
aground I tilted the horizontal control and the machine seemed to
leap into the air like a frightened gull. So suddenly did it rise that it
quite took me by surprise."[5] He set down on the water, tried it again,
and found that it worked as well the second time.

In 1912 he went further by inventing the flying boat. He built a test airplane with a fuselage shaped like a pontoon, but it produced too much drag to take off. Observing the wake from a motorboat, he considered that he might diminish this drag by having the bottom make a sharp upward step partway along its length. It worked; the new shape rose into the air quite readily, and Curtiss saw that he had made another invention. With this "step bottom," a plane could fly over the ocean while reserving the means to come down safely in an emergency.

The Wrights might have introduced innovations of their own, but they were bogged down in litigation. This involved far more than *Wright* v. *Curtiss,* for while that was the most important lawsuit, it certainly was not the only one. The brothers were like a carpenter with a hammer who thinks everything in the world is a nail. To them, almost everyone in aviation was a potential patent infringer. Their patent indeed was broad; it embraced every successful system of flight control. Anyone who wanted to use such a system was welcome to do so, provided that he purchased a license from the Wrights and paid the pertinent fees and royalties. However, not everyone cared to do this, while some inventors took exaggerated views of their own originality. French planebuilders such as Bleriot were subject to suit in two countries, for infringing the Wrights' French patent and for selling aircraft within the United States. The brothers even sued the organizers of air shows, who had to purchase their licenses as well.

The Wrights also found themselves on the receiving end. Other inventors held their own patents and were quite prepared to assert that Wilbur and Orville had committed their own infringements. Their attorney had secured duplicate patents not only in France but in eight other European countries. In actions separate from those of infringement, every such patent was open to challenge as being invalid, on grounds either that the Wright control system had actually been invented earlier, or that the brothers had compromised their patent through prior disclosure.

Legal fees were no problem; the Wright Company paid the bills. But every one of these actions had to be litigated either in the United States or in Europe, and this took an increasing share of the brothers' time. They had to make court appearances in a number of cities, pre-pare depositions, and present expert testimony to judges who were aeronautical innocents. Lawsuits take on lives of their own, particu-larly when initiated by other parties, and the brothers found them-selves enmeshed in legal webs that offered few opportunities for escape. They won nearly all of these suits, both as plaintiffs and as defendants, but they knew that they had not invented the controllable airplane merely to devote their lives to subsequent court proceedings.

Legal and business activities continued to impel the brothers to spend long periods apart, but the family remained close and its mem-bers were glad to be together when they could. Early in May 1912, with spring having returned, Katharine packed a picnic lunch as Wilbur, Orville, and their father Milton joined her for an afternoon outdoors. When they got home, Wilbur complained that he had a temperature. He continued his activities for several days but found himself growing weaker. He took to bed, where his condition deteri-orated further. Two weeks later he rallied, but soon he worsened anew. He died on May 30th, and Milton's diary notes amounted to a eulogy:

> His life was one of toil. His brain ceased not its activity till two weeks of his last sickness had expired. Then it ceased. . . . A short life, full of consequences. An unfailing intellect, imperturbable temper, great self-reliance and as great modesty, seeing the right clearly, pursuing it steadily he lived and died.[6]

The diagnosis was typhoid, which Wilbur believed he had con-tracted by eating improperly prepared seafood during a recent trip to Boston.

Death was no stranger to the Wright household. The family had lost their beloved Susan in 1889, while Orville had seen a number of his fellow pilots plummet to their own destruction. Still, the brothers had drawn so much emotional satisfaction from their family ties that neither ever married. During the months that followed, there were times when Orville had to remind himself that his brother had not merely stepped into another room.

Wilbur was forty-five years old at the time of his death. Orville was four years younger and had much of his life still ahead. He also now held considerably greater responsibility within the Wright Company, where he took over as president. *Wright* v. *Curtiss* still was high on the agenda of unfinished business, and on February 27, 1913, Judge Hazel rendered his decision.

It represented complete vindication for the Wright interests. Holding that their patent indeed was broad enough to apply to Curtiss's ailerons, Hazel handed down a permanent injunction barring Curtiss from building, selling, or publicly flying his airplanes. Curtiss was free to negotiate with Orville, seeking a settlement that might permit him to continue his business, but instead he posted a bond and took the case to the U.S. Circuit Court of Appeals. Hazel stayed his injunction pending this appeal, and the litigation continued.

Eleven months passed, and this appellate court handed down its own ruling. Once again Orville won all he had asked for, as it upheld Hazel's decision in full. Nevertheless, Curtiss spotted a loophole. The injunction only covered aircraft that moved their ailerons simultaneously in opposite directions. He introduced a system that moved only one aileron at a time, leaving the other flush with its wing. The Wrights had thought of this; it was in Claim 1 of their patent. However, that claim had not been litigated during the action of the previous years, leaving Orville to start again with an entirely new lawsuit. He filed that suit late in 1914. Curtiss then pleaded that as a defendant, he was in need of judicial relief. He won a stay of the appellate injunction, and went back to building ailerons of the type he preferred.

Wright v. *Curtiss* thus had consumed uncounted hours for both the Wrights and their attorneys, and the only people who made any money were the lawyers. Indeed, Curtiss put the litigation to his advantage. Early on, knowing little of aeronautics, he had set up a company in partnership with no less than Augustus Herring, who had spent time with both Chanute and Langley and had visited the Wrights at Kitty Hawk. Herring was quite prepared to let people believe that this background gave him the secrets of the universe. He loved to talk about his patents, which were nonexistent, and his inventions, which were imaginary.

But he knew how to win the confidence of men of experience, to keep them from asking questions. The new firm was the Herring-Curtiss Company, and Herring had a good lawyer. He persuaded Curtiss to invest in the firm by signing over his successful factory and the land it sat on, in exchange for stock in Herring-Curtiss plus a mortgage; no cash changed hands. Herring also made himself the majority stockholder. Hazel's injunction of 1910 gave Curtiss a way to get rid of this incubus, as it destroyed the company's credit and led creditors to push it into involuntary bankruptcy. After he won dismissal of the injunction on appeal, he set up a new firm. He repurchased his factory and other holdings at a trustee's sale, and soon was back in business.

Herring had approached the Wrights following their flights at Kitty Hawk in 1903 and had offered a somewhat similar arrangement based on his "patents." The brothers had ignored him, showing that they were smarter than Curtiss, but a decade later the success of the legal delaying actions made it increasingly clear that the Wright and Curtiss companies would compete on the merits of their products. Curtiss had spent far less time than the Wrights in litigation, and his aircraft were correspondingly superior.

From the outset, his ailerons had held preference within the world of aeronautics, for while wings with ailerons were rigid, warping wings had to be flexible, which compromised their strength. Even so, the Wrights continued to warp their wings. An important reason was that they had put so much effort into defending the merits of this approach during litigation that abandonment of wing warping threatened to undermine their legal position by admitting that Curtiss's method was better. The Wright Company did not begin to use ailerons until late in 1915.

Curtiss held a further advantage in pilots' control apparatus. The Wrights abandoned the hip cradle in 1907 when they installed upright seating, but they introduced instead a complex system of hand-operated levers. One of them went back and forth to work the elevator. Another went back and forth to warp the wings. Many Wright aircraft were two-seaters and the location of the two controls was reversed for the left- and right-hand positions. Students therefore trained as left- and right-hand pilots; a man could easily get confused if he sat in the wrong seat. The wing-warping lever also had a movable end. It operated the rudder, bending left or right by twisting the wrist.

The Curtiss system, available only on his airplanes, was far more natural. An aviator placed a yoke around his shoulders, which had wires that controlled the ailerons. Like a motorcyclist leaning into a turn, he bent his body to the left or right and made the plane bank in the same direction. He held a steering wheel, turning it like the one in an automobile to swing the rudder right or left. That wheel was mounted atop a control stick—between the pilot's knees, not off to one side as in a Wright aircraft—which moved back and forth to work the elevator. Everyone used the same arrangements; there were no left- and right-hand pilots under Curtiss.

There also were serious questions concerning the safety of the Wright designs. As early as 1910, such aircraft accounted for nearly one-fourth of that year's thirty-five fatalities. During the first few years of Army aviation, Wright machines brought the death of six of the first seven men to die in air crashes, and eleven of the first twelve. The Model C of 1913, which amounted to a Model B with a more powerful motor, was responsible for seven of those twelve. A military investigation concluded that its elevator was too weak, condemning the Model C as "dynamically unstable for flying."

Many of these crashes had occurred when an airplane stalled. Orville introduced a pilots' instrument to indicate angle of attack, in the form of a vane that deflected to follow the airflow. He hoped that it would advise aviators when they were climbing too steeply and thereby serve as a stall-warning indicator. It didn't; the accidents continued.

In a parallel effort, he launched a renewed attempt to achieve stability in flight. The vision of an aircraft with built-in stability had died hard, for although it was easy to install wings that had plenty of dihedral, their stability brought a loss of aileron effectiveness and made the planes hard to maneuver. Orville, followed closely by Curtiss, believed that the answer lay in an autopilot. Such a device might maintain an airplane in a steady attitude even if the pilot took his hands off the controls.

During 1913, Orville introduced an arrangement that used a pendulum to detect deviations from straight and level flight, or from properly banked turns. This pendulum swung to one side in response to such wanderings, activating a mechanism that warped the wings to restore normal flight. Orville's invention tried to control pitch with a vane like that of the angle-of-attack indicator. The vane could be set at a desired angle for use during climb and descent as well as in level flight. Any swerve from the desired flight path deflected this vane and brought corrective action from the elevator. Orville showed off this system late that year, making seven circuits of a field while he flew with his hands off the control levers. His craft maintained its bank angle and flew at nearly a constant altitude.

Curtiss addressed the problem of stability by approaching Elmer Sperry. His firm of Sperry Gyroscope was building gyrocompasses for the Navy and was also working on a gyrostabilizer to prevent ships from rolling heavily in swells. He sent his son Lawrence to develop a gyrostabilized automatic pilot for aircraft, which saw demonstration in France in mid-1914. Lawrence, piloting a Curtiss flying boat, took his hands off the controls and stood up in the cockpit as his mechanic made his way outward along the wing. The craft remained steady in flight, and a crowd of spectators went wild.

By bringing the gyroscope to aviation, Curtiss showed that he certainly was far from being merely a patent infringer. He was an innovator of the first rank. The gyro proved to be the critical element in cockpit instruments for safe flight through clouds, in successful automatic pilots, and, decades later, in inertial guidance systems. However, Sperry's early gyros tended to drift in direction after a few minutes, thereby losing effectiveness, while Orville's system added nothing to what a skilled pilot already could do. The search for safety therefore took other forms.

Pilots were accustomed to sitting in the open air, but airflow around their bodies was turbulent and contributed to unsteadiness in flight. Cockpits within fuselages addressed this, promoting smoother flow of air. Other problems resulted from pilots' preference for pusher propellers, mounted toward the rear. These gave an unobstructed view toward the front, with both Curtiss and the Wrights building aircraft of this type. Nevertheless, a senior Wright engineer named Grover Loening would not abide them. When he entered the Army in 1914 as an aeronautical engineering officer, he lost little time in condemning all pusher designs. They stalled too easily, and when they crashed, the engine often broke loose and fell on the pilot.

Army officials quickly switched to tractor designs, with the propeller in front, and recorded a dramatic improvement in safety. Some early tractors came from the California planebuilder Glenn L. Martin, who sold the first of them to the Signal Corps during July. Even so, the Wright Company took time before it got the word. It did not break with the past until late in 1915, when its Model K finally rejected a design layout that dated to 1903. The K introduced tractor propulsion as well as ailerons, finally catching up with an aeronautical world that had been using both for some time.

In this fashion the design of aircraft went well beyond the concepts of the 1909 *Grande Semaine,* which had continued to show strong Wright influence. Only a few years later, the appearance of the craft had changed dramatically. Pilots now sat in cockpits; airplanes had fuselages. Elevators now were at the rear, with the motor and propeller in the front. Seaplanes and flying boats were offering new vistas, for any river, bay, or lake could serve as an airfield, with no need to worry about potholes or stumps and ditches hidden in tall grass.

At the personal level, Orville and Curtiss remained a study in contrasts. Both had money galore, with Orville holding not only his own assets but his share of Wilbur's estate, which had totaled nearly $280,000. Curtiss was happily married and had a son, born in 1912. Orville was in his mid-forties, but seemed to be a great deal older. He now lived in a beautiful mansion, set on a 17-acre lot and showing a columned portico that recalled the one at the White House. Yet he rattled around within the vastness, accompanied only by his father, who died in 1917, and his sister Katharine. Carrie Kayler was still with them as the housekeeper; she had married, and her husband became part of the household. Still, Orville's ties to Katharine became the emotional mainstay of his life.

His health was not good. Having been maimed in the Fort Myer crash, he continued to walk with a limp, for he had unhealed injuries that X rays had not yet disclosed. Severe pain from those injuries at times could still lay him low. In December 1915 his agony became so intense that he had to be brought home in an ambulance, and remained in bed for eight weeks.

He had tried to carry on following the death of Wilbur, but he found that he was not well suited for the life of a company president, and he avoided its responsibilities as much as he could. He hoped to keep his hand in as an inventor, but the attempt at building an automatic pilot was one of his last contributions. Knowing that the company needed good leadership, he began making arrangements during 1914 for a quiet retirement.

He started by borrowing money and buying up most of the outstanding shares of the Wright Company. In 1915 he sold all his stock to a group of Manhattan investors, thereby transferring ownership. He relinquished his presidency, taking in return a post as a senior consulting engineer, but found that even this arrangement did not work well. After a year he allowed the consultancy to lapse. He was richer than ever, having received $1.5 million as his share of the transaction, but for the first time since 1899, he no longer held any serious involvement with aviation.

Patent litigation continued for a time and again displayed important differences between Orville and Curtiss. Curtiss by now had patents of his own, dealing particularly with flying boats, but he freely made his inventions open to all. He filed no suits for patent infringement. Against the Wright Company, he didn't need to; Orville had developed a heartfelt loathing of Curtiss and resolved that his own flying boats would not resemble those of this rival, which meant that those Wright aircraft were considerably inferior. However, Curtiss's aversion to patent litigation went deeper, for he had wisely concluded that lawsuits represented a fool's errand and that he was better off working to develop better aircraft. In a letter to the Navy's Captain Chambers, Curtiss wrote that "the best plan is to let the patents go, and go after the business."

Orville felt differently. As sons of a bishop, he and Wilbur had been raised to believe that the legal system existed to protect those who were in the right. Yet his latest foray against Curtiss did not go far, for Curtiss's attorneys had become skilled in delay. Moreover, Curtiss found a useful new tactic when the British entered World War I in 1914, and started to purchase his flying boats for use in antisubmarine patrols. Working at a new plant in Buffalo, he assembled aircraft that were completely bereft of ailerons. There was not a single aileron in the entire factory. He manufactured those control surfaces at a separate facility in Canada, a nation that did not recognize the validity of the Wright patent. Airplanes and ailerons then went separately to England, where American court decisions held no force. Workers there installed the ailerons to create finished warplanes.

The new lawsuit became moot during 1917, following America's entry into the war. The U.S. Congress voted $640 million for production of aircraft, described at the time as the largest single appropriation ever allocated for a single purpose. Attorneys within the industry shaped a cross-licensing agreement, whereby a number of patent holders placed their rights within a common pool. Planebuilders paid a royalty of one percent into this pool, from which funds were drawn to compensate the holders of patents for the value of those rights. In exchange for the royalty payments, planebuilders could draw on those patents at will. With this, the legal war between the Wrights and Curtiss finally came to an end.

The years-long litigation nevertheless left a residue of bitter feelings, accompanied by a prolonged challenge to the Wrights' role as inventors. The question of whether the Wrights really invented the airplane is with us still, resembling the issue of whether Shakespeare wrote the works of Shakespeare. To this day, these remain minor scholarly subspecialties, offering further ways for people in the academic world to bring home the bacon. They have their uses, challenging historians to document their conclusions with greater care and to strengthen the basis whereby they know what they claim to assert. But during the early twentieth century, the challenge to Wilbur and Orville had to be taken seriously. It shaped attempts to overturn their patent rights; it also forced them to defend their work against claims from rival inventors who held their own patents. This point of view also led the Smithsonian Institution to make the formal assertion that it was not the Wrights but rather Samuel P. Langley who had built the first craft that was capable of flight.

A key man at the Smithsonian was Albert Zahm, who had been chairman of the Department of Physics and Mathematics at Catholic University in Washington. He held a strong interest in aerodynamics and had operated the nation's first large wind tunnel. He had maintained a friendship with the Wrights, arranging for Orville to stay at the prestigious Cosmos Club during the 1908 trials of the Army's airplane. However, their friendship cooled in the course of the patent litigation.

At the outset, Zahm made it clear that he would offer his services as an expert witness to the highest bidder. The Wrights took the view that any man who could be bought in such a fashion was not to be trusted, and declined his overture. Still, Wilbur wrote to Zahm that while he might testify for Curtiss, "such service carried out in a spirit of fairness need not interrupt the friendship which has always existed between us." Six weeks later, Zahm appeared in court. The Wrights rebutted his statement by revealing that Zahm himself had filed a patent application that contradicted his own testimony. The courtroom then erupted in laughter when Zahm tried to explain why he could not produce this application. Having been rebuffed by the Wrights and then made to look ridiculous in court, Zahm thereafter was their enemy.

The wreckage of Langley's Great Aerodrome had been gathering dust in a back room of the Smithsonian, but in 1913 that institution set up a new aeronautical office and named Zahm as its head. This led to discussion of whether the Langley machine might be restored and made to fly after all. When Judge Hazel's injunction against Curtiss was upheld on appeal in January 1914, the question gained urgency. If Langley's craft indeed could fly, this might constitute new evidence, undercutting the Wrights' claims to have been first in flight. Such evidence might give weight to a motion seeking to reopen the litigation, with the injunction being stayed pending its outcome.

In the wake of the appellate ruling, a meeting took place between Curtiss, his leading attorney, and Zahm. This brought the Smithsonian into the fray. It had every reason to remain neutral and to avoid favoring either party, but it now came out in support of Curtiss, in a matter where he stood to benefit financially. As he wrote in a letter of mid-March, "I think I can get permission to rebuild the machine, which would go a long way toward showing that the Wrights did not invent the flying machine as a whole but only a balancing device, and we would get a better decision next time."

He was grasping at straws, but the injunction was in force and he was ready to use all means to defeat it. He was well aware that even Hazel's preliminary injunction, stayed by appeal and overturned within months, nevertheless had wrecked the credit of the Herring-Curtiss Company and left it bankrupt. He and Zahm therefore shaped a two-part strategy. They expected to begin by restoring the Great Aerodrome—now renamed *Langley*—to its 1903 configuration, so far as this was possible. Curtiss then would attempt to have it fly. After that, he intended to modify it extensively while installing a more powerful motor, to show that an airplane of this type could not only take to the air but could turn in a respectable performance.

Events soon led Curtiss to make his modifications earlier than he had anticipated. For the initial flights, he wanted to fly with Manly's 1903 engine. It had been dunked in the Potomac and then had been left unattended for ten years, which did not improve its performance. Rated initially at 52 horsepower, it turned out only 40 horse, and even then it required a modern carburetor and radiator, a new intake manifold, and magneto ignition in place of the original arrangement that used batteries. Still, this loss of power suited Curtiss. If the *Langley* could fly with reduced power in 1914, it would have flown all the better with full power in 1903.

Next came the problem of landing gear. The Great Aerodrome had none; it was built to take off using a catapult and then to come down onto the Potomac without floats for support. Curtiss fitted it with his pontoons, which were of a type that had not existed in 1903. He braced them with wire in ways that strengthened the wings, to keep them from collapsing again. The pontoons added weight and drag, which suited him as well; if it flew with these impediments, it would have done even better without them, eleven years earlier. Still, there now was reason to doubt that *Langley* could ever become airborne. He addressed this issue by refitting the wings to improve their lift-to-drag ratio. He also modified Langley's propellers for greater efficiency.

Power for propulsion had always been Langley's strong suit, and the overall effort would have been far more honest if Curtiss had simply replaced the Langley motor with a modern version of the same horsepower, ballasted to duplicate the weight. In lieu of the catapult, he might have built a fast speedboat to carry the airplane and then tried for a takeoff from Lake Keuka, with *Langley* restored impeccably to its 1903 configuration. As it was, this airplane now amounted to a hodgepodge of the old, the new, and the modified.

Even so, it flew after a fashion. The first attempt came on May 28th, with the craft floating on its pontoons and taxiing into the distance until it was too far away for good photography. Zahm was there as the Smithsonian's official observer, and he declared that it had made a flight of 150 feet. On June 2nd the experimenters indeed had a motorboat, a small one that kept pace with the aircraft as it taxied anew, and this time a photo taken from the boat showed daylight under both pontoons. *Langley* had flown! Clement Ader had done about as much in his *Eole,* in 1890, but Curtiss and the Smithsonian now had grist for their mills.

The next phase in the experiments came later that year, featuring installation of a new motor of 80 horsepower along with a single propeller that represented a substantially more efficient design than Langley's. Despite the weight and drag of the pontoons, *Langley* soared into the air and flew like a swan, covering distances as great as 3,000 feet. It then went back to the Smithsonian, where during 1918 it was restored to its original configuration of 1903 and placed on public display.

The Langley, *a substantially modified version of the* Great Aerodrome,
flies at Lake Keuka in 1914.

An accompanying label described it as the "first man-carrying aeroplane in the history of the world capable of sustained free flight. Invented, built, and tested over the Potomac River by Samuel Pierpont
Langley in 1903. Successfully flown at Hammondsport, N.Y., June 2,
1914." A more credible description would have stated that its initial
flights in 1914 introduced wing shapes, structural bracing, and pontoons that lay beyond what Langley was prepared to build in 1903, with
its ability to fly nevertheless existing largely in the mind of the behold-
er. The subsequent flights showed that after installing an engine of 1914,
it displayed the performance of early French machines of 1907.

Orville was far from pleased with these proceedings, but for several years he took no action. He had admired Langley, who had died in
1906, and did not want to raise criticisms that could be seen as attacks
upon the dead. He was not certain of the extent of Curtiss's modifications. He respected the integrity of the Smithsonian as a leading
national center for science. He was unprepared to assert that its officials knew what Curtiss had done, thereby making themselves parties
to his personal and financial interests.

But his attitude changed markedly during 1921, when a friend from England, Griffith Brewer, came to visit. Brewer had been present in Hammondsport during 1914 and had personally watched the *Langley* undergoing its modifications. He asserted that because he was British and had no formal ties to Orville, he could attack the Smithsonian without having his criticisms dismissed as mere petulance. Orville had before-and-after photos of Langley's machine, in both its 1903 and 1914 configurations; careful scrutiny enabled the men to compile a detailed list of the improvements. The work took two months and resulted in a paper written by Brewer titled "Aviation's Greatest Controversy." He sent copies to Zahm, Manly, and Curtiss, asking for comments. Another copy went to Charles Walcott, director of the Smithsonian.

Walcott's response left Orville outraged, for it showed that this official certainly had not been an innocent dupe. He had been involved in the affair up to his eyebrows. Walcott had not developed links to Curtiss, but he had a strong desire to vindicate Langley, who had been his predecessor within that institution. He also had no wish to break with Zahm, whom he had trusted.

Brewer's paper soon reached print, along with the replies from Walcott and the others, and stirred considerable interest. It challenged statements by Zahm that the original Great Aerodrome had been "unmodified." It gave a long list of changes that Brewer and Orville had discerned. The paper also stated that the *Langley* "did not do a true, free flight" with its original engine. Walcott remained unmoved. Further entreaties from Orville went nowhere, so in 1925 he played his trump card. He announced that he intended to send his 1903 Flyer to London, where it would be displayed in the Science Museum.

The continued existence of that airplane was purely a matter of happenstance. The Wrights had been accustomed to abandoning their gliders, leaving them to the winds and storms of Kitty Hawk once they were no longer needed. In this fashion the gliders of 1900 and 1901 vanished without a trace, while that of 1902 decayed until only a single wingtip could be salvaged. The 1903 machine might have met the same fate, particularly because it had been damaged severely following its last flight, but the brothers thought they might have further use for it, so they returned it to Dayton. They probably would have left it amid the sand dunes if they had known that they would build a new craft for 1904—which they used in full, then burned to keep it from taking up room. The 1903 Flyer remained within its crates, surviving a major flood in 1913 that left those wooden boxes submerged under twelve feet of mud and water. Still it could be salvaged, and was first exhibited publicly at Massachusetts Institute of Technology during 1916. It was Orville's personal property, to be displayed as he wished.

This move placed Walcott on the defensive, for it asserted that this national treasure could win its proper appreciation only in a foreign land. He and his successor, Charles Abbot, made some effort to accommodate Orville's wishes, but now it was Orville who remained unmoved. He met with Abbot and called for a published retraction of a number of false and misleading statements that the Smithsonian had issued since 1914. Abbot hemmed and hawed, and the Flyer remained in London.

As the controversy continued, and as everyone other than the Smithsonian continued to heap honors on Orville, this issue began to threaten that institution's credibility. It was one thing for Walcott to make a mistake, which Orville at first had thought had happened. It was another thing for him to stand fast and for his successor to offer mere palliatives, out of uncritical admiration for Langley. During the 1930s Abbot made several further attempts to deal with the matter, but Orville rejected them as too little, too late.

He particularly disliked statements, written by Zahm and published by the Smithsonian, that were blatantly false and misleading. For example, the Smithsonian's *Annual Report* for 1914 asserted that *Langley* "has demonstrated that with its original structure and power, it is capable of flying with a pilot and several hundred pounds of useful payload. It is the first aeroplane in the history of the world of which this can truthfully be said." The "useful payload" was the pontoons and their supports, while the "original structure" had collapsed at takeoff in 1903.

Abbot approached Orville anew in 1940, asking him to declare specifically what he wanted as a published statement. He replied that it must include a public apology: "I sincerely regret that the Institution employed to make the tests of 1914 Glenn H. Curtiss, who had just been adjudged an infringer of the Wright patent by the U.S. Court." This was more than Abbot could accept. He had already written, "If it is insisted that the Smithsonian Institution must confess to knavery before this controversy can be settled, we dismiss the subject."

A biographer of the Wrights, Fred Kelly, finally resolved the issue. He hoped to work closely with Orville and sought to win his confidence by approaching Abbot with draft text of a statement that held Orville's approval. Published in 1942, it appeared in full within the Smithsonian *Annual Report*. It included a five-page list, with an illustration, of the changes Curtiss made in the spring of 1914, even before installing his 80-horsepower motor. It also carried the apology that Orville had demanded:

> I sincerely regret that the Institution employed to make the tests of 1914 an agent who had been an unsuccessful defendant in patent litigation brought against him by the Wrights. . . .
>
> I point out that Assistant Secretary Rathbun was misinformed when he stated that the Langley machine "without modification" made "successful flights."
>
> I sincerely regret the public statement by officers of the Institution that "The tests" (of 1914) showed "that the late Secretary Langley had succeeded in building the first aeroplane capable of sustained free flight with a man."[7]

Orville gave ground as well. The hard condemnation of Curtiss was softened considerably. Nor did he insist on a statement that the 1903 Great Aerodrome had been incapable of flight. This compromise settled the controversy, clearing the way for the return of the Wrights' 1903 Flyer and for its display within the Smithsonian itself.

Orville by then was deep within the sunset of his years. He had returned to aviation following America's entry into World War I in 1917, but with the war's end he retreated to a personal laboratory that stood a short distance from his old bicycle shop in Dayton. He continued to dabble in aeronautics, but his most significant invention proved to be a toy for children called Flips and Flops. He accepted memberships on prestigious advisory boards, but contributed little to the organizations they directed.

As his personal twilight deepened, the stars in his sky winked out one by one. Following the death of Wilbur in 1912, he had lost his father in 1917. His brother Reuchlin, who lived across town, followed three years later. Then in 1926 his sister Katharine, who had become his emotional mainstay, declared that at age fifty-two she intended to marry an old friend and move to Kansas City. Stricken by what he regarded as a form of betrayal, Orville cut off relations with her and resisted her entreaties for reconciliation. He did not relent until she too went to her deathbed, dying of pneumonia in 1929. Lorin, his last surviving brother, then succumbed in 1939 and left him truly alone.

Yet he retained his sharp mind and his interest in aviation as he continued to follow advances in this field. In 1946, less than two years before he died, he was a guest of honor aboard a four-engine Lockheed Constellation, one of several models of airliners that set the pace following World War II. He even made his way to the cockpit and briefly took the controls. He then told a friend, "Wilbur and I produced and flew the first airplane powered by a conventional internal combustion engine, and I have just had the pleasure of flying one of the last models of a commercial plane that is powered by an internal combustion engine. All future commercial airline planes will be powered by some type of a jet propulsion engine."

He died early in 1948, following a heart attack, with the disposition of the 1903 Flyer still unresolved. The dispute had been settled in 1942, but the war was still on, and he took no initiative even with the return of peace. However, his will proved to contain the required stipulation. On December 17, 1948, forty-five years after the Flyer had lifted from the sands of Kitty Hawk, a formal ceremony installed it in a place of honor within the Smithsonian Institution.

The attendees then repaired to a nearby hall, where the Collier Trophy was being awarded. Taking its name from the Wrights' old friend Robert Collier, it was one of the most prestigious in aeronautics. In

1948 it was granted in recognition of the recent achievement of super-sonic flight. Its recipients included the Air Force's Chuck Yeager, who had broken the sound barrier in a Bell X-1 rocket plane. On that evening the world of aviation granted full distinction to its founders, while at the same time honoring men who were reaching toward new frontiers.

TEN

INVENTIVENESS
AND INVENTION

THE CONTRIBUTIONS OF FRANCE to aviation have been glorious, and are reflected to this day in its terminology. An airplane has a *fuselage* along with an *empennage* or tail. It maintains control using *ailerons*. Engines are enclosed within *nacelles* or housings, while the structural framework uses *longerons*, longitudinal members. The construction may be *monocoque*, "single shell," dispensing with internal structure and using a stiffened skin for its strength. A craft may have *canards*, small control surfaces set well forward of the wing. With the dictionary of aeronautics being largely written in French, one is led to ask just how the Wrights invented the airplane.

The influence of Wilbur and Orville is easy to trace. Following the death of Lilienthal in 1896, Ferdinand Ferber remained for a time as the only Frenchman still attempting to fly with gliders of that German design. A magazine article that he read in October 1901 led him into

340

correspondence with Chanute, who sent him a copy of Wilbur's recent address to the Western Society of Engineers. This paper discussed the gliders of 1900 and 1901, which had a forward elevator but lacked a tail. Ferber turned away from gliders of Lilienthal's type and began to build versions of the *type de Wright*. He made little headway, but his attempts drew interest among other would-be aeronauts.

Then in April 1903, Chanute spoke of the Wright 1902 glider at the Aero Club in Paris. This one had the movable rudder. Chanute provided photos that he had taken at Kitty Hawk. He helped the staff of *L'Aerophile* to prepare a detailed set of drawings, which appeared in print in August 1903. This encouraged Ferber to continue his own experiments, as he added a tail of his own design. Ernest Archdeacon crafted his own glider based on Chanute's articles, with a forward elevator and a rear-mounted rudder, and engaged Gabriel Voisin to fly it as his test pilot. A young engineer from the Sorbonne, Robert Esnault-Pelterie, sought to build a precise duplicate of the Wrights' 1902 craft.

If the drawings in *L'Aerophile* had come directly from Wilbur and Orville themselves, and had been accompanied by a detailed discussion of their control system that included wing warping, then these French amateurs might have gotten somewhere. As it was, both Ferber and Archdeacon ignored the need for control of roll, while Archdeacon crafted a downsized glider with reduced wingspan and substantially less wing area. After a fair amount of practice, Voisin covered little more than 65 feet of distance during his best glides. But this experience whetted appetites, and led these men to try to improve their designs by using their own originality. Esnault-Pelterie tried to follow up the published hints on wing warping that had come from both Chanute and Wilbur Wright. When his version of this control system failed to work well, he began experimenting with ailerons and became the first aviator to attempt to fly with these wing-mounted control surfaces. Ferber tried to add built-in stability by crafting his wings with dihedral. He thereby launched an involvement with inherent stability that characterized a number of French designs during the next several years.

After 1903 the leaks of information from Dayton dried up. A few additional hints reached print, as when a published drawing of the

Wright 1905 Flyer disclosed that it had a biplane forward elevator. For the most part, though, the French were on their own. They responded credibly, doing enough original work to give them some claim to independent invention, and by the time Wilbur flew at Le Mans in 1908 the French were building true airplanes of their own design. Wilbur's disclosure of his flight-control system, against a background of this inventiveness, then gave France what it needed to surge to the forefront.

Yet with the Wrights having undoubtedly invented the airplane in America while furnishing both inspiration and valuable technical guidance in France, the question remains: How did they do it? Right at the outset, Wilbur drew on his recent background by conceiving that an airplane was to amount to a flying bicycle. This approach was both imaginative and conservative. It also was in line with the work of other engineering leaders of the day, who approached new problems by using existing technology. Chanute, a civil engineer, had made a highly valuable contribution to aeronautics by building biplane wings that used the Pratt truss, which until then had served for railroad bridges. At a vastly higher level, John Stevens, chief engineer of the Panama Canal project, had spent his career as a railroad man. He saw the Panama effort as a large-scale exercise in the use of locomotives and rolling stock, and hired only fellow railroad men for the key posts.

Yet while the concept of the airplane as a bicycle drew on the brothers' background, it also stood as a brilliant leap of originality. Aeronautics was a topic that people were reading about at the time; that was how the Wrights learned about it in the first place. Certainly there was no shortage of mechanics who had hands-on experience with bikes. Even so, only the Wrights made the connection. It escaped both Chanute and Langley, and while these gentlemen were learned savants who rode in carriages, one must not think that they viewed bicycles with the dismissive attitude of Eustace Tilley, the high-collared dandy of *The New Yorker* who deigns to notice a butterfly. Langley and Chanute, like Francis Bacon centuries earlier, were quite prepared to take all knowledge for their province. Their colleague Alexander Graham Bell had studied entomology, drawing on this background in naming Curtiss's *June Bug*. If any of those men had appreciated that the bicycle held an important clue to the secret of flight, he would have followed it up.

The concept of the airplane as a bicycle held consequences, which the Wrights were quick to appreciate. A bicycle needed the continued attention of its rider to remain upright. They expected that an aircraft in flight would demand similar full-time attention, exerted through a control system, which led them swiftly to the issue of control and to the first thoughts of wing warping. Riding a bike also demanded practice; one could not simply hop on and pedal away. Hence it was clear that a flying machine would require even more practice, to be attained through careful trials using gliders. Full flight control, wing warping, and preliminary work with gliders then defined their approach to the engineering of an airplane.

Having modest means, they were prepared to build a new glider or airplane every year, but could not afford to emulate Chanute or Louis Bleriot by spreading their resources over a number of strongly different design concepts. They started with a particularly simple layout, a biplane kite with wing warping that also used a forward elevator, then scaled it up for their gliders of 1900 and 1901. In 1902 they added a tail, first as a fixed and then as a movable rudder. This slow process of development was also conservative, for it gave them maximum opportunity to learn from each year's flying machine along with minimum need for change from one year to the next. In turn, the required changes could be weighed and assessed with particular care.

The Wright brothers were brothers, which also contributed to their success. They could argue the issues in full. Indeed, they spoke only half in jest of times when Wilbur converted Orville to his point of view, while Orville convinced Wilbur that he had been right. Such interaction was essential; it enabled each man to challenge the other, to break an unproductive line of thought, and to compel one another to justify lines of reasoning in detail. No one else had that. Lilienthal had worked alone. Chanute was like a professor with students, who carried out work that he assigned while raising few challenges and fewer useful original ideas. Langley worked productively with his colleague Charles Manly, but they took separate responsibility for the engine and the airframe, and no one at the Smithsonian was senior enough to tell Langley that he was barking up a wrong tree.

The Wrights developed a knack for asking the right questions and coming up with appropriate answers. The question, *What is an airplane?*, was one that they addressed by viewing it as akin to a bicycle. When work during 1901 made clear that they needed better data on wings, they had the skill and imagination to craft their balances, which were essential in obtaining useful wind-tunnel data. They answered another question, *What is a propeller?*, by viewing its blades as rotating wings. The brothers have often been described as geniuses, and if indeed this is true, their genius lay in their ability to raise and to address the most important issues.

Mechanical skill was another important aspect of the Wrights' achievement. They designed and built their wind tunnel, balances, and model wings. They took the data, used it in crafting designs for the 1902 glider and the 1903 Flyer, then built these aircraft and flew them. This personal involvement with all phases of the work contrasts sharply with both Langley and Chanute, who relied on other people to build and fly their machines. The Wrights did not rely uncritically on published data; they obtained their own. By working as designers, builders, and test pilots, they channeled flight experience into design improvements, as when they introduced the movable rudder.

Much of their joint effort consisted simply of good hard work, and it is worth speculating on how they might have proceeded if they had not had the insight of the twisted box as early as 1899. Chanute was in Chicago, not far from Dayton, and one may envision the brothers beginning by building and flying hang gliders in accordance with Chanute's Pratt-truss designs. Yet because they were bicycle men, it is quite likely that they soon would have discerned a need for control. That is what happened in France, where experience with their early powered machines led both Voisin and Bleriot to introduce means of control, inadequate as they were. Wilbur and Orville might have had to try various forms of control before they came up with one that worked, but their bicycle background could have left them with little doubt that this was the critical problem.

As it happened, their conservatism served them well for a time. The Wright craft that were built under license in France and that flew at Reims in 1909 differed only in detail from the Flyer of 1903. The *Vin Fiz* of 1911 sported a rear-mounted tail at the end of an open framework, but it still used a pusher engine and warped its wings, while its pilot, Calbraith Rodgers, sat in the open as if at Kitty Hawk. By then the Wrights' conservatism was no longer helping them, for other inventors now were bringing forth improvements of considerable importance.

As early as 1909, Leon Levavasseur introduced his Antoinette VII. In addition to a full empennage it had a fuselage, as distinct from an open-framework boom extending to the rear. The engine was tractor-mounted, while the pilot sat in a cockpit. Two years later, Edouard Nieuport placed his motor within a housing and used a streamlined fuselage to set a speed record of nearly 83 miles per hour. In 1913 Louis Bechereau introduced monocoque construction with his Deperdussin racer. That same year saw a dramatic move toward large size, as Russia's Igor Sikorsky unveiled the world's first four-engine aircraft. In Great Britain, the B.S. 1 of Geoffrey de Havilland had a streamlined fuselage with its own enclosure for the motor. This plane would not have looked out of place twenty years later.

In 1915, with the world at war, increasing demand for high performance finally led the Wright Company to introduce tractor-mounted motors and ailerons. The writer Sherwood Harris summarizes the state of the art:

> Within a dozen years after the Wrights' first flight, sleek, streamlined monoplanes were buzzing around the racecourses of Europe at close to 125 miles per hour. The world altitude record was an astonishing 25,755 feet. A German pilot had won the world's endurance record by flying continuously for twenty-four hours and twelve minutes, and in Tsarist Russia a giant, multi-engined plane designed by young Igor Sikorsky had flown with sixteen persons aboard. The first landing and takeoff had been made from a warship, the seaplane was well-developed and the first experimental helicopters had appeared. The English Channel had been flown from France to En-

gland, from England to France, and by a woman; pilots had learned to roll, "loop the loop" and do other fancy maneuvers; and—more ominously—the first bombs had been dropped from an airplane on an enemy in combat.[1]

Many of the most advanced aircraft during the prewar years had been monoplanes. These had included the pathbreaking designs of Bleriot when he flew the Channel, as well as of Levavasseur, Nieuport, and Bechereau. But the ruthless air combat of the Western Front had weeded out such designs in favor of the biplane, which had greater structural strength and greater agility when maneuvering. For use in peacetime, biplanes also stood out. The high strength of their wings, which followed from their sturdy crossbraced construction, gave a marvelous lightness to such designs. A biplane with good engines could lift a load as heavy as that aircraft's empty weight.

At the Wright Company—the Wright Aeronautical Company after 1919—creative conservatism proved to be a two-edged sword. It had enabled the brothers to pursue a single approach in considerable detail, understanding it well enough to use it as a basis for their invention of the airplane. Yet this same conservatism then left the company trapped with a set of configurations that were increasingly obsolescent, while the world passed them by. That was why the airplane as an invention could belong to the Wrights while many of its most important features had names that were taken from the French.

Yet the company still had its opportunities, the most important of which proved to lie in engines. After the war the Navy began to build aircraft carriers, and soon found that air-cooled engines offered major advantages for the warplanes. Water-cooled versions had become standard, and had drawn on the experience of the automobile industry. For the Navy, though, they were inadequate, because carrier takeoffs still remained close to the limits of the feasible.

Catapults for naval aircraft lay well in the future. With the ship steaming into an onrushing breeze, a pilot would roll down the flight deck, lurch toward the sea, then pull out of the dive and begin to climb. There was always the danger of crashing into the ocean, with the bows of the onrushing carrier close behind. A naval aviator thus needed every advantage, and air-cooled engines offered quite a few. They were lighter than the water-cooled counterparts, enabling a pilot to accelerate more rapidly. They also dispensed with radiators that leaked, hoses that burst, cooling jackets that were prone to corrosion, and water pumps that sometimes failed. By enhancing reliability, air-cooled motors diminished the likelihood of engine failure, which inevitably led to a ditching and loss of the airplane.

During the war, Army orders for aircraft had been substantial, whereas carrier-based aircraft did not yet exist. The Army liked liquid-cooled motors, which used well-understood designs, and in 1920 only one outfit was working seriously on the air-cooled type. Its owner, Charles Lawrance, had designed engines for racing cars and now had a small company that was working out of a three-story loft in Manhattan.

His 200-horsepower motor was just what the Navy could use. However, his firm was too small to carry out the development and production that the Navy wanted. Navy officials responded by arranging for Lawrance to sell his company to Wright Aeronautical, which was large and had a well-established position in building airplane motors. In 1922 Lawrance became a vice-president at Wright. He responded by bringing out the Wright Whirlwind as a new model for 1924. It went on to power many aircraft, including Charles Lindbergh's *Spirit of St. Louis.*

This naval initiative launched a train of developments that brought air-cooled engines to the forefront, replacing the liquid-cooled types for most purposes. A competing firm, Pratt & Whitney, sprang to life with additional naval support and offered its Wasp and Hornet motors. Wright responded with its powerful Cyclone. The new engines placed the company on a solid financial footing, and in 1929 the financier Clement Keys arranged a merger with its old and bitter rival, Curtiss Aeroplane and Motor Corporation. Glenn Curtiss and Orville Wright were still alive when the new Curtiss-Wright Corporation came into existence as a major aeronautical powerhouse. It did not escape their attention whose name came first.

By then the design of airplanes was about to enter a time of rapid and dramatic change. The standard concepts of the 1920s continued to come forth as fabric-covered biplanes, for aircraft of this type had proved themselves during the war, and it was not clear for some time that anything better was necessary. What brought the change was a burgeoning demand for speed. Within a few years those World War I carry-overs became museum pieces, giving way to all-metal monoplanes.

The monoplane as a concept was old; the problem was to make it work. Lacking the crossbraced structure of a biplane, a monoplane wing relied for strength on spars, girder-like members running from wingtip to wingtip that could carry the airplane's weight in flight. Designers supported these spars by erecting kingposts and attaching bracing wires, but the merciless air battles of the war drove such makeshifts from the skies.

An obvious response lay in making the spars thick. Leon Levavasseur tried that as early as 1911, but his plane proved to be so heavy that no existing engine could get it off the ground. The increasing power of wartime engines gave new life to thick-spar concepts, which became an important theme in the work of the planebuilder Anthony Fokker. Late in the war he brought out the D-VIII fighter, demonstrating the strength of its wing by having two dozen men sit and stand along its length. The Fokker monoplanes nevertheless remained heavy, and while they flew well, they proved to be no faster than biplanes.

John Northrop, a California planebuilder, went on to turn the monoplane into a serious contender. His first airplane, in 1920, took shape as a biplane with a gracefully curving and well-streamlined wooden fuselage. He continued to work with wood and in 1927 he brought out the Vega, which combined a streamlined monocoque fuselage with an unbraced wing of the Fokker type. To save weight, he used an air-cooled engine.

The Vega was an immediate hit. It cruised at 135 miles per hour with its initial Wright Whirlwind motor, a speed that increased to 170 mph with the more powerful Pratt & Whitney Wasp. William Randolph Hearst ordered one, as did the pilots Amelia Earhart and Wiley Post. It found work as an airliner, carrying six passengers, and it also set records. Wiley Post's model, *Winnie Mae,* led the field in a race from Los Angeles to Chicago. At the 1927 National Air Races, it took a Vega to beat a Vega.

Aluminum construction also made headway during those same years, but the competition from wood was formidable. Straight-grained spruce, often used in biplane wing spars, was very light in weight and had a strength of 10,000 pounds per square inch. Aluminum alloy was six times denser but not necessarily six times stronger. Even so, the German designer Hugo Junkers viewed it as the material of the future. Beginning in 1917 he built a succession of all-metal fighters, first biplanes and then monoplanes. Following the war he built an aluminum airliner, the four-passenger F-13. He corrugated its skin for greater strength, but still it was heavy and cruised at only 87 mph.

It was important to reduce this weight, and Adolf Rohrbach, a countryman of Junkers, showed what to do. During the war he introduced "stressed skin" construction, which pointed a direction for monoplane wings that could combine high strength with light weight. Conventional design demanded that the wings' internal structure should carry the loads. Rohrbach argued that the skin could carry stress as well. The internal structure, with its spars and ribs, then would have its loads relieved, and could be made lighter in weight.

Even so, aluminum remained unpopular, for the alloys of the day tended to corrode. Then in 1927 a researcher at Alcoa, Edgar Six, showed how to bond a layer of pure aluminum, which resists corrosion, to an ingot of high-strength alloy. His process permitted the rolling of ingot into sheet while retaining the protective layer as a coating. The result was Alclad, which gave clear promise for use in aircraft construction.

Corrosion had delayed the general use of aluminum; rot soon brought an end to the use of wood. This happened after 1931, for in March of that year, a Fokker airliner lost a wing as it flew over Kansas. Seven people died in the crash, including the coach Knute Rockne of Notre Dame, who then was at the height of his fame. The accident investigation showed that moisture had accumulated in the wing interior, causing deterioration of the glue that bonded the birch and spruce spars. The wing was covered with plywood rather than fabric, in another use of Rohrbach's stressed-skin approach, and the decay could have been found only by peeling back those sheets of wood for an inspection.

That was the end of those Fokker aircraft. Fokker himself continued to build airplanes in the Netherlands but stopped doing so in America. His wooden wing construction was proscribed. Many of his remaining airplanes were scrapped, with the airline TWA removing engines from a number of them and setting them afire. New equipment now was a matter of urgency, and the Boeing Airplane Company came to the forefront.

Airmail service was a mainstay of commercial aviation, and in 1930 Boeing had built the Monomail, combining an air-cooled engine with all-aluminum construction and a monoplane wing. Boeing engineers then set out to design an improved bomber. Two teams of engineers set to work, one pursuing a biplane concept and the other an all-metal monoplane that incorporated features of the Monomail. After a few weeks the chief biplane designer threw in the towel: "I can't make my clunk do what a low-wing monoplane can do."

The bomber that resulted, the B-9, introduced the twin-engine configuration that became standard for contemporary airliners. It made its first flight in April 1931 and soon raised both eyebrows and speed records, turning in a top speed of 186 mph. Bombers were traditionally the slowest of the Army's planes, with the B-3, a twin-engine biplane, lumbering along at a speed of 90 miles per hour. But the B-9 was five miles per hour faster than the best operational fighters. These also were biplanes; the ones that attacked King Kong in the 1933 movie were some of the Army's best. But the success of the B-9 opened new vistas for monoplane fighters as well.

Ironically, the B-9 did not go into production. It lost out to the Martin B-10, which had a similar twin-engine layout and was faster still. But Boeing recouped with a new airliner, the 247, which carried ten passengers.

To look at it even today, across a span of seven decades, is to appreciate the revolution in aircraft design that had taken place in only a

The Boeing 247 airliner.

few short years. Only half a decade earlier, the famous Ford Tri-Motor had displayed external bracing struts, fixed landing gear, engines that lacked streamlined enclosures, and a boxy fuselage covered with corrugated aluminum skin. The 247 had none of these inadequacies. It mounted two engines rather than the three of that Ford, but its excellent streamlining gave it a speed of 155 mph.

It might have swept the skies, but at Douglas Aircraft, designers responded with the fourteen-passenger DC-2, followed by the DC-3 that had twenty-one seats. This was twice as many as in the 247, and because both of these craft were twin-engine monoplanes, the difference in revenue for a DC-3 was largely profit. C. R. Smith, president of American Airlines, declared that "the DC-3 freed the airlines from complete dependence on mail pay. It was the first airplane that could make money just by hauling passengers."

Fitted with new thousand-horsepower engines from both Curtiss-

Wright and Pratt & Whitney, the DC-3 launched its career in June 1936 with an initial flight from Chicago's Midway Airport to Newark. The passengers included old C. R. himself and the flight was nonstop, breaking the four-hour mark with help from a tailwind. With this, American launched its "Flagship" service between those two cities. By summer's end the airline was offering coast-to-coast service, 16 hours eastbound and 18 hours when heading west against prevailing winds. Passengers could work through lunchtime in Manhattan and then depart Newark at four in the afternoon, sleeping in a berth during the night and arriving the next morning at seven a.m. in Los Angeles.

The DC-3 went on to dominate commercial aviation. As late as 1958, on the eve of the first big jets, the DC-3 existed in greater numbers within the domestic fleet than any other airliner. It attracted passengers with low fares, spreading its operating costs over its number of seats. It then kept them coming back for more by delivering them safely.

Safety in the air called for instruments, in an era when pilots were accustomed to flying by the seat of their pants. If it separated from the seat that was installed within the airplane, the craft was in trouble and might even be upside down. Aviators trusted their senses. Britain's Sir Sefton Brancker, a leader in aeronautics, said of instruments that "personally, I am the greatest believer in using them for training. After a little experience with instruments as a guide, any intelligent man will find himself working without them instinctively."

But pilots' instincts proved to be worse than useless when they flew into clouds or dense fog that hid all view of the sun and ground. Like a car that tends to wander off the road, the plane would begin to turn. As it turned it banked; the design of the wings caused this to happen automatically. Then, turning on its own, the plane dipped its nose and picked up speed. The pilot would have felt an unbanked turn, the kind a car makes when rounding a corner, but not a banked one. However, he had no trouble noticing the increasing airspeed, and would conclude that the airplane was in a dive. He would respond by pulling back the control stick—and with the plane actually in a turn, this steepened the turn and made things worse. Soon the engine was racing and the propeller was snarling, while his seat-of-the-pants feelings kept urging him to pull back some more. If he could break out of the clouds and see the ground again, thereby gaining a visual reference, he could bring an end to this downward spiral and save the airplane. If he couldn't, it would either break up in midair or dive into the ground.

Orville Wright had built an autopilot in 1913 that used a pendulum to detect deviance from proper flight. It was worthless in such a situation, for in a banked turn, the pendulum continued to point toward the cockpit floor, even if the plane was nearly on its side. Some airmen reasoned that a ship steers through fog by using its compass; why not an airplane? The problem was that a compass needle does not point to true north; left to its devices, it would point steeply downward toward a location deep within the earth. This brought "northerly turning error," whereby a pilot flying northward could turn right—and the compass needle would show that the change in direction was to the left.

Lawrence Sperry had brought the gyroscope to aviation with his own autopilot. A gyro indeed could sense a turn, even when it was banked. In 1918 he mounted a gyro within an instrument panel. It worked nicely—but after he came out of the turn and took up a new heading, the needle stubbornly stayed at its new reading. He fixed that by attaching a spring to the gyro. Now it indicated rate of turn rather than the turn itself, deflecting more in a sharp turn than in a gradual one, then returning its needle to the upright position. This was the first turn indicator, which soon became standard equipment in cockpits. A variant, the turn-and-bank indicator, placed a ball within a curving glass tube that resembled a carpenter's level. The ball stayed centered during a properly banked turn but shifted position to indicate a sideslip.

Though available through the 1920s, these instruments did not exactly take the world of aviation by storm. Pilots continued to fly by the seat of the pants, often saying that the turn indicator wasn't something anyone could trust. It worked all right as long as an airplane was in the clear, but when it flew into clouds the thing went crazy and showed a turn.

Charles Lindbergh was one of the first to take the new instrument seriously. He used it twice while flying the mails between St. Louis and

Chicago, on occasions when he was caught in impossible weather. Both times all he could do was climb to a safe altitude and bail out. But those experiences taught him the key: to absolutely believe the indicator and to disregard his own senses. He did these things during his flight to Paris in 1927, when he flew through fog and clouds for long stretches. Twice he started to fall off in a spin, but both times he recovered by trusting his turn indicator. His enormous prestige then encouraged other aviators to do likewise. This not only improved safety; it introduced all-weather flying, which was essential if aviation was to become a serious activity.

The growing role of aviation relied on the increasing power of engines, which drew on the development of high-octane gasolines. These brought major improvements in horsepower, fuel economy, and lightness of weight. They served as a major underpinning of the sweeping changes that led to the DC-3. For comparison, the Liberty engine of World War I had 1,650 cubic inches in cylinder displacement, the volume swept by its pistons. Using the fuels of the day, it developed 400 horsepower. The Rolls-Royce Merlin of World War II had the same displacement but produced up to 2,200 horsepower, using vastly better grades of gasoline. Samuel Heron, a longtime leader in this field, states that "about half the gain in power was due to fuel."

The focus of fuel development was the struggle to boost engine compression ratio, which measures the degree to which a piston can compress a fuel-air mixture as it moves upward in the cylinder. Piston motors produced more power and gained better fuel economy by achieving high values for this ratio. But the achievable values were limited by a motor's ability to resist knock. Knock is a detonation of the fuel-air mix that resembles an explosion; one early researcher described it as "the noise that could be heard across a ten-acre lot."

During World War I, all that anyone knew was that kerosene made motors knock badly while gasoline often did not. The gasolines of the day were distilled directly from crude oil and had octane numbers as low as 50. But the octane scale lay well in the future, and a principal measure of fuel quality was its volatility, or ease of evaporation. Volatile fuels had a reputation for avoiding knock. Sir Harry Ricardo, a British researcher, later recalled that "the discriminating motorist never bought a drop of gasoline without first dipping his finger in the can and blowing on it to test its volatility."

Concern for this property led to the main advance in this area: the knock-suppressing qualities of tetraethyl lead. Two research chemists, Thomas Midgely and T. A. Boyd, began by noticing that the trailing arbutus, a wild flower with red leaves, blooms early in the spring. This, they thought, might be because the red color was absorbing sunlight particularly well. They were working with kerosene, and decided that if this fuel were dyed red, the unburned kerosene-air mix within a cylinder, ahead of the flame front, might absorb heat from the combustion and vaporize more fully, demonstrating improved volatility and resisting knock like gasoline. They proceeded to test this idea by using iodine from the lab shelf as a colorant. Sure enough, knock was greatly decreased. But when they tried ordinary red dye, it had no effect at all on the knock. Still these investigators had found that knock might be suppressed by using an additive that was not itself useful as fuel. This opened a wide range of compounds to study.

Substances resembling aniline proved more effective than iodine but produced a smelly exhaust. Tellurium was even better but was also smellier, stinking like "a mixture of garlic and onions." Midgely and Boyd then proceeded systematically by using the periodic table, and by 1921 they learned of the usefulness of tetraethyl lead. It had a rich, bitter odor, and had been known during the war. Used as a fuel additive, it gave resistance to knock when mixed with gasoline in quantities as small as a few cubic centimeters per gallon.

The next advance came at the new firm of Ethyl Gasoline, set up to market tetraethyl, where the chemist Graham Edgar defined the octane scale in 1927. He found that iso-octane, which has a molecule with eight carbon atoms, gave far better knock protection than any available gasoline. It was out of the question to use iso-octane itself, for it cost up to $25 per gallon at a time when the wholesale price of motor fuels was measured in pennies. Edgar nevertheless declared that if a fuel prevented knock as well as iso-octane, it would be rated at 100 octane.

For some time, people had been aware that gasolines distilled from California crude had particularly good antiknock properties. Investigation now showed that they had octane ratings as high as 73. The Army responded in 1930 by issuing a specification that called for aviation gasoline of 87 octane, which was made by adding tetraethyl to this California fuel. Further research showed that modest increases in octane could give dramatically disproportionate improvements in horsepower. In 1932 a Wasp was under test at an Army laboratory, putting out 720 horsepower when using 91-octane gas. It nevertheless continued to knock at full throttle, and the investigators responded with a California grade that contained far more tetraethyl than usual. Heron later recalled that "to everyone's surprise, and particularly my own, this fuel permitted 900 horsepower." This particular blend was useless for operational squadrons, for much smaller amounts of tetraethyl were damaging engine exhaust valves. Still, these results spurred new interest in 100-octane fuel.

Iso-octane now drew renewed attention. Its high cost came about because it was available only from the Rohm & Haas Corporation, which prepared it as a synthetic organic chemical by using an elaborate process. Shell Oil succeeded in providing a thousand gallons of this fuel, in a less pure grade, and the results were outstanding. They showed that a rise in octane from 91 to 100 boosted the power of a Wasp or Cyclone by up to thirty percent. Shell and Standard Oil went on to build plants to produce iso-octane in quantity, at affordable prices. In 1936 the Army's chief of staff ordered that 100-octane fuel was to serve as the standard aviation gasoline for its warplanes.

In addition to drawing help from chemists, the engines of that era spurred a move toward flight at higher altitudes. High-flying military aircraft were harder to shoot down. For airliners, flight at altitude took these aircraft above the clouds, while giving a measure of relief from heavy turbulence that often caused passengers to become severely nauseous. For both types of craft, the reduced air pressure of the high sky diminished the drag and gave higher flight speeds. In turn, those higher speeds gave increased range for both bombers and the airlines.

The lessened air pressure reduced the drag, but it also sharply cut the flow of air that engines needed when burning their fuel. This brought a substantial drop in horsepower. To keep these motors running at full power, they needed air pumps to compress the atmosphere at high altitude and feed it into the cylinders. The device that did this was called a turbocharger. It placed a turbine in the hot engine exhaust, drawing power from this exhaust that otherwise would have gone to waste. The turbine spun a rotating compressor that served as the pump.

The French inventor Auguste Rateau devised the first unit for use with aircraft as early as 1916. It was a major installation in its own right, virtually a separate engine on top of the one it assisted. But though it lacked neatness it had plenty of capability, and showed this in a series of spectacular flights. At the Army's McCook Field, home of its engine laboratory, altitude records became a specialty. In February 1920, Major Rudolph Schroeder reached 33,130 feet. He could not breathe properly at that height; he had an oxygen supply, but he blacked out when it failed and did not regain consciousness until his plane descended into denser air. A year later, with better equipment, Lieutenant John Macready went to 40,800 feet. No ordinary motor could have achieved such heights, but the turbocharger pumped the rarefied air to sufficient pressure to make the difference.

Even so, these represented no more than individual sorties. For serious military use, the turbocharger had to perform dependably day after day, and it lacked the necessary reliability. The problem lay in poor heat resistance of the turbine blades, which faced temperatures in engine exhaust that were as hot as a flame and caused the blades to lose strength.

Lieutenant E. T. Jones, head of McCook's Power Plant Laboratory, rescued the turbocharger by reinventing its design. He introduced the "side type," mounted flush with the fuselage and exposing its turbine to the open air. This helped the turbine blades to stay cool, and prevented the turbocharger from being abandoned as a lost cause. Army researchers nevertheless kept their eyes out for new alloys for blades that could withstand higher temperatures. In this fashion, proponents of the turbocharger built up a considerable body of experience dealing with rapidly rotating turbomachinery under conditions of great

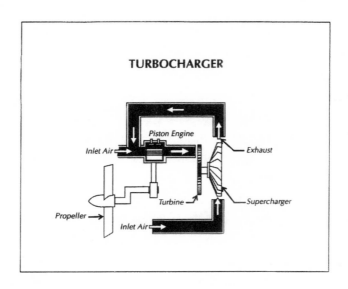

The turbocharger used the power of an engine's exhaust to drive its supercharger. This increased the engine's performance while using energy in the exhaust that otherwise would have gone to waste.

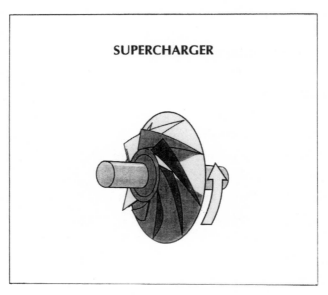

A supercharger was a rapidly-spinning air pump.
Rotating within a closely fitted housing, it pumped more air
into an engine for increased power at high altitude.

heat and stress. In time this fed directly into development of the turbojet engine.

The firm of General Electric became actively involved with turbochargers. It had been building industrial blowers since 1907, which
gave its people a good knowledge of compressors. This expertise was
at hand in 1936, when the firm of Haynes Stellite brought out a class
of nickel-base alloys known as Hastelloy. Their purpose was to resist
acids in the chemical industry, but they proved far superior to the best
conventional materials for use in turbine blades.

The combination of good turbines and side-type installation made
the turbocharger an important military asset during World War II.
General George Kenney, who went on to command Douglas
MacArthur's air arm in the Pacific, described its advantages in March
1942. "America is producing the best military planes in the world
today," he boasted. "At high altitudes the Lockheed P-38 and the
Republic P-47 can lick anything. There are only two honest 400-mile-
per-hour planes in the world, and we've got both of them. There are
only two heavy bombers that can operate above 30,000 feet: the Boeing B-17 and the Consolidated B-24." He took particular note of the
B-17: "Its new turbocharger attached to the engine has made it a superior high-altitude plane, carrying a heavy bomb load at 34,000 feet."[2]

Air power came into its own during that war, giving decisive support to the campaign against Germany while forcing Japan to surren-
der unconditionally without a single Allied soldier setting foot on its
home islands. Yet in important respects, everything that happened up
to 1945 was mere prelude. For during the war, the jet engine burst
upon the world.

The concept of the turbojet grew out of a similar engine, the gas
turbine, that flourished in experimental labs and then died, early in
the century. The problem lay in its low efficiency and high fuel consumption. From time to time people thought of reviving it for use in
aviation, but it was not well-suited for use at the modest speeds of that
day, and these studies largely gave reasons to leave it in its grave. But
by the mid-1930s the rapidly increasing speeds of the best aircraft
spurred new thoughts of adapting the gas turbine for flight. Even early

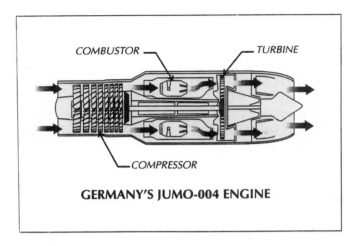

Germany's Jumo-004 was the first jet engine to fly in combat. Its simple layout set the standard for more powerful types that followed.

designs offered light weight along with temptingly good levels of thrust. They still burned fuel in prodigious quantities, but they did not knock like piston motors. Hence there was no need to use exotic chemicals such as iso-octane; cheap kerosene did nicely. The first engines found a role in early jet fighters, which required the highest possible speed.

Two young inventors, Frank Whittle of the Royal Air Force and Hans von Ohain in Germany, created the first such engines while working independently. They particularly addressed the problem of burning large flows of fuel in compact combustion chambers. Engine-building firms—Germany's Heinkel and Junkers, England's Rolls-Royce and de Havilland, America's General Electric—went on to build versions that were suitable for use as standard service types. These companies drew particularly on experience with turbochargers and with a similar rotary air compressor, the supercharger. (It differed from the turbocharger by dispensing with the turbine, but was less effective because it took power from the engine itself and used that power with only modest efficiency.)

The Messerschmitt 262 became the world's first jet fighter to see action in combat. Anselm Franz, the chief designer of its engine, later recalled an early test flight with the pilot Fritz Wendel at the controls:

> The engines were turned on and Wendel carefully brought them to full power. Now he released the brakes, the plane rolled, and he held her down to the ground. Suddenly the airplane left the ground and, propelled by those two jet engines, as seen from where we were, climbed almost vertically with unprecedented speed until it disappeared in the clouds. At that moment, it was clear to me that the jet age had begun.[3]

With a top speed of 541 mph, the Me 262 might have swept the Allies from the skies. However, it faltered because of its own need for heat-resistant metals. Prototypes of its engine made free use of cobalt, nickel, and chromium, which gave good temperature resistance. But these were in short supply within wartime Germany, forcing engineers to turn to inferior substitutes. The 262 was unmatched in the air, but it spent little time in the air, for it needed frequent replacements of engines and parts. On the ground it was a sitting duck.

Germans laid much of the groundwork, but Americans reaped the rewards. This happened just as the war was ending, when Yankee specialists set out to start afresh in seeking an appropriate shape for a jet plane. Boeing was in the forefront, with a large new wind tunnel capable of testing designs at airspeeds close to the speed of sound. Within that firm, George Schairer was a senior aerodynamicist. In May 1945 he joined a group of specialists and traveled to Germany to observe firsthand what that country had achieved in its wartime research. He stopped en route at the Pentagon and learned that Robert Jones, one of his colleagues, was arguing that it was possible to reduce drag for greater speed by using sweptback wings. This idea was new. Would it work? Could it be understood in the light of known aerodynamic principles? Schairer and others in the party soon were discussing the matter, continuing their talks during the long flight across the Atlantic.

They were heading toward the mother lode of aeronautics, for German scientists not only had founded scientific work in this field but had made many of the main discoveries, giving leadership that lasted for decades. These German scientists were friends of Schairer and his associates, who were eager to resume their prewar ties. The visitors found their way to a major research center, where Schairer saw that the library was intact. Soon he was finding drawings and wind-tunnel data concerning . . . an aircraft with swept wings. Adolf Buse-mann, a theorist at that institute, had gotten there first.

Swept wings became a hallmark of jet propulsion, so much so as to appear in time on road signs pointing the way to an airport. They appeared on Boeing's B-47 bomber, powered by six jet engines, and on the North American F-86 fighter that ruled the sky during the Korean War of the early 1950s. Moreover, while these engines brought

The shape of things to come. The XB-47 bomber of 1947
was the first large swept-wing aircraft.

dramatic new prospects for flight at high speed and altitude, wartime electronics was contributing to safety.

Radar, another war baby, came to aviation and soon found use in traffic control. A controller could sit at a scope and see all the airplanes in the vicinity, then use radio to give instructions. Radar signals pierce the thickest fog with ease, and even the early systems were good enough to enable an operator to direct a pilot to the runway. It was somewhat like being blindfolded and having a friend call out directions so you could walk a straight line across a floor.

This gave rise to Ground Controlled Approach, which became the military blind-landing system. In service, it repeatedly brought planes in safely when even birds might have preferred to walk. During the Battle of the Bulge in 1944, with ceiling and visibility close to zero, GCA brought two fighters in for landings. Someone asked one of the pilots when he saw the runway. He replied, "I didn't; I just felt a bump."

Radar and GCA were military developments. The Civil Aeronautics Administration, a Washington agency with responsibility for commercial airlines, brought out its own blind-landing arrangement known as the Instrument Landing System. ILS featured a glide-slope beam, which marked the approach glide path by going off into the distance at an angle of three degrees above the horizontal. It also had a localizer beam, in line with the runway, that allowed a pilot to point his plane in the proper direction. Using ILS, fifteen planes could land in an hour.

Radar, GCA, and ILS all enhanced safety in bad weather, but the eyes of the public were on the new jets. New engines set the pace, and while General Electric started during the war by relying on British designs, the company set up its own development laboratory and began work on original concepts. These included the J-47, with 5,000 pounds of thrust. This posed a strong challenge to Pratt & Whitney, which had spent the war working on piston engines. That company built its own jet-engine lab, but its executives knew they needed more. They also faced competition from Westinghouse, which came to the jet-engine business following long experience with steam turbines used in generating electric power.

"We faced a mighty tough situation," Leonard Hobbs, Pratt's director of engineering, later declared. "We were five years behind the other companies. We decided that it was not enough to match their designs; that to get back in the race we must leapfrog them—come up with something far in advance of what they were thinking about." He set his sights on an engine of 10,000 pounds of thrust, and he wanted more. Turbojets still were fuel guzzlers, showing poor fuel economy, which meant that there was no prospect for using these engines in airliners and heavy bombers. He decided to seek reduced fuel consumption along with the thrust.

His research director Perry Pratt came forth with the key concept: the "twin-spool" engine. This placed a turbojet within a turbojet. It had two compressors, one behind the other, each driven by its own separate turbine and shaft. High compression had proven to be critical in improving the power and fuel economy of piston motors, and the same was true of turbojets. The new engine, called the J-57, achieved an internal pressure of twelve atmospheres.

This engine truly launched the jet age. It powered new fighters such as the North American F-100, the first to break the sound barrier in level flight. New versions, rated first at 13,500 and later at 18,000 pounds of thrust, powered commercial jet airliners beginning with the Boeing 707 and Douglas DC-8. These quickly won favor by providing comfort with their speed, for they flew above the weather and eliminated the harsh vibration of piston motors that had been quite wearying. The Boeing B-52 brought jet power to the realm of heavy bombers, flying for the Strategic Air Command and mounting eight J-57s.

The writer Tom Wolfe recalls the military jets of the 1950s:

To take off in an F-100 at dawn and cut in the afterburner and hurtle twenty-five thousand feet up into the sky, yet with full control, full control of *five tons* of thrust, all of which flowed from your will and through your fingertips, with the huge engine right beneath you, so close that it was as if you were riding it bareback, until you leveled out and went supersonic, an event registered on earth by a tremendous cracking boom that shook windows, but up here only

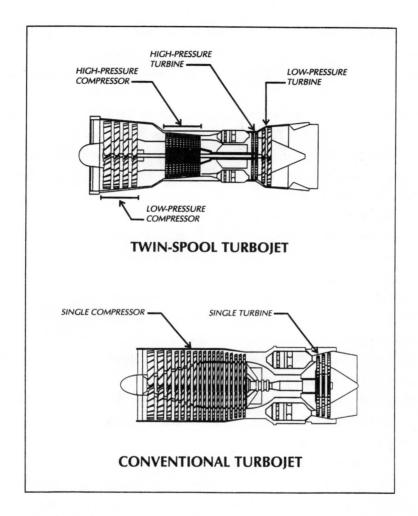

HIGH-PRESSURE
TURBINE

HIGH-PRESSURE
COMPRESSOR

LOW-PRESSURE
TURBINE

LOW-PRESSURE
COMPRESSOR

TWIN-SPOOL TURBOJET

SINGLE COMPRESSOR

SINGLE TURBINE

CONVENTIONAL TURBOJET

Twin-spool jet engines such as the J-57, top, gave more thrust and better fuel economy than conventional designs.

by the fact that you now felt utterly free of the earth—to describe it, even to wife, child, near ones and dear ones, seemed impossible.[4]

For the Air Force, even the J-57 wasn't enough. Gerhard Neumann, an engineering manager at General Electric, crafted a lightweight engine called the J-79. At Lockheed, the chief designer Clarence "Kelly" Johnson fitted it into a new fighter, the F-104, that was built to fly beyond Mach 2. This was as fast as an airplane built of aluminum could go without having this metal soften due to aerodynamic heating. The new engine had enough thrust to enable a 104 to carry over a ton of fuel and still accelerate while pointing straight up.

Indeed, the J-79 gave this fighter the performance of a rocket plane. On December 12, 1953 the test pilot Scott Crossfield reached 1,327 mph in his Douglas Skyrocket, which became the first airplane to fly at more than twice the speed of sound. Only four years later, in January 1958, Lockheed began delivering operational F-104s to the Air Force. In May one of these fighters topped Crossfield's mark with a new speed record of 1,404 mph. Next, in 1959 an F-104 flew to an altitude of 103,395 feet. This approached the record of 125,907 feet set in the rocket-powered Bell X-2 three years earlier, and quite surpassed altitude marks set in other rocket planes of that era.

For the Air Force, though, this was too much of a good thing. Operational pilots spent very little time soaring into realms where the sky turned a deep purple, the sun glared as a blindingly brilliant disk of metallic whiteness, and the cloud-dappled surface of the earth plainly showed its curvature. It was far more important to attack ground targets, and the original F-104 needed a good deal of modification to make it suitable for this role.

After that, the Air Force retained the Mach 2 capability in subsequent fighters but made them considerably larger, to carry more ordnance. Indeed, the increasing power of jet engines brought major changes in what constituted aircraft of a particular type. During World War II, the B-17 served as a heavy bomber. It was a large airplane with four engines, and weighed up to 50,000 pounds when fully loaded with fuel and munitions. A decade later the B-47 was four times heavier but counted as a medium bomber. The true heavy bomber of the 1950s, the B-52, weighed in at close to half a million pounds.

The same trend took hold in fighters. The F-16 took shape as a single-engine warplane, with a maximum loaded weight of 42,000 pounds. This approached the weight of the B-17; yet the F-16 was rated as a lightweight fighter. Standard-size fighters of the post-Vietnam era—the F-14, F-15, and F/A-18—ranged up to 81,000 pounds. In addition to carrying substantial weapons loads, they could fly two or three missions in a day, whereas the B-17 flew more like two or three per week.

The search for higher thrust was unrelenting. Moreover, when the jetliners entered commercial service, the noise of their engines brought widespread outrage. The head of the new Federal Aviation Agency had to get an unlisted phone number after people started waking him up with telephone calls at three and four o'clock in the morning. "The jet has to adjust to civilized community life," said the director of aviation for the New York Port Authority. "It can't come in raw and screaming; it's got to be housebroken first."

The three main engine-builders—Rolls-Royce, Pratt & Whitney, and General Electric—responded by introducing fanjet engines, which also were called turbofans. This design added a whirling fan to the basic turbojet, which had numerous closely-spaced blades and looked like a farmer's windmill. The turbofan represented a new application for the twin-spool principle, for the fan used its own turbine to drive it. Pratt & Whitney built its own fan arrangements for installation on the standard J-57. The conversion took place during engine overhauls, without returning them to the factory.

Early fanjets continued to resemble standard turbojets. In no way did they show the wide gaping mouths of later such engines, as on the Boeing 747. Even so, they added important new improvements in thrust, fuel economy, and noise reduction. In addition to being quieter in their own right, their higher thrust promoted steeper takeoffs, which gave more altitude over which their roar could fade.

Their improved fuel economy also gave new life to transatlantic nonstop flight. Prior to the jets, this became feasible only during the mid-1950s, which was very late in the piston era. From the outset, around 1960, turbofans increased the range of big jetliners to over four thousand miles. This opened the way to direct service to all of Europe's major cities, on routes such as New York to Rome. It also gave a start in nonstop transpacific service with direct connections from Seattle to Tokyo. Yet while leaping across oceans, fanjets also powered jetliners of considerably shorter range: the Boeing 727 and 737, the Douglas DC-9. This was important, for most traffic indeed was on the short routes. In cities such as Chicago, far more people wanted to fly to New York than to London. The smaller jetliners made this possible, and with this, the triumph of the jet was complete. Having taken over the full range of military missions, civilian engines now covered all important combinations of size and range.

Decades earlier, the turbocharger had brought turbines and compressors to that era's piston motors long before they became basic elements of the turbojet. Fanjets returned the favor, adding a type of propeller—the fan—to the basic turbojet. It was not long before engineers began to look ahead to new engines with fans of vastly greater size, and again General Electric took the initiative. That firm had introduced the first U.S.-built turbofan, and had used it to convince skeptics of these engines' merits, only to find that Pratt & Whitney walked off with most of the sales. As one senior manager put it, "We converted the heathen, but the competitors sold the bibles!" To win back lost souls, GE had to pursue research. This effort won strong support at the Pentagon, where Defense Secretary Robert McNamara wanted big engines that could power an enormous military cargo plane, the C-5A.

The first such engine, the General Electric TF-39, introduced a fan with eight-foot diameter. Its thrust was 40,000 pounds, twice as much as the standard fanjets of a few years earlier. In September 1965, Lockheed won the contract to build the C-5A, which mounted four of these new engines. This cargo jet showed that aircraft indeed were breaking all bounds in size, for if placed in a football stadium, it was long enough to extend from the goal line to the opponent's eighteen-yard line, with its wings overhanging both benches. In service, it carried heavily armored tanks.

Commercial air traffic was expanding rapidly. Pratt & Whitney responded to the TF-39 with its own big fanjet, the JT-9D. In turn, soaring demand for airliner seats led William Allen, president of Boeing, to commit to a bold new project: the 747. It entered service in 1970, but it was ahead of its time, and sales remained slow during the

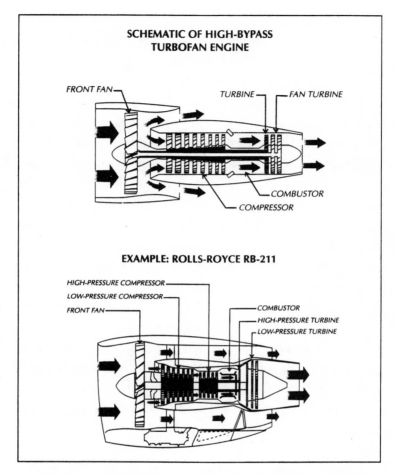

**SCHEMATIC OF HIGH-BYPASS
TURBOFAN ENGINE**

FRONT FAN

TURBINE — FAN TURBINE

COMBUSTOR

COMPRESSOR

EXAMPLE: ROLLS-ROYCE RB-211

HIGH-PRESSURE COMPRESSOR

LOW-PRESSURE COMPRESSOR

FRONT FAN

COMBUSTOR

HIGH-PRESSURE TURBINE

LOW-PRESSURE TURBINE

*Big turbofan engines, such as the Rolls-Royce RB-211, gave
high thrust for widebody airliners such as the Boeing 747.*

early years. But during the 1980s and 1990s it emerged as the plane
the world needed, with Boeing selling over a thousand of them. With
sticker prices as high as $177 million, the company's total revenues
approached the gross national product of a modest-sized country.
Boeing brought out new versions that were larger still, with longer
range. The 747-400, the current model, became the world's first true
transpacific airliner, able to carry full loads along routes that faced
headwinds as great as two hundred miles per hour. In day-to-day
service, it carried 412 passengers with their baggage as well as five pal-

lets of cargo. In August 1989 one of them flew nonstop from London to Sydney, staying in the air for over twenty hours while covering 11,156 miles. In the history of aviation, only three airplanes had ever traveled farther on a single load of fuel.

The 747 certainly was dramatic, and its widebody cabin became popular for its spaciousness. Yet even before it flew, Frank Kolk, a vice president at American Airlines, insisted that another important route to the future involved slightly smaller aircraft that could offer widebody comfort while mounting only two engines, giving air carriers less equipment to purchase and maintain. He too was ahead of his time, for engines such as the JT-9D lacked the high thrust and demonstrated reliability that could qualify them for this role. The first follow-on widebodies, the Lockheed L-1011 and McDonnell Douglas DC-10, therefore mounted three engines.

But the concept of a widebody twinjet opened a market opportunity in Europe, where French planebuilders spurred the development of an industrial consortium, Airbus Industrie. Its A-300, followed by the A-310, emerged as the first airliners of this new type. The advantages of two rather than three engines caused sales of the Lockheed and McDonnell Douglas trijets to dry up. Boeing then entered the game with its own widebody twinjet, the 767, which went into service in 1982.

After that, Boeing followed in 1995 with its 777. It stands today as the ultimate twinjet, with size and passenger capacity that rival the early 747s. Its nacelles are wider than the fuselages of early jetliners such as the 707; the engine housings of a 777 could easily accommodate six-abreast seating with an aisle. From New York, it has the range for nonstop flight to the tip of South Africa and to nearly all of Asia. Only Australia or Singapore would require a refueling stop.

In general appearance, one would no more compare this twinjet to the Wright Flyer of 1903 than look for similarity between the aircraft carrier USS *Nimitz* and a Viking long ship. The vessels both have hulls, the airplanes both use wings; and that is about it. Yet like all successful winged craft of the past century, the 777 continues to show its inheritance from Wilbur and Orville. It relies on ailerons for flight control, without which it would fall out of the sky. In turn, those control surfaces closely resemble the ones that Glenn Curtiss mounted to his *Gold Bug* in 1909, and which subsequently were found to stand as an application of ideas treated in the basic Wright patent. Orville lived long enough to take the controls of a Lockheed Constellation, which mounted four piston engines and flew nonstop from coast to coast. He was still alive and healthy in December 1947, on the forty-fourth anniversary of the flights at Kitty Hawk, when the B-47 made its initial flight, rising on jet power and sporting swept wings that showed the shape of things to come. Through it all, he had the satisfaction of knowing that he and Wilbur had introduced the methods of control that unlocked the secret of flight, making possible everything else that followed.

NOTES

CHAPTER ONE: ENTER THE WRIGHTS

1. Crouch, *Bishop's Boys*, p. 54.
2. Ibid., p. 82; Young and Fitzgerald, *Twelve*, p. 12.
3. Young and Fitzgerald, *Twelve*, p. 13; Howard, *Wilbur*, p. 8.
4. Howard, *Wilbur*, p. 11; Crouch, *Bishop's Boys*, p. 110.
5. Crouch, *Bishop's Boys*, p. 113.

CHAPTER TWO: PROPHETS WITH SOME HONOR

1. Gillispie, *Montgolfier*, p. 42.
2. Ibid., p. 62.
3. Cayley's paper is reprinted in Pritchard, *Cayley*, Appendix III.
4. Ibid., p. 206.
5. Maxim, *Development*, pp. 851–52.

CHAPTER THREE: TEACHERS AND FIRST LESSONS

1. Vaeth, *Langley*, p. 45.
2. Moolman, *Kitty Hawk*, p. 94.
3. A photographic reproduction of this letter appears in Combs and Caidin, *Kill Devil*, photo section following p. 168. See also Young and Fitzgerald, *Twelve*, pp. 16–17.

4. Combs and Caidin, *Kill Devil*, pp. 78–79.

5. Ibid., pp. 82–83.

6. Young and Fitzgerald, *Twelve*, p. 28; Crouch, *Bishop's Boys*, p. 194.

7. Jakab, *Visions*, p. 92; Young and Fitzgerald, *Twelve*, p. 27.

CHAPTER FOUR: HITTING A WALL

1. Young and Fitzgerald, *Twelve*, p. 29.

2. Crouch, *Bishop's Boys*, p. 208.

3. Wilbur Wright's paper is reprinted in Jakab and Young, eds., *Published*, pp. 114–32.

CHAPTER FIVE: "WE NOW HOLD ALL THE RECORDS!"

1. Anderson, *History*, p. 226; Jakab, *Visions*, p. 141.

2. Combs and Caidin, *Kill Devil*, p. 156.

3. Young and Fitzgerald, *Twelve*, p. 44.

4. Combs and Caidin, *Kill Devil*, pp. 159–60.

5. Jakab, *Visions*, p. 178.

6. Jakab and Young, eds., *Published*, p. 135.

7. Ibid., p. 136.

8. Ibid., pp. 137–38.

9. Crouch, *Bishop's Boys*, p. 240.

CHAPTER SIX: AMBIGUOUS SUCCESS

1. Combs and Caidin, *Kill Devil*; Jakab and Young, eds., *Published*, pp. 287–88.

2. Jakab and Young, *Published*, p. 41.

3. Combs and Caidin, p. 181.

4. Crouch, *Bishop's Boys*, p. 252.

5. Vaeth, *Langley*, pp. 83–85.

6. Jakab, *Visions*, p. 203.

7. Jakab and Young, eds., *Published*, pp. 91–92.

8. Ibid., p. 44.

9. Vaeth, *Langley*, pp. 89–90.

10. Kelly, *Wright Brothers*, pp. 96–97.

11. Ibid., pp. 99–100.

12. Ibid., p. 101.

CHAPTER SEVEN: RETURN TO DAYTON

1. Young and Fitzgerald, *Twelve*, p. 69.

2. Combs and Caidin, *Kill Devil*, p. 231.

3. Crouch, *Bishop's Boys*, p. 275.

4. Young and Fitzgerald, *Twelve*, p. 73; Crouch, *Bishop's Boys*, pp. 278–79.

5. Hallion, *Prometheus*, pp. 110–15.

6. Kelly, *Wright Brothers*, pp. 149–50; Combs and Caidin, *Kill Devil*, pp. 242–43.

7. Kelly, *Wright Brothers*, p. 150; Combs and Caidin, *Kill Devil*, pp. 243–44; Howard, *Wilbur*, p. 164.

CHAPTER EIGHT: INTO THE WORLD

1. *Scientific American,* January 13, 1906, p. 40.

2. U.S. Patent 821,393.

3. Kelly, *Wright Brothers*, p. 153.

4. Ibid., pp. 153–54.

5. Ibid., pp. 154–55, for both letters.

6. Walsh, *Kitty Hawk*, p. 199.

7. Kelly, *Wright Brothers*, pp. 158–59.

8. Ibid., p. 162.

9. Hallion, *Prometheus*, p. 116.

10. *Scientific American,* p. 86.

11. Young and Fitzgerald, *Twelve Seconds*, p. 97.

12. Combs and Caidin, *Kill Devil*, pp. 281–82, 286.

CHAPTER NINE: NOON INTO TWILIGHT

1. Kelly, *Wright Brothers*, p. 253.

2. Howard, *Wilbur*, p. 296.

3. Ibid., p. 297; Young and Fitzgerald, *Twelve*, pp. 113–14.

4. Combs and Caidin, *Kill Devil*, pp. 269–70.

5. Roseberry, *Glenn Curtiss*, p. 314.

6. Young and Fitzgerald, *Twelve*, p. 129.

7. Kelly, *Wright Brothers*, p. 332.

CHAPTER TEN: INVENTIVENESS AND INVENTION

1. Harris, *First to Fly*, back of dust jacket.

2. Moss, *Superchargers*, pp. 101–2.

3. Boyne and Lopez, *Jet Age*, p. 74.

4. Wolfe, *Right Stuff*, pp. 30–31.

BIBLIOGRAPHY

BOOKS AND REPORTS

Adams, G. Donald, *Collecting and Restoring Antique Bicycles.* Orchard Park, NY: Burgwardt Bicycle Museum, 1996.

Anderson, John D., Jr., *A History of Aerodynamics.* New York: Cambridge University Press, 1998.

Botting, Douglas, *The Giant Airships.* Alexandria, VA: Time-Life Books, 1981.

Boyne, Walter, *Messerschmitt 262: Arrow to the Future.* Washington: Smithsonian Institution Press, 1980.

Boyne, Walter, and Donald Lopez, eds., *The Jet Age.* Washington: Smithsonian Institution Press, 1979.

Brooks, Peter W., *The Modern Airliner.* Manhattan, KS: Sunflower University Press, 1982.

———, *Zeppelin: Rigid Airships 1893–1940.* Washington: Smithsonian Institution Press, 1992.

Canfield, Leon H., and Howard B. Wilder, *The Making of Modern America.* Boston: Houghton Mifflin, 1964.

Combs, Harry, and Martin Caidin, *Kill Devil Hill: Discovering the Secret of the Wright Brothers.* Boston: Houghton Mifflin, 1979.

Constant, Edward, *The Origins of the Turbojet Revolution.* Baltimore: Johns Hopkins University Press, 1980.

Crouch, Tom D., *A Dream of Wings: Americans and the Airplane, 1875–1905.* Washington: Smithsonian Institution Press, 1989.

————, *The Bishop's Boys: A Life of Wilbur and Orville Wright.* New York: W. W. Norton, 1989.

————, *The Eagle Aloft: Two Centuries of the Balloon in America.* Washington: Smithsonian Institution Press, 1983.

Crown, Judith, and Glenn Coleman, *No Hands: The Rise and Fall of the Schwinn Bicycle Company, an American Institution.* New York: Henry Holt, 1996.

Davenport, William Wyatt, *Gyro! The Life and Times of Lawrence Sperry.* New York: Scribner, 1978.

Davies, R. E. G., *A History of the World's Airlines.* London: Oxford University Press, 1964.

————, *Airlines of the United States Since 1914.* London: Putnam, 1972.

"Dependable Engines . . . Since 1925." Pratt & Whitney, July 1990.

Durant, Will, *The Reformation.* New York: Simon & Schuster, 1957.

————, "The Age of Faith." New York: Simon & Schuster, 1950.

Durant, Will and Ariel, *Rousseau and Revolution.* New York: Simon & Schuster, 1967.

Dwiggins, Don, *The Complete Book of Airships—Dirigibles, Blimps & Hot Air Balloons.* Blue Ridge Summit, PA: Tab Books, 1980.

Ege, Lennart, *Balloons and Airships.* New York: Macmillan, 1974.

Fairlie, Gerard, and Elizabeth Cayley, *The Life of a Genius.* London: Hodder and Stoughton, 1965.

Gibbs-Smith, Charles H., *Aviation: An Historical Survey from Its Origins to the End of World War II.* London: Her Majesty's Stationery Office, 1970.

————, *Ballooning.* London: Penguin Books, 1948.

————, *The Invention of the Airplane (1799–1909).* New York: Taplinger, 1965.

Gillispie, Charles C., *The Montgolfier Brothers and the Invention of Aviation.* Princeton, NJ: Princeton University Press, 1983.

Gunston, Bill, *Fighters of the Fifties.* Osceola, WI: Specialty Press, 1981.

Hallion, Richard, ed., *The Wright Brothers: Heirs of Prometheus.* Washington: National Air and Space Museum, 1978.

Harris, Sherwood, *The First to Fly.* New York: Simon and Schuster, 1970.

Heppenheimer, T. A. *Turbulent Skies: The History of Commercial Aviation.* New York: John Wiley, 1995.

————, *A Brief History of Flight*. New York: John Wiley, 2001.

Heron, S. D., *History of the Aircraft Piston Engine*. Detroit: Ethyl Corp., 1961.

Howard, Fred, *Wilbur and Orville: A Biography of the Wright Brothers*. New York: Knopf, 1987.

Hughes, Thomas Parke, *Elmer Sperry: Inventor and Engineer*. Baltimore: Johns Hopkins Press, 1971.

Jackson, Robert, *Airships*. Garden City, NY: Doubleday, 1973.

Jakab, Peter L., *Visions of a Flying Machine: The Wright Brothers and the Process of Invention*. Washington: Smithsonian Institution Press, 1990.

Jakab, Peter L., and Rick Young, eds., *The Published Writings of Wilbur and Orville Wright*. Washington: Smithsonian Institution Press, 2000.

Jane's All the World's Aircraft. 2001–2002 and earlier editions. Alexandria, VA: Jane's Information Group, 2001 and earlier.

Kelly, Fred G., *The Wright Brothers: A Biography*. New York: Dover, 1989.

Kirschner, Edwin J., *Aerospace Balloons: From Montgolfiere to Space*. Fallbrook, CA: Aero Publishers, 1985.

Langewiesche, Wolfgang, "Flying Blind." In *Great Flying Stories* (Frank W. Anderson, Jr., ed.). New York: Dell, 1958.

Lewis, Peter, *British Aircraft 1809–1914*. London: Putnam, 1962.

Loftin, Laurence K., *Quest for Performance*. NASA SP-468. Washington: U.S. Government Printing Office, 1985.

Mansfield, Harold, *Vision: A Saga of the Sky*. New York: Madison, 1986.

McCullough, David G., *The Path Between the Seas*. New York: Simon & Schuster, 1977.

McGurn, James, *On Your Bicycle*. New York: Facts On File, 1987.

Miller, Jay, *The X-Planes, X-1 to X-29*. Marine on St. Croix, MN: Specialty Press, 1983.

Miller, Ronald, and David Sawers, *The Technical Development of Modern Aviation*. New York: Praeger, 1970.

Moolman, Valerie, *The Road to Kitty Hawk*. Alexandria, VA: Time-Life Books, 1980.

Moss, Sanford A., *Superchargers for Aviation*. New York: National Aeronautics Council, Inc., 1942.

Nayler, J. L., and E. Ower, *Aviation: Its Technical Development*. Philadelphia: Dufour Editions, 1965.

Nolan, Michael, *Fundamentals of Air Traffic Control*. Belmont, CA: Wadsworth Publishing Co., 1990.

Pedigree of Champions: Boeing Since 1916. Seattle: Boeing, 1985.

Perry, David Brun, *Bike Cult: The Ultimate Guide to Human-Powered Vehicles*. New York: Four Walls Eight Windows, 1995.

Prendergast, Curtis, *The First Aviators*. Alexandria, VA: Time-Life Books, 1981.

Pritchard, J. Laurence, *Sir George Cayley*. London: Max Parrish, 1961.

Robinson, Douglas H., *Giants in the Sky*. Seattle: University of Washington Press, 1973.

Roseberry, C. R., *Glenn Curtiss: Pioneer of Flight*. Garden City, NY: Doubleday, 1972.

Schlaifer, Robert, and S. D. Heron, *Development of Aircraft Engines and Fuels*. Boston: Harvard University, 1950.

Solberg, Carl, *Conquest of the Skies*. Boston: Little, Brown, 1979.

Stien, E. P., *Flight of the Vin Fiz*. New York: Arbor House, 1985.

Tuchman, Barbara, *The Guns of August*. New York: Macmillan, 1962.

Turner, P. St. John, and Heinz J. Nowarra, *Junkers: An Aircraft Album*. New York: Arco Publishing, 1971.

Vaeth, J. Gordon, *Langley: Man of Science and Flight*. New York: Ronald Press, 1966.

Walsh, John Evangelist, *One Day at Kitty Hawk*. New York: Thomas Y. Crowell, 1975.

Wolfe, Tom, *The Right Stuff*. New York: Bantam, 1980.

Young, Rosamond, and Catharine Fitzgerald, *Twelve Seconds to the Moon*. Dayton, Ohio: United States Air Force Foundation, 1983.

PAPERS AND PERIODICALS

Crouch, Tom D., "How the Bicycle Took Wing." *American Heritage of Invention & Technology,* Summer 1986, pp. 10–16.

———, "Capable of Flight: The Feud Between the Wright Brothers and the Smithsonian." *American Heritage of Invention & Technology,* Spring 1987, pp. 34–46.

Culick, F. E. C., "The Origins of the First Powered, Man-Carrying Airplane." *Scientific American,* July 1979, pp. 86–100.

"Genesis of the First Successful Aeroplane." *Scientific American,* December 15, 1906, p. 442.

Kaplan, Ellen, ed., "Pratt & Whitney: In the Company of Eagles." East Hartford, CT: Pratt & Whitney, 1990.

Maxim, Hiram, "The Development of Aerial Navigation." *North American Review,* September 1894, pp. 344–52.

———, "A New Flying-Machine." *The Century,* January 1895, pp. 444–56.

————, "Birds in Flight and the Flying Machine." *North American Review,* October 1895, pp. 405–11.

"McDonnell Douglas Commercial Family DC-1 through MD-80." Long Beach, CA: McDonnell Douglas, 1985.

Pritchard, J. Laurence, "The Dawn of Aerodynamics." *Journal of the Royal Aeronautical Society,* March 1957, pp. 149–80.

————, "Francis Herbert Wenham, 1824–1908." *Journal of the Royal Aeronautical Society,* August 1958, pp. 571–96.

Schairer, George, "The Engineering Revolution Leading to the Boeing 707." Seattle: AIAA 7th Annual Applied Aerodynamics Conference, 1989.

Slade, Joseph W., "The Man Behind the Killing Machine." *American Heritage of Invention and Technology,* Fall 1986, pp. 18–25.

Somerscales, E. F. C., and A. A. Zagotta, "History of the Internal Combustion Engine." ICE, Vol. 8. New York: American Society of Mechanical Engineers, 1989.

Steiner, John E., "Jet Aviation Development: One Company's Perspective." Seattle: Boeing, 1989.

Worrel, Rodney K., "The Wright Brothers' Pioneer Patent." *American Bar Association Journal,* October 1979, pp. 1512–18.

"The Wright Aeroplane and Its Fabled Performances." *Scientific American,* January 13, 1906, p. 40.

"The Wright Aeroplane and Its Performances." *Scientific American,* April 7, 1906, p. 291.

Wright, Orville, and Wilbur, "Flying Machine." U.S. Patent 821,393. *Official Gazette,* May 22, 1906, pp. 1257–58.

INDEX

Page numbers in *italics* indicate illustrations.